"Or Does It Explode?"

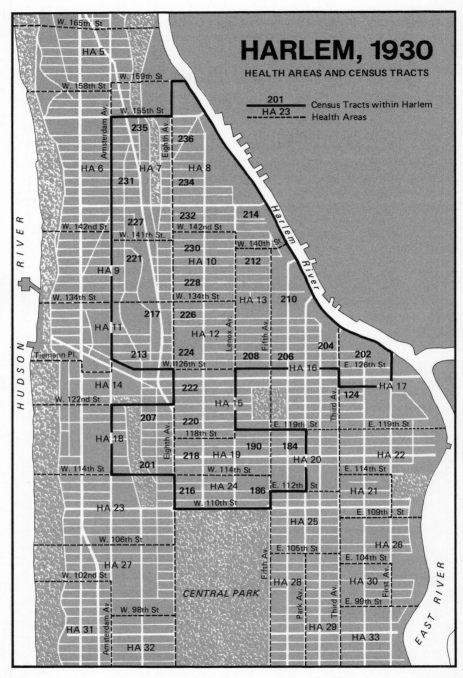

Harlem, 1930. Health Areas and census tracts. New York City Department of Health and Neighborhood Health Development, "Health Center Districts, New York Handbook of Statistical Reference Data: Ten-Year Period, 1931–1940," 1944.

"Or Does It Explode?"

BLACK HARLEM IN
THE GREAT DEPRESSION

Cheryl Lynn Greenberg

New York   Oxford
OXFORD UNIVERSITY PRESS
1991

Oxford University Press

Oxford   New York   Toronto
Delhi   Bombay   Calcutta   Madras   Karachi
Petaling Jaya   Singapore   Hong Kong   Tokyo
Nairobi   Dar es Salaam   Cape Town
Melbourne   Auckland

and associated companies in
Berlin   Ibadan

Copyright © 1991 by Cheryl Lynn Greenberg

Published by Oxford University Press, Inc.
200 Madison Avenue, New York, New York 10016

Oxford is a registered trademark of Oxford University Press

Library of Congress Cataloging-in-Publication Data
Greenberg, Cheryl Lynn.
"Or does it explode?" : Black Harlem in the great depression /
Cheryl Lynn Greenberg.
p.   cm.
Includes index.
ISBN 0-19-505868-2
1. Harlem (New York, N.Y.)—Politics and government.   2. Harlem
(New York, N.Y.)—Economic conditions.   3. Afro-Americans—
New York (N.Y.)—History—20th century.   4. Depressions—1929—
New York (N.Y.)   5. New York (N.Y.)—Economic conditions.
6. New York (N.Y.)—Politics and government—1898–1951.
I. Title.
F128.68.H3G74   1991
974.7′100496073—dc20   90-41827   CIP

2 4 6 8 9 7 5 3 1

Printed in the United States of America
on acid-free paper

For Madelyn and my parents

Acknowledgments

The most rewarding part of preparing this book has been the exchange of ideas with friends and colleagues; it is a pleasure to have the opportunity to thank them. First, I would like to gratefully acknowledge the help of the archivists and librarians of the many libraries I visited who alerted me to interesting materials, taught me the intricacies of their catalogues, and who occasionally bent the rules to facilitate the process of my research. At the National Archives I want to thank Jimmy Rush—the only researcher I know who keeps the *Strawberry Statement* at his desk for easy reference—Jerry Hess, and Jerry Clark. Kenneth Cobb at the Municipal Archives in New York City was wonderfully patient and helpful as I moved through box after box of Mayor LaGuardia's materials, getting in the way of their re-cataloguing process. Robert Morris and the entire staff at the Schomburg Center for Research in Black Culture, also in New York, made me feel more like one of the family than a "client" and always kept an eye out for interesting material I might have missed. I have never encountered a friendlier, more helpful staff than at the Schomburg Center.

Putting my ideas down in a coherent form proved its own challenge. The manuscript began as my dissertation, and its subsequent improvements have a great deal to do with good advice. But it also seems to me that so many people have read this manuscript that it would be inappropriate for me to accept all the blame for any errors that remain in the text. I freely share both praise and criticism for this book with many colleagues and friends. My dissertation defense committee—John Garraty, Herbert Gans, Charles Hamilton, Joshua Freeman, and Eric Foner—gave me such strong encouragement and good advice that I actually looked forward to continuing my work on the project. I was also immensely aided by discussions with many people. Nancy Weiss Malkiel, John L. P. Thompson, Elaine Soffer, Ira Fagin, J. Matthew Gallman, and Barbara Sicherman all talked with me at length or read parts of the manuscript, pointing out inconsistencies in my thinking and helping me refine my arguments. They combined a critical review of my work with warm support. John Thompson and my father, Irwin Greenberg, also provided invaluable statistical help. Without them the text and footnotes would have been much simpler to read, but much less substantial. I would also like to thank Trinity College for providing me with a summer grant, and help in preparing the manuscript for publication.

Several people deserve special mention. Thomas Kessner, John B. Kirby, Joshua Freeman, and J. Ronald Spencer read and edited the entire manuscript, and miraculously, they have remained my friends. Their close and careful reading of the text combined good sense, historical clarity, and a warm generosity of spirit. Whatever strengths of argument or style this book may possess are due in large measure to them.

The best decision I made in this long endeavor was the first: to ask Eric Foner to serve as my dissertation advisor. Not only did he read and comment on every draft, he did so promptly and thoroughly. He never failed to provide encouragement and ideas. His impressive store of knowledge and historical insight spurred me to think more deeply and carefully and rekindled my enthusiasm and my sheer love of learning. His contributions are evident in my arguments and in the underlying structure. This would be a far weaker book without him.

He also recommended Oxford University Press to me, and it was there that I met my editor and my friend Rachel Toor. She read and critiqued my manuscript twice, and throughout the entire process of writing and revision, remained my lifeline to sanity. I treasure both her help and her friendship.

Dan Lloyd, my last and most devoted reader, taught me new questions to ask and showed me new ways to approach the answers. His creativity has strengthened all of my work. That he has had such an impact is hardly surprising; our courtship has been virtually simultaneous with this book. During all this professional and personal rewriting he has sustained me with love and chocolate; I am so thankful for our life together.

This book is for my parents and my sister Madelyn—whom I depend on in ways too numerous and personal to list here—and for Kelly, who loved to sit on the manuscript whenever he got the chance.

Hartford, Connecticut   C.L.G.
May 1990

Contents

Illustrations appear following page 92

"Or Does It Explode?"

Introduction

At 3:00 P.M. on March 19, 1935, Lino Rivera stole a penknife from Kress's Store on 125th Street. A store employee caught him. The sixteen-year-old struggled to free himself and bit his captor, who summoned the manager. While the store called an ambulance for the bitten employee, a woman who had observed the scuffle began to scream that the boy had been hurt or killed. A crowd quickly gathered. In an unfortunate coincidence, a hearse pulled up behind the store. Immediately, the rumor sped through the crowd that the boy was dead. The police, arriving on the scene, arrested the woman for disorderly conduct while the store manager explained that the boy had been released unharmed. The crowd began to disperse.

Early that evening, several men gathered in front of the store carrying signs and giving speeches protesting the alleged brutality. A rock shattered the store window and the riot began. Two local groups arrived with pamphlets:

Child Brutally Beaten—Woman Attacked by Boss and Cops—Child near DEATH.
ONE HOUR AGO A TWELVE YEAR OLD NEGRO BOY WAS BRUTALLY BEATEN BY THE MANAGEMENT OF KRESS FIVE AND TEN CENT STORE.
THE BOY IS NEAR DEATH.
HE WAS MERCILESSLY BEATEN BECAUSE THEY THOUGHT HE HAD "STOLEN" A FIVE CENT KNIFE.
A NEGRO WOMAN WHO SPRANG TO THE DEFENSE OF THE BOY HAD HER ARMS BROKEN BY THESE THUGS AND WAS THEN ARRESTED.
WORKERS: NEGRO AND WHITE. PROTEST AGAINST THIS LYNCH ATTACK ON INNOCENT NEGRO PEOPLE.
DEMAND THE RELEASE OF THE BOY AND WOMAN!
DEMAND THE IMMEDIATE ARREST OF THE MANAGER RESPONSIBLE FOR THIS LYNCH ATTACK. . . .

The Young Liberators

The Young Communist League's words were equally inflammatory:

The brutal beating of the 12 year old boy, Riviera [sic], by Kresses' special guard, for taking a piece of candy, again proves the increasing terror against the Negro people of Harlem. Bosses, who deny the most immediate necessities from [sic] workers' children, who throw workers out of employment, who pay not even enough to live on, are protecting their so-called property rights by brutal beatings, as in the case of the boy, Riviera. . . . Our answer to the brutal beating of this boy . . . must be an organized and deter-

3

mined resistance against the brutal attacks of the bosses and the police.
WORKERS' [*sic*] NEGRO AND WHITE; DEMAND THE IMMEDIATE DISMISSAL AND ARREST
AND PROSECUTION OF THE SPECIAL GUARD AND THE MANAGER OF THE STORE.
DEMAND THE RELEASE OF THE NEGRO AND WHITE WORKERS ARRESTED. . . .
DON'T LET THE BOSSES START ANY RACE RIOTS IN HARLEM. . . .[1]

Although neither called for violence, both leaflets inflamed the rioters. The crowd, eventually numbering in the thousands (including onlookers), spread east and west on 125th Street, breaking store windows and looting from Fifth Avenue to Eighth. The seven police officers on routine patrol in Harlem were joined by reinforcements and by the Chief Inspector. Ralph Ellison offered a vivid description in his novel *Invisible Man:*

I could see a crowd rushing a store . . . , moving in, and a fusillade of canned goods, salami, liverwurst, hogs heads and chitterlings belching out to those outside . . . ; as now out of the dark of the intersecting street two mounted policemen came at a gallop . . . charging straight into the swarming mass. And I could see the great forward lunge of the horses and the crowd breaking and rolling back like a wave, back, and screaming and cursing, and some laughing . . . as the horses . . . went over the curb . . . to where another crowd looted another store. And my heart tightened as the first crowd swung imperturbably back to their looting with derisive cries. . . .

They came toward me as I ran, a crowd of men and women carrying cases of beer, cheese, chains of linked sausage, watermelons, sacks of sugar, hams, cornmeal, fuel lamps. If only it could stop right here, here; here before the others came with their guns. I ran.

By the end of the night, seventy-five people, mostly black, had been arrested for "inciting to riot, felonious assault, malicious mischief and burglary, all the direct result of the disturbance." Fifty-seven civilians and seven policemen were injured, and 626 windows broken.[2]

Mayor Fiorello LaGuardia charged a commission to investigate the causes of the riot, appointing an impressive array of experts from the black and white communities, including E. Franklin Frazier, Countee Cullen, A. Philip Randolph, and Hubert Delany. Moving beyond the superficial explanation that the riot erupted because of local resentment at the perceived mishandling of a black child at the hands of a white store owner, the commission examined the general conditions in Harlem that provided the root causes for such resentment.

The commission found no evidence to sustain the common perception that Communists or other radical groups provoked the riot; they uncovered "no evidence of any program or leadership of the rioters." Rather, the "outburst was spontaneous and unpremeditated," the visible manifestation of a frustrated, unfocused, and desperate anger. The riot began as an assault on white property, but escalating emotion soon made protesters less discriminating. "As they [the crowds] grew more numerous and more active, the personality or racial identity of the owners of the stores faded out and the property itself became the object of their fury."

Police conduct worsened rather than calmed the situation. The police tried to "suppress the excitement rather than to explain the cause of it," and thus did not counter the protesters' rhetoric with facts that might have defused tensions. Once the riot began, the police made "derogatory and threatening remarks," and in some cases acted with unwarranted brutality. One boy who was running was shot and killed without warning. This, the commission found, was entirely in keeping with the widespread perception in Harlem that the police often behaved poorly and irresponsibly there. As Alain Locke commented, "Many in the Harlem community . . . suspect . . . police brutality and intimidation." The commission blamed much of the rioters' anger on "brutality and lack of courtesy by police."[3]

But black resentment went beyond police brutality. The Mayor's Commission also cited discrimination in business and schools, overcrowding, unfair rents, and "inadequate institutional care," and argued:

> The citizens of Harlem understand that the invasion of their rights and the slight regard that is shown for their lives is due not only to the fact that they are Negroes but also to the fact that they are poor and propertyless and therefore defenseless.

Alain Locke concurred: "It was not the unfortunate rumors [which began the riot] but the state of mind on which they fell."

Harlem residents, frustrated and resentful, took matters into their own hands the day of the riot. In describing the riot, Adam Clayton Powell, Sr., concluded: "The Negro used to be the most lovable, forgivable [sic] being in America, but the white man's prejudice, hatred and lies have changed the Negro's psychology. He is just as full of hell, hatred and lies as the white man." Perhaps this is so; the commission saw the event in a more positive light. Riots and other unplanned episodes had shown blacks "the power of their organized number . . . strengthening the belief that the solution to their problems lies in organized action."

The riot was, essentially, the raw expression of anger taught by political organizations whose collapse left a vacuum. Black men and women from all walks of life had been politicized and sometimes even radicalized by Depression-era political organizing. They had identified the problems they faced, discovered the problems were communal, and learned how to respond. When the most organized and potent of these political coalitions, the "Don't Buy Where You Can't Work" campaign, collapsed at the end of 1934, many found themselves without a forum for expressing grievances. So when a street corner orator turned the rumor of Rivera's death into an issue of racial discrimination, the people listening were ready to believe— and act. Without an organized structure for opposition, Harlemites expressed their anger through violence. The riot was as much of a political act as were organized protests and campaigns.

Both poverty and discrimination brought Harlem to the boiling point in 1935. As Nannie Helen Burroughs concluded:

> The causes of the Harlem riot are not far to seek. They lie beneath mountains of injustices done the colored man . . . through years of "patient sufferance" on his part. . . . If that's Red then the writers of the Declaration of Independence were very Red. They told Americans not to stand injustice after "patient sufferance." The colored man has reached the endurance limit. . . . Day after day, year after year, decade after decade, black people have been robbed of their inalienable rights. . . . In Harlem the cornered rats fought back. That "long train of abuses" is a magazine of powder. An unknown boy was simply the match. . . . Colored folks feel that Harlem is their last stand.[4]

Harlem's riot thus ripped away the veneer of civility to reveal the impact of bigotry on African-Americans. Past discrimination had long denied skills and education to blacks, while continued discrimination barred them from jobs and training and confined them to higher-priced, more poorly maintained areas. Racism created and perpetuated Harlem's poverty—race and class were inextricably linked in the black experience. Yet segregation and discrimination also produced strong social and political networks within the black community. These served not only to meet immediate needs, but also to mobilize thousands to demand a better life. This activism, both organized and spontaneous, demonstrated that a determined people could win effective improvements in their condition.

The response of white leaders and officials came quickly in the face of forceful protest, although it slackened whenever black organizations relaxed their vigilance. Perhaps the clearest example of the link between protest and response, the 1935 riot prompted the Mayor's Commission's thorough investigation, and that group's widely publicized findings ultimately brought better government services to Harlem. Several black political efforts, stalled until that point, moved forward as white leaders suddenly became more responsive. Although in the end the fundamental problems facing Harlem persisted, the limited gains African-Americans did achieve in turn spurred political struggles on behalf of broader agendas.

In these changing times some whites came to view more sympathetically the problems facing the black community. The combination of a strongly anti-discriminatory mayor, the economic pressures of the Depression, the liberalizing nature of the New Deal, black political action, and the growing hatred of Nazism, all helped change the attitudes of many whites about blacks. While life was difficult in the Depression, these changes in both the black and the white communities ultimately altered urban race relations. The riot, in short, brings to light both the impact of discrimination and segregation on the black community, and the interactions among racial oppression, black political activity, and white response. These two themes are the focus of this book.

This study explores employment, relief, and black political action—central experiences for Depression-era Harlemites. Chapter 1 sets the stage for the Depression by looking backwards. Harlem had become the main area of black settlement and an impoverished ghetto before the 1930s. Its inhabitants came from places that had denied them education and access to skills, a cycle of deprivation that continued, with some alterations, in New York. Most blacks held unskilled jobs that provided them with little income and even less possibility for upward mobility. As a result, the social and physical conditions of Harlem—housing, health, crime—were far worse than elsewhere in the city. Despite these difficulties, the people of Harlem developed a vibrant community life replete with civic, religious, and political organizations. These allowed Harlem's citizens to work toward ameliorating some of the harshest conditions through organized movements of social protest.

The Depression pushed African-Americans still further into poverty. Chapter 2 describes black unemployment and its consequences in the pre–New Deal Depression, and charitable efforts by blacks and whites. Generally first to be fired, blacks were rehired only after whites. New York blacks had the highest unemployment rate of any group in the city. In the early years of the Depression, public agencies responded too slowly and private philanthropic efforts provided most of the available aid. Yet their resources were quite limited. In this milieu it fell to black organizations, particularly black churches, to expand long-existing services to the black community. Both the scope of relief and the criteria of the various agencies for granting aid reflected the sensibilities of a pre-Depression era.

Chapter 3 seeks to understand the impact of the Depression on those blacks who held employment and to illuminate the differences that gender, nationality, and occupational level made within that experience. The Depression made the barriers to economic advancement still more rigid, as it wore down the minimal gains that blacks had been able to achieve in the 1920s. Black men at higher economic levels lost their jobs to white men, and black women lost theirs to white women. Black mens and women, then, worked at different jobs but shared their place at the bottom of the economic ladder, in the most marginal occupations. Proportionately more blacks worked in unskilled and menial jobs than did any other population group.

Even at the bottom, though, the struggle to retain employment intensified. While traditional "Negro" jobs, such as porter and domestic, offered neither decent wages nor mobility, they had at least provided some job stability, because few white workers wanted them. The Depression sent whites into these fields—suddenly every job became a "white man's job." Blacks who managed to keep their jobs earned less than their white counterparts. Black women earned even less than black men and more often worked in temporary or part-time jobs. Essentially, the experience of black women in that era was a continuation of what had come before: both race and sex discrimination continued to dictate and limit their choices. Gender, race, and class all conspired to determine economic options.

Chapter 4 examines the roots of black political action, the politicization of black men and women in the New Deal era, and several specific case studies, including efforts to win union membership for blacks. Many strongly held and competing political visions flourished in Harlem. Those preaching black nationalism struggled with advocates of socialism, communism, trade unionism, and religious faith for a popular following. To the people of Harlem, however, these visions were not necessarily mutually exclusive. Many individuals embraced several of these positions, moving from one to another as the occasion demanded. The breadth of alternatives encouraged broad-based community activism, as everyone could find a congenial perspective. Yet fluid and wavering allegiances limited the ability of any one group to pursue its vision completely.

Such efforts did bring change; limited successes did begin to weaken the racial segmentation of the job market. As the decade progressed, black organizations became more daring in their activities and demands. While retaining their focus on economic opportunity, they began insisting that whites play a role in improving the discriminatory climate.

These themes emerge most clearly through the "Don't Buy Where You Can't Work" campaign, the topic of Chapter 5. Its successes provided Harlem's first real strides toward equality of economic opportunity. While its specific goal was the employment of black clerks in white-owned stores, the implications of this campaign were much broader. Through the coalitions established during this effort, the women and men of Harlem explored the potential for political action within the constraints of a segregated community. The differing tactics, visions, and styles of members of the "Don't Buy" campaign provide insights into the workings of Depression-era political activity against a backdrop of circumscribed economic opportunity and political power.

The Depression also forced many blacks onto public and private relief rolls. After Franklin Roosevelt's election, the landscape of relief agencies changed completely from the hodgepodge of previous and ultimately inadequate private efforts; Chapter 6 explores the experience of blacks on relief in the New Deal period. Public funds became available in large amounts for the first time for both work and home relief. In many instances private agencies refocused their energies toward non-financial services. Yet some elements of relief-giving remained the same. Black would-be recipients had to rely on the mercy and good will of the relief bureaucracy to allocate services equitably. Not surprisingly, the expectation of fair distribution was rarely met. Not only were relief allotments generally lower than subsistence levels, racist practices meant blacks received aid less often than whites and were more often placed in inappropriately low job classifications.

On the other hand, relief agencies brought desperately needed improvements to Harlem. Roads and parks were repaired; a new school built; a health center funded and staffed; and recreation, education, and vocational programs established or expanded. Thousands of needy families received enough aid to avoid starvation, eviction, or family dissolution. It is crucial to weigh these benefits against the drawbacks, particularly in the context of New York in the 1930s. The process of relief administration was affected by local black political action, national governmental decisions, widespread racism, and such force for equity as the benign administration of Fiorello LaGuardia could bring to bear.

The findings of Chapter 6 suggest that the welfare state did not hurt the poor by providing too much, as many conservatives currently argue, but rather by providing too little. When relief agencies operated at their best, communities lived in better housing, enjoyed better health, and were fed and clothed adequately. In some instances relief kept intact families that might otherwise have separated. The persistent poverty of this community had more to do with inequalities in the welfare system and the society that administered it than it did with the existence of public aid.

African-Americans were far from pawns in the relief process. They fought back against abuses, extracting the benefits they deserved from relief agencies. Black organizations, from the churches to the Communist party and the NAACP, shaped Harlem's dissatisfactions into sharply focused movements for fair hiring by relief agencies, higher relief grants, and a job placement system that put all who applied into jobs appropriate to their skill level.

Mayor LaGuardia and many of those he appointed to head city departments played a significant role in the success of black demands for equitable treatment. So did the local administrators of several New Deal agencies. The mayor appointed African-Americans to high-ranking government positions and took their advice seriously, and a grateful Harlem rewarded him with overwhelming electoral support.

Chapter 7 examines how families lived in Harlem in light of these economic and political conditions. What impact did segregation have on housing and food costs? How did Harlem families meet their needs, given low wages and relief grants? What did Harlem community life look like under these constraints? Harlemites responded to poverty with personal strategies, such as working several jobs or committing victimless crimes like peddling or playing the numbers; family alternatives like swapping, borrowing, and extended kinship networks; and community efforts, including black-run day-care centers and homes for the aged. Yet health, housing, and crowding in Harlem remained worse than anywhere else in the city.

Family plays a central role in this study, and the findings here suggest that our understanding of family history and women's history is limited if blacks and the poor are marginalized within it. Black families in Depression Harlem were not always constituted in the same way as traditional white middle-class nuclear families were, yet female-headed households or extended families did not suffer the hardships of the Depression in a more sustained or dramatic way than others.

I intentionally avoided one subject related to family life. Depression-era discussions of illegitimacy were filled more with defensiveness or cries of moral outrage than with reliable data. Statistics and the reminiscences of residents reveal that illegitimacy was more openly admitted in the black community, but no data speak to what the actual rate of illegitimacy was for either race. Was it more common in the black community, or simply more effectively hidden in the white? At the time, legitimacy was of concern to officials not only because of their moral sensibilities, but also because it determined eligibility for relief programs and the like. For this study, however, the important question is not whether the parents of children were legally married, but rather how children were cared for, and what impact, if any, male absence had on the economic life of the family.

The study concludes with an overview of employment, relief, and black activism in the early war years. The increases in defense production did little to help blacks until a threat to march on Washington, D.C., persuaded President Roosevelt to issue Executive Order 8802 forbidding companies holding government defense contracts to discriminate on the basis of race. This, in turn, spurred other political efforts. The appreciable benefits that came to Harlemites still never matched the promises held out by white leaders. The early war years brought substantial improvements to Harlem in some areas, but altered little or nothing in others. This contradiction prompted Harlem's second riot in under a decade, and it is with this that the book closes.

Several themes emerge from this exploration of Depression-era Harlem. These can be summarized apart from the details that undergird them. Perhaps most central is the complexity of Harlem's black community. Southern-born, northern-born, and foreign-born blacks shared the experience of discrimination, but their different backgrounds meant they did not always hold the same assumptions or values.[5] Class also divided them. Segregated by race, well-to-do and poor cohabited in Harlem, yet remained divided by neighborhood or street. The social interactions of these groups did not overlap any more than they did in the white community, and their attitudes toward political questions often differed.

Still, everyone in Harlem faced similar deprivations and limits; these differences within the community primarily affected what choices individuals had in responding to those difficulties. This study suggests that certain generalizations about life in the Depression can be applied to Harlemites as a whole. By and large, traditional black family and social structures continued to provide the basis for survival in that period. Fluid household membership embracing many outside the nuclear family, a strong sense of community rooted in black churches, and black political and self-help organizations all sought to enlarge the boundaries that constrained Harlemites. Harlem provides a case study for examining in some detail these personal and communal strategies.

Faced with the challenges of the Depression, discrimination, and unemployment rates of close to 50 percent, blacks in Harlem built on existing traditions of response, expanding and transforming them. Some issues, generally those involving poverty per se, produced individual and private responses. Others, particularly those that highlighted and challenged racial inequality, more often brought Harlemites together in large groupings. The dynamics of these shifting modes of action are here explored at length. What beliefs, structures, and patterns of association determined affiliation in these social and political groups and guided their course of action?

The goals of most Harlem blacks remained identical to those held before the Depression: an end to discriminatory practices and better access to the benefits whites in American society routinely enjoyed. While the Depression made these goals more urgent, it did not bring a wholesale reconsideration of them. Few Americans of any race explicitly challenged the basic assumptions governing opportunity in the United States. Although many struggled to further humanize the economic system in the Depression, few sought the complete overthrow of capitalism or questioned the allocation of social benefits according to income. White liberals tended to couch racial distinctions in class terms, thereby masking the extent to which race and class overlapped in America. Because most on the left accepted this perspective, the interlocking structures of racist institutions remained invisible and virtually impenetrable. It was only within these frameworks that most black efforts for improvement operated, whether individual-, family-, or community-based.

What did change in the Depression was the balance between political and philanthropic activity, and the increased willingness of many in the black community to use confrontational tactics to achieve broadly agreed-upon goals. While community organizing was not new to the Depression, the 1930s saw the growth of a widespread, activist political culture in Harlem that spread from traditional organizations, such as the NAACP and the black churches, to the black community at large. Three factors were central in encouraging such a politicization. The Depression intensified hardship, while the responsiveness of New Deal programs to pressure groups highlighted the importance of an organized and forceful political voice. Perhaps most critical, the administrations of President Roosevelt and Mayor LaGuardia held out the possibility of racial equality. Without that hope, no incentive to organize could be persuasive enough.

Thus thousands of black women and men became politically active in the 1930s, forming new groups like the Harlem Cooperating Committee, the Harlem Housewives League, and the Afro-American Federation of Labor, and spurring other organizations like the YWCA, the Association of Colored Graduate Nurses, and black social clubs to work with them for social change. Women played a tremendously important role in this, a role most scholars have only recently begun to recognize. Groups that began by serving the immediate needs of their constituents shifted toward a broader political perspective, demanding more government aid or better protections against discrimination. Coalitions of organizations further spread this new political culture and brought more substantial successes. Failures, too, played a part—in delineating the limits of existing political goals and social critiques, and in revealing the structural problems that lay beneath the surface. This politicization process fundamentally altered the nature of black protest.

This work fills several gaps in the historical literature, and provides a testing ground for the hypotheses of several important books about blacks during the Depression. Most examinations of Harlem or of blacks in New York City end with the 1920s. Perhaps the most prominent of these is Gilbert Osofsky's *Harlem: The Making of a Ghetto,* an indispensable tool for understanding the background of Depression Harlem. Others, such as Nathan Huggins' *Harlem Renaissance,* David Lewis' *When Harlem Was in Vogue,* and Jervis Anderson's *This Was Harlem,* focus primarily on art and culture. Broader studies of blacks in the 1930s—for example, Harvard Sitkoff's *A New Deal for Blacks,* Raymond Wolters' *Negroes and the Great Depression,* and John Kirby's *Black Americans in the Roosevelt Era*—suggest the impact of the New Deal on black communities across the United States. The first two also focus primarily on black elites and their impact on national politics. This book provides an opportunity to test and apply their more general findings in a specific community and examine closely the lives of ordinary people. Similarly, Nancy Weiss's *Farewell to the Party of Lincoln* offers invaluable insights into the workings of the dramatic switch in black political allegiance from the Republican to the Democratic party during this time, and her findings are fleshed out by the specific detail of Harlem.

All of these works provide the crucial backdrop to the story told here. I am interested in the daily life of a community—the single largest black community in the nation. Distinct from the works just cited, this book focuses on the way national policies affected the lives of their supposed beneficiaries and the ways these national trends operated in or were challenged by Harlem. While our approaches are different, all of these works grapple with similar questions about the black community. In what ways did race and class interact in the Depression? What was the dynamic that sustained or weakened the hegemony of interlocking racist institutions and assumptions in white society in this period? What issues and concerns prompted blacks to action? What forms did that action take? In what ways did the black experience in the Depression set the stage for later developments in the struggle against racism?

I follow the path that has been laid out at least in part by others: St. Clair Drake and Horace Cayton's *Black Metropolis* examined Depression Chicago, for example, and Julia Kirk Blackwelder explored issues of poverty, class, and race in *Women of the Depression: Caste and Culture in San Antonio.* Harlem, however, has not received scholarly scrutiny for the most part. The research that has been done on Harlem in the Depression, most notably Mark Naison's *Communists in Harlem During the Depression* and Larry Greene's doctoral dissertation, "Harlem in the Great Depression," has concerned itself with specific aspects of that experience, in these cases political and institutional. I have relied heavily on their work and generally support their conclusions, but my focus is a broader one, which attempts to place those experiences in the context of the larger community.[6]

While these historical questions and studies informed my effort, a body of material that was not a work of history at all made perhaps the most significant contribution. In many ways the Mayor's Commission on Conditions in Harlem was the springboard for this study. From the start the group demonstrated an energy for detailed investigation and an integrity that impress all those who have encountered its work. The fourteen members with a staff of thirty collected thousands of pieces of information, ranging from numbers and types of black businesses in Harlem, to arrest records for Harlem precincts. The records include public testimony from more than a hundred witnesses, community surveys, statistics on health and education, and notes and reports on housing, health, education, employment, and relief. These data appear throughout this book, and inform many of its conclusions.[7]

The commission's conclusions about the riot bring us full circle, reminding us of the link between violence and Harlem's larger problems, tying the riot to discrimination and to poverty: "There is solid ground for the bitter resentment of the people of Harlem. . . . The very susceptibility which the people in the community showed toward this rumor [of Rivera's death] was due to the feeling of insecurity produced by years of unemployment and a deep-seated resentment against the many forms of discrimination which they had suffered as a racial minority."[8] It is an examination of that experience that is the subject of this book.

CHAPTER 1

Depression in
the Age of Prosperity

Harlem. For many Americans in the 1920s the word evoked images of "hot, throbbing jazz," of "happy-go-lucky negroes" rubbing shoulders with "angry black poets."[1] This was the era of the Harlem Renaissance, of flowering black culture and pride. Practically every famous black figure of the time had moved to Harlem: poets like Langston Hughes and Countee Cullen; novelists and writers like James Weldon Johnson and Claude McKay; activists and intellectuals like W. E. B. DuBois and A. Philip Randolph. White America praised black writers and musicians, and frequented black clubs and speakeasies.

Not only the black cultural and intellectual mecca, Harlem was also an important center for black political activity. The National Urban League, the National Association for the Advancement of Colored People, and Marcus Garvey's Universal Negro Improvement Association had their headquarters in Harlem. The Brotherhood of Sleeping Car Porters and the Trade Union Committee for Organizing Negro Workers began there. Black political clubs flourished, as did an outspoken and activist black press.

Black migration to Harlem brought more than artists and intellectuals, of course. As Nathan Huggins notes in *Harlem Renaissance,* "Harlem for blacks, like New York for whites, was synonymous with opportunity." In the twenties the black proportion of Manhattan's population rose from 5 to 12 percent. New York attracted hundreds of thousands of southern black migrants, as did Chicago and a handful of other cities. West Indians also came to Harlem; in 1930, 55 percent of all foreign-born blacks in the United States lived in New York City. As African-American playwright Loften Mitchell reminisced, "[In] the Harlem of my first recognition . . . southern Negroes fled from physical lynchings and West Indians from economic lynchings. They met in the land north of 110th Street and they brought with them their speech patterns, folkways, mores and their dogged determination."[2]

This mix of diverse peoples made Harlem a uniquely exciting African-American community. Black leaders noted Harlem's vibrant energy, its existence as a separate "city within a city, the greatest Negro city in the world." Mitchell described it as a "distinct nation that was much like a small town." "It had movement, color, gaiety, singing, dancing, boisterous laughter and loud talk," wrote James Weldon Johnson. Claude McKay called Harlem "the queen of black belts."[3]

13

Despite civil rights laws, Jim Crow policies were widespread in New York and black economic development lagged behind white. Nevertheless, black writers in the 1920s insisted that the improved economy, the commitment of many in New York City government to legal equality, and the economic and artistic strides made by blacks would soon establish racial equality. "I know of no place in the country where the feeling between the races is so cordial and at the same time so matter-of-fact and taken for granted," commented Johnson. Through hard work and perseverance, many argued, blacks themselves would destroy forever the negative stereotypes many whites still held about their race.[4]

This belief proved too optimistic. Economic and artistic advancement was not sufficient to dislodge entrenched racial discrimination or lessen Harlem's widespread poverty. Segregation inevitably meant high rents, while lack of skills and discrimination in training, hiring, and promotions resulted in low occupational levels for most Harlemites, leaving them with incomes well below the city's average. Consequently, health and housing conditions there were notoriously poor, and overcrowding in Harlem was worse than almost anywhere else in New York City. Such economic and environmental conditions placed tremendous strains on families. Crime and juvenile delinquency rates exceeded those of more affluent areas. In reality, Harlem crumbled into a slum while optimists noticed only advancement. It lived in depression before the Depression.

"A Self-Contained City"

New York City blacks had not always lived in Harlem. Only in the early twentieth century did it become the city's primary area of black settlement. At the time the complex interactions between segregation and urban growth created a center for black life there that was also a ghetto. Harlem held diverse black populations within it who were knit together both by black institutions that nurtured them and by white racism that limited their opportunities.

In 1904 the IRT (Interborough Rapid Transit) subway line reached Harlem, provoking a flurry of speculative building there. Hurried construction often meant poor-quality housing, and building owners found it difficult to fill the new apartments. At the same time, existing residents of Harlem, who were primarily Jewish, began moving into the suburbs as their economic status improved. This left older, well-built homes vacant as well. In areas not undergoing population shifts, white landlords continued to discriminate against blacks. In Harlem, however, the numerous vacancies pressured local landlords to accept any interested tenants. Most of New York's black community was at that time clustered in poorer housing in the West Fifties and Sixties and so Harlem was attractive to them. They were willing to move into homes others found undesirable, because segregation limited the choices for black renters.

A black real-estate agent, Philip Payton, bought property on 134th Street and Fifth Avenue in 1904 and opened good-quality Harlem buildings to black tenants for the first time. In spite of some white protest, several white real-estate owners followed suit. The influx of blacks sped the process of white emigration. Faced with vacant apartments and with dwindling numbers of white tenants, landlords would not refuse blacks. When they did, blacks pooled their resources and bought the buildings themselves. By 1925, African-Americans owned an estimated 60 million dollars' worth of Harlem real estate.[5]

A community began to form at what is now Central Harlem at 135th Street east of Eighth Avenue. As the black population grew, the boundaries spread outward in all directions. Fewer than 4,000 blacks lived north of 125th Street in 1905. By 1920, 84,000 blacks were living there. They constituted the vast majority of the community's population in the center of Harlem and a substantial minority at its edges. This expansion did not occur in gradually widening circles as some theories on urban growth suggest; rather, the black population spread unevenly from the center of Harlem into nearby areas.[6] Blacks moved south and northwest first; the move to the east and west was slower because whites in those areas left later and more sporadically. By 1930, black Harlem included most of Manhattan between Park Avenue and Amsterdam Avenue, north from Central Park to 155th Street. It held close to 190,000 blacks: two-thirds of New York City's black population and over 80 percent of Manhattan's.[7]

The new black community, while offering pleasanter surroundings than other black areas in the city, was no less segregated. In 1927, Dr. Kelly Miller, a sociologist and a dean at Howard University, described Harlem as

a solid Negro community . . . with as definite lines of demarcation as if cut by a knife. There was no compelling law. Indeed, the tradition and practice of New York State are against any form of racial discrimination by law, and yet this process has gone on and still continues as effectively without the law as with it.

As black newcomers came to the city, then, Harlem was simultaneously an attractive location and one of the few neighborhoods open to them. The migrants therefore joined the rush of Harlem settlement and squeezed within Harlem's narrow confines. Black Harlem did expand geographically, but at a much slower rate than its population did. As in other cities with a growing minority population, residential segregation seemed to increase. Population in black areas rose, but the neighborhood could not expand quickly enough because whites in nearby areas resisted the spillover. Louise Kennedy, a scholar of black migration in this period, hypothesized that white resistance tended to become fiercer in such circumstances because the threat of integration grew with the black population increase. Thus black areas became more densely populated and lines of segregation actually hardened.[8]

Segregation also meant Harlem contained within it most of the services a community required. As E. Franklin Frazier described it: "Not only has the location of the Negro community been determined by economic and social forces inherent in the growth of the city, but . . . the expansion of the Negro community has assumed the pattern of a self-contained city."[9] Harlem had access to at least some services from four nearby hospitals: Harlem, St. Luke's, Community, and Sydenham. Two other clinics offered additional health care for adults, and several more provided health services for babies, children, and pregnant women. The New York Urban

League, a branch of the public library, the YWCA and the YMCA, the Abyssinian Baptist Church and the Mother Zion Church were all located within two square blocks. Harlem held fourteen public schools and six public playgrounds. Music and dancing could be had at the Apollo on 125th Street, the Savoy Ballroom on Lenox Avenue, Small's Paradise on Seventh Avenue at 135th, and the Rockland Palace on 155th Street; and theater at the Alhambra and the Lafayette, both on Seventh Avenue. Main shopping areas were found on the avenues and on 125th, 135th, and 145th Streets. Harlem residents enjoyed the popular pastime of "strolling" up and down Broadway and Seventh Avenue. As Loften Mitchell wrote:

> Seventh Avenue . . . was kept immaculate by community pride. . . . No one dared to be caught dressed sloppily on Seventh Avenue—colored folks' Broadway. . . . Seventh Avenue on Sunday afternoon was where you strolled. . . . Strolling, despite its seeming casualness, was exacting. You had to walk with your right leg dipping a bit, resembling a limp. Your fedora was snapped smartly over your right eye. You and your young lady started just below 116th Street, moving north up Seventh Avenue. Three hours and a half after the start of your stroll you made it to Henry's Sugar Bowl on 135th Street. There you had a malted and met other friends. Then—you started "strolling" downtown.[10]

Much of the growth of black Harlem came from the migration of southern-born and foreign-born blacks. In the twenty years before the Great Depression, New York City's black population more than tripled (from 92,000 to 328,000), while the white population rose 41 percent. Migration caused most of this increase; less than a quarter of New York City blacks in 1930 had been born in New York State. According to the Mayor's Commission on Conditions in Harlem, since 1910, southern-born blacks constituted almost two-thirds of the black population there.[11]

Southern black migrants came north for many of the same reasons whites did. The boll weevil and soil exhaustion pushed them from the land. With the outbreak of World War I in Europe and the subsequent immigration restrictions, many migrants to northern cities found opportunities in manufacturing and industry. Letters from friends or relatives in the North boasted of a better life. Blacks had other reasons as well. They came in hope of escaping southern discrimination, Jim Crow laws, lynching, poll taxes, and segregated schools. As Alain Locke wrote:

> The wash and rush of this human tide on the beach line of the northern city centers is to be explained primarily in terms of a new vision of opportunity, of social and economic freedom, of a spirit to seize, even in the face of an extortionate and heavy toll, a chance for improvement of conditions . . . a mass movement towards the larger and the more democratic chance—in the Negro's case a deliberate flight . . . from medieval America to modern.[12]

While many cities in the North offered economic and social opportunities for these southerners, Harlem as a "race capital" provided special attractions as a destination. According to the Reverend Adam Clayton Powell, Sr., Harlem "became the symbol of liberty and the Promised Land to Negroes everywhere." A black former South Carolinian explained, "Well, that's the way it is about New York. Every person, I don't care who he is or where he is, wants to see New York some day. They have all kind of ideas about what it is like." As one contemporary migration study concluded: "The metropolitan area of greatest attraction to [black] migrants . . . was New York City." Nor were the newcomers disappointed in their expectations; few moved back once they had settled in Harlem.[13]

Foreign-born blacks also joined the swollen ranks of the new arrivals. Eighteen percent of Manhattan's black population in 1930 came from foreign countries, mainly from the Caribbean. Of the 99,000 foreign-born blacks in the United States in that year, 55,000 lived in New York City. Almost half had arrived in the previous decade. Although they were viewed as a monolithic population by whites and native-born blacks, each national group perceived itself as different from the rest: Jamaicans, Bermudans, Antiguans, Virgin Islanders.

When these southern and foreign migrants arrived in New York, they joined an established community of blacks, many of whose families had been in the city for a century or more. Both segregation practices and personal preference dictated that the newcomers settle into existing black neighborhoods, but relations between them and the established black community were often strained. While northern blacks recognized their common bond of racial oppression with black southern migrants, and understood the southerners' desire to better their condition, they also looked down on the newcomers' seemingly backward and ignorant ways. Charles Johnson, editor of the National Urban League's journal, *Opportunity,* wrote in 1925 that the differences between southern and northern Negroes were "greater than the differences between whites and Negroes," noting especially the southerners' seemingly "primitive and reckless" behavior. Louise Kennedy concurred: "There are various indications that numbers of northern blacks did not eagerly welcome the migrants but, instead, sought to keep aloof from them."[14]

Perhaps the sharpest tensions, however, arose between native-born and foreign-born blacks. Many of the latter were poor, but a good number came from "middle, artisan and laboring classes," according to W. A. Domingo, a contemporary West Indian journalist and president of the West Indian National Council. With a different historical experience of race relations and often arriving with skills or education, they generally felt little kinship with American blacks and disdained their occupations. They had "contempt for body service and menial work" and for the Americans who performed them. More often than native-born blacks the foreign-born pursued higher education, entered skilled jobs, and opened businesses. As one means of distinguishing themselves, many refused to relinquish their foreign citizenship even after years of living in New York.

The antagonism ran both ways. There is evidence of a great deal of prejudice and resentment directed by American blacks at this foreign-born community. Many resented the foreigners for being dismissive and overbearing toward other blacks and too radical politically. They called the foreigners "monkey chasers" and "coconuts" and were called "handkerchief heads" in return. Discriminatory housing practices elsewhere in the city necessitated that both populations cohabit in Harlem nevertheless.

As a result, Harlem was not a monolithic community. The different groups tended to cluster in smaller, separate neighborhoods there. In some, Jews or Italians

remained. In others, such as Sugar Hill and Striver's Row, upper-class blacks settled. Puerto Ricans, West Indians, and southern black migrants often lived separately. Single black men and women generally preferred to live in Central Harlem,
while families with children more often chose apartments toward Harlem's edges.[15]

"A Class as Well as a Race"

What did unite Harlemites was race. More than any other factor, race determined
residents' occupational and social opportunities. As was true in the rest of the
United States, Harlem's blacks worked primarily in low-paying jobs with little
opportunity for mobility. Eugene Knickle Jones of the Urban League noted,
"Negroes represent a *class* as well as a *race*."[16] The low occupational level of Harlemites reflected the legacy of racism and segregation that prevented most blacks
from obtaining much education or skill, and that continued to prevent those with
skills from obtaining appropriate employment. Black men and women did not have
the same jobs, but both remained at the bottom of their respective occupational
ladders in what has come to be called a split labor market, which reserved the best
jobs for whites.

Southern-born blacks in particular lacked education and skills; further, many did
not consider education as a means to success. In the South, because of the poor
quality of their public schools, many blacks lacked even the most basic skills. A
majority came to New York without having completed grade school, and few had
any vocational training. Often coming from the land, many southern-born black
men had experience only as agricultural laborers. Poverty and the discrimination
of white employers had made education a luxury; historically, educated southern
blacks had found they had little economic advantage over the non-educated. Some
blacks therefore had turned away from the newly freed slaves' commitment to education.[17]

While the desire to get an academic education did reassert itself once they were
in the North, black adults had access to only three of the city's adult education
classes. The YMCA, the YWCA, and the New York Urban League supplemented
these with a few classes of their own, but overall opportunities for adult education
in Harlem were minimal. In contrast to their desire for academic learning, southern
blacks apparently continued to show little interest in vocational training, perhaps
because they hoped for other opportunities in the North. The Urban League
reported that few black students enrolled in vocational courses. These limits on
black education, both externally and self-imposed, ensured that blacks would
remain at unskilled jobs even if higher positions did open to them.[18]

But such positions did not open to blacks. While New York City's economic
structure defined the limits of opportunity for every worker, primarily race determined employment level. Blacks fared worse than any other group in the labor
force. Opportunities for advancement were few, and earnings low. Both employers
and unions continued to maintain racial barriers to mobility, compounding the difficulties blacks faced in trying to transcend past discrimination.

Blacks had long been barred from many training and apprenticeship programs, and from skilled and white-collar positions. Both employers and trade unions practiced such exclusion. Louise Kennedy, studying the employment patterns of urban blacks, noted, "the attitude of organized labor is one of the most persistent and effective checks to the Negro's advancement in skilled work." Since most trades in New York were unionized, and most unions excluded or discriminated against blacks, advancement for them was almost impossible. Jake, the protagonist of Claude McKay's *Home to Harlem*, explains the situation from the black worker's perspective:

"I ain't no white folks' nigger and I ain't no poah white's fool. When I longshored in Philly I was a good union man. But when I made New York I done finds out that they gived the colored mens the worser piers and holds the bes'n a'them foh the Irishmen. No, pardner, keep you' [union] card. I take the best I k'n get as I goes mah way. But I tells you, things ain't none at all lovely between white and black in this heah Gawd's own country."

His friend Zeddy went further, condoning the actions of blacks who "scabbed." Here, fiction mirrored fact. Black men and women had gained entry into certain industries only as strikebreakers, many times crossing the picket lines of unions that had excluded them. Black longshoremen in New York got their start this way, for example. As Zeddy put it, "I'll scab through hell to make mah living.... White mens don't want niggers in them unions, nohow.... Ain't white mens done scabbed niggers outa all the jobs they useter hold down heah in this city?" These sentiments were widely held in the black community. If black workers' loyalty lay with anyone, it lay with the employer who provided the job, despite the fact that employers were often no better, refusing to hire blacks or to promote them once hired.[19]

Distinct from the problem of discrimination, but compounding its effects, the economic structure of New York itself and the timing of most blacks' arrival there limited black opportunities for mobility. New York, with its preponderance of skilled and white-collar jobs and of small manufacturing firms, provided few opportunities for unskilled or unschooled labor. The city lacked most of the large industries that provided some upward mobility for African-Americans in other cities at this time. The proportion of the total population engaged in manufacturing in 1930, 35 percent, was lower than the figures in other large northern cities, including Chicago, Cincinnati, Detroit, and Philadelphia. Many of the manufacturing positions that did exist had already been taken by the eastern and southern Europeans who had arrived in New York before the migration of large numbers of blacks. While some African-Americans had been in New York all along, racist practice generally dictated that employers choose white workers over black as long as the supply lasted, thus reinforcing a segregated occupation structure.

Aided by the demands of world war, New York's blacks did move increasingly into factory employment, as blacks did elsewhere in the country. But they entered at the bottom, taking the unskilled jobs. Even had there been no restrictions placed on black advancement, they could not have improved their position. It had taken the white immigrants almost a generation to rise in manufacturing; by the 1930s, when blacks would have had the same length of time to begin the rise through the industrial ranks, the city was in a deep depression, and production had contracted.

If New York City lacked substantial opportunities in manufacturing, what it did have, and in abundance, were service jobs. Low paid, offering no mobility, these jobs did not attract whites and were generally filled by blacks, who had few other options. In fact, a larger proportion of black men in New York than in the nation as a whole worked in service occupations.

All these forces contributed to the lack of opportunity for New York's black workers. In 1920, two-thirds of all gainfully employed blacks in New York worked in occupations classed as unskilled.[20] Past discrimination, New York's economic structure, and contemporary racism in the form of a segmented and discriminatory job market accounted for the low economic status of New York's black community.

While these forces operated in determining job opportunities for both men and women, each sex had distinct employment experiences. Black men most often worked as laborers, porters, or did other sorts of menial tasks, as Table 1.1 indicates. There were some differences between native-born and foreign-born black men. In his study of blacks from 1925 city census data, Herbert Gutman found that proportionally more West Indians held skilled positions than did native-born blacks. The same proportion of Americans and West Indians worked in business and the professions, but since native-born blacks far outnumbered the foreign-born, the tiny black middle class of Harlem was made up predominantly of the former.

Black men in the city did find more economic alternatives than they did in many other places. Of the 321 specific occupations listed by the 1920 census, in New York

TABLE 1.1

Gainfully Employed Males: Rate by Occupation Level and Race
for Non-agricultural Jobs, New York City and U.S., 1920[21]

	New York City			United States		
	Black	White		Black	White	
		All	Foreign-born		All	Foreign-born
Managers, officials, proprietors	1.5	18.4	16.2	2.0	11.5	11.5
Clerks & kindred	8.3	11.8	10.9	2.8	15.9	7.2
Skilled & foremen	7.9	⎡	22.3	8.5	22.3	22.3
Semi-skilled	14.5	53.0	25.6	14.7	21.1	23.7
Laborers	28.5	⎣	13.0	54.5	19.2	26.9
Service	35.0	8.1	6.9	14.0	2.3	3.9
Public officials	0.1	⎡	0.2	<0.1	0.7	0.2
Public employees	1.4	3.3	1.3	1.2	2.2	1.4
Professionals	2.8	5.4	3.6	2.4	4.7	2.8

all but five included at least one black. Those from the poorest areas of the South noticed the differences. Migrants from St. Helena, South Carolina, interviewed by Clyde Kiser reported that they "are engaged in a wider variety of occupations, the tempo of work is swifter, and contacts with employers more impersonal than in other cities. . . . Possibly more than those in any other city [Kiser speculated], the migrants in New York have tended to rise or fall to levels of occupation commensurate with their training, intelligence, and skill." Therefore, from the point of view of blacks themselves, especially southern migrants, their economic status had improved.

Nevertheless, they fared much more poorly than whites. Newly arrived European immigrant men quickly moved into jobs in higher occupational categories than those in which most black men could be found. This opportunity differential operated despite equally low levels of education in the two communities, and a higher proportion of illiterate adults among the immigrants.[22]

Black men remained at the bottom in industry, and excluded from most skills. Although the number of black machinists in the city rose fivefold between 1910 and 1920, in the latter year they still constituted less than 1 percent of all city machinists. In the same year New York blacks made up less than 2 percent of all carpenters and masons, lower than the black proportion in those fields nationally. Twenty-one percent of Manhattan's black men worked in manufacturing and mechanical industries in 1920, up from 12 percent a decade earlier. Still, the white proportion in those fields was twice as large, and far more white men than black held skilled and supervisory positions.[23] Discrimination, therefore, meant educated and skilled black men could only find menial jobs. A. Philip Randolph worked as a porter for Consolidated Edison after college. Black journalist George Schuyler commented with stunningly savage imagery: "Turn a machine gun on a crowd of red caps . . . and you would slaughter a score of Bachelors of Arts, Doctors of Law, Doctors of Medicine, Doctors of Dental Surgery."[24]

This gloomy economic picture remained unchanged through the twenties. The general prosperity of the period had little impact on black men's occupational status; by and large the black community remained lower class. In no type of employment did the black male population vary more than two percent from the beginning to the end of the decade. Herbert Gutman found three-quarters of his sample of black city dwellers (both migrants and long-term city residents) held non-skilled and service jobs in 1925, approximately the same as the 1920 rate. Nine-tenths of all employed black males worked in blue-collar occupations, slightly higher than the 1920 figure. His estimates of blacks in business and the professions show the earlier rates unchanged. As was true elsewhere in the country, the percentage of black males in skilled labor changed little between 1920 and 1930. The proportion of black men in manufacturing in 1930, 22 percent, had risen only one percent in a decade. While overall white workers did not experience a tremendous improvement either, their increases in clerical, professional, and semi-skilled work surpassed those of blacks.[25]

Low occupational levels meant correspondingly low wages. Investigations found $33 a week the minimum income necessary to maintain a "fair American standard" of living for a family of four in Manhattan. Clyde Kiser reported black

unskilled laborers in New York City in 1928 earned $20 a week, while skilled work-
ers ("of whom practically none belonged to trade unions") rarely made over $30.
Ottley and Weatherby placed a black "workingman's" earnings at $18, and noted
that the coveted job of Pullman porter paid only $67 a month. The New York
Urban League's (NYUL) 1927 study found black males in Harlem earned an average of $24 per week. The vast majority of black men in that study worked in man-
ufacturing and mechanical industries and many reported frequent layoffs. Only 1
percent of the sample earned more than $175 a month, or approximately $40 a
week. Over half earned under $23 per week.[26]

Many of the black men who earned so little made no less than whites working at
the same jobs; wages for unskilled jobs were universally inadequate. The average
weekly wage for all city workers in "common labor" in 1927 was approximately
$27, and $37 for industrial workers as a whole. Still, blacks and immigrants worked
more often than did native whites at laboring jobs and the lowest industrial levels
because discrimination and lack of skills constrained their choices. Every report
examining black or immigrant industrial workers, for example, found they earned
between $24 and $31 in this time period—generally not because they were paid less
for the same work but because they worked at the lower skill levels. Both race and
foreign nativity proved economic liabilities in New York.

In some cases blacks did earn less than whites for the same work. Unlike industrial work, service jobs often did differentiate pay by race. Adam Clayton Powell,
Sr., reported a sign in an employment agency that read:

An elevator boy wanted—Colored; hours 8 A.M. to 8 P.M. daily, $65 per month.
Elevator boy wanted—White; hours 8 A.M. to 7 P.M. daily, $90 per month.

As Powell commented, "Even in New York it costs an elevator man 365 hours of
extra labor and $300 a year to be colored."[27] By and large, then, "even in New
York" the race problem compounded the class problem.

Black women who worked faced many of the same difficulties in finding rewarding
employment. In the black community, wives worked more often than single
women, a pattern different from that of whites. The bulk of working white females
were unmarried and under twenty-five, while the proportion of black working
women steadily increased with age until sixty-four. Thus marriage, which freed
most white women from the need to work, had no such effect for blacks. The NYUL
found men the sole breadwinners in less than a fifth of the African-American families it surveyed. Two-thirds of all mothers and wives worked outside the home, four
times the native-born white rate. Owen Lovejoy of the Children's Aid Society estimated that 88 percent of black married women in Harlem worked outside the home
or sought such work. Some of these women, and others, also worked by taking in
lodgers. This higher rate of black female employment was true for the country as a
whole: over 40 percent of all black women worked in 1920, more than twice the
proportion of both native-born and foreign-born white women. The distinction was
particularly marked for wives; a third of all married black women worked during
the 1920s, compared with less than 10 percent of white wives.[28]

Evidence suggests that black wives went to work more often than white not only because their husbands' wages were lower, but also because of a different attitude in the black community toward women's participation in the labor force. Black wives worked five times as often as equally poor foreign-born women; obviously economic need was not the sole condition motivating black women to work. History and culture played a role as well. Black women knew from centuries of experience that they were as capable of working as men were. Though they may have held as tenaciously as whites to a middle-class dream of being housewives, their history offered a competing model of a black mother. Mary White Ovington described her: "an industrious, competent woman, she works and spends, and in her scant hours of leisure takes pride in keeping her children well-dressed and clean."[29]

Black women sought work in every area open to them, but they faced significant obstacles. First of all, black women were able to enter only those few fields open to white women—and not all of those. As black social worker and assistant school principal Elise McDougald argued in a 1925 article, the black woman labored under the dual burden of race and gender. She suffered from inadequate wages and economic barriers because of her sex, but the benefits of being female (such as protection from heavy work) did not apply to her because of her race. Prevalent ideals of beauty excluded her. As a black, and penalized by past and present discrimination, she was further handicapped by the "low wages of her men," lack of training, and recent entry into urban occupations. All of these placed her at the bottom of the economic scale.[30]

Thus black working women faced different but not better economic opportunities than black men did. Barriers such as racial discrimination by employers and unions, and lack of training, applied to them as well. Although the number of black

TABLE 1.2

Gainfully Employed Females: Rate by Occupation Level and Race for Non-agricultural Jobs, New York City and U.S., 1920[31]

	New York City			United States		
	Black	*White*		*Black*	*White*	
		All	*Foreign-born*		*All*	*Foreign-born*
Managers, officials, proprietors	1.0	7.8	3.8	1.8	3.6	5.5
Clerks & kindred	2.7	2.7	16.1	1.5	33.3	14.4
Skilled & foremen	0.3	⎡	1.1	0.2	0.9	1.5
Semi-skilled	30.0	2.9	43.2	14.0	31.6	42.1
Laborers	0.7	⎣	0.7	4.1	2.3	3.6
Service	63.1	22.7	29.6	74.6	13.3	26.6
Public officials	—	⎡	—	<0.1	0.3	<0.1
Public employees	—	0.1	0.1	<0.1	<0.1	<0.1
Professionals	2.3	9.8	5.4	3.9	14.8	6.4

women doing skilled work or in the professions increased between 1910 and 1920, only two percent of all working black women held professional jobs in the latter year. Less than four percent worked in clerical, proprietary, or managerial occupations, even though that category included boardinghouse operators. By contrast, over a quarter of employed white women worked in clerical or similar jobs, and another 10 percent were professionals. In the twenties the proportion of black women working in the professions and doing clerical work rose slightly, but the contraction of industrial production and the onset of the Depression swelled the ranks of domestic and personal service workers, and cut the proportion of black women working in manufacturing by almost a third. Thus the commonest experience for black working women before the Great Depression was in unskilled, domestic, and service work.[32]

Close to 70 percent of all employed black women in Manhattan in 1920 worked in domestic and personal service. George Stigler concluded in his study of this topic:

> The low social status of domestic service, the absence of vocational or educational requirements, and the discrimination practiced in other lines of employment seem adequate to explain the fact that immigrants and negroes have constituted more than half of the female servants since 1900.[33]

These domestics earned approximately $15 a week during the 1920s. Those in service jobs who did not work for private families often earned even less and worked in worse conditions. Nor did they generally make as much as their white counterparts. As was the case with men's work, service jobs for women tended to provide better pay and job conditions for whites than for blacks. The median weekly wage for black laundry workers in 1928 was $8.85, compared with $16 for white workers. According to the Trade Union Committee for Organizing Negro Workers, "to say that they [black laundry workers] are being most brutally exploited is to put it very mildly. In many instances, these young girls are forced to work from 7:30 A.M. until 7:00 P.M., with ½ to ¾ of an hour for lunch; they work six days per week and receive from eight to ten dollars as a weekly wage." The committee reported on one large Harlem laundry whose owner fired his white workers who had worked five and a half days a week with an hour off for lunch. He replaced them with blacks who were made to work six days a week, with forty-five minutes for lunch, for the same wage.

Nor was there much hope for advancement. As the *New York Age* reported in 1925, black women pressers at the Leo Cooper Company could not rise to the better-paying positions: "The colored girls are only given opportunty for washing soiled dresses and ironing them." The company kept its windows closed, although the irons used steam heat, and the week before the reporter's visit, two women "were taken ill on account of the unfavorable conditions and were given medical treatment." Yet these women could not afford to quit, the *Age* reported. One woman had a sick husband and a five-month-old baby. Others supported "aged parents" or "have children that are being boarded in private families or have debts that necessitate their helping their husbands. Still others are unable to do the hard day's work in private families, and can find no other kind of employment."[34]

Some did manage to find other work. Twenty-three percent of New York's black women worked in manufacturing and mechanical industries, higher than the proportion of black men. In fact, the rate of black women working in industry rose faster than that of black men, a phenomenon true in a good many cities. World War I opened the factory doors to black women, most of whom preferred the life of industrial labor to the long hours, confinement, and contant supervision of domestic service. They entered the garment trades; leather and dyeing industries; stock rooms; and paper, toy, and candy factories. Still, their late entry into industrial work and widespread discrimination ensured that they, like black men, remained in its lowest ranks. Except in the garment trades, where the International Ladies' Garment Workers Union (ILGWU) actively recruited members of all races, workers had difficulty rising from their unskilled jobs to skilled ones. As in the laundry trade and other services, Mary White Ovington wrote, "The colored girl in New York meets with severer race prejudice than the colored man and is more persistently kept from attractive work. She gets the job that the white girl does not want."[35]

Skilled black women also had difficulty obtaining employment in their fields. As a 1919 YWCA study noted: "One would have to wait many days to hear of even one request for a Colored bookkeeper or stenographer. . . . These [trained black women] finally entered factories doing unskilled, monotonous work—their spirits broken and hopes blasted because they had been obliged to forfeit their training on account of race prejudice." Ninety percent of black women interviewed by the YWCA who had entered industry reported they did so to make more money or to gain skills, but they soon discovered that prejudice barred their progress.

Like male factory workers, most of these women worked a forty-eight- to fifty-hour week. In the needle trades, the industry with the highest wages, the YWCA found half of the black female employees earned $12 a week, "a starvation wage in these days of high prices." In nearly every industry: "White workers on the same processes received from $2 to $5 a week more than their Colored sisters. . . . Throughout the trades, differences in the wages of the Colored and White were unmistakable." Though some employers explained these differences with laments of lower black productivity, others admitted they paid blacks less no matter how good their work. A paper-bag manufacturer who owned two factories paid $8 a week to workers in his all-black factory. In the second, where both whites and blacks were employed, he "was forced to pay a minimum of $15.00."

In part, the ability of employers to pay lower wages to black women than to white can be attributed to the fact that only 12 percent of these black industrial workers belonged to unions. The ILGWU, the Amalgamated Clothing Workers' Union, the Fancy Leather Goods Union, and a few others demanded equal pay for black and white, "largely, no doubt, from a desire to protect their own interests," the YWCA study drily commented. Where blacks belonged to unions their wages were higher. Why, then, did so few black women join unions? The YWCA concluded that "industrial ignorance and the lack of understanding of the value of collective bargaining have caused Colored women to accept low wages, as well as unpleasant work."[36] Economic need also forced these women to accept non-union jobs.

Nor did union membership necessarily seem attractive to them. Almost three-quarters of the black women interviewed had never heard of unions or had never been asked to join. A small number had tried to join a union and were rejected or made unwelcome. In this, the experience of black working women and men converged. With the exception of the ILGWU, unions did little to recruit black workers, and because blacks had traditionally been excluded from unions, even those who could join did not always view it as desirable. As a result, however, over half of the interviewed black women workers in 1919 reported incomes of less than $10 a week. By 1928, their average weekly wage had risen to approximately $13, but 84 percent of white women earned more. At the upper level, no black women reported wages over $20, while 22 percent of whites did.[37] While both black men and women earned less than their white counterparts, women also earned less than men, putting black women at the very bottom of the earning scale.

Government work could have provided a real alternative to black men and women unable to find decent positions in the private sector, but the city did not fulfill these expectations. Few professionals or other white-collar workers found satisfactory opportunities in municipal agencies. Nor were many particularly successful in establishing lucrative private businesses or services in Harlem.

New York City provided many services to the public, services that required workers at every level. Many qualified blacks expected to receive municipal jobs appropriate to their skill level, especially given the Progressive era's civil service reforms. Unfortunately, in reality these reforms did little to speed black progress, because many in control of city agencies used the new system to maintain their power. For example, the police, dominated by the Irish, manipulated unionization and civil service rules to keep the non-Irish out of the leadership ranks. Lacking political power, blacks were denied a foothold in the bureaucracy. Since each agency was essentially self-governing, those not in power had difficulty advancing. The Police Department assigned black policemen to black areas only, and set a no-promotion policy in regard to them which remained in force through the end of the 1920s.

Black professionals hoping for municipal employment fared little better. Black doctors and nurses were barred from practicing in public hospitals. Five years of black protest led by a coalition of the NAACP, the National Urban League, the *Amsterdam News,* and several churches finally forced the city in 1918 to agree in theory to accept black interns into public hospitals, but only one was in fact given a post. Every public hospital was governed by a private board, each of which refused to accept blacks. Although Harlem Hospital did agree to hire black nurses in 1923, no hospital staffs allowed black doctors.[38]

Mayor Hylan, who governed New York City from 1918 until 1926, suggested the creation of an all-black hospital to circumvent these difficulties. Fearing neglect by the city and second-class care, the black doctors (now organized into the North Harlem Medical Association) and their supporters refused. A 1925 compromise saw five black physicians appointed as visiting staff at Harlem Hospital and a promise to give blacks preference for interning positions. The coalition continued to agitate until the Harlem Hospital bureaucracy was reorganized in 1929 and admitted blacks as permanent staff. Even then, few blacks practiced in any public hospital other than Harlem Hospital.

The 1929 solution was a partisan victory. Appointments were made on a party basis: a black doctor already at Harlem Hospital was fired while new black doctors were appointed, based on political affiliation. The reorganization itself was done so the Democrats could regain control over the administration of city hospitals. Thus Harlem Hospital finally employed blacks because of political expediency; it proved no more responsive to the needs of the black community than before.[39]

Individuals in other ethnic neighborhoods who found it difficult or undesirable to rise through municipal or wage work used the resources of their own communities, opening local businesses serving local needs. Excluded at every turn from New York's mainstream, Harlem's small pool of black professionals and businessmen and -women, many of them foreign-born, served their own community as well.

Yet even there, blacks faced special difficulties. Black businesses were generally poorly capitalized and thus could not compete effectively against better-financed whites. Instead, blacks moved into low-profit fields and competed against one another for a small share of the market. A survey conducted in 1928 found 330 barber and beauty shops and 198 food stores and restaurants run by blacks in Harlem. Another 129 offered laundry and tailoring services. Together they accounted for half the black businesses there. The following year another study surveyed two-thirds of Harlem's census tracts and found almost 40 percent of black businesses were in personal service. A third of the net sales of all Manhattan's black businesses came from groceries, restaurants, and other eating places. Given the preponderance of black businesses in these fields, it is hardly surprising to discover that as a whole black businesses in Manhattan had yearly net sales of only $10 per capita (of the black community).[40]

This predominance of service establishments mirrored national trends. Restaurants, laundries, and beauty shops required less training and capital, neither of which many blacks had. Banks showed a reluctance to provide loans to black businesses, whether because of racial antipathy or a high rate of failure by such businesses in the past. This kept blacks out of capital-intensive businesses. It also meant black stores were more poorly stocked than most of those owned by whites, so prices were often higher, and credit less available to customers.

If blacks had had needs peculiar to themselves that only other blacks could provide (like Jews who needed kosher meat, for example) black stores could have competed successfully against white, even with higher prices. By and large, such was not the case. Beauticians, undertakers, and a few others offered services the white community was unwilling to provide (or, in the case of laundries, offered services traditionally performed by blacks, and at a lower price). Black restaurants offered Harlemites familiar cooking and an alternative to unpleasant treatment at white downtown establishments. All this helps explain why the bulk of black businesses fell into these categories. Yet even in these fields white businesses in Harlem outnumbered black. For most services, larger and better-financed white establishments competed successfully against black ones in the same neighborhood. They could often offer the same products at a lower price, or provide a more varied selection.

Thus, even in their own communities, black women and men in business found economic success difficult to achieve. Blacks ran less than 20 percent of all Harlem's businesses in 1929: 1,908 out of a total of 10,319, according to one study. A 1928 editorial in the *American Recorder* (tellingly entitled "Boost Harlem") surveyed Harlem's business community and concluded:

> It is, indeed, quite true that business enterprises in the community are in the hands of alien races. . . . While it is true that many white people would not live among colored people they do not find it difficult to trade with them in their own locality. . . . Every effort of the colored man to conduct business in his own community is destroyed by the powerful competition of white businessmen.[41]

The twenties, so prosperous for many in the country, had been no better to Harlem business and professional workers than it had to those in lower-paying and lower-status employment. The fundamental structure of opportunity had not changed for either group.

Standard of Living

As a result, most Harlem families remained poor in the 1920s. Although black wages and earnings in New York were higher than in the South, so was the cost of living. Clyde Kiser pointed out that "the rent and food cost alone in New York . . . is sufficient to reduce an annual family wage of $1,000 in New York to a parity with the average family income of $427 in St. Helena." As it was a segregated neighborhood, Harlem had higher rents and food costs, while black earnings were lower. Therefore, although most white families were able to make ends meet in the 1920s, black family income generally remained too low to provide an adequate standard of living, even when several family members worked.

As noted above, the National Industrial Conference Board calculated that an industrial worker's family of four "living at a fair American standard" in Manhattan in 1926 needed $33 a week: $12 for food, $4 for clothing, $8 for rent, $2 for fuel and light, and $7 for sundries. To test its assumptions, the board examined the spending habits of the city's native-born white industrial workers' families. Those with four members actually spent $32 per week because they spent slightly less on rent than anticipated by the board. A single male living alone should expect to pay $19 a week, the Conference Board estimated, and a single woman living at home, $13. (The board estimated slightly lower costs for women because their food expenses were expected to be lower.) The $37 average industrial weekly wage and contemporary observations suggest many New York working-class families were in fact able to sustain a "fair American standard of living." As the New York City Department of Health optimistically reported in 1926: "The sale of milk at various [baby health] stations is falling off. There is apparently a great deal less poverty in the city now than ever before."

If the average white industrial worker's family earnings came close to the standard set by the board, black earnings did not. President Hoover's Conference on Home Building and Home Ownership found that Harlem families during the 1920s earned an average of $1,300 a year ($25 a week), well under both the "fair American standard" and the average New York City family's earnings of $1,750.[42]

Despite this, many influential black leaders blamed black financial instability on foolish spending habits. The Reverend Adam Clayton Powell, Sr., preached in a 1928 sermon:

> Extravagance is the outstanding sin of the members of our race. We eat too much, drink too much, sleep too much, frolic too much, talk too much, show off too much, and bury too much money in the graveyards.[43]

The denial of social status concomitant with economic level often led to ostentatious spending by moneyed Harlemites, a phenomenon widely reported by blacks and whites of the period. To blame the debts of the hard-working black poor on extravagance, however, is to ignore the basic inadequacy of pay scales for menial work and the reality of segregation and discrimination, which intensified the problem. Not only was the average Harlem wage lower than that of other workers, living expenses were higher. Most important, few Harlem apartments rented for the low rate the Conference Board had estimated.

Harlem's housing problems illustrated the implications of discrimination and poverty. Because of the city's segregation practices, Harlem landlords could raise rents without fear of losing their black tenants. As Judge John Davies of Harlem's Municipal Court testified at a 1925 hearing of the Mayor's Committee on Rent Profiteering: "It is common for colored tenants in Harlem to pay twice as much as white tenants for the same apartments." This discrepancy in rents was not new. A 1915 study by the National Urban League (then the National League on Urban Conditions Among Negroes) found that in Harlem, black families paid $4.71 per month per room, while German Jews living in the same area paid only $4.03. Furthermore, rents in Harlem surpassed those for comparable dwellings elsewhere in the city. A United Neighborhood Houses study in 1928 found the typical white Manhattan working-class family paid $316 a year for rent. In Harlem, a comparable black family paid $480. Between 1919 and 1927, average New York City rentals rose 10 percent. In a Harlem block, rents rose almost 100 percent, from $22 to $42 per month. Landlords held black tenants essentially captive.

The rental differences between Harlem and the rest of the city did not reflect any higher quality in Harlem houses. In 1927 the New York Urban League conducted a survey of Harlem, which found that residents there spent $14 to $18 per room per month for a heated apartment. The average rent for such an apartment in Manhattan as a whole went from $12 in old buildings to $15 in new ones.[44]

Indeed, a large proportion of Harlem families lived in poorly maintained apartments. The NYUL study classified more than half the Harlem apartments it surveyed as "bad" or "poor," with rents exceeding those in the rest of Manhattan. One-fifth of those interviewed by the NYUL lived in apartments with only cold water. Over 10 percent had no bath. Many others with both heat and bath reported these were in disrepair. A 1929 survey of Harlem's Twenty-first Assembly District showed a quarter of the tenements there violated Tenement House Department regulations.

Not surprisingly, given such conditions, black residents moved frequently within Harlem. Almost half the surveyed population had lived at their current address for less than a year. The most frequent reason given was the constant search for adequate housing. The fact that blacks had lived in their apartments for less time than many white tenants, however, cannot account for higher Harlem rents either. According to the Housing Commission, if a tenant in 1927 had occupied a typical three-room city apartment for two years, the rent would be $36.25. In Harlem, however, after two years of residency, the NYUL found the same apartment would cost $55.70.[45] This finding also suggests the higher Harlem rents could not be due to differences in apartment size.

Because Harlemites earned less than other city dwellers and faced higher housing costs, they paid more of their incomes for rent. The United Neighborhood Houses study found that while New York City dwellers paid an average of one-fifth their income for rent, those in Harlem paid over one-third. The NYUL survey found almost half the families studied paid at least 40 percent of their income just for rent; Owen Lovejoy found that rent cost more than half of black average income.[46] High rents made it still more difficult for Harlem's families to earn a decent living; an adequate minimum income in Harlem would need to be higher than the required minimum elsewhere in the city.

Harlem's residents met expenses by relying on such expedients as "rent parties." Tenants invited acquaintances, cooked food, and hired musicians. Clyde Kiser cited one example of an invitation from 1929:

> Shake it and break it. Hang it on the wall.
> Sling it out the window and catch it before it falls.
> At A SOCIAL WHIST PARTY given by _____ at _____.
> Saturday evening, March 16, 1929.
> Music by Texas Slim. Refreshments.

This party cost twenty-five cents for admission. Refreshments were sold and the total collected helped pay the rent. Some noted this cooperative practice with approval, some with skepticism. Kiser commented:

> Not so much from the desire to help a family pay the monthly rent as from an assurance that there will be found wild dissipation, music, orgiastic dancing, "hard licker," and pickled pigs' feet, do the Harlemites crowd into the rooms and "make whoopie." Originally an attempt by a destitute family to raise funds for rent and at the same time to provide entertainment for their friends the "rent party" has become a systematized practice organized and bordering on the "racket." In many cases, however, it is still a serious and imminent need which motivates them.

Black families also took in lodgers to help meet payments. Several of the families surveyed by the NYUL went so far as to offer "hotbeds." Night workers slept in a bed by day; day workers slept in the same bed that night. Most households did not go to such extremes. Still, the NYUL found 3,314 lodgers in their survey, an average of more than one per household. Fifty-four percent of the apartments contained at least five people; since the average family size was just under four, many households must have contained members who were not part of the nuclear family. To put it another way, almost three-quarters of all Harlem families had two or fewer children, but only 46 percent of all Harlem households contained four members or less. Conversely, very few black families (5 percent) had six or more children, but almost a third of all black Harlem households contained at least seven people. Gutman found a third of such "augmented" households included members of the extended family, while two-thirds held unrelated lodgers. While every study provided a slightly different figure for the proportion of black families with lodgers, it seems clear that black families used this income-producing strategy more often than white families. According to historian Gilbert Osofsky, while 26 percent of black apartments contained at least one lodger, 11 percent of white Manhattan apartments did. Nor were lodgers new for black families. A 1915 Urban League study found 59 percent of the families surveyed had lodgers. Over half of those 1915 households also included children.[47]

In Harlem mutual benefit was derived from boarding. By offering space to non-settled individuals, families supplemented their income while providing desperately needed accommodations for new migrants, unmarried workers, or poor single parents. A 1927 survey, for example, found accommodations in YWCAs and similarly supervised housing for only 226 single black working women; thousands more sought rooms in boardinghouses or with private families.

Yet the taking in of lodgers also made that area one of the most densely populated in New York. The average density in the white neighborhoods of Manhattan in 1925 was 223 people per acre. The comparable black density was 336 per acre. In 1930, the New York Housing Authority found the population density of one Harlem block to be 671 per acre, and 620 in another. The block of 140th to 141st Street between Seventh Avenue and Eighth Avenue was "reputed to be the most crowded dwelling area in the world."[48]

All in all, then, while the quality of Harlem's housing may have been no worse than that in much of Manhattan, segregation meant higher rents and poorer upkeep by landlords. This, given the residents' lower incomes, brought overcrowding, high death rates and poor health, a large transient population, lack of privacy and recreational space, and high crime. As Gilbert Osofsky noted in his excellent study of the subject: "The most profound change that Harlem experienced in the 1920s was its emergence as a slum." Poor housing was not necessarily the cause of Harlem's problems, but it was certainly a physical manifestation of them.

Poverty, overcrowding, and poor housing conditions led to startlingly high illness and mortality rates. Black rates of malnutrition, disease, and death far exceeded white. In 1925, there were 16.5 deaths for every thousand blacks in New York City. That figure was 40 percent higher than that of the city generally, and 13 percent higher than that of Manhattan. The racial difference is more striking considering the relative youth of the black population. If the black rates were standardized for age, the death rate per thousand blacks would be 18.3.[49]

Harlem's illness and mortality rates were almost identical to the black rate in the rest of the city and nationwide, indicating that Harlem's black residents shared the lower life-expectancy common to all African-Americans of the period. White mortality rates in Harlem were higher than Manhattan's, but lower than those of Harlem blacks, and can be accounted for by the large proportion of elderly men and women in the white Harlem population.[50]

This higher death rate for both Harlem and New York City blacks appeared in almost every category, as Table 1.3 indicates. Maternal mortality was two times the general city-wide rate, infant mortality (death of a child under one year) and still-births almost double, tuberculosis deaths over three times higher. According to a 1920 study of urban areas of New York State, death rates for every age group until eighty were higher for blacks than for whites.

Deaths from homicide in Harlem were 73 percent higher than elsewhere in Manhattan, and almost four times higher than in New York City as a whole; more than two-thirds of those murdered in Manhattan were black. Conversely, Harlem's suicide rate was well under Manhattan's. Blacks were less than 40 percent of all Harlem suicides, although two-thirds of its population. Throughout New York City, blacks resorted to suicide far less often than their white counterparts did. It is not clear why this is true, but such findings are not unique to New York. It reflects, perhaps, the lower expectations of a long-suffering population. More positively, the low suicide rate demonstrates the power of a "survival culture" and strong communal solidarity nurtured under slavery and carried forward into freedom.[51]

In some cases, these high black rates were lower than national figures. The general death rate for blacks nationwide was 18.2 per thousand, and black mothers died in 12 deliveries per thousand births in the United States. In all other categories, though, Harlem's rates exceeded the national averages for blacks. In this, Harlem's experience mirrored the pattern of other black ghettos of the urban North. Contrary to contemporary claims that they were healthier because they had better access to health care, blacks in northern cities taken as a whole had a death rate of 22.1 per thousand. Most other specific death rates, such as infant mortality and tuberculosis,

TABLE 1.3
Death Rates from Selected Causes for New York City,
New York City Blacks, Manhattan, and Harlem, 1925

	Rate per 100,000 Population Unless Noted:			
	New York City			
Cause	*Total*	*Black*	*Manhattan*	*Harlem*
General death rate (per thousand pop.)	11.4	16.5	14.3	16.2
Pulmonary tuberculosis	75.5	258.4	111.8	180.6
Pneumonia	132.8	282.4	163.9	220.7
Suicide	14.8	9.7	21.0	16.4
Homicide	5.3	19.5	11.0	18.7
Syphilis	7.2	41.0	?	?
Infant mortality (per thousand live births)	64.6	118.4	72.9	114.4
Maternal mortality (per thousand total births)	5.3	10.2	4.8	8.2
Stillbirths (per thousand births)	47.6	82.7	55.0	71.8

were also higher than in the rest of the country. Except for its overall mortality rate, Harlem reflected this higher urban rate: its infant mortality, stillbirths, tuberculosis, and pneumonia all surpassed nationwide black levels.[52]

Harlem's appallingly high death rates are no puzzle; its limited access to health care explains them. For the most part, the few free clinics run by the City Health Department or by private organizations provided the only medical facilities available to blacks. Few could afford private hospital or convalescent care even if such institutions had accepted black patients. Fees for private doctors were similarly difficult for most Harlemites to pay.

Several health agencies had made a start in providing free health care in Harlem, but the problems were far larger than the resources provided. In 1915, the Department of Health and private social agencies cooperated in creating "a constructive program of service to reduce Negro infant mortality in New York City." They opened clinics and educated black mothers about nutrition and health care. In two years, black infant mortality dropped from 202 per thousand births to 173. Projects elsewhere in Manhattan had also demonstrated the improvements in infant health that could be achieved. The Association for Improving the Condition of the Poor established a free prenatal care clinic in 1917, in the Columbus Hill section (west of Columbus Circle) where many blacks still lived. Between 1917 and 1923, it compared the health of these babies with the health of those born in Harlem to mothers who did not attend a clinic. Sixty-eight of every thousand Harlem babies born alive died within a month. In Columbus Hill, mothers receiving any prenatal care had 34 deaths per thousand. With three or more months of prenatal care, the rate dropped further, to 21. With better services, the black infant mortality rate could have been halved.[53]

In 1922, a Harlem Tuberculosis and Health Committee was established. It, too, provided clinic care and spent $4,000 for "educational work among negroes." In 1923, the New York Urban League opened two buildings on West 136th Street to house a division of the Visiting Nurses Association and the Tuberculosis and Health Committee. It reported a drop in Harlem's infant mortality rate: "The death rate of infants . . . reflected in direct proportion the amount of health work done." Recognizing the need for convalescent care, the Urban League also provided twelve beds for women, at $12 a week. The East Harlem Health Center, established in 1920, helped bring the death rate down in that area from 15.8 deaths per thousand in 1920 to 10.1 in 1927.

Despite all this activity, Harlem still had fewer clinics per capita than did the rest of Manhattan. With 14 percent of the borough's population, and a higher proportion of its deaths, Harlem contained only 9 percent of Manhattan's free clinics. It had 14 percent of Manhattan's prenatal and baby health clinics, comparable to its population but not to its infant death rate—almost a quarter of Manhattan's total. For all other clinics, Harlem's allotment fell far short of Manhattan's average. As the Welfare Council noted in its 1926 report on public health, because there were no special black hospital facilities, because blacks could not afford private hospitals, and because there were not enough integrated public hospitals, there were not enough beds available to provide for their needs. James Hubert of the Urban League added that only one-twentieth as many convalescent beds were available for blacks as for whites. As late as 1929, the Association for Improving the Condition of the Poor still lamented that "there is no group in the community in greater need of intensive health service than the colored people."[54] Much of this inequality was due to the dearth of voluntary agency work in Harlem. Few non-black agencies in the 1920s developed programs that targeted the black community, and black agencies lacked adequate funds.

Contemporary analysts understood that the high black death rate could not be blamed solely on inadequate health care. Even with an equal proportion of prenatal and baby care clinics, Harlem's black infant mortality rate remained higher than the national figure, while New York's white infant mortality rate was lower. Winthrop Lane, contributing editor of a journal of "constructive philanthropy" called the *Survey* (later renamed *Survey Graphic*), argued that as blacks learned better sanitation, mortality would decline. Dr. Nathan, who studied health conditions in North Harlem, attributed the high death rates to blacks' "comparatively low economic status" and its concomitant ills. Examining infant mortality, which she noted "is generally recognized as the most sensitive index of health conditions available, especially in congested centers of population," she found "a striking correspondence of low infant mortality in those areas where breathing space is available."[55] Harlem's overall high rate, she concluded, was "mute testimony to the effect of poverty, ignorance and congestion. . . . High infant mortality among the colored may also be due in some degree to gross infraction of the recognized laws of infant hygiene. . . . The prenatal clinics in Harlem are excellent, so far as their work goes, but at present only a comparatively few mothers are receiving effective guidance in antenatal hygiene." She also found a higher mortality among newly urbanized blacks and among those coming from warmer climates. Overall,

> Causes which might account for [the] large proportion of stillbirths [and infant deaths] are inadequate prenatal and neonatal care, illegitimacy, venereal diseases and the tendency of too many mothers to work at hard labor until the very day of confinement. . . . Mothers should be kept from arduous work and should be provided with adequate medical care, as well as with financial assistance, when urgently needed. Considering the limited facilities to be found in North Harlem at the present, it seems extremely doubtful that these aims will be attainable in the near future.[56]

Crime and Its Context

As Nathan suggested, Harlem's problems resulted from a complex combination of economic, demographic, and social factors. These same factors affected juvenile delinquency, child neglect, poor school performance, and adult crime. Economic privation, lack of supervision, and the paucity of recreational facilities in Harlem contributed to the rise of black delinquency in the 1920s.[57]

Because both parents generally had to work, children required outside supervision. Some private agencies provided such services. The New York City Colored Mission and the Protestant Episcopal City Mission conducted nursery and vocational schools, boys' and girls' clubs, and fresh-air outings, which, the Colored Mission's report noted condescendingly, "have helped many of our little brown-skinned friends." The Children's Aid Society opened the Henrietta Industrial

School for Negro Children in 1892. Three years later the Kindergarten Association for Colored Children was established. By 1905, the Negro Fresh Air Committee was building playgrounds. Yet in the 1920s, Harlem's few day nurseries served only approximately 6 percent of children with two working parents. Ten percent were cared for in private homes. Another third of all parents left their children with relatives or friends. Half the children, however, were left alone. The Children's Aid Society claimed Harlem had "only 15 percent of the recreation facilities it needs." The Joint Committee on Negro Child Study found only one boy of the fifty they interviewed on the street had had contact with any form of organized activity—in this case, the Boy Scouts.[58]

The lack of adequate services contributed to the high rate of juvenile delinquency in Harlem. The examination of these statistics is important for its illumination, not only of the community's problems, but also of the racism many believed integral to the system of criminal justice. The NYUL found that in the 1920s, proportionately three times as many black children as white appeared in Children's Court as alleged delinquents. Blacks made up 8 percent of all cases arraigned in court in 1925, and 11 percent in 1929, although they were only 3 percent of all city juveniles.

This was hardly surprising, since most black children lived in impoverished families, and poor children were more often charged with juvenile delinquency. Not only did poverty give them more reason to commit crimes, police were also more likely to arrest poorer children for activities passed off as pranks or high spirits when committed by wealthier youngsters. Owen Lovejoy also attributed high rates of black delinquency to the unsettling effects of migration. He pointed out that in 1915 the black community contained far fewer migrant families. Two percent of the total city population, blacks constituted less than 2 percent of that year's delinquents.[59]

If the 1925 statistics are indicative of the decade's general pattern, in the 1920s police arrested black youths primarily for breaches in public order: deserting home, being "ungovernable and wayward," or disorderly conduct. For white children, the picture was more mixed. While plenty of white children were also charged with various forms of disruptive behavior, authorities charged white boys most often with

TABLE 1.4

Arraignments of Black and White Youths in Children's Court:
Most Common Delinquency Charges, by Charge, Race, and Sex, 1925[60]

	Boys		Girls	
	Black	White	Black	White
Total cases	582	7895	308	2727
Total delinquency cases	418	5719	125	708
Percent of delinquency cases accused of:				
disorderly conduct	28.2	19.8	3.2	2.5
deserting home	17.2	12.2	34.4	42.7
stealing	16.8	20.4	6.4	12.7
burglary	10.0	20.0	0.0	0.3
ungovernable and wayward	8.4	6.7	49.6	35.2

criminal activities: stealing and burglary. Twice as many white girls as black, proportionately, appeared in court for stealing.

Although this suggested to many that black juvenile delinquency, while more widespread, was not as truly criminal, a closer look suggests a more complex picture. Authorities arrested more blacks for disorderly conduct than for burglary, but in proportion to their population, both figures were higher than for whites. For example, police arrested 30 white boys out of every 10,000 for stealing, compared to 45 black boys per 10,000.

Although disorderly conduct was certainly not as significant a form of delinquency as stealing, 76 black boys were arrested per 10,000 for that charge, compared to 29 per 10,000 white boys. In proportion to their population, police arrested black girls for stealing more than twice as often as whites. They were arrested for deserting home four times as often, and were considered "ungovernable and wayward" almost seven times as often. Overall, proportionately more than twice as many black children as white were arraigned in Children's Court in the mid-twenties. This rate held both for "serious" truants and for those charged with lesser offenses.

There were other differences between the races. Significantly fewer black cases than white were dismissed before trial. In 1924 and 1925, for example, a third of all black delinquency cases were dismissed, compared with almost half of all such white cases. Of those standing trial, a higher proportion of blacks than whites were found guilty.[61]

Estimating black delinquency rates from court statistics, however, raises certain problems. Police could not have caught and arrested all children who committed crimes. They may have been more likely to apprehend black children than white for petty crimes, or the court more likely to convict them. The higher proportion of guilty verdicts for blacks suggests either judges and social workers discriminated against black children or that the higher number of black juvenile arrests reflects a higher rate of criminal activity among black youths. The data provide no clarification, but certainly both factors contributed to the high black juvenile delinquency rate, given the racism of the time and the poverty and inadequate services of Harlem.

"The figures themselves," Clyde Kiser pointed out, "make one suspicious that the high rate for Negroes and the preponderance of minor offenses are due to the prosecuting of Negroes accused of minor offenses and to the quashing of those against whites." Sylvia Robison added that the number of arrests of black youths might be higher "because of a tendency on the part of white authorities to suspect Negro children more frequently than they would suspect white."

On the other hand, some black leaders suggested the figures might be skewed in the opposite direction. Ira deAugustine Reid pointed out the broadly known fact that the police were less vigilant in Harlem, and might therefore ignore the misbehavior of some black children. He further suspected that black victims were less inclined to accuse black children of crimes than whites would be to accuse white children because the youth would be turned over to a white police officer and because blacks had less faith in the criminal justice system. Finally, since fewer facilities served blacks, perhaps police recognized they could do little, and so would issue reprimands rather than arrest children for whom no services existed.[62]

Whether too many or too few black children entered the juvenile justice system, there is no question that discrimination continued to operate after they were found guilty. Available evidence suggests racial differences when judges sentenced children "adjudged delinquent." Overall, a black child was five times as likely as a white to receive the most lenient judgment of a suspended sentence. But a far higher percentage of blacks than whites were placed in institutions, and they were generally sentenced for longer terms. Almost twice as many black delinquents as white served a sentence of over five years. Whites received probation five times as often as blacks.

The two groups of youths were treated similarly in discipline cases (ungovernable behavior and disorderly conduct), but not for illegal acts (ranging from burglary to stealing subway rides). One might suspect the higher proportion of suspended sentences for blacks related to their higher rates of arrest for minor infractions, but the evidence does not support such a conclusion. The sentencing differences are not due to the types of crimes committed. For example, the largest proportion of both suspended sentences and commitment for blacks came from stealing and burglary cases. At the other extreme, three black children were arraigned for riding subway cars illegally. One child's case was dismissed; one received a suspended sentence; the third was placed in an institution.

White children did have greater access to private services than blacks did; fewer white than black delinquent children ended up in Children's Court in the first place, because more were helped by private agencies before appearing there. Not only does this fact help to account for the higher black arrest rate, it also may explain why more whites than blacks were let off with probation, in order to attend private programs. Of children remanded for care before 1930 and still serving a sentence in that year, the majority of blacks were held in institutions, while the majority of white children were receiving "field agency" services. Presumably, also, sentencing judges trusted white home life more than black, and were thus more likely to consider probation for white delinquents. These patterns had been true throughout the 1920s. In 1923, for example, while less than 6 percent of all arrests, blacks constituted 18 percent of the population in institutions for delinquents, indicating both the higher proportion of black children remanded to institutions, and their longer sentences.[63] All in all, the experience of black delinquents in the criminal justice system reveals in chilling detail both the lack of adequate facilities for youngsters in Harlem, and the racism of the white power structure.

Children's Court also heard cases of neglect. The proportion of the youth population appearing in court for neglect did not vary from year to year for either race until 1929. Still, the proportion of black neglect cases each year was more than twice as high as the proportion of blacks in the population. Half of these black children were under seven years old. Not unexpectedly, like delinquents, neglected children of both races came primarily from poor families.[64]

The forces promoting delinquency and neglect also acted on the adult population. More than 15 percent of all prisoners in the Greater New York area jails were black, although blacks made up less than 5 percent of the total adult population. Several factors contributed to this result. Studies showed that most of those in police or court records were single or childless, often lodgers, between 20 and 44 years old. More blacks than whites fell into these categories, which accounts for some of the race differential. Still, the proportion of black arrests far exceeded white, even cor-

recting for age and marital status. Several black observers suggested that the proportion of black criminals was high because police were more prone to arrest blacks
than whites. But poverty seems the most significant explanatory factor. As with
youths, poor adults were arrested and convicted more often than the wealthy. Furthermore, many impoverished blacks were imprisoned because they could not
afford to pay their fines or make bail. Finally, crime rates (numbers of crimes
reported) were in fact higher in Harlem and other poor areas, hardly a surprising
finding.[65]

While violent and property crimes certainly occurred, more arrests involved participation in illicit trades. The Thirty-second Police Precinct (in Central Harlem)
reported that officers arrested few blacks for serious offenses. The most widespread
criminal activity in Harlem involved the "numbers" or "policy" game. Although
it was illegal, "all of Harlem played . . . the humble laundrywoman and the disrep-
utable pool player, as well as the respectable schoolteacher," Claude McKay wrote.
Players chose a three-digit number and bet a certain amount; say, a nickel. This
information was given to a "runner" who passed it to the organizer or "banker."
Combinations of the day's stock market figures determined the winning numbers.
Those guessing all three numbers correctly won 600 times their original wagers—
in this case, $30. Since 1,000 combinations were possible, and the return was 600
times the wager, policy men made huge profits. Runners, too, took a percentage of
the winnings. The larger economic issue was unimportant for most players, however. Numbers offered a chance for everyone. Not surprisingly, "the success of the
numbers game attracted white 'bankers' to Harlem. . . . A vast new field of exploitation was opened up in Harlem . . . in the decade following the world war."[66]

White adults who looked to Harlem for their illicit pleasures compounded the
crime problem there. Bootlegging and prostitution flourished, encouraged by the
thousands of white visitors eager for thrills. "Harlem has become a 'slumming
ground' for certain classes of whites who are looking for picturesqueness, for 'thrills'
and, too frequently, for a convenient place in which to go on a moral vacation,"
lamented the Committee of Fourteen, which combated city vice.

This phase of the situation is being exploited by certain white men and women who are
operating resorts and dives to cater to visitors from downtown. The "easy morality" of
the Negro may or may not be a fair allegation, but it certainly is not a convincing explanation of a condition over which white officials have control and in which white customers are a major factor.

The committee's investigator in Harlem, working for five days in 1928, found a
greater number of violations of vice and prohibition laws than did all four other
investigators combined, each of whom worked for six days in other areas of the city.
Appalled by "the prevalence and the openness of vice conditions in this district,"
the committee charged that Harlem was a place "to which the white officials of the
city government have been somewhat indifferent." Of the eighty-five speakeasies
the investigator visited, whites owned eighty-one. All served both black and white
customers, and all but seven welcomed prostitutes. As Claude McKay described it,
"Harlem was the paradise of bootleggers. . . . Prohibition had made defiance of the

laws general and racketeering respectable. Some of the most law-abiding citizens patronized bootleggers."

In his visits to sixty-one houses of prostitution, the investigator for the Committee of Fourteen found fifty also sold illegal liquor. These houses were primarily run by black men or women, "with both white and colored inmates for both white and colored patronage." Five offered the services of children under fourteen. As the investigator concluded, "The situation cannot be dismissed as a 'Negro problem' for Harlem is in large measure a reluctant victim of conditions which have been imposed from outside."

Interestingly, Harlem seems to have been a center for prostitution even before it became black. The committee complained about several sections of Harlem in 1905, then inhabited primarily by Italians. This area "was so bad as to be objectionable to decent men, not to mention women."[67]

Each year of the 1920s, between 20 and 30 percent of all the city's prostitution arrests occurred in Harlem. In 1925, black women were 22 percent of all women arrested city-wide, but 36 percent of all prostitutes arrested (although, again, the reliability of arrest statistics as true indicators of crime rates is suspect). Although the committee reported "notable progress" in suppressing this trade in Harlem in 1928 and 1929, the practice continued to flourish, if recurring laments are any indication. In fact, the progress the committee claimed was merely that Harlem's vice was "driven under cover," and so approximated the "largely clandestine" situation elsewhere in the city.[68]

Drug sales also worried officials. An article in the *Lincoln News* in 1929 claimed: "Cocaine Main Harlem Drug."

The sale of dope and drugs in Harlem still continues to be a problem to the Police Department. . . . One can still purchase cocaine, the most common drug, within a two block radius of Lenox Avenue and 135 Street. . . . The habit is continually spreading. . . . Heroine and morphine may also be purchased . . . a little quantity of heroine sells for $32 and liquid morphine is a close second.[69]

Slouching Toward Depression

The increasing crime rate and the large numbers of black child-neglect cases did not occur in a vacuum. While white America boomed and roared through the 1920s, the signs of decline that would become the Great Depression were already visible in Harlem and other poor communities. Factory employment rates in New York City decreased steadily every year from 1923, evidence of a continuing shift away from large industry there. As the New York Urban League reported in October of 1927, "there seems to prevail an unusual amount of unemployment. Already the number of applicants [for jobs] . . . surpassed that of last year—2,798 to date." The next year, although it stopped accepting applications for domestic service, the League's total applicant pool rose by another thousand. Its placement rates, however, declined from 34 percent in 1927 to 28 percent the next year. The Association for Improving the Condition of the Poor claimed the city had the highest unemployment since 1914, the first year statistics were kept.[70]

Private welfare organizations documented the economic decline and its impact on the poor well before other Americans saw it. "The Association [for Improving the Condition of the Poor] began to feel the effect of this [decline] early in 1927 with the increased number of cases applying or being referred to it for some kind of assistance." In spite of their optimism that "the present recession is . . . apparently but a temporary event," charitable organizations reported ever-increasing applications for aid. Expenditures by all social agencies, public and private, rose steadily between 1925 and 1929, especially for direct aid, health, shelter, and employment. This increase could not be accounted for by inflation or by population growth. In constant 1914 dollars, the eight public agencies and thirty-nine private ones spent 53 cents per inhabitant in 1925 and 61 cents in 1929. The number of families "under care" with the Charity Organization Society almost doubled between 1925 and 1929; the proportion of families applying because of unemployment rose from 39 percent of its total caseload in 1925 to 65 percent in 1928.[71]

By February of the latter year, conditions were so severe that the Welfare Council, a cooperative body of the city's largest public and private social work agencies, held a conference for all such organizations to create a permanent committee on unemployment. The agencies' reports "showed a serious falling off in placement of workers in jobs and a corresponding increase in the number of homeless men, seamen and families applying for assistance." The six largest agencies reported a 17 percent increase in applications over the previous year; the New York State Employment Service reported its job placements declined 36 percent in the same period. Looking only at adult males, job placements declined over 50 percent. The danger, the conference noted, lay with the effects of long-term unemployment. The unemployed worker suffered "constant anxiety and undernourishment, . . . loss of self respect, . . . mental and moral degeneration, and from being merely unemployed the worker becomes unemployable." The new committee recommended government action during crisis periods to provide work for the unemployed when industry could do no more.[72]

Its pleas fell on deaf ears. Not only did government provide no work for the unemployed, it did little to help them at all, save for offering free placement services from the New York State Employment Service. Few qualified for state or municipal aid save the blind and disabled, and women with legitimate children under sixteen, whose husbands were dead, permanently incapacitated, in state prison, or had deserted them. These women received money from the Board of Child Welfare, which, because of inadequate appropriations, in fact supported only widows. Even with these restrictions and a two-year residency requirement, the number of new cases rose every year, doubling between 1925 and 1929.

Overwhelmingly poor and unskilled, Harlem blacks felt the earliest effects of economic decline. The New York State Employment Service received 5,600 applications for employment in its Harlem office in 1926, and 6,600 two years later. Although the total Family Court caseload declined in the 1920s, the number of black cases rose, primarily for abandonment and non-support.[73]

Harlem had some help through the troubled economic times from private agencies, but received less attention than did similarly poor white areas. The Charity Organization Society, one of the largest social organizations operating there and 12 percent of whose families under care were black, recognized this imbalance when it announced the opening of a second Harlem office. "'We are opening this second office in Harlem,' said Mr. Purdy [the director of the COS], '. . . because we realize that for the size of the population living in Harlem they are not receiving nearly the leadership and help they should from our civic and welfare agencies.'" Many private services refused any aid to blacks. In all of New York City, only five institutions for juvenile delinquents accepted blacks, three for neglected children and two for the "feeble-minded." Almost a fifth of black Protestant dependent children in 1925 were placed in Catholic institutions because of insufficient Protestant facilities for them. Others were sent to orphanages or returned to unhealthy home environments for lack of alternative care. Several facilities such as Children's Village closed their doors to blacks in the 1920s. The NYUL reported to its executive board that several summer camps that formerly accepted black children at no charge had recently stopped. The children were well dressed by their eager parents, so the camps concluded that they were not poor enough to be "deserving of free camp facilities." Harlem held too few job placement bureaus, emergency shelters, and milk stations. Social work agencies rarely operated there.[74]

So long as the economic decline was limited to a few areas with minority populations, most agencies and the government paid little attention and provided few programs to aid the unemployed. Thus the Great Depression came as a great shock to the majority of Americans. Not so for Harlem. As black journalist George S. Schuyler commented, "The reason why the Depression did not have the impact on the Negroes that it had on the whites was that the Negroes had been in the Depression all the time."[75]

CHAPTER 2

A View from the Bottom: 1930 to 1933

The stock market crash and ensuing economic contractions affected everyone, but the resulting hardships burdened some groups more than others. While every occupational class suffered losses in income and job availability, the unskilled saw the sharpest cut in employment and wages. Because they were concentrated so heavily in those ranks, blacks as a group suffered greater losses than did whites. Furthermore, racism and discrimination intensified during this period of hardship, which meant blacks received fewer of the existing opportunities in each occupational class. The small middle class of Harlem found its numbers reduced by a wave of layoffs and business failures that affected blacks even more than whites and forced hundreds of white-collar workers into the ranks of the laboring classes and the unemployed.

Initial Effects

The first full year of the Depression, 1930, threw almost 10 percent of the employed United States population out of work. It struck one in six in New York City, and one in four among Harlem's blacks. The next year unemployment was higher still.[1] Public and private aid, which expanded to meet the increased need, did not reach all the poor and unemployed. The Harlem community, hardest hit, mobilized on its own behalf to supplement the inadequate services and monies provided by municipal and charity relief programs. Churches and fraternal, social, and political organizations joined together to aid the poor. However limited their resources, Harlem groups fed, clothed, and supported thousands of the black destitute. Unwilling to remain merely victims, blacks rejected passive acceptance of hardship and acted to ameliorate what conditions they could.

That first Depression year was tragic for many throughout the city. The unemployment rate. quadrupled. Social workers representing agencies as diverse as the Department of Health and the Association for Improving the Condition of the Poor reported to the Welfare Council that they "saw much more distress last winter [1930–31], both in extent and in degree, than they had ever seen before, and that standards of living had fallen noticeably in the last two or three years." Many families were inadequately clothed, and "lack of sufficient food . . . was a common experience." The social workers had "the impression of more malnutrition and a lowered vitality among the people they see . . . and of more sickness than usual." Available evidence supports their findings. Public school medical examinations in 1930 revealed 16 percent of all students suffered from malnutrition, up almost 20 percent from the year before. The next year unemployment doubled again, and the proportion of malnourished students rose another percentage point. By the next year it had risen again, to 21 percent.[2]

The Depression inevitably disrupted family life in the city. Juvenile delinquency rose. So did the numbers of cases of child neglect. The Charity Organization Society reported an increase in its desertion cases. "The general opinion" of city social workers "is that it was the exceptional family that got through the winter without serious strain on domestic relationships and a marked deterioration of family life."[3] The Department of Public Welfare reported that the number of applications to commit a child as a public charge rose from approximately 8,000 in 1925 to 10,000 in 1928 as the first hints of Depression reached the poor, to 13,000 in 1930, and 16,000 one year later. In December of 1932, the department reported 23,000 children under institutional or foster home care, far higher than pre-Depression figures. As the City Budget Office noted: "The large increase in the number of children is due largely to the breaking up of homes of destitute families."[4]

As a poor community, Harlem suffered the worst ravages of a collapsing economy. With economic hardship came strains in family life and health, and a rising crime rate. In this sense the experience of Harlem reflects in microcosm the experiences of poor communities made poorer by the Depression. Yet because of discrimination, past and present, blacks also faced problems unique to them.

As New Yorkers commonly knew, blacks were always "first fired, last hired," an experience shaped by both race and economic class. Coming from the South and often lacking urban skills and education, blacks were concentrated in unskilled and service occupations hardest hit by the Depression. Economizing families cut down on domestic help, for example, and by December of 1930, factory production had declined almost 25 percent. As the Joint Legislative Committee on Unemployment pointed out, the "heavy burden of unemployment . . . [fell] on unskilled workers." The early Depression had a less drastic effect on the professions, but few blacks worked in those fields.[5]

Racism also affected blacks' employment situation. Past discrimination, in its denial of adequate education, training, and opportunities, relegated blacks to the lowest occupations, where layoffs were high. Present racism meant the preferential hiring and retention of white workers over black. Because of both, blacks as a group suffered more privation during the Depression than whites.

Every contemporary study documented that in establishments with both black and white workers, employers laid off blacks first. Since blacks had entered factories and shops more recently, they lacked seniority when the Depression struck. Furthermore, since most factories had been unionized by the time blacks received industrial work, and since most unions excluded blacks from skilled or foremen's positions, blacks were let go earlier as the least skilled in the work force. Sometimes employers fired blacks first simply because of their color. The Welfare Council reported that African-Americans lost their jobs in the early Depression three to four times faster than whites, and returned to private employment half as quickly.

For the same reasons, black unemployment was higher than white in every city in the country. In fact, althought their unemployment rate still exceeded that of whites, blacks in New York fared better than those in other cities.

Even those Harlemites who were still employed faced difficulties. Many blacks who lost their jobs did find other work, but often at a lower occupational level. According to a 1932 survey of Health Area 12 in Harlem, in two years of Depression the proportion of black workers in the professions and in skilled and semi-skilled fields had already fallen slightly, while the proportion of blacks doing unskilled work showed an increase. New jobs coming into the Harlem Branch of the New York State Employment Service were at a lower occupational level than work the unemployed had done previously.

Women and men felt this decline in economic options differently. The proportion of black Manhattan women working in manufacturing dropped by a third, to 17 percent, in 1930. (Still, that figure was higher than those for other manufacturing centers, such as Chicago, Cleveland, and Philadelphia.) As elsewhere in the United States, in Manhattan the number of black women who worked as servants had increased dramatically by 1930, rising approximately five times faster than the number of white domestics did. For men, the number of business owners fell, and the ranks of laborers swelled.[7]

Compounding the employment problem, earnings at every occupational level dropped precipitously because of falling pay scales and reduced working hours; employed as well as unemployed Harlemites faced the specter of starvation. Although living costs declined, they did not decline as drastically as wages. Black laborers saw the greatest drop in their income, in some cases to a third of pre-Depression earnings, but no occupational group fared much better. Skilled workers suffered an almost 50 percent salary reduction, while black professionals, who suffered least as a group, saw their income fall by over a third. Their 1932 median earnings of $1,440, highest of any occupational category, were still lower than the median income of all blacks in 1928. The decline in laboring wages is most significant because 84 percent of all African-American family heads surveyed reported

TABLE 2.1
Percent Unemployed in Selected Cities,
by Race and Sex, 1931[6]

| | Males | | Females | |
	Black	White	Black	White
Manhattan	25.4	19.4	28.5	11.2
Chicago	43.5	29.7	58.5	19.4
Detroit	60.2	32.4	75.0	17.4
Birmingham	36.0	18.2	30.6	14.8

themselves in that category; the unskilled alone accounted for 45 percent of the total.

Black domestic workers placed by the State Employment Service in 1931 earned a maximum of $15 a week; most received a good deal less. Factory workers earned $7 to $12 a week, chauffeurs made $15 to $25. Short-term laborers earned $2 to $6 a day.[8] At those rates, few could support families, even with both parents working. While some white workers also earned this little, whites as a group were not as badly off, because white families who lived on such low wages constituted a smaller proportion of their community.

Black children also sought to bring in money any way they could. Black juvenile theft rose, as did child labor. Five percent of the total youth population, blacks made up 12 percent of the alleged delinquent population in 1930, and 11 percent in ensuing years. Twenty-five of every thousand black children between the ages of seven and sixteen were arrested for delinquency, compared with ten per thousand in the (better-off) white community. For both races, these numbers surpassed pre-Depression rates. Larceny and burglary outpaced disorderly conduct as the most common delinquency charge for black boys. Hundreds of children were arrested for selling newspapers after 7:00 P.M. and shining shoes on the street. The rise in juvenile delinquency, then, occurred primarily because legal employment was hard to find: 43 percent of black youths between sixteen and twenty-four and 33 percent of white were unemployed and seeking work.[9]

Thus, despite all their efforts, black families saw a real decline in their total income. In 1932, the Milbank Memorial Fund estimated Harlem's median household earnings at $1,019, a decline of 43 percent from three years earlier, while costs of basic necessities declined only 17 percent in that same period. In 1928, 4 percent of the 1,800 Harlem families the Fund surveyed earned less than $600 a year; by 1932, 24 percent earned that little. Fifteen percent of Harlem's black families earned over $3,000 in 1928, a modest figure, which plummeted to 3 percent in 1932.[10]

In fact, available evidence suggests blacks as a group earned less even than poor whites. The League of Mothers' Clubs studied both black and white tenement families in New York in 1932, and found that the median income of all employed families totaled $1,049. While these earnings had dropped by a third since 1928, the figure was still $30 higher than the median for the entire city's black working population, and $220 more than that for black tenement-house families.[11]

Problems besetting whites as a consequence of economic hardship, then, occurred still more frequently among blacks in these early years of the Depression. Hunger, overcrowding, crime, illness, poor housing, and homelessness stalked Harlemites. As Beverly Smith complained in the *Dunbar News:*

> The . . . average white New Yorker . . . thinks of it [Harlem] as a region of prosperous nightclubs, of happy-go-lucky Negroes dancing all night to jazz music and living during the day by taking in each other's policy numbers. . . . The fact is that this community of 220,000 Negroes is the poorest, the unhealthiest, the unhappiest and the most crowded single large section of New York City.

The Urban League, active in aiding the black unemployed, told its own stories of hardship. It reported receiving word of ten to twenty eviction cases every day. According to its employment bureau, "men and women stand in line from 1:00 A.M. till 9:00 in near zero weather and fight their way past policemen in order to get a chance at $15.00 a week jobs."

The dislocations created by unemployment seem to have reached further inside black society than white. A Welfare Council investigation of black homeless men in the city found they were ten years younger than white homeless on average. Their physical and mental health was better. The black homeless mirrored the characteristics of the general black population. White transients, on the other hand, were older than the average white population, and were more often ill; they came from the fringes of white society. The education level of blacks receiving government aid was identical to that of the general black community, suggesting that unemployment reached those with skills as well as those without. The worst ravages of the early Depression reached all strata of black society; the inroads into white society were less far-reaching.[12]

Economic hardship took its greatest toll on children, as evidenced by the growing number of black parents brought to court for child neglect. While the numbers of white cases did not grow until 1932, suggesting that many white families had savings to fall back on or otherwise avoided the Depression's full impact for a time, the number of black cases rose every year from the Depression's start. Blacks constituted 8 percent of all neglect cases in 1929 but 14 percent of such cases three years later. Many were children like Walter Adams, age four, whose father was charged with neglect for leaving the child alone while he worked. Alfonso Doctor, two and a half, appeared in court because his parents had abandoned him. Both of these children were placed under the care of the Department of Public Welfare. The court placed fifteen-year-old William Hopkins, who had no home and had attempted suicide, with the Children's Society. The Charity Organization Society reported a doubling of the number of black desertion cases in the first two years of the Depression, a far higher increase than for whites. As the New York State Temporary Commission on the Urban Colored Population concluded, the high rates of black child-neglect and abandonment "indicate widespread family disorganization primarily due to economic insecurity."[13]

"Even the most optimistic social worker with Negro families," wrote one former optimist from Harlem's Utopia Children's House in 1933, "must admit that conditions are appalling. During the past year, we have discovered a number of cases of mothers going without food themselves, sending their children to the Utopia House to be fed. These mothers were afraid to make their true conditions known for fear the city would take their children from them." It would be difficult to disagree with the assessment of the Association for Improving the Condition of the Poor that "no group . . . has been more seriously affected by the economic depression than the negroes."[14]

Certainly objective figures indicate Harlemites lived under worse physical conditions than other city residents. As had been true in the past, black illness and mortality rates surpassed white. Infant and maternal deaths and deaths from tuberculosis and pneumonia remained significantly higher for Harlem blacks than for any other city group.

While poor conditions were not new to Harlemites, their neighborhood's quality of life had declined in the early Depression years. Harry Shulman, in his study of city slums, reported that apartments on the Harlem streets he studied "had deteriorated physically" in the five years since his 1926 study. A 1933 article in the Unemployed Council's newspaper, the *Hunger Fighter,* graphically depicted living conditions on one Harlem block:

> Rain pours through the ceiling. Rats dart from great gaps in the walls, windows are smashed, sickness flourishes especially because the garbage is never collected from the dumbwaiters. These are some of the horrors of the Negro worker's life disclosed by the Upper Harlem Unemployed Council after canvassing only three houses at 16, 18, 20 West 116 Street.[15]

Charitable Efforts

There was little Harlemites could do. Since they had earned such low wages before the Depression, few of the estimated 20,000 to 50,000 Harlem unemployed had financial reserves to rely on while looking for work. As a result, while applications by city residents to private relief agencies rose 75 percent between 1929 and 1931, black applications tripled. Less than 5 percent of the city's population, blacks constituted more than twice that proportion of all relief cases. Only the unique and dire hardship of the Depression led most to such an extreme remedy. Three-fourths of these black families had never before applied for any type of aid. Thus the nature and extent of relief in New York City was a crucial issue for Harlemites.[16]

Because of the dramatic increase in the number of poor, public and private agencies expanded their programs. Of the two, private aid expanded far more quickly, because of government reluctance and public budget constraints. Only when private efforts proved unequal to the immense task of relief before them did the state and city finally step in, providing services never before offered by public programs. (The federal government under President Hoover never did; the President advocated private and local aid and gave little help to relief efforts.) These public and private agencies, run primarily by whites, had real limitations both in the numbers they were able to help, and in how they granted that aid. Nevertheless, for many this support made the difference between starvation and survival.

In December of 1929, 25,000 families and individuals in New York City received some sort of financial assistance from either public or private sources, including veteran, blind, and old age assistance; mothers' aid; public home relief; private relief; and, after April of 1931, state-funded public work relief. By December of 1930, aid reached 91,000 families, and a year later, 164,000. Just after Franklin Roosevelt's election to the presidency, but before New Deal money became available to supplement state and local funds, fully 217,000 city families and individuals received relief. Even more people needed financial help but did not receive it because of residence requirements, budget limitations, and other restrictions. The

Welfare Council estimated that 100,000 New York families needed but were not receiving aid.[17]

Although under pressure to help relieve the suffering of his constituents, Mayor James Walker (in office from 1926 to 1933) proved reluctant to commit public monies to relief. Instead—and only after a Communist party–led march of 35,000 unemployed to City Hall in March and a more confrontational October rally at the Board of Estimate—he appointed an Official Committee for Relief of the Unemployed and Needy in October of 1930, which solicited contributions from municipal employees. That winter the committee spent $1.5 million providing financial and in-kind aid to resident families with dependents, distributed through local police precincts. At first the needy received baskets of food. Later the city provided food tickets redeemable in local stores. The committee also distributed clothing and coal, and prevented over 100,000 evictions by providing rent money.[18]

The Board of Education mounted its own aid program in 1930. Teachers and administrators voluntarily donated 1 percent of their monthly salaries to provide lunches, shoes, clothing, and occasionally funds to thousands of needy children and their families. That first year, for example, they gave away 100,000 pairs of shoes. They increased their contribution to 2 percent the next year to meet the growing need, and raised a million dollars.[19]

This quasi-public support only partially met the needs of unemployed and underemployed New Yorkers. In their turn, many of the private charitable organizations that had worked with the poor of the city since long before the Depression increased their own efforts. Most, specifically committed to improving the material condition of the poor, provided monthly allowances, health care, temporary employment, or help in obtaining government relief.

Because private agencies were the first to distribute aid widely to the needy, they helped define the context in which this relief, and all subsequent relief, was given. But most of these agencies had begun in or were shaped by the Progressive era, and continued to reflect the style and goals of organizations of that time. For example, the Progressive focus on the needs of the poor rather than their rights led private agencies to involve themselves in every aspect of a client family's private life. Many aid recipients reported feeling invaded and controlled. Only in 1938 did the Commissioner of the New York State Department of Social Welfare first reconsider this balance: "I am beginning to feel that it [social service] is overlooking the fact that our clients have rights—and very real rights. Sometimes they exercise some of those rights that we do not like, but that is not the point. They are their rights."

These voluntary agencies revealed their traditional attitudes when they discussed their clients. Some social workers interviewed in 1932 complained that "'certain types *demanded* relief, when previously they *asked*.'" Others voiced concern over the number who received help but did not truly need it:

> The publicity about hard times and lack of work "has given many lazy people an excuse for not trying to get work"; . . . and has given them "an excuse to seek help when in truth in normal times they would not work when they could." . . . It "induced the professional beggar to go from place to place seeking help"; made men unwilling to look for work or "unwilling to work for reduced wages."

Finally, these voluntary organizations felt an unwavering commitment to the economic system. While they urged legal changes to ensure more fairness and better conditions in the workplace and on relief, none challenged capitalism itself. Nor could they have been expected to; these groups were staffed primarily by middle-class professionals who wanted a more just society but would not question the system that put them in power. They sought not to remake society, but to bring its lower ranks up toward the rest. For example, when debating the merits of home relief when wages were so low, organization leaders expressed concern that generous relief payments would deplete the ranks of workers available for the lowest jobs. They did not, as one alternative, argue for a higher living wage for both relief and low-level employment. As the Charity Organization Society put it, there were two problems for relief agencies. The first was the effect of inadequate relief on long-term family life. The second: "What problems of continuing dependency will be created if relief is disproportionate to the normal earnings of the family? What problems are created for industry if relief becomes higher than the current wage rate?"[20] This set of concerns and attitudes—paternalism, distrust of those claiming need, and a commitment to the existing economic order—would continue to dominate the views of philanthropists and administrators about the giving of home relief, both public and private.

Whatever their limitations, however, private agencies did fulfill the mandate they had taken upon themselves: to aid the poor materially. Groups such as the Association for Improving the Condition of the Poor (AICP) reported a tripling of their caseloads between 1929 and 1932. The AICP, possibly the largest private philanthropy in the city, had served thousands of poor families since well before the Depression. During the 1920s, it gave approximately 7,000 families a year financial or medical help and 506 elderly, widowed, or tubercular families received a "monthly allowance." In 1929 and 1930 the numbers appealing for help skyrocketed. In the year of the Crash, 12,000 applied for aid, and over twice as many the following year. The numbers of those actually served rose more slowly, as the AICP expanded its fund-raising and its service program. In 1930, 10,000 of those applying received medical or financial aid over the course of the year and 1,455 families received a monthly sum. "Emergency or temporary relief," a new category of aid, helped almost 4,000. The Charity Organization Society, a comparable agency, also saw a dramatic leap in applicants and in cases accepted. Again, the Depression itself was the clear cause of the increase. The proportion of applicant families citing unemployment as the reason they required help rose from 39 percent in 1925 to 63 percent in 1930. By 1933 it had reached 90 percent.[21]

Other private agencies saw themselves as performing non-financial functions, but in the emergency added financial help to the services they provided. Some, like the Children's Aid Society, focused on the needs of young people, both social and physical. The Society ran shelters for homeless children, took poor girls and boys on beach and country outings, and offered its charges social clubs, recreation, programs and facilities, clothing, lunch, and health care. It placed orphaned children in institutions or foster care. During the early years of the Depression it supplemented these programs with direct monetary aid to needy families and served hot lunches to children who used its playgrounds.[22] Other organizations aided deserted women, offered vocational training, or provided shelters and meals for the home-less. Churches, large and small, ran employment bureaus, served as food and cloth-ing distribution centers, referred the needy to appropriate agencies for help, and ran programs for young people. Almost all of them added direct financial aid of some kind to their list of services.

Recognizing the limited contributions they could make singly, several private agencies organized in 1930 under Seward Prosser, chairman of the board of Bank-ers' Trust. This Emergency Employment Committee managed to raise $8.5 million from private sources. The committee and its Emergency Work Bureau spent the whole amount that summer providing various services, including jobs for 26,000 individuals with dependents. Reorganized as the Emergency Unemployment Relief Committee (E.U.R.C.) under the president of Manufacturers' Trust, Harvey Gibson, its Emergency Work and Relief Bureau received 112,000 applications for assistance in six weeks. Though it believed over half the applicants were "in imme-diate or impending need," the Bureau was only able to raise enough funds to employ 32,000. Overextended, the committee approached bankruptcy early in 1931:

We have been employing a large number of men. . . . These men have been heads of families with children, and they have been paid $15 a week for three days' work. . . . At this rate the funds at our disposal will be exhausted before the month of March is gone. We should increase the number of such men who are given employment now with the stress of the winter in front of us, and with several thousand heads of families who have applied for work who are practically as needy as those to whom we have given employ-ment. We are utterly unable because of the lack of funds at our disposal to do this. . . . We do not see any likelihood of further funds from voluntary sources.[23]

Just in time, the state government took action. Governor Franklin Delano Roo-sevelt established the Temporary Emergency Relief Administration (TERA), funded under the new Wicks Act of 1931. Raising personal income taxes by 50 per-cent, the Act for the first time provided money to fund jobs and aid for the unem-ployed. New York City received almost half of this revenue.

Thus replenished, the Bureau continued its work. By 1932, over 90,000 city fam-ilies received home relief from the coalition. It sent another 48,000 to work at other agencies, with wages paid by TERA funds. All told, the Emergency Work Bureau spent $33 million by the end of 1933.[24]

From the start, the Work Bureau made jobs available only to city residents receiving no other aid, and paid all workers at the same subsistence rate. Rather than place all workers in manual labor, the Bureau tried to place them in their nor-mal occupations. The staff of the Bureau came from the ranks of the unemployed. Cobblers repaired the worn-out shoes of the needy, and musicians entertained in public parks. Recreation and case workers did programming and service work in private agencies. This last provided a double bonus; over 1,400 nonprofit organi-zations, their capacities stretched to the limit, received qualified staff paid for by the Bureau. Thus they could devote more money to their own relief efforts. The Emergency Work Bureau set up evening vocational schools and organized a Women's Bureau. This group placed women in white-collar jobs in libraries, hospitals, and other public services, and set up sewing rooms to employ seamstresses who sewed clothing for relief families. Taking care of immediate needs as well, the Bureau staff fed two sandwiches to every applicant waiting on line.[25]

Traditional sources of public aid still existed, of course, and expanded to meet the growing needs of city dwellers. The number under care at the Department of Public Welfare (which aided the blind, homeless, transient, elderly, the disabled, veterans, and neglected and delinquent children placed under state care) and at the Board of Child Welfare (which supported deserted or widowed mothers with legitimate dependent children) increased significantly with the onset of the Depression. The Department of Public Welfare, having recently established "outdoor" relief (providing relief for needy families in their own homes rather than only in institutions), opened Home Relief Bureau offices all over the city. Applications for help immediately deluged them, half from those who had never before applied for any aid. By July of 1932, the Home Relief Bureau cared for 50,000 families. The Board of Child Welfare saw the number of new cases rise from 3,000 in 1930 to over 9,000 in 1932. "Never in the history of the Board of Child Welfare has there been such volume of work," the agency reported.[26]

Municipal agencies often cooperated with private organizations in providing services. The Health Commissioner appointed a Committee on Neighborhood Health Development in June of 1929 made up of Health Department officials, private health and welfare associations, and medical societies. In its first year the committee established, with the cooperation of private clinics, a city-wide system of public health centers, including one in Harlem. The New York State Employment Service and the new City Free Employment Agency explored possibilities for new jobs in the private and public spheres. These agencies could do little, however, because so few jobs were available at all. The city's employment agency, for example, placed only 27 percent of its male applicants in 1932.

The city also helped care for the thousands made homeless. Thirty-nine public and private agencies operated shelters cooperatively under the Welfare Council's Central Registration Bureau. These shelters provided a bed, food, and clothing when necessary. The numbers using such facilities and the average length of stay both rose dramatically in the first years of the Depression. By March of 1933, more than 10,000 men appeared at city shelters each night.[27]

This aid undoubtedly eased the worst of the devastation. Yet several barriers limited its effectiveness. Most important, of course, was the limited funding. Private organizations could not raise sufficient money to help all who required it. The city government did not pick up the slack, as the City Affairs Committee, the self-styled "non-partisan committee of civic reconstruction," objected: "The Walker administration has consistently refused to appropriate any large sum of money for the direct relief of the unemployed despite the obvious inability of private charity to carry the burden." The committee accused the mayor of making no effort to speed public works projects, and of providing inadequate relief funding. The mayor responded that legal and financial restraints prevented his taking more extensive action, but the committee argued that if he could raise taxes to increase city payrolls, he could do likewise to provide revenue for relief. It reminded him that he had the legal right to provide "emergency relief," power granted him during the World War. He still chose not to act.

State aid helped, but not enough. In the two years from November of 1931 to November of 1933, state TERA provided $97 million to New York City aid programs. But in the first year, municipal relief alone cost $58 million, while private relief agencies (the EURC, the Mayor's Official Committee, the School Relief fund, and eleven major private relief agencies) spent approximately $25 million more. In total, the AICP estimated that over $80 million was spent for relief by public and private agencies in the city just in 1932, up 800 percent from 1929. The need was still greater.

Relief families suffered as a result of this inadequate funding. In calculating the amount of aid to be given, a family's total assets were deducted from a minimum budget, and the shortfall provided by the relief agency. As the Mayor's Committee on Unemployment Relief admitted, that minimum budget came to less than the subsistence standard, so even families receiving aid lacked sufficient funds to live on. According to the Charity Organization Society, a family of five in 1932 needed a minimum of $87.75 a month, while the average Emergency Home Relief family received only $22.04.[28]

Yet better funding alone would not have solved the relief problem. The newly established Home Relief Bureaus under the Department of Public Welfare had not yet developed an efficient procedure to process applications. In the first month of 1932 they received so many applications that they closed to new requests in February and again from April to June. They reopened at that time, announcing the department had approved relief for two-thirds of its 158,000 applicants. Yet of that 100,000, only half actually received any aid that month.

The general view of the crisis as temporary further weakened relief programs. The Wicks Act established the TERA for eight months only and would have expired in June of 1932 had the legislature not extended its life. The city set its public relief budget for a five-month period. Each time state or city money ran short, the Emergency Work and Relief Bureau had to solicit private donations to make up the difference. Few suspected how enduring the Depression would prove. In 1932 the Bureau received applications from thousands "in desperate immediate need," yet found "signs of improvement on the business horizon." It therefore perceived its efforts "to be no longer one of attempting to stem an endless and overwhelming tide of distress. It is, rather, that of intensifying present relief efforts for a time."[29]

The reality, of course, differed substantially from this perception. The Welfare Council warned:

> In spite of all that is being done, thousands of men, women and children will face starvation unless every dollar of public and private funds that can possibly be secured be made available at once. . . . After two years of depression, the index of employment continues to go down. It is the belief of this Committee that unprecedented destitution exists in this city.

In 1932, 6 percent of New York City's population received public relief. The next year the proportion doubled and the figures continued to grow.[30]

Relief for Harlem

As a predominantly poor population, black Harlemites had to rely heavily on outside help. Yet relief, when available, was inadequate for most New Yorkers. Did blacks fare even worse than whites in its distribution? There is little evidence of explicit racial discrimination in the administration of the home relief programs of public or private agencies that served blacks, or in their distribution of funds. As a group, though, blacks did receive less than whites. First, blacks did not have the same range of options whites did, as many private agencies refused to serve them at all. A second and subtler problem was that the agencies that did serve clients without regard to race predicated their aid on certain class-based criteria that, while not intended to be racially discriminatory, had a disproportionate impact on blacks.

These biases were not overt; in theory, all were treated alike. Explicit regulations in most of these agencies mandated equal treatment of blacks and whites. The Association for Improving the Condition of the Poor insisted it "does its work . . . without reference to creed, color, or race." New York State relief money was to be given "without discrimination on grounds of political creed, religion, race, color or noncitizenship." Emergency Work Bureau staff announced to those standing in line their intention to "treat every man alike, no matter what his race, his religion or political creed. . . . The talk was repeated each morning."[31]

The agencies appear to have upheld such rules. In a 1931 article in *Opportunity,* James Hubert noted "in the main, the welfare agencies of New York City are 'color blind.' Both public and private funds are disbursed on a basis of need and are not influenced by race or color." In a letter to the President's Emergency Committee for Unemployment, T. Arnold Hill of the Urban League wrote: "I would not say that relief resources for Negroes in New York City are adequate at the present time. I believe, however, that relief for Negroes is as adequate as for whites, but I doubt the adequacy of it for either group." Black teachers and city employees interviewed by a reporter from the *Herald Tribune* "perceive fair and equal treatment" from social agencies. New York was not unique in this; E. Franklin Frazier found no discrimination in home relief benefits for blacks in any northern cities he studied.[32]

Whether "equal" treatment was in fact "fair" treatment, however, is not as clear. The Harlem area received approximately 8 percent of the Gibson Committee's total relief budget, according to the Governor's Commission on Unemployment Relief. Higher than the proportion of blacks in the city's population, it was not as high as the proportion of blacks among the city's unemployed. Thus, noted the commission, "the needs of the community [Harlem] swept this sum away much more rapidly than anyone had anticipated." Critics argued, and continued to argue throughout the Depression, that relief agencies should provide services based on the proportion of blacks in the ranks of the unemployed rather than in the total population.

Rigid rules such as those pertaining to residency excluded many needy individuals and families. Since more blacks than whites had recently moved to the city, and more lived alone and therefore did not qualify for family aid, blacks fared worse than other groups. This inequitable distribution cannot be attributed to outright discrimination as the practices of some later work programs can, but it does suggest that the black community, because of its peculiar makeup, did not receive funding proportionate to its needs. A 1932 survey of randomly selected families and individuals found that only a quarter of the totally unemployed black households interviewed received some form of financial relief. Two-thirds of the white unemployed did.[33]

The fairness issue should be explored also from a class perspective. To the extent that the Gibson Committee acted on its explicit commitment to seek employment for white-collar workers, opportunities for blacks were more limited than they otherwise might have been. For example, the Women's Bureau concentrated on projects for skilled and professional women, a decision that excluded even more blacks than it did whites. The Urban League protested that 18 percent of blacks registered with the Bureau received jobs, compared with 27 percent of whites. While this is explainable, at least in part, by the lack of skills among the black applicants, it raises questions about why the Bureau focused on skilled work projects rather than on others that could benefit more women. Several other rules and restrictions also affected blacks disproportionately; the Board of Child Welfare's policy not to provide funds for illegitimate children, for example, hurt black women more than white to the extent that unmarried black women had children either more often or more openly.

Personal choice may also help explain the low rate of Harlemites receiving help. The NYUL found a surprising "reluctance with which many applicants seek or accept charity, even when there is no other way out."[34] Whites certainly felt reluctance as well, but if this statement is true, it may account for some of the difference between the numbers in need and receiving relief.

Public and private aid to Harlem did rise as the Depression worsened. The two police precincts in Manhattan distributing food and other goods to the largest number of families both served Harlem. Some private white or multiracial organizations also provided increased aid to residents there. For example, the Quaker New York City Colored Mission, which had served the black community long before the Depression, stepped up its efforts after the Crash. Mission workers, who saw themselves as aiding those "who struggle along in and out of the self-supporting class," provided some monetary grants and a free employment service. So did a few others, including the Charity Organization Society and the Children's Aid Society. Blacks constituted more than 22 percent of all families on public home relief in 1933, and between 30 and 40 percent of those receiving aid from private agencies. Even this could not bring an adequate living standard to Harlem. The community's needs were too great.[35]

Ancillary services remained meager as well, especially for children and the homeless. The situation was particularly acute for children dependent on the state. Although an increasing number of black children were committed to institutional care because their parents were unable to care for them, many institutions continued to refuse to accept them.

The largest institution providing care for dependent black children was the Colored Orphan Asylum (COA), established by a group of Quaker women in 1836. Originally on Twelfth Street near Sixth Avenue, it moved to the quieter suburbs of Fifth Avenue and Forty-third Street in 1843. Twenty years later, draft rioters torched the orphanage and threatened to kill all the children inside. While the sight of these children marching solemnly out of the burning building in their long nightgowns affected the rioters enough to let the children pass unharmed, the COA moved to the quiet of 143rd Street, and in 1907, to Riverdale in the Bronx. Children lived in the orphanage itself, or were "boarded out" in foster homes (which in many cases then became adoptive homes). Because of the unwillingness of other institutions to accept black children, the COA continually expanded its services. The Children's Court requested the COA to accept older children, for example, which it agreed to do in 1926. From that point it accepted boys up to age fourteen and girls to age twelve.

Even before the Depression, then, the problems of finding space for black dependent children posed a serious problem for authorities. With the rise in the number of these black children in the early 1930s, the Colored Orphan Asylum became overcrowded, and the average stay for black children at temporary shelters far exceeded that for whites. "The depression was felt soonest and most bitterly among the negroes in Harlem. . . . Our greatly increased enrollment of destitute children is the product of this fact," commented a COA official. Temporary shelters, run by the Society for the Prevention of Cruelty to Children, held dependent, neglected, and occasionally delinquent children until a more permanent place could be found for them. In 1933, the average stay for blacks was 40 percent longer than for whites.[36]

This problem of space was due in large part to the fact that many white private child-guidance agencies refused service to black children. This meant fewer resources for Harlem's poor, and contributed to the community's higher black juvenile delinquency rate. If one includes in delinquency statistics the number of children served by private agencies as well as those appearing in Children's Court, the black proportion among the delinquent population declines because more whites than blacks received such alternative care. The percentage of blacks in the delinquent population in 1930, for example, drops from 12 to 10, and for Manhattan alone, from 26 to 21. The point here is not that agencies' refusals of service skewed statistics, but rather than Harlem had higher delinquency rates because it had access to fewer preventive youth services. Much of the large increase in black delinquency figures came from higher numbers of arrests for illegal child labor and for neglect, both direct functions of poverty. Yet blacks had access to fewer services that fought such poverty. As Sylvia Robison, who studied juvenile delinquency, discovered:

Negro children are conspicuously absent in the case loads of the unofficial agencies, where they represent only 2.4 percent of the total. . . . Obviously the lack of provision of alternative agency care for Negro children bears some relation to their higher incidence in the court room.[37]

Nor did more benevolent services equitably serve Harlem children. The few white organizations that had been providing recreational facilities there continued their work, but in the Depression these few agencies saw their resources spread too thin, as so much needed to be done for these children and so few agencies helped to do it. The Children's Aid Society (CAS), which had worked in the black community since the group's founding in 1897, ran a supervised playground and Children's Club on 133rd Street, "entirely staffed by Negro workers." The Society boasted that over a thousand children utilized the facilities each day. The organization also provided medical, dental, and occasionally financial services, because workers there saw such suffering among their charges. As the organization reported in 1932, "so prevalent has malnutrition become in Harlem that the Society has undertaken to feed daily at its Harlem Center a hundred of the most undernourished." It expanded that program the next year to include lunch for mothers who brought their children to the center. The Society also employed a social worker from the Emergency Work Bureau who helped find jobs for the children's parents after employees discovered that the fathers of nine of every ten children using the center were unemployed. This last program enjoyed only limited success; the social worker placed only eight men in 1932.[38]

The CAS and a handful of other smaller child-care agencies could not hope to provide care for every child who needed it, nor complete care to any. These private organizations with their limited budgets, supported by voluntary donations, were strained to the limit. As a result, although such services reached thousands, thousands more needed such aid. Doing the best they could was not enough.

Harlem's black homeless were served even less adequately. In theory they could travel downtown to stay at a free lodging house, but as the Unemployed Council complained,

> there is no municipal lodging house in upper Manhattan nor any other flop houses, and the Negro workers together with thousands of white workers in Harlem have no money with which to even pay subway fare down town: and when they manage to get downtown to apply for lodging they cannot get in because of the discrimination.

The only lodging house in the area was the Colored Branch of the Salvation Army Shelter. It provided beds for 166 a day in 1933, but hundreds more slept in subways, empty basements, or out on the streets of Harlem, as a Columbia University study documented. The Colored Mission offered clean sleeping quarters for "respectable women," but it had few beds and generally offered shelter only for a single night.[39]

"To Feed a Hungry God": Black Self-help

Obviously, external aid, whether public or private, did not meet the needs of thousands in Harlem. Local black churches, together with black social, political, and self-help organizations, developed or expanded their own programs to help ease some of the widespread suffering. Because the immediate need was so great, most of these programs focused on providing basic necessities of food, shelter, health care, and jobs—that is, supplementing the efforts of white relief organizations. African-American organizations also had other, unique goals, particularly a commitment to improve their people's economic and civic opportunities. Long a priority for the community, these political efforts continued in this period, but many black groups considered meeting immediate needs of paramount importance, given the economic disaster. Only after the New Deal began and funded material relief programs would these organizations shift their energies back to the larger issues underlying black poverty. For four years, until their resources were almost completely depleted, Harlem organizations kept thousands from starvation and total destitution. Several coordinated their efforts in order to provide effective services. "Perhaps never before has any community presented a more united front than have the leaders in Harlem in their effort to meet the unemployment emergency," James Hubert of the New York Urban League noted with pride in 1931.

Existing agencies such as the New York Urban League continued to provide diverse services but now served a far larger population of the needy. The League's job-placement bureau experienced a dramatic jump in applicants seeking work and accelerated its efforts to find jobs for them. Its success rate was abysmal, however; only 9 percent of their applicants received jobs of longer than a week's duration in 1933. In part, the League's screening process accounted for the poor record. It rejected positions that paid what it considered unacceptably low wages, and offers to hire blacks as strikebreakers. Still, even if the League had filled every job opening it received, it would have placed only 30 percent of its applicants.[40]

The Urban League had long offered other services in addition to job placement. It described itself as a "community agency . . . link[ing] up the social and civic work to be done with the potential workers in the community. . . . The group as a whole is in readiness for any call and limits itself by no fixed objectives. . . . It functions, in other words, a little like a nascent community council." It organized programs to encourage vocational opportunity, better housing, playgrounds, and public health in Harlem, and housed a dental clinic, an optometry clinic, and branches of the Tuberculosis and Health Association and the Henry Street Visiting Nurses. Almost a hundred clubs and organizations, from the Boy Scouts to the Harlem Housewives League met there. The League sent 200 Harlem children a year to summer camps, taught adult education and vocational classes, and aided attempts of black workers to enter existing trade unions or organize their own.

In response to the Depression, the Urban League also handled requests for clothing, food, and rent. In the year 1932 alone it moved 67 families into better quarters, distributed clothing to 1,264, fed 4,000, fought 54 evictions, paid rents for 68 families, put 253 individuals up for a night, provided emergency cash loans, helped 175 fill out relief applications, gave shoes to 855, and accommodated 194 in convalescent homes. The League provided 158 Easter dinners, 216 Thanksgiving baskets, and 121 Christmas baskets. Although the Urban League did not view itself as a relief agency, its annual reports for this period explained that the need was so great that such additional activities "seemed imperative." The League also sponsored a drive to raise additional funds to help Harlem's suffering people.[41]

Other black agencies were far smaller. Most of these agencies had begun operation well before the Depression, reflecting the long-standing need of the black community for such services. The White Rose Mission provided various support programs for black women but had space for only a few at a time. The Utopia Children's House (UCH), established in 1921 by local black women to "combat the increasing percentage of delinquency among Negro underprivileged children through a program of prevention," provided all-day supervision for preschoolers, and after-school programs for older children at 170 West 130th Street. The UCH provided its charges with a daily hot lunch, clothing, health care, recreational outings, and food for their families. The workings of the UCH demonstrated the ways private and public agencies could work together successfully to provide services for the needy. Initially funded by local contributions and a grant from John D. Rockefeller, Utopia Children's House bought its building in 1924 and soon became self-supporting through voluntary contributions. In the early Depression, state TERA provided money for dental care, the Board of Education paid for half of every child's lunch, and the recreation staff came from the Emergency Work Bureau.

A few other recreation and day-care centers were also available in Harlem, including the Hope Day Nursery for Colored Children, at 33 West 133rd Street, "owned, managed and controlled by colored women . . . [and] supported by voluntary contributions." It had first opened in 1902. All were small, however, and could not begin to meet the needs of Harlem residents.[42]

Unmarried mothers and their children in Harlem also had access to only a few services. The Katy Ferguson House on West 130th Street, staffed primarily by Harlem women and partially funded by the Department of Welfare, offered free care for single black mothers and their babies, one of four such institutions in the city willing to take blacks and the only one run by them. It housed only sixteen women at a time, and always had a waiting list. The other institutions serving unmarried black mothers were the Salvation Army Home, which accepted six black women at a time; the Hopewell Society with five; and the Brooklyn Nursery and Infant Hospital, which took two. These last two segregated the mothers by race. Two others, the New York Foundling Hospital and the New York Nursery and Children's Hospital, accepted only babies. The need for all such services exceeded the supply, but budget constraints limited the scope of these organizations.[43]

Supplementing the efforts of local black organizations, Harlem churches mobilized to raise their own contributions for the needy. Certainly they were well positioned to undertake such work. Black churches served not only as spiritual centers for the black community, but as social and political centers as well. In a segregated and poor society, churches filled numerous niches. Nonetheless, while the black churches had long provided needed services, the sudden and dramatic increase in these efforts with the onset of the Depression prompted James Hubert to announce: "The response from the churches in creating jobs, distributing food and clothing, indicates the dawning of a new day in the Negro church."

Although the largest congregations numbered in the thousands, almost two-thirds of all Harlem churches had fewer than a hundred members and met in storefronts or private apartments. Despite drastic differences in wealth, most churches, from the largest to the smallest, participated in the critical task of relieving suffering. The United Holy Church of America at 457 Lenox Avenue, "one flight up," offered food and clothing "without any red tape" to needy families. Although it could only afford to help fifty families, its relief work was "up to the standards prevalent in the city."[44]

Churches of all sizes provided day nurseries for the children of working mothers, children's clubs and activities, job placement services, health clinics, and aid for the elderly. Several sent children to summer camps or fed them lunch. Generally, the larger the church, the more programs it offered. Sister Josephine Becton, head of a Spiritualist church, and a medium and mystic, ran a home for mothers and children. Other large congregations, such as St. Mark's Methodist Episcopal, St. James Presbyterian, Emanuel African Methodist Episcopal (AME), and Mother AME Zion could afford to provide dozens of services to large numbers of needy people. Mother Horn, who could be heard on the radio every Sunday and Wednesday night leading her congregation of 3,000 at the Mount Calvary Assembly Hall of the Pentecostal Faith Church for All Nations, claimed to have fed 48,000 people in one year.[45]

Perhaps the most colorful religious figure in Harlem, Father Divine provided his own form of relief for the hungry. This spiritual leader had thousands of followers who believed him to be God. Divine (born George Baker) grew up in the South. Harassed and arrested for preaching black equality and his own divinity, Divine decided to try the North, and arrived in New York in 1915. He and a few followers settled in Sayville, on Long Island, where his divine identity was kept secret. His generosity to the poor, though, brought busloads of Harlem visitors to his home, especially after the Depression began. As the number of followers multiplied, Divine's white middle-class neighbors became alarmed, fearing a "Harlem colony." Divine was tried and found guilty of disturbing the peace in 1932, and sentenced to a year in jail. In just retribution, Divine's followers believed, the sentencing judge fell dead three days after the sentencing. Divine murmured, "I hated to do it," left prison on bail (his sentence was later reversed on appeal), and moved to Harlem.

Until the early 1940s, when lawsuits over real estate persuaded him to move his headquarters to Philadelphia, he reigned in Harlem. He and his followers, primarily female, lived communally and chastely, segregated by sex but not by race (most, but not all, of his followers were black). They pooled resources to maintain the fifteen group houses, known as "heavens," scattered throughout Harlem and in several locations outside New York. With this collective income, each heaven provided daily banquets for all who wished to partake. At these meals, one observer noted, were "melons, hams, chicken, green apples, corn, bananas, sweet and white potatoes, cabbage, celery, squash, tomatoes, peppers, lettuce, rice, cakes, pies, coffee, and milk." Reportedly, almost 3,000 a day came and ate, members and nonmembers alike.[46]

Prominent in efforts to feed and clothe the poor was the Abyssinian Baptist Church. Not only did it have the largest congregation of any church in Harlem, with 8,000 members in 1929 and almost 15,000 members by 1938, it also benefited from the leadership of its deeply committed pastor, Adam Clayton Powell, Sr. Like Divine, Powell grew up in the South. He was converted from gambling to Christianity at age twenty and became a minister. He began his pastoral work in the Ebenezer Baptist Church in Philadelphia in 1892, then moved to a New Haven, Connecticut, church. Already he had begun preaching and writing about "the race problem." He was well known by 1908 when New York's Abyssinian Baptist Church, then on West Fortieth Street, asked him to serve as minister. It was he who bolstered church membership and urged the church to follow the black migration to Harlem. In 1922, ground was broken on West 138th Street, and the building was completed a year later. There he continued his efforts to improve conditions for his people, building a home for the elderly, raising funds for black schools and hospitals, and preaching education, hard work, and compassion for the needy.

Early in 1931, Powell urged his church and others in Harlem to do even more than they had been to relieve suffering. "The axe is laid at the root of the tree and this unemployed mass of black men, led by a hungry God, will come to the Negro churches looking for fruit and finding none, will say cut it down and cast it into the fire." Taking his own advice, he pledged four months of his salary to charitable efforts. As he described it, "before I could finish the delivery of the sermon, the audience was rushing forward placing money on the table 'to feed a hungry God.' One woman left her pocketbook containing her week's wages and walked home. The trustees counted in cash and pledges twenty-five hundred dollars including my thousand dollars. It was the most impressive climax to a sermon I had ever witnessed." With this money and donations in kind, Powell expanded the church's relief program, which provided clothing, food, coal, and kerosene to the needy. In less than four months, church members collected and distributed 17,928 pieces of clothing, 2,564 pairs of shoes, plus uncounted toys; hired married men to do temporary jobs for church members at 50 cents an hour; and fed 2,000 daily in the church's soup kitchen. Powell offered use of the Community House as a shelter for the homeless. In the years 1930 and 1931 alone, the church provided aid to over 40,000 individuals. The relief efforts were coordinated by Adam Clayton Powell, Jr., son of the minister.[47]

Perhaps the most impressive action by the churches came as a cooperative effort. In November of 1930 under the direction of the Reverend Shelton Hale Bishop of St. Philip's Protestant Episcopal Church, prominent church leaders organized the Harlem Cooperating Committee on Relief and Unemployment. Like the Mayor's Official Committee, it asked all working Harlem adults to contribute a percentage of their weekly wages to it. Opening an office on West 135th Street, the committee helped families and individuals to apply for aid from private and public agencies. If their needs could not be met elsewhere, the organization provided what it could, from rent money to meals. The committee described its goals in an article in the *New York Age:*

> to save deserving tenants who are out of employment from being dispossessed, and to pay their bills for gas and electric current. . . . [Our program] is not intended to overlap or supplement any other agency of relief but to cooperate in meeting applications that would not otherwise be cared for.

The committee certainly succeeded in its task. Of the 22,000 applications for help that it received between December of 1930 and July of 1931, 20,000 were helped in some way: with money, food, clothing, carfare, or referrals to appropriate health or service agencies. Under its auspices, seventeen churches provided meals for 2,400 a day. The committee paid rents for 1,372 families who would otherwise have been evicted from their apartments. According to Powell, Bishop's committee, "working night and day," aided "the 35,000 unemployed men and women of the race." "Nothing in New York City in the way of feeding the unemployed was comparable to what the churches in Harlem did for the Harlem people," beamed Bishop.

Like other black organizations, the committee sought to minimize any impression of patronizing benevolence and instead emphasized community solidarity and self-help. According to Bishop, the Harlem Cooperating Committee clearly demonstrated "that Negroes would do something for themselves and could do it creditably. . . . People of different minds and occupations were together contributing what they had to give to the welfare of the community." Bishop hoped that those receiving the aid would feel, not that givers were "handing down something from above but that people like themselves who just happened not to be unfortunate were helping those that just happened to be."[48]

Catholics, with two all-black churches and five others in the Harlem area, provided services for their own needy. As in Protestant churches, of course, their religious education programs continued unabated. In addition, they operated an institution for dependent black children and another for unwed mothers, and a day nursery for children of working parents. The Handmaids of Mary, an entirely black order there, staffed the orphanage and several of the church's social service programs.

The Catholic churches provided clothing, food, and vocational education to all who sought help. Because so many white agencies did not accept blacks, many black Protestants as well as Catholics took advantage of the proffered services. The orphanage in particular received large numbers of applications from Protestants, since black delinquent and neglected children had few alternatives for placement. Whenever they had room, Catholic institutions in Harlem willingly accepted any children needing help.[49]

While most black organizations focused primarily on providing economic and emergency aid, the economic crisis also prompted collective political self-help. In 1930, for example, one hundred black Harlem grocers banded together in a Colored Merchants' Association (CMA), modeled on a 1928 Alabama organization. To compete more effectively with white chain stores, they agreed to buy and advertise cooperatively and to study and apply new sales and business techniques. In this way they could appeal with confidence for the patronage of black consumers, "not . . . on the basis of race pride, but rather on the basis of quality, price and service." Several owners remodeled their stores, and a CMA warehouse opened on West 138th Street, selling canned goods inexpensively to participating grocers.

Although a few reported increased sales, this experiment fell into decline by 1933 because such stores still could not compete with white-owned chains, which generally offered customers easier credit and a wider selection of goods. As of 1931, whites still owned over 80 percent of Central Harlem businesses. Only a quarter of them employed any blacks, usually as menials. The black employees in Harlem stores earned an average of $89.60 a month, compared with $110 for whites. This demonstrates both the lower profits of black businesses (where many of these black employees worked) and the tendency of white businesses to hire blacks for only the lowest-paying jobs.[50]

Other organizations struggled to improve the opportunities for black employment in city agencies and to end racial discrimination there. The NAACP fought several campaigns to improve black access to desirable occupations. While, as the NAACP's James Allen testified before the Mayor's Commission on Conditions in Harlem, "our organization is not to place jobs," the NAACP did take action to demand equal access for blacks to jobs where the law clearly supported it, as in the case of municipal work. Walter White carried on an increasingly bitter correspondence with the Commissioner of Hospitals, William Greeff, over the matter of training programs for black nurses, until the commissioner left office. In 1932, black nurses could practice at only four city hospitals, and only Harlem Hospital accepted blacks in its training programs. White pointed out that "such discriminatory practices not only violate the spirit and the letter of the charter of the State of New York, but violate as well the Civil Rights Act of New York." He further argued it was immoral at a time of such economic hardship to deny taxpayers public employment they were qualified for: "During this period of distress and unemployment the Negro is suffering to a much greater extent than any other racial group. Barring colored women from employment as nurses works an economic handicap not only upon them but upon the Negro race generally." Commissioner Greeff protested that such charges were "unfair."

When the NAACP threatened "to resort to every legitimate means" to remedy the discriminatory policies, Greeff retorted that he was moving as fast as possible. Although he was "not . . . unsympathetic" to black problems, he also had to create and maintain "proper morale" among the staff. Since nurses worked together "as one family," he complained that the problem could not be solved as easily as White implied. "Were I to accede to your request, I know that there would be great disturbance to that morale." Greeff proved as capable as White of using the current crisis to justify his position. "I am not willing at the present time, when by reason of the economic situation the hospital load is at its greatest, to thus handicap the care which we are able to give to the sick poor."[51]

Feeling that actions of groups such as the NAACP did not go far enough in challenging existing discrimination, the Communist party established Councils of the Unemployed. By 1930, an Upper Harlem Council of the Unemployed was organized, and began protesting evictions, employment discrimination, and inadequate relief allowances. Berating the city for its neglect of Harlem homeless, the council concluded with a call to action.

> In sections where Negro workers are jim crowed like Harlem, there are not even any places where thousands of Negro women, children and men can sleep this winter. The Negro workers of Harlem have been sleeping with their fellow white workers in Mount Morris Park between Madison and Lenox Avenues, 121st and 124th Streets, and many Negro workers have been sleeping under the sky in Morningside Park between 129th and 140th Streets.

Other Negro and white workers in Harlem have been sleeping in hall ways, under steps, in cellars, standing in different joints until driven out, in pool rooms, on house tops during the summer. But this winter they must find and secure suitable places to sleep.

The Harlem unemployed are now appealing to their fellow workers . . . to force the landlords, Negro and white, to stop evictions. . . . Negro and white workers! Unite in Unemployed Councils to smash boss discrimination and terror against Negro jobless![52]

The Communists may have been trying to persuade their fellow workers that capitalism itself oppressed them, but there is no evidence that most blacks at this time agreed with their analysis. In fact, a 1931 survey of 427 families in Harlem found a "striking. . . lack of perception of the general economic trend. None seemed to realize that they were in the midst of an economic depression, nor had any of them any concept of the economic ills of the nation. . . . These people may be described as being not only not class conscious, but economically unconscious." These families knew hard times had come to them; in 1926, half of the fathers in this survey earned over $40 a week, while in 1931, only one did. Like many others in the United States, however, they felt this to be a personal failure, not a failure in the system.[53] Black intellectuals and political leaders had not succeeded in transmitting their critical perspective to the larger community. Organized groups responded to the crisis with an understanding of the economic and social forces operating to keep black people poor. Yet the community as a whole did not immediately embrace these views.

The reluctance of many in Harlem to join these protest efforts reveals the general community's lack of interest in political action. The immediate and widespread need for food and shelter overwhelmed other concerns in the early years of the Depression. Furthermore, most blacks—indeed, most Americans—did not view government as responsible for the well-being of the populace. Primarily a migrant population, most Harlemites sought the American Dream through the traditional vehicles of capitalism and individualism. The ensuing years would see a growing belief that government had certain basic obligations to its citizens; it would culminate several decades later in a civil rights movement that defined fairness and government obligation in very different ways than did this early-Depression black community. This shift, though, still lay in the future. For the moment, hardship was the central issue.

Yet, while Harlem organizations worked to alleviate immediate needs, by 1933 they faced the same depleted budgets as the rest of the city did. Private funds ran out everywhere. Many churches closed their kitchens. Relief applications swelled, but relief money contracted. The Urban League received even fewer industry requests for employees.[54] Economic improvement was nowhere in sight. Harlem verged on collapse.

In that year, however, the political landscape changed completely. The newly elected president, Franklin Roosevelt, would institute his New Deal programs. The year following, Fiorello LaGuardia would become mayor of New York and bring the city its own version of a new deal. By 1934 the Depression was far from over, but the specter of disaster receded. Now the problem would not be whether relief was available, but to whom it would be distributed, and by what means.

This, in turn, would reinvigorate black political efforts. Because public agencies took over the task of providing for basic material needs, black organizations then shifted their focus to organizing the community to demand equal opportunities. Since most adult Harlemites moved in and out of the work force during the Depression, their fates were linked both to the job market and to relief programs. The organizations blacks participated in therefore challenged racism in both areas during the New Deal years. Questions of what constituted "fairness," and to what extent context and history ought to determine current practice, arose with urgency as New Deal agencies expanded and private employment opportunities narrowed. The meaning of "fairness" was of course ambiguous; government, private employers, unions, and black organizations each viewed their own stance as the most equitable. It was within this ambiguity that black political action emerged in the New Deal years.

CHAPTER 3

Barely Making Ends Meet:
At Work in the Great Depression

Traditionally, the Negro worker in America has been beset by many handicaps. Restrictions in the free exercise of the ballot, residential segregation, segregated and inferior schools, exploitation and neglect, and numerous other limitations might be noted. But the disastrous effects of all these combined problems have not equalled that of the practice of discrimination in the field of employment.[1]

At any given time during the 1930s, a majority of Harlem families contained at least one working member, whose employment opportunities were dramatically affected by the Great Depression. The black occupational structure had changed since the 1920s, generally to the detriment of black workers. African-American economic opportunities, always limited, narrowed still further. While black skilled, unskilled, and white-collar workers, men and women, and the foreign-born and native-born experienced these changes in different ways, all shared this shrinking of opportunity and the consequent low wages. Although unemployment rates were lower in New York than elsewhere, and earnings a bit higher, Harlem's experiences with employment paralleled the urban black experience across the country.

Those black families who survived on their earnings without resort to external aid generally required the full-time employment of several members for most of the year, and had few non-working dependents. If any of these conditions changed, economic catastrophe usually ensued. Thus black workers and their families could at any time move up or down a continuum of economic well-being that ranged from self-sufficiency to underemployment, unemployment, debt, or relief.

Unemployment was the greatest threat for both races. Throughout the 1930s, levels of joblessness remained staggering. Across the country, 25 percent of all job seekers could not find work in 1933. As late as 1940, when the expansion of war industries was under way, 15 percent of the labor force, or over eight million people, remained jobless.

Through most of the Depression, for both sexes and for every age, New York City's rate of unemployment surpassed the national average and mirrored the rates of other cities. One-third of all New York men and women employed in 1930 were out of work in 1935—an estimated one million. This affected not just the unemployed but also those dependent on them. In 1933 approximately 37 percent of the total city population lived in unemployed families.

65

For black communities, and Harlem in particular, unemployment rates were worse still. Federal Writers' Project researchers found that by the time New Deal programs began, the majority of Harlem's population was "on the verge of starvation, as a result of the depression and of an intensified discrimination that made it all but impossible for Negroes to find employment." More black men than white reported themselves in the labor force, but 40 percent of them registered as unemployed in 1937, compared with 15 percent for whites. To put it another way, blacks constituted 5 percent of New York's population, but 15 percent of the unemployed. Of those blacks who had jobs, significantly fewer than whites held private-sector employment rather than public. Similarly, more black women than white worked (52 vs. 41 percent) but proportionately fewer of them held private employment. Black women were also less likely than black men to get public-works jobs.[2]

Blacks endured higher unemployment rates than whites for the same reasons they had lost their jobs more quickly in the early Depression: lack of skills and the discrimination of employers. Semi-skilled and unskilled jobs, where blacks were highly concentrated, had the highest unemployment rates all decade long. While 12 percent of the city's employed worked at manual labor or as servants, fully 35 percent of workers on relief in 1934 claimed these as their usual occupations. By contrast, for example, 13 percent of the employed population reported themselves as professionals or semi-professionals, but these two categories represented less than 5 percent of the unemployed. Of those in municipal lodging houses in 1937, 72 percent were laborers, 18 percent skilled, and less than 1 percent professional. Furthermore, the less skilled stayed at city shelters the longest: female domestic workers spent an average of 46 nights per person; factory women spent 28, male laborers, 22. By contrast, clerks stayed eight nights and the few professionals who needed shelter stayed an average of three. In 1935, of African-American household heads unemployed and on relief, 27 percent named domestic and personal service as their usual employment (compared with 7 percent of white males), and 47 percent considered themselves unskilled or semiskilled (41 percent of whites). Of 313 "unattached" Harlem female Home Relief applicants studied in April of 1935, 205 were domestics; almost half had been unemployed for more than a year.[3] Still, low occupation levels alone cannot account for the greater unemployment in the black community, for blacks' unemployment rate exceeded that of whites in every occupation. Discriminatory hiring and firing policies played their part as well.

Those blacks fortunate enough to keep their jobs or find new ones found opportunities for upward mobility almost completely closed in the 1930s. In fact, blacks were pushed still farther down the occupational ladder. Black skilled and white-collar workers often found themselves forced out of their jobs by employers preferring whites. If they could find new jobs at all, they moved into unskilled and menial labor. Even higher-level service workers faced increased competition for their jobs from desperate whites and downwardly mobile blacks; the Depression compressed Harlem's class structure into the lowest economic levels. There, families maintained economic independence only precariously, moving on and off relief rolls as their economic fortunes changed.

Data from relief agencies help illuminate the economic structures of the black community and this process of attaining and losing economic independence. The Federal Security Agency studied New York family income and composition in 1935. City agencies and private organizations conducted their own investigations of black and white non-relief families. The Bureau of Labor Statistics (BLS) did two large surveys between 1934 and 1936, one on income and expenditures of all New York City families, and a second, smaller study of blue-collar (or, as the BLS called them, wage-earning) and low-salaried clerical workers. The raw data from the latter offer an opportunity to ask new questions about black employment patterns.

Investigators for this study (called here the BLS Harlem sample) polled a random sample of wage-earning and low-salaried clerical families not on relief and having at least two members. They inquired about family composition, occupational level, number of weeks worked, and earnings. In the sample, blacks constituted one hundred of the families surveyed, eighty-one of whom lived in Harlem. Of these eighty-one, twenty-four came from the West Indies or Puerto Rico, while the remainder were American-born.[4] While these families cannot be relied upon as being a typical group of working Harlemites, the information does provide hints about employment and consumption patterns in the larger black community. Supplemented with evidence from published studies, these data illustrate important patterns of employment and income in the black community. Cumulatively these investigations present a clear and compelling picture of poverty, hardship, and the struggle for economic survival of the employed lower- and middle-class blacks of Depression Harlem.

Family composition was varied in the BLS sample and reflected community patterns. Six of the thirty-four two-member families were not husband and wife, but two related adults. Women without husbands present headed eleven families, all of which had at least one adult child or other adult relative. No households had male heads without wives. The average female household head (as distinguished from other women living in the economic family) in this survey was thirty-eight years old; her husband, if present, was forty. Of the 47 families containing more than two members, 16 included children sixteen or under, three of whom were nieces or nephews of the household head. A total of 34 families had children of any age. Twenty-six families included non-nuclear relatives, and in seven of these the household head also had children. One surveyed family, for example, included two parents, ages forty-eight and forty-two, their five children (two under age sixteen), a daughter-in-law, and their grandchild. Extended families and other complex arrangements, rather than complete and isolated nuclear families, proved the norm in this group; economic self-sufficiency was not exclusive to two-parent, non-extended households.

Over half of the families in the BLS Harlem survey had two wage-earners even if they were not husband and wife; this was probably the only way the family could manage financially. The family described above required four earners, three of them working all fifty-two weeks of the survey year, to break even; the family had $28.58 in savings at the year's end. By contrast, most white families that managed to stay off the relief rolls did so on one income. For all native-born white families in the BLS's larger income and expenditure survey, 80 percent had only one earner.

Only 60 percent of black families in that survey relied on one income (a figure equivalent to that for foreign-born white families), despite their smaller size. At every income level, more black families than white had additional earners.[5] Clearly, more whites than blacks held jobs with high enough earnings to support a family alone.

Another BLS survey family of two parents and their two adult children illustrates the plight of such low earners. Both parents and one son worked, but their wages and hours worked were so low that the family's expenses exceeded their earnings. The mother, a thirty-six-year-old cleaner in a shirt manufacturing company, earned $12 a week and worked for twenty-eight weeks that year. Her husband, forty-three, worked as a stockman in a retail store. He worked forty-two weeks at $20 a week. One son, nineteen, a delivery boy, worked for forty-eight weeks but earned only $3 a week for the work. His brother could not find employment at all. The family's rent came to $362, or $30 a month—quite reasonable for Harlem. Another $429 went for food that year, and approximately that much for all other expenses combined. Their modest budget and small family, however, could not prevent them from ending up almost $60 in debt by the end of the survey year.

Other families similarly sought to increase the number of earners, or potential earners, per household. Many families or couples moved in with others and pooled their incomes during the Depression. For both races, the majority of families with four adult members had two or three workers, so such living choices were not motivated solely by economic desperation. Yet when neither member of a couple could find employment, sharing a household with employed friends or relatives made sense, and this phenomenon seems especially marked in black families. In fully a quarter of black households containing four adults, only one person held employment—twice the rate for white.[6]

The numbers are too small in this survey to draw definite conclusions, but the evidence suggests black children did not often leave school for employment. Despite the family's need for every possible dollar, black parents kept their children in school. None of the BLS survey families reported labor of children under eighteen. Either black families were willing to defer the additional income in favor of education, or adolescents could not find jobs. All but one of the children under eighteen were listed explicitly as students or appeared to be, because the highest grade level they had completed was the appropriate one for their age. Of course it is possible that children who left school to work moved out of their parents' house. But none of the lodgers in the survey who provided their ages was under twenty-three, and living alone was costly. If the children married, they would appear in the survey as household heads themselves, but none in the survey were so young. If teens and young adults did not appear as members of separate households or as lodgers, they must have remained at home. So for the families in this survey, at least, children remained in school. In fact, in New York, the same proportion of black and white children over fourteen were enrolled in school. According to the census bureau, only 1 percent of all black children under sixteen held gainful employment, lower than figures for most other cities.[7]

Adults, then, did most of the paid work, and they worked hard. Two-thirds of male household heads in the Harlem sample had worked fifty-two weeks in the surveyed year. So did 13 percent of the wives and 21 percent of young people between the ages of sixteen and twenty-one. Another large group of women and other supplementary earners in these families worked part-time. Several adults in the survey worked at more than one job during the year. One man held such varied positions as machine operator, photographer, and wholesale foods salesman; another worked as a cab driver and shoe shiner; a third as typesetter and insurance salesman. No husbands had been unemployed or at home all year, and over half of all wives had had some work.[8] Obviously families whose employment histories were not as successful were unable to remain self-sufficient.

Black women's labor proved crucial to family self-sufficiency during the Depression.[9] In 1931, 60 percent of all Manhattan black women over fifteen worked, a figure higher than before the Depression and higher than for whites. Almost half of all married black women worked, compared with 18 percent of wives from white wage-earning families. Single black women now surpassed married women in the job market—79 percent of them worked—not because wives left (although the figures are slightly lower than in pre-Depression days, suggesting high unemployment), but because more single women joined, testifying to greater need. Three-quarters of black widows and divorcées worked as well. In the BLS sample, non-wives earned the same wages wives did and worked more weeks of the year.

While the fact that black men earned so little undoubtedly led to more black women working than white, the data suggest that, as was true before the Depression, black women also worked for reasons other than economics. The figures for black women at work did not change significantly from one family income category to the next, while the proportion of white working wives declined slightly as family income rose. Of the eighty-one wives in the Harlem survey, forty-five worked. There was no statistical relationship between black husbands' earnings and whether their wives went to work. Level of education or number of children also made no significant difference in determining whether or not these women held outside employment. Better-educated women were no more or less likely to work than were their less-educated sisters; just under half of the women with fewer than five years of schooling stayed home, compared with 43 percent of women with high school educations. Black cultural values must have played a part in the decision as well. In the black community, women continued to view paid employment as part of their appropriate role in the family.[10]

"Any Job Was a White Man's Job"

Black workers, both male and female, faced significant barriers to achieving economic self-sufficiency. The Depression worsened their opportunities for upward economic mobility and brought increased competition at the lowest occupational levels. While the split labor market operated with renewed vigor at the higher levels, excluding blacks, it began to break down at the bottom, where whites competed with blacks for previously all-black jobs.

Barriers to skilled and white-collar employment in private industry became still more rigid. As Alfred Smith, black "racial adviser" for the FERA and WPA, pointed out in 1935: "Industrial bans based on color and aimed at the Negro have always existed. . . . [But their] number has grown and the ban now extends in some instances to 'reemployment' of Negro workers." He found this discrimination or "displacement of Negro labor" in all types and levels of employment. Employers' concerns about racial disturbances among workers, their fear that blacks would not perform their tasks well enough, the lack of adequate training among blacks, and the traditions of certain jobs' "belonging exclusively to the white race" all contributed to the problem; these sentiments intensified with the pressures of the Depression. The Mayor's Commission on Conditions in Harlem, gathering information on these exclusionary practices, asked a trained African-American riveter, Luther Burton, to describe his experiences.

Q. So you had at least 30 years of practical experience? Now tell us about this particular job that we have under discussion.

A. On the 3rd of April, I was called up to 200 W. 135th St. Mr. Simmons [of the New York State Employment Service] told me "to get your gangs together and be back here in the morning." . . . [He] sent us down to this job in Eastview. . . . When we got there Mr. Kennedy, the superintendent, I says to him, "Are you Mr. Kennedy?" He says yes. "What are you men here for?" "There's a riveting gang here for you. We comes to work." "No, you can't work here." "Why," we says. He said, "This company never worked colored and never will." "Why, give us a chance and let us show you how we work." "No, you won't work here. This company never worked no negroes in the State of New York. . . . Furthermore, if I had you fellows to work, I have only four gang of riveters and they will quit." . . . [A company representative then defends the decision:] "You fellows aren't experienced." "How do you know we are not experienced. Mr. Kennedy, he didn't try us out." . . . he said, "I'll tell you what, I'll give one man a job." "Well, what about the three others?" He said, "I don't know." . . . and with that we left the employment office. . . . I have had the experience of many such jobs. . . . Some jobs when you go to the foreman and ask him for a job, he laughs at you. There are really good skilled Negroes, experienced mechanics walking the street who can't get jobs.[11]

Other times, the discrimination took the form of different pay scales for black and white. Yet even at lower wages, blacks could not keep their jobs for long. Mr. Haines, president of the Mechanic's Association, described one example of a widespread practice:

On the YMCA job . . . we find that colored men were hired. They were requested to work for less than the prevailing rate of wages. These men went to work and they made a shift of the men one week and the next week they hired other men. What transpired with the first batch of men I don't know. The second group of men who went on the second week demanded the prevailing rate of wages when pay day came. These men then were laid off and the other men also and no other colored carpenters had another opportunity to work on that YMCA job. . . . If that is not discrimination, then I don't know what it is.[12]

The Mayor's Commission on Conditions in Harlem found barriers to black advancement in every field. White businesses and hotels outside Harlem never hired black clerical workers; they rarely did even within that community. In fact, outside of Harlem blacks found it difficult to obtain even traditionally black jobs, like barbers and waiters. As the commission put it, the city had two types of businesses: those that hired blacks for menial labor, and those that refused to hire blacks at all. "Discrimination and non-economic factors," it concluded, "are responsible to a large extent for the present state of affairs." In 1938, the New York State Commission on the Urban Colored Population echoed the Mayor's Commission's sentiments, finding "the operation of deliberate as well as unconscious forces restricting the Negro to certain of the less desirable types of employment and generally barring him from the more desirable fields."

Unions proved as discriminatory as employers, reserving employment and training positions for whites. "Many more men would have been placed in skilled jobs were it not for the union qualifications attached to such orders," complained the director of the New York State Employment Service's Harlem branch.[13]

Trade unions had had a long history of racial exclusion; the issue was as old as the union movement in America. Some trade unions excluded blacks altogether, either explicitly in their constitutions or quietly by "tacit agreement." Others put blacks in separate locals. While some early groups, such as the Knights of Labor, welcomed black members, most did not. Early unions were often fraternal organizations as well as labor collectives; "whites only" was as much an issue of social taboo as it was an attempt to control or restrict the skilled labor supply. Even if an international union did not exclude blacks, locals often did. Internationals gained power and prestige according to their size; it was to their advantage to incorporate blacks—indeed, any new workers. Locals, by contrast, maintained power by strictly limiting entry into the occupation. They therefore often found exclusion the more advantageous choice. Even when unions advanced the rhetoric of equality, individuals had to implement it, so personal racism had its effects on the local level as well.[14] This was as true for New York City as it was elsewhere.

Sometimes unions circumvented criticism about their racial policies with tokenism. As James Allen, president of the local branch of the NAACP, testified before the Mayor's Commission:

... The matter of discrimination against [black] members of the trade union ... is one with which we should be seriously concerned. I have a letter here in regard to the matter when we took up the question of Negroes in the Columbia University Library. A man came into my office one day with a very pitiful and sad story. . . . He stated he carried a union card for 20 years, he was a man with a family and children, he had been refused work on this project. He thought at first he would apply to the union giving his side of his story. We wrote a letter to the president of the union. . . . We also wrote the contractors and were given the same run-around story of employing one or two colored. [quoting letter:] "We are pleased to advise you that up to one month ago, one colored laborer was working on the above building. At the present time two are employed. This indicates that we are not discriminating against the colored race."

Q. Is there such an indication in your mind?

A. Not at all.

Mr. Haines testified to similar practices used against black mechanics and carpenters. Not only did the unions themselves restrict membership and jobs, they took no action when presented with discrimination by foremen.

> It has been my duty for a period of years to present cases of discrimination from time to time with no results. . . . There have been but seven [black mechanics] who were fortunate enough to get on the [city] jobs. By that I mean this: That they were hired on the job, but there is such a subtle system of discrimination that they will hire two colored men today, give them a few days' work and then they will displace them for two more colored men the next week and lay them off and use two more colored men.
>
> *Q.* As to white workers, they don't use that policy?
>
> *A.* No, sad to say. When those questions come before the Building Trades council, we are placed at a disadvantage so that we cannot hope to achieve anything.

As the New York State Temporary Commission concluded: "That many unions are guilty of unfair [racial] practices, especially toward the Negro group is a matter of proven fact." Even if the international union did not exclude blacks by decree, city locals often did.[15]

Public utilities and transportation services, falling somewhere between public and private, practiced their share of racial discrimination in hiring policies. Although the Civil Rights Law, Section 42, explicitly forbade any public utility to "refuse to employ any person in any capacity . . . on account of race, color, or religion of such a person," this provision was routinely ignored. As Hubert testified before the Mayor's Commission:

> Mention is made of the Metropolitan Life Insurance company. Now the Metropolitan, like the Consolidated Gas and the Telephone Company and the milk companies, are willing to have Negroes use their commodities. They are quite willing to distribute milk in Harlem, but they are not using Negroes to deliver the milk.

One of the largest utilities told the New York State Temporary Commission outright that it would continue to exclude blacks: "In a few cases . . . it was frankly admitted that the exclusion of Negroes was deliberate." The Mayor's Commission on Conditions in Harlem believed utilities excluded blacks because of tradition and custom, because they believed blacks to be less efficient, and because they feared the negative reaction of white workers. The Metropolitan Life Insurance Company and the New York Telephone Company admitted this to an interviewer for the Federal Writers' Project.

New York Telephone employed a few black laborers, but refused to hire blacks at any other levels, most particularly as operators or repairmen. As the company explained:

> Due to the peculiar nature of its work and its ultimate contact with the public, certain types were, in the course of time, favored in hiring. For example, a phone operator can have no accent. As a result certain racial strains were barred almost automatically. Again, the company has to be extremely careful in their people who go into the homes

of the city to install and repair phone equipment. This seemed to result in automatically ruling out colored men. Perhaps in this manner the company acquired the reputation of being prejudiced against certain groups.

James Hubert of the Urban League told the story of a black woman who wanted to take the test to be a telephone operator. After finally receiving permission to do so—no easy task—"the examiner said she made one of the best records, best tests with a very high rating. In spite of that, she has never been called for employment. . . . That is just a sample of what the Negro has been up against."

The subways proved similarly unfair. As James Allen testified in 1935:

[In] 1932 when the new subway was being built by New York . . . the [NAACP] office sent about trying to secure information relative to qualifications so that Negroes could have a chance to make application. I have here a book of 250 applicants some who came there with qualifications such as graduates of the Massachusetts Institute of Technology who were appointed as common laborers, or porters.

As late as 1940, the NAACP continued to plead with the Transport Workers Union, the BMT (Brooklyn Manhattan Transit), and the IRT to "integrat[e] . . . qualified Negroes as conductors, motormen, platform guards, clerks and executives."[16]

Thus private, quasi-public, and union hiring practices conspired to restrict black occupational mobility. Although the earlier shift of blacks to industry did not reverse itself during the Depression, blacks in New York City remained trapped in the "lowest paid and unskilled" levels there, according to the Mayor's Commission. Three percent of all industrial workers, blacks were 9 percent of its unskilled ranks. The State Commission lamented the hundreds of "financial and mercantile enterprises" that refused to hire blacks—doubly a problem because these jobs were in expanding fields. It noted apprehensively that the country was shifting away from industrial production and toward clerical and professional occupations just at the time blacks were moving into industrial labor. Yet, like the Mayor's Commission, it found no evidence that blacks even in this field found employment at any but the lowest ranks.[17]

The hardening of barriers at the upper levels meant many employed blacks did not work at jobs they had been trained for. The proportion of skilled blacks working in their fields had increased between 1925 and 1930, but declined thereafter. Only one-third of New York's skilled black workers surveyed by the Department of the Interior's Office of the Adviser on Negro Affairs in 1936 currently held employment in an appropriate occupation, down from two-thirds in 1930. The same was true nationwide. Another third of all skilled blacks were unemployed in 1936, according to the Department of the Interior, a rate far higher than that for whites. Nor did professionals fare better. The National Urban League found 60 percent of black doctors in Harlem were on work relief in the fall of 1934.

Professional and white-collar blacks found themselves more often unemployed than their white counterparts, and many could only find work at laboring jobs. Although only 74 percent of black applicants at the New York State Employment Service in Harlem sought unskilled or semiskilled work, fully 88 percent of all black placements fell into those two categories. The office reported few companies willing to accept black applicants for skilled, clerical, or professional opportunities. The NYUL reported that 80 percent of requests sent to its placement service came for domestic workers, a tenth for industrial, and few for professional. About half offered only temporary positions. Only 15 percent of those seeking jobs, however, had worked at domestic service before. A third had held industrial jobs, and fully a tenth were professionals.[18] Class divisions, then, broke down for many blacks in the Depression—not because lower-class blacks moved up, but because middle- and upper-class blacks found their occupational positions increasingly difficult to maintain.

Compounding this long-standing discrimination, the Depression also brought increased competition with whites for even the poorest jobs. Victims of a labor market structure that relegated them to the lowest-level jobs and kept them there, blacks had at least maintained a certain amount of job security before the Depression. Few whites had competed with them for menial and service positions. The widespread hardship of the Depression, which hurt whites as well as blacks, destroyed even that precarious foothold in the market. White unemployed workers sought employment where they could get it, even if it meant accepting jobs they earlier would have refused. White men fought to be janitors and porters; white women joined the ranks of domestic and laundry workers. As Alfred Smith described it:

> The Negro gainful worker is being displaced by white gainful workers. . . . He is no longer in possession of traditionally "Negro jobs" and he no longer shares the role of cheap labor with a comparatively small foreign labor element. . . . [During the Depression] any job was a white man's job. . . . The effect of displacement of Negro maids, domestics of all kinds, elevator operators, barbers, bellboys and the like . . . has been as serious in aggregate as the displacement of Negro workers in large industries.

Claude McKay also noted this displacement: "Elevator operators, waiters, porters, maids had seen their jobs downtown shrink away during the Depression and their places taken by white workers."[19]

This phenomenon was not unique to New York but occurred across the United States. One of Richard Wright's characters, a black postal worker in Depression-era Chicago, complained to his friend:

> "Slaughter [from the NAACP] was saying that the white clerks around here's done got up some sort of organization to run us and the Jews out."
> "Well, the white folks didn't want this job [mail sorting] when times was good," [his friend responded].
> "No white man wanted to work nights and breathe all this dust."
> "And now 'cause the Depression's on, they want to kick us out."

The Urban League noted: "One of the indirect factors responsible for such a large volume of unemployment among Negroes is the displacement of Negro workers by white persons . . . increased competition between Negroes and whites for jobs ordinarily held by Negroes." The new competition drove blacks into the lowest of these menial jobs; Arnold Rose's research for Gunnar Myrdal's study *An American*

Dilemma documented a shift of black workers out of the higher service occupations such as waiter and barber and into lower ones such as bootblack, porter, and laundry worker. All this helped account for the higher black unemployment rate and lowered wages and occupational status for those who kept their jobs.[20]

At Work

The implications of these pressures on black occupational distribution is plain: a narrower concentration of jobs at the bottom of the economic pile, and less stability even there. The strengthening of the barriers to skilled and white-collar employment, coupled with the increased difficulty in finding any work at all, meant an even higher proportion of employed New York City blacks worked in domestic and personal service in the 1930s than had done so in earlier years. While the percentage of blacks working in these fields had declined after 1910, it rose again with economic hard times. As late as 1940, of those employed, 27 percent of Central Harlemites fell into each of the two categories, figures that considerably exceeded the proportions for Manhattanites overall. A third of all Manhattan workers in that year described themselves to census takers as clerks or managers, compared with only a tenth of workers from Central Harlem. Employed Harlemites held professional positions only a third as often as workers in the rest of the city. A third of all blacks in manufacturing, mechanical, and transportation fields in the Depression decade worked as "laborers." Another third held jobs as unskilled workers, stevedores, or dockhands. Basically, job opportunities had worsened.

Blacks in Harlem had a less favorable distribution of jobs than any other ethnic, immigrant, or poor group in the city, although they fared better in New York than blacks did in the nation as a whole. The fact that so many supported themselves and their families in these poorly paid jobs demonstrates that even at that level, it was possible to make ends meet. Still, it was more difficult; the proportion of non-relief families in these fields was lower than their proportion in the general working black population.

TABLE 3.1
Occupation Level of Those Employed, by Percent,
Manhattan and Selected Health Districts, 1940[21]

	Central Harlem	East Harlem	Lower East Side	Manhattan
Professional, semiprof.	4.0	7.2	9.7	12.6
Clerical, managerial	11.0	21.0	29.5	32.0
Skilled	5.2	10.9	9.1	6.9
Operatives, kindred	18.8	26.3	25.6	16.4
Service (excl. domestic)	27.3	19.6	18.3	19.0
Domestic service	27.2	7.2	1.6	8.7
Laborers	5.9	6.7	5.5	3.8
Not reported	0.6	1.1	0.7	0.6

The BLS Harlem sample confirms these findings and provides a glimpse inside the statistics. Almost half of all husbands in that survey worked at unskilled service jobs: porter, elevator operator, "general helper." Seven percent worked as laborers. A fifth of all working wives held service jobs, another third were domestics. Unskilled laundry work accounted for 4 percent of wives and 2 percent of husbands. Another 31 percent of wives and 27 percent of husbands worked in semi-skilled positions.[22]

Discrimination ensured that black men and women generally worked in menial jobs regardless of age, education, or skill. In the BLS sample, a working woman's education played almost no part in determining her occupation. A majority of all employed wives worked in domestic or personal service, regardless of the number of years of schooling they had had. The same was true of the women who came to the Universal Negro Improvement Association for help. This group had virtually identical education patterns to those of the larger Harlem community and therefore represents a typical black group in terms of the range of economic opportunity open to them. Sixty-two of these 89 women held jobs as domestics or "cleaners," a fifth of whom had high school educations. Similar findings were reported by a study of 39 non-relief black families in Harlem and Brooklyn. Of 23 women in that study, 14 women worked as domestics, and that group, along with waitresses, contained the best-educated women of any female occupational group.

The data further suggest that those women who did hold white-collar jobs generally held those at the lowest ranks. They rarely had a great deal of education either, which presumably excluded them from the more skilled clerical and white-collar fields. Only five wives in the BLS survey held clerical jobs, and three of them had less than seven years of education. In the UNIA files, only four women worked as typists or clerks, one with fourteen years of education, one with eleven, the last two with eight and three years. Although the samples are too small to generalize from, the data suggest that no matter what one's education, for women at least, the likeliest occupations were in the unskilled and service sectors.[23]

Men encountered similar limitations. Within the UNIA's client group, education did not determine occupation for men any more than it did for women. Male laborers and handymen (over half the sample) ranged from unschooled to high school graduates. Only two other men had higher educations than the best-educated handymen. The study of thirty-nine non-relief black families in New York also revealed that education played virtually no role in determining males' occupations. While those in white-collar jobs did have slightly higher education levels, porters were the next–best-educated group. Of the five porters, two had been to college. Except for male clerks, half of whom had at least a high school education, education made no difference in terms of occupation for any group.[24]

Some scholars have suggested that the lower occupational status of blacks is explainable by their lower levels of education and training than whites. While blacks were slightly less educated than whites on the average (seven and eight years of education, respectively) it does not explain why well-educated blacks also generally did not do well in the job market, nor does it explain why equally poorly educated white immigrants fared better. The NYUL's employment service reported that it did find education had some effect on occupational level, especially for professional work. An applicant with a college degree was more likely to receive a clerical job than was one with an elementary school education. Still, 21 percent of black college graduates they placed worked in factories, and many well-educated women could only find domestic work. In other words, it was more difficult to obtain a high-ranking job with little education, but a good deal of education did not at all guarantee appropriate or desirable work.[25]

Although they were equally affected by the destruction of the racially segregated job market at the lower levels and faced similar obstacles to advancement to higher ranks, black men's and women's employment experiences still differed in the 1930s. Racial divisions in the labor market began to break down as whites increasingly competed in unskilled and service fields, but gender divisions did so far less often. While whites were willing to abandon racial job stereotypes when economically pressed, men continued to resist crossing gender barriers. White men replaced black men, white women replaced black women. Thus white men demanded jobs as porters, but neither white men nor black sought work as chambermaids or in other traditionally female service jobs. At the highest occupation levels, race determined entry. At lower levels, gender proved a stronger line of differentiation than race in the Depression. The exceptions to this rule generally involved white women's moving into black male jobs. For example, the National Urban League noted: "In Penn Station in New York City white girls have replaced colored male employees in the check room of the Savarin Restaurant." For white women, presumably, some black men's jobs could seem more desirable than their only other alternative—black women's jobs, the worst of all. Thus gender obstacles exacerbated racial barriers, and when either were crossed it was to the blacks' disadvantage.[26]

A higher proportion of black men than women held clerical, managerial, and proprietary jobs and worked in skilled positions and as laborers. Yet, because of their race, neither had opportunities for occupational mobility. Black women's heavy concentration in domestic service, similar everywhere in the country, was comparable with black men's in other service fields, but unlike the white pattern for either sex. In other words, black women had "drifted back to domestic and personal service" since the Depression began, and black men had returned to their different but equally low positions as laborers and unskilled workers.

Black women generally found jobs more rapidly than black men did, but they were more often temporary, low-paid, and unpleasant. Similarly, white women fared better than white men in their search for jobs, but also earned less at them. In fact, white men had the longest periods of unemployment, probably because as a group they resisted manual labor for a longer time. Thus the lower one's occupation (in experience or expectation), the less unemployment one experienced, but the worse one fared once a job was obtained.

Women enjoyed a lower layoff rate and found new employment more readily because in many cases the Depression did not affect jobs taken by women as deeply. Domestic workers suffered a 13 percent unemployment rate, compared with 27 percent in the construction industry. Telephone operators, 95 percent female; and private launderers, 99 percent, enjoyed low unemployment rates, while occupations that contained virtually no women, such as carpentry and road work, had sig-

TABLE 3.2
Occupational Distribution of Manhattan Residents, by Race and Sex, 1940[27]

	Men		Women	
	% Black	*% White*	*% Black*	*% White*
Professional and semiprofessional	3.8	11.8	3.7	18.1
Proprietary, managerial, official	5.6	15.3	0.9	4.7
Clerical	7.4	10.2	2.4	24.2
Sales	3.3	10.5	1.1	6.1
Skilled	7.3	10.9	0.3	1.0
Semiskilled	18.4	15.8	18.0	16.5
Domestic service	2.4	0.7	60.0	13.2
Other service	40.3	18.8	13.0	15.2
Labor	11.1	5.2	0.3	0.2
Not reported	0.5	0.7	0.3	0.7

nificantly higher rates. Still, within occupations shared by both men and women, female unemployment surpassed male.[28]

Some of the gender differences in unemployment can be accounted for also by the greater tendency among unemployed women to stop searching for work and call themselves housewives. Additionally, many more women than men worked part-time (not necessarily by choice). While underemployed they would not count among the unemployed, but they earned little and had less stability.

The competition between black women and the white women who now flocked to the service-job market intensified the downward pressure on women's wages and working conditions. Employers had little incentive to pay more or to improve conditions. An examination of domestic and laundry work, two of the commonest jobs black women held, illustrates the deterioration of wages and working conditions caused by the increasingly rigid racial barriers to better-paid occupations, and the breakdown of the racially split labor market in the lowest levels of women's work. Every occupational problem blacks faced in the Depression—the worst tasks, lower wages for the same work, and displacement by whites—was present in these two fields. Conditions in laundry and domestic work had never been good, one reason only black women took those jobs. Employers, the general public, and even some of the employees themselves, viewed women's work as temporary or as a second income and therefore devoted little energy toward improving the workplace. Also, women in service found it generally more difficult to organize than did workers in factories, since many of their jobs were done alone (such as domestic work). The resulting situation in the two fields was so dreadful as to prompt numerous governmental and philanthropic investigations.

Black domestics with steady jobs earned very little. With no laws regulating wages or working conditions, servants and maids averaged weekly incomes of between $6 and $10, and in the worst cases worked every day for twelve to fourteen hours. Complaints of ill-treatment were common.

But black women in even this lowest field faced new competition from whites in the 1930s, and many lost their steady positions. As one article on domestic workers described it, black domestic workers "have been so downtrodden since the depression, when white girls were given the jobs over which for years they had had a monopoly, that they are happy to get any sort of work." Desperate black domestics searching for work traveled to particular street corners in the Bronx, locally known as the "slave market," seeking temporary work. Community groups, from the National Negro Congress to the YWCA, the League of Women Shoppers, and the Communist party, complained about the intolerable conditions at these Bronx markets.[29] An article in *Crisis* told of black women "there by 8 AM, on certain street corners, to barter labor for 'slave wages' . . . human love is also a marketable commodity." Rain or shine, women congregated. Many women had lost steadier work. Others came because family income could no longer meet expenses. Competition was fierce and wages correspondingly low. The state found fifteen to twenty cents an hour to be a typical wage in these markets. Others found it to be even less. Some women who applied for home relief after trying their luck in these slave markets were actually rejected by relief officials because the wages they reported were so low the case workers suspected they had lied about their pay or they had been supplementing it with profits from illegal activities. It was impossible, relief officials concluded, for these women to have been able to survive on so little. Obviously, the "slave market" was aptly named.

One black woman explained that she came to the street corner market because at employment agencies white women always received the jobs. She complained of employers who cheated her out of her wages by turning the clock back or by paying less than the agreed rate, yet she had no choice but to keep returning. As the *Crisis* article pointed out, "an embryonic labor union now exists in the Simpson Ave. 'mart' . . . [these women are] largely unaware of their organized power, yet ready to band together for some immediate and personal gain." That potential was never realized in the Depression, in part because "they still cling to that American illusion that anyone who is determined and persistent can get ahead." More significantly, desperately poor workers were always available, no matter how low wages fell.[30]

For women fortunate enough to escape the slave markets, few alternatives proved better. In the laundries, where huge numbers of black women labored, high temperatures, unsanitary bathrooms, poor ventilation, and other Health Code violations were common. The New York State Department of Labor estimated in 1936 that wages for women working in laundries were often as low as $6 a week for sixty hours of work. Three-quarters of all women in laundries earned less than $15 a week working a median of forty-three hours. (Not that men there fared much better; the median wage for women was $13, and $14 for men, who worked even longer hours.) After the Supreme Court declared the Minimum Fair Wage Law unconstitutional in 1936, laundry wages declined still further, until in many cases, workers were earning even less than they would have received on relief.[31]

Black women workers fared worse than white, even in the same jobs. One black laundry worker complained to an interviewer from the League of Women Shoppers: "Us colored girls gets treated worst of all. If there's a vacancy in the better jobs they never give us a chance. . . . They give it to a white girl." To keep wages low, many employers tried to divide their employees with familiar racist tactics. A black worker told this story:

> In our laundry they had only white girls first. Then later they started taking on colored girls but this is the way they did it: a colored girl would come in and the boss said, "We can't take you on. The white girls don't want to work with you." The colored girl would start to go and he'd say, "I'll take you, but you got to work for less money than the white girls." They incited one against the other and later they cut the white girls, saying they could get colored girls cheaper.

The Shoppers League noted "race antagonism" was "nourished [by employers] to such an extent that the Negro and white workers are not permitted to eat together even if they wish to." As black Socialist and union organizer Frank Crosswaith wrote in 1939, black women domestic and laundry workers were "among the most exploited and dehumanized of all the workers in New York City."[32]

Thus, even though black women may have been able to retain their jobs or find new ones more easily than men, they consistently worked under even worse conditions. They earned less and more often worked at part-time or temporary jobs. The Harlem office of the State Employment Service reported that it placed less than a quarter of its 3,700 black male applicants in 1932, contrasted with 40 percent of black female applicants. Yet most of the greater opportunities for women came for temporary work in domestic and personal service, with low pay. Such work constituted 80 percent of all positions it had available in 1931. Similarly, the Charity Organization Society's Employment Service reported that over half of all its female applicants from the Harlem area found jobs, compared with a third of male applicants. Yet the women working full time (again, the vast majority in domestic service) earned on the average a weekly wage of $18.56, while full-time positions for men paid $22.79.[33]

In the BLS Harlem sample also, women on average earned less than men for jobs at the same skill level and worked for fewer weeks in the year. Black men working in unskilled jobs, for example, earned an average of $18 a week, and worked for forty-two weeks. Women on the same level averaged $9.62 a week and thirty-four weeks of work. This large differential in earnings was due to the extremely low wages of domestic workers, all female. Men in clerical jobs did fifty-one weeks' work, at a rate of $21.08, whereas their female counterparts worked five fewer weeks at $18.63 per week.

The inadequacy of such earnings is indicated by the New York State Department of Labor's finding that a woman worker living at home with her family in 1937 had to earn $1,056 a year, or over $20 a week, in order to achieve a minimum "adequate living budget," and $1,193 if she lived alone. The budget estimate included a small clothing allotment, rent and household expenses, personal and medical care, recreation, insurance, food, and "other living essentials." Even two incomes did not necessarily allow a family to meet expenses. Mrs. Johnson, a thirty-three-year-old day domestic, earned between $4 and $6 a week. Her husband worked irregularly, earning only $10 or $15 a week as a laborer. Other relatives lived with the couple, and all pooled their incomes when they were able to find work, but it was not enough; the Johnsons had to send their two children south to live with relatives. They could not earn enough to keep their family together.[34]

Black clerical and blue-collar workers earned these abysmally low wages at virtually every occupational level, if the BLS Harlem sample is typical. Neither black men's nor women's wages improved much as they moved up the occupational ladder or gained work experience. Age also played less of a role in predicting income for black working people than it did in the white community. The larger BLS survey found that as age increased for whites, so did earnings. The correlation was far weaker for blacks. Either they changed jobs more frequently, thus losing the benefits of seniority, or in black jobs, experience did not raise pay. For black males in the Harlem sample, there was only a weak relationship between age and weekly wages, and for black females, none at all. On the other hand, a stronger correlation existed between weekly wage and occupational level for black women, a correlation inexplicably absent for men. The data suggest, then, that men earned slightly more as they gained experience, but the pay scale did not vary according to the level of job they held. The pay women received, on the other hand, was somewhat determined by occupation (probably because domestic work paid so much less than other jobs), but not affected by their age. Perhaps their employment history was more sporadic and therefore age did not reflect job experience, or perhaps they worked primarily in jobs in which raises simply were not given. Most domestics, for example, probably worked for a fixed wage regardless of the number of years in the field.

The study of thirty-nine non-relief families, the UNIA's files, and the NYUL and WPA placement services all corroborate these findings. The two services reported that the weekly salaries offered for different occupational fields were almost identical. The average offered weekly wage for commercial jobs was $12.46; for industrial, $12.70; and for domestic, $12.13. Mr. Judd, a twenty-four-year-old shoemaker, estimated his weekly earnings at $15, while a thirty-six-year-old male laborer named Johnson reported the same wage. Thomas Pelmore, a mechanic, earned $18 a week, as did a shipping clerk. Higher-level clerical and professional jobs did pay better salaries. At the ranks where most black workers were concentrated, however, pay scales were low and showed little variation by field.[35]

Noting that white incomes at the unskilled and semi-skilled levels were also quite low, the National Negro Congress (NNC) argued that not only racial discrimination but low overall pay scales for labor left black families with barely enough to survive. As a black member of the NNC wrote:

Certain phases of economic problems bear much more heavily on us because of the incident of race. But the heavier burdens are imposed on us because we are workers. . . . The pressure of the Depression naturally affected the *weakest* socio-economic group— the Negro. Hence our plight was far worse than that of the others—but it was an ECO-NOMIC not RACIAL problem. With this understanding we will not fall into the error of believing economic problems are resultants of racial prejudice.

The NNC, organized in 1936 by dissident NAACP members, trade unionists, Socialists, and Communists to promote economic change, and directed largely by the last two groups during the Popular Front period, was united by the idea that working-class and black concerns were linked. Thus this group saw economic issues as the paramount concern. Nevertheless, the truth was more complex. Both economics and racism affected black status in this period. Not only did blacks work primarily in low-paying fields (an economic problem) but blacks were also barred solely because of their race from opportunities that would help them improve economically.[36] Furthermore, evidence suggests black workers earned less than whites at the same occupational levels. In 1935, black laborers (at all levels) had average weekly wages of just over $20, while their white counterparts earned almost $32, or $1,641 a year. Within those groups, women of both races earned less than either group of males. Among clerical workers, black men earned $31 weekly, and white men almost $41. Again, black and white women earned less still.[37]

For native white male wage-earners and clerical workers, lower earnings were primarily due to underemployment rather than low wages at full-time jobs, since the average number of weeks worked rose as their income category did. The lowest-earning white group was employed an average of only twenty-seven weeks during the year, and the highest group worked fifty-two weeks. This relationship did not exist for black men. Black men at every income level save one had worked an average of forty-nine to fifty-two weeks in the survey year. For every job type and income level the average number of weeks worked by blacks exceeded that for whites. Thus in general blacks worked much longer to earn the same wages. Nor was this unique to New York. "Wages paid to Negro gainful workers are in most instances smaller than wages paid to white gainful workers doing identical work. The differential wage is less widespread in the North than it is in the South, although it exists in all sections," wrote Alfred Smith.[39] While Harlem blacks may have been earning higher wages than blacks did in the South, they still earned less than their white counterparts locally. The split labor market, then, had in fact divided two ways: by race and by gender. For black men and women, the racial divisions in the lowest levels of the job market lessened in the 1930s, and they faced increased competition from whites in unskilled and service fields. But gender distinctions in occupation remained.

TABLE 3.3
Percent of Families Earning at Each Income Level, by Occupation and Race,
Blue-collar and Clerical, New York City, 1935[38]

Annual Income	Clerical		Skilled		Semi-skilled		Unskilled	
	White	Black	White	Black	White	Black	White	Black
$500–$900	2	0	4	50	7	15	11	11
$900–$1500	32	56	29	0	35	63	46	57
$1500–$2100	41	32	34	50	37	11	32	25
Over $2100	25	12	33	0	21	11	11	7
Total in occupation level (%)	26	16	20	2	40	27	14	55

Harlem's occupational structure varied not only by gender; it was also marked by distinctions based on nationality. The immigrant and native-born black communities experienced the effects of the Depression in very different ways, although both shared the discrimination and poverty common to their race. Two foreign-born communities actually co-existed in Harlem: a well-trained and educated middle class of business and professional workers, who constituted a higher proportion of blacks in those fields than their number in the black population; and a poorly educated, unskilled class at the bottom of black working-class society. As a whole, foreign-born black families did better than the native-born, with a median annual income of $1,020 compared with $980. This reflects the strength and proportional size of the foreign-born middle class, as the working-class immigrants earned even less than did their native-born counterparts. Considering only the blue-collar and low-salaried clerical workers of the BLS Harlem sample, foreign-born (usually West Indian) family income averaged just under $25 a week, compared with over $31 for the native-born, although both groups averaged an almost identical number of workers per family. Over the survey year, black American-born families earned $756 per working person, compared with $618 for the foreign-born. While the proportion of West Indians in unskilled labor was slightly higher than that of American-born blacks, and the latter worked, on average, for more weeks in the year, these differences do not completely account for the discrepancy. The foreign-born also earned less than the native-born workers in the same fields. A Virgin Islander who worked as a laundress, for example, reported earning $2 a week; her husband earned $12 weekly as an elevator operator. Both wages were low even by Harlem's standards. Despite the fact that both worked all fifty-two weeks, they and their two children were in debt at the year's end.[40]

Foreign-born blacks in the BLS Harlem survey had completed slightly less education on average than native-born blacks, but for neither group was there any relationship between education and occupation level or weekly wage. The UNIA's case records reveal almost identical education levels for the two national groups, and the same proportion in service jobs: approximately two-thirds of all those employed.[41] West Indian and native-born black families did differ in composition, but this did not explain the income differences either. With the same family size, but more children under seventeen, foreign-born families had fewer potential workers. Yet they had as many actual workers, because more of the employable members of foreign-born families held gainful employment. Of all potential workers in the foreign-born family (those between the ages of sixteen and seventy), only 18 percent had not in fact held any job that year, compared with 31 percent of American-born blacks.[42]

Other factors help explain the lower earnings of the foreign-born. Fewer West Indians than American-born blacks worked all fifty-two weeks of the survey year. This suggests that more foreign-born blacks held temporary jobs, which generally paid less than permanent ones. Furthermore, although both populations had approximately the same proportion of women, foreign-born women worked almost twice as often as their native-born counterparts. Thus they made up a higher proportion of the employed adults in the West Indian group, meaning that the foreign-born work force included more members of a lower-paid group. Whatever the reason for their lower average earnings, the foreign-born working class had even less money to support their families than did the native-born.

Regardless of gender or nationality, virtually all African-American blue-collar and clerical workers struggled through the Depression. Given low earnings and high unemployment and underemployment, total black family income was inevitably quite low, leaving many in desperate circumstances. A 1935 National Health survey of the city found 22 percent of black non-relief families and 14 percent of white earning less than $1,000 a year. Only 2 percent of black families earned over $3,000 (slightly lower than in 1932), while almost a tenth of white New Yorkers did.[43] The average BLS-surveyed Harlem worker earned less than $14 a week, or $716 a year; the average family as a whole earned $1,529. That family's costs came to $1,557, however. Using a different survey group, E. Franklin Frazier discovered the same inadequacy of black earnings. A "maintenance budget" estimated by the WPA's Division of Social Research in 1935 required $467 per family member. Dividing the family income by the number in the family, New York City families earned $611 per person, but the average non-white family earned $401.

The low earnings of both men and women at blue-collar jobs made adequate family support difficult. For example, one woman interviewed by the BLS reported earning $12.40 a week as a presser in a laundry, and she worked for twenty-six weeks that year. Her husband, a university porter, earned a bit more: $20 a week. He worked all fifty-two weeks that year, as did their son, an usher at $15 a week. This family lived with a nephew who also worked as a porter, earning $8 a week for thirty-four weeks. The family had a lodger who paid $2.50 each week. An elderly friend also lived with them. Their total income, $2,597, did not meet expenses. This family, with four working members and a lodger, came up $73 short at the end of the year.[44]

Harlem did not contain only blue-collar and low-wage clerical workers. Some black professionals and business owners successfully maintained their economic positions during the Depression era. Yet they, too, suffered setbacks, even if they did not have to join the competition for blue-collar work. According to the Urban League: "Negro workers of the white collar and business class have been . . . distressed, handicapped on the one hand by common prejudice against their employment by white employers, and on the other hand by the lowered income of the wage-earners of their own race." While the number of black-owned shops actually increased in Harlem during the 1930s, a phenomenon not true nationwide, individual business owners still struggled. The number of stores rose, but profits declined. Businesses were hurt by the fall in purchasing power in the black community; undercapitalized businesses suffered the most, and black business failures were frequent. While the rise in the number of black stores demonstrated that black occupational advances did not all vanish in the Depression, these gains did not spill over to the rest of the community. There were more black businesses in Harlem than there were hired employees in them.

The professional class in Harlem—a WPA researcher found approximately 300 practicing doctors, 1,300 nurses, 175 dentists, 200 lawyers, 600 teachers, and 250 ordained ministers in its ranks—did not fare much better. Their rate of unemployment surpassed that of whites in similar fields. At work neither they nor the black business group earned as much as whites, though they still did better than clerical and blue-collar Harlemites. Black business and professional workers, male and female, earned less than half of what their white counterparts did in 1935: $1,274 ($24.50 a week) for black women and slightly more for black men, compared with $2,648 ($51 a week) for white women and $3,594 ($69 a week) for white men. This race differential is no less unexpected for professionals than for business owners, since black professionals also generally served their own, poorer community and could not charge as high a fee for their services. Income differences were smaller between occupational groups (blue-collar, clerical, business) than they were between the races.[45]

Government work offered one alternative for black professional and white-collar workers. An anti-Tammany "Fusion-Republican," Mayor LaGuardia, who assumed office in 1934, represented the progressive forces in the city far more than his predecessor did. An advertisement appearing in *Opportunity* in 1929 (during an unsuccessful run for mayor) and signed by several prominent Harlem residents praised LaGuardia for the fair-minded positions he had evinced while in Congress: "A Man of All the People and For All the People Regardless of Race, Color or Creed. . . . LaGuardia stands four-square on Negro advancement. . . . LaGuardia believes in equal opportunity, justice, and fair play to all. . . . LaGuardia is outspoken in his defense of our race." The advertisement told the truth. LaGuardia prided himself on championing the underdog. He steadfastly defended the rights of ethnic groups to receive the full range of opportunities America had to offer. While less consistent on racial issues (his anti-Japanese sentiment is startlingly out of character in this regard), he did support the equal access of blacks to municipal benefits. Unlike earlier administrations, LaGuardia's enforced strong civil service protections against racial discrimination. Because private industry had no such standards, the city government became the largest employer of white-collar blacks in the New Deal period. The New York State Temporary Commission noted approvingly that:

> The assurance of equal treatment in the city service has attracted many Negro applicants. There are to be found in this service Negro policemen, firemen, public health nurses, teachers, clerks, ticket agents and trainmen on the city-operated subway, and a considerable number of employees in numerous other classes. Under the competitive system of promotion in force over many areas of the service, moreover, Negroes have secured promotion in some cases to major positions. There is a Negro police lieutenant, two Negro police sergeants, and a Negro fire chief of battalion.

And they received substantially higher paychecks than did blacks in private employment. Mr. Paynes, a Home Relief Bureau supervisor, earned $60 a week, while Mr. Hobbs, a post office clerk, brought home $46. With the exception of a musician, these men earned the two highest salaries reported in either the BLS Harlem survey or the study of thirty-nine non-relief black families. This racial liberalism extended to the highest appointed positions in LaGuardia's administration. The NAACP's Roy Wilkins reminded blacks: "All races and creeds and classes has he gathered to his government. . . . Hubert Delany . . . Myles Paige . . . Eunice Carter . . . Jane Bolin . . . ," all black.

Under such leadership, city officials in LaGuardia's administration did much to counter traditional discrimination and racism in government programs. The mayor required city departments to explain if they passed over any eligible appointee for a less-qualified one. This process, designed to catch instances of racial or ethnic discrimination, seemed effective, according to both city officials and concerned citizens' groups like the NAACP. When the Department of Welfare chose not to make a black temporary administrative supervisor permanent, the commissioner, William Hodson, took the unusual step of writing a letter to the head of the Committee on Negro Welfare of the Welfare Council defending the decision. He also issued a press release to the same effect:

> An administrator is responsible for the distribution of more than $2 million a year and directs a staff of 200, and deals with community pressures. . . . It is no disparagement of [the temporary supervisor] to say that he has not fully met these requirements. . . . [He] has certain definite good qualities which are well known to his friends and associates. On the other hand [the candidate] has not been able to control the administrative operations in his district with that degree of authority and precision which is required. . . . This judgement upon [him] is . . . the unanimous opinion of the responsible heads of Divisions. . . . This I think will be assurance . . . that no personal or racial discrimination has entered into our final conclusions.

Commissioner Hodson went on to point out his personal commitment to fight discrimination and reminded the public in his press release that almost half the investigators and more than a third of all Welfare Department employees he appointed were black. When Walter White of the NAACP complained that New York's Family and Children's Court placed black and white probation officers on separate lists and black officers received only black probationers, both contrary to stated procedure, LaGuardia immediately ordered an investigation. Municipal employment was one of the most important reasons why Harlem's black middle class was not completely decimated in the Depression.[46]

Systemic Racism

These advances could not have occurred without both good-faith efforts by government officials and a tenacious black community. Racism, though, remained so deeply embedded in the system and was so often invisible or even unconscious that victories generally came only after arduous battles, and sometimes not at all. Black nurses had been excluded from all but one city training program and could work at only four of twenty-six public hospitals or health services. Efforts to change this policy had failed with Commissioner Greeff. Black political organizations tried again when LaGuardia took office.[47] In that one episode are illuminated the many opportunities for discrimination available to racist agencies and administrators. Assumptions made everywhere in the system perpetuated inequality.

Alyce Greene, a black nurse, applied in 1934 to New York City's Department of

Hospitals, Division of Nursing, to do post-graduate work at Bellevue. The Director of Nursing there wrote in reply that "at present there are no post-graduate courses in New York City for Negro nurses." An NAACP investigation found no mention of race in departmental requirements, and protested the decision to the new commissioner of the Department of Hospitals, arguing that blacks paid taxes and were therefore entitled to equal access to government services. This situation "is only one manifestation of an attitude of intolerant racial prejudice which seems to run throughout the Department of Hospitals." Commissioner Sigismund Goldwater replied that while he agreed no unfair preferences should be shown, each hospital had control over its own programs and his intervention would "introduce a deleterious influence" into the department. An angry response from the NAACP brought no further comments or action. Several citizens' and professional groups, including Alpha Kappa Alpha, a black sorority, and the National Business and Professional Women's Club, added their protests but to no avail; there the matter rested for a time.[48]

The NAACP returned to the battle at the end of 1936. After noting that the Department of Hospitals was the only city agency that practiced such overt and widespread discrimination, the NAACP's Board of Directors resolved: "It is unbecoming of the government of the city of New York to practice racial intolerance and there can be no question about its ability . . . to stop it." Goldwater, still commissioner, replied:

> I point, not without pride, in [*sic*] the progress that has been made during the past three years. If complex administrative programs could be carried out as readily as well-meaning resolutions can be written, the lot of the hospital administrator would be a far happier one.[49]

He took a slightly different tack from this foot-dragging defense of the status quo in his letter to Mayor LaGuardia, who had also received the NAACP resolution:

> While I do not see how the principle advanced in the attached resolution of the NAAC [*sic*] can be disputed, the literal adoption of the suggested program without reservation or qualification of any kind would utterly wreck the Department of Hospitals, in that it would throw the responsibility for nursing throughout the Department upon a group which is inadequate in numbers and in ability to assume so stupendous a task.

He asked LaGuardia to reassure the NAACP that the department was "sympathetic towards its demands and that substantial progress has been made."

Although LaGuardia wrote exactly this to NAACP's Walter White, that group remained unpersuaded. For all Goldwater's claims of progress since 1933, no additional city hospitals or nursing programs had begun accepting blacks. The New York State Temporary Commission on the Condition of the Urban Colored Population held hearings on the subject in December 1937 at which a representative of the National Association of Colored Graduate Nurses testified that black nurses still worked in only four hospitals, and that very few had been made supervisors. Only Harlem Hospital trained black nurses, and that institution was all black.[50]

Commissioner Goldwater countered at the same hearings that "the number of

Negro nurses in attendance in the City Hospitals today is disproportionately large, so large that there have been protests against the discrimination in favor of Negroes." He claimed that 18 percent of all city hospital nurses were black. While this figure may have been accurate, it sidestepped the central issue. Black protest focused on the breadth of opportunity available to black nurses, not their proportion in the nursing population. Goldwater himself bolstered his critics' argument, complaining that the black nurses were concentrated in a few hospitals. He used this as a defense of his heroic efforts to integrate nursing staffs; whenever black nurses joined a staff, he claimed, white nurses fled. More likely, given the context in which all this took place, whites were transferred out to make room for blacks who were barred from other hospitals. The Temporary Commission found no evidence that white nurses fled hospitals when blacks joined the staff "as has been sought to be conveyed." As for white complaints of reverse discrimination, if such were made, they were not kept by the mayor's staff.[51]

Goldwater's position hardened as he continued his testimony, explaining the problem in terms of the poorer training black nurses received, which made them unqualified to serve. Unwilling to repeat in public his comment to LaGuardia that black nurses were "inadequate . . . in ability," he instead ascribed this view to unnamed (but influential) others:

> Now, that situation is reflected in the very current view, and I am not quoting my opinion on this, but there is a very current opinion, a widely current opinion among those who observed the department constantly, that by and large a great number of Negro nurses do not function as efficiently as a large number of the other group.[52]

This criticism may have been valid, although it begged the question of how blacks were to receive adequate training when they were not admitted to most nursing and medical schools in the city. Yet his conclusion that their poor training, not discrimination, explained why blacks could not obtain positions in so many public hospitals was patently absurd. If no blacks were qualified, none would work in any city hospitals. Why was a nurse who was trained adequately for Harlem Hospital not trained well enough for Bellevue? The Temporary Commission concluded that deliberate segregation was a widespread practice in city nursing programs.

Goldwater actually claimed that all the nursing schools and hospitals would accept qualified blacks, but had never found any. "If I ever heard of a qualified black applicant . . . rejected for a less good white," he claimed he would have intervened. When confronted with his behavior in the case of Alyce Greene, he explained that although the candidate's credentials appeared good, the staff felt on the basis of personal evaluation that she was "extremely unfitted" for the job. He simply upheld their judgment. Three years earlier, of course, not only had he not offered such an explanation, but he had explicitly refused to intervene on policy grounds.[53]

As a result of the hearings, two black nurses were placed at Bellevue—the first two ever appointed there. By 1941, the National Association of Colored Graduate Nurses noted, black students were receiving nursing scholarships, and black nurses had joined the staffs of city health and welfare agencies, prisons, and two public schools. Eleven municipal hospitals had accepted black nurses, and five employed black supervisors. Two voluntary hospitals also hired black nurses, and two Belle-vue specialty training programs accepted them (though no blacks had yet been accepted in its basic nursing program). Private charities employed black nurses and a bi-racial staff worked at the municipally run Central Harlem Health Center.[54]

Progress had been slow and resistance fierce, because until the hearings even well-meaning whites never challenged the fundamentally racist assumptions that under-lay policy decisions. Only a combination of tenacious interest-group pressure and a public investigation that laid the racism bare brought any change. Organized black protest succeeded only when backed by representatives of the power struc-ture; in this case, the city and state governments. Mayor LaGuardia's firm stance on non-preferential hiring also played a crucial role as a force behind the scenes.

The government did virtually nothing, however, to counter the discrimination in private industry. State and city services did little to try to change racist employers' minds about hiring blacks for skilled or white-collar positions. For example, the largest agency, the New York State Employment Service (NYSES) gave blacks a fair proportion of available jobs but did not serve black interests as well in other ways. While it had a policy of not asking employers whether they had racial or reli-gious preferences for employees they sought, the NYSES instructed its agents not to object if the employer stated a preference without being asked. In October of 1935, to cite an example of race-specific placements for just one month, the New York State Employment office received 333 calls, specifying: "271 whites, 11 Jews, 7 white or colored men, 5 colored men and one Italian or Filipino were wanted. Seven Jews, 17 white or colored women, and 14 colored women were wanted." The "or" category was primarily for domestic work. As a result, the vast majority of black applicants received only domestic and service work, since most employers chose not to hire them for higher-ranking occupations.

According to a NYSES memorandum, few white-collar jobs were offered to blacks. The Service received 126 requests for white-collar workers between August and December of 1936 and directed only three to the Harlem office. Half of the requests the Harlem office received came for domestic service; less than 1 percent for clerks. The NYSES did nothing to counter this, and thus served to validate and reinforce racist preferences.[55]

As a result of frequent protests by the black community against such discrimi-natory placement policies, in 1936 the NYSES hired William Wilkinson to deal specifically with black concerns. When investigating complaints, if he found dis-crimination of any sort, "whether they are . . . omissions or deliberate discrimina-tion," he was to restructure procedures or redress the grievances. According to his superior, "It is the earnest desire of the administration that all offices throughout the state deal fairly with, and give full consideration to, applicants of all groups regardless of race, religion or color." Furthermore, a division in the Harlem branch devoted itself to "open[ing] new jobs to the race, contacting business houses, pri-vate agencies, and even getting departments of the government to make provisions against discrimination on jobs paid for by public funds."[56]

As the New York State Temporary Commission uncovered the same discrimi-natory patterns well after these two efforts began, clearly neither program enjoyed much success. While the government took notice of complaints, real commitment to change was not evident, in part because the NYSES never demanded race-blind hiring requests and continued to pre-select which jobs would be offered at the Harlem branch. Carita Roane, head of the Service's Harlem branch, inadvertently revealed the limited nature of her efforts when she offered an example of her work to improve black placements:

> When the Cushman chain bakeries decided to increase their personnel, offering a course of training . . . the management was approached by the NYSES and urged to include colored girls. However they declined to do this. This policy is pursued vigilantly wherever and whenever possible.

If this was "vigilance," it is no wonder job opportunities for blacks were as poor as they were. Agency personnel could have refused to accept race-specific employment requests, or sent all job announcements to all branches. In its report, the State Temporary Commission cited examples of work places that had integrated without incident, like the IND (Independent) subway, and concluded that employers' fears of angry white employees or clients "are frequently baseless or seriously exaggerated." If it did nothing else, the NYSES could have made the same point to prospective employers. It did not.[57]

The lack of legal constraints on preferential hiring and firing by private employers or unions also limited the ability of governmental agencies to bring about real change. Nor did the city council or the state legislature propose such a law, despite James Hubert's plea to the Mayor's Commission: "At least, if you have legislation, you have made one step towards a solution of it and since I am for legal action, I would like to suggest that this Commission consider very carefully such legislation as would prohibit discrimination against people on the basis of color."[58]

Various stratagems of misdirection served racists well in maintaining the status quo that favored whites. The practices used in New York City were not as blatantly discriminatory as those in the South and thus proved more difficult to confront and fight. Even whites who did not consider themselves to be biased against blacks acted in discriminatory ways because they accepted common assumptions about black abilities and race relations. In New York City, when officials tried to justify racist practices, they generally suggested that society, unnamed others, or blacks themselves were to blame for the poorer opportunities of blacks. Goldwater testified that others distrusted the competence of black nurses. In that way he denied being a racist himself, while upholding a clearly racist policy. He claimed to be only reflecting reality. But by accepting that reality and using it as an excuse to discriminate, he perpetuated a racist order. He employed this strategy again when he warned that white nurses fled hospitals that accepted blacks. Even if it were true (and it seems not to have been), it does not justify further discrimination. But by blaming others, he managed to suggest that the blame—and therefore the responsibility—did not lie with him.

Others blamed blacks themselves. Because employment agency personnel believed blacks were only suited for menial tasks, they sent only those jobs to their Harlem branch. This only perpetuated the problem, since without other opportunities, blacks could not hope to rise from unskilled labor. Somehow blacks had to prove themselves capable of higher-level work without being provided the opportunity to do so.

Finally, racists could appeal to arguments in support of the status quo. The phone company feared black repairmen would terrify white housewives, and foremen argued white unionists would quit rather than work with blacks. Goldwater feared to disrupt the smooth working of his agency with difficult questions about race. Commissioner Greeff had used a similar excuse a few years earlier, pleading the exigencies of the Depression. At best, these defenses of existing practice allowed others to continue racist behavior undisturbed. When the status quo is racist, any defense of it perpetuates racism, even if that defense is couched in other terms entirely.

Such assumptions were widely shared by whites in power during the Depression. They were not obvious in their racism and were therefore insidious. First, these beliefs were difficult to challenge as racist, since the racism was masked. Second, because they did not recognize the racism, even well-meaning policy makers accepted these views without question and were guided by them in setting policies, which, unintentionally but inevitably, had a racist impact. But political activism begins with seeing through these practices and reformulating the grounds on which economic opportunity should be based, and these arguments on behalf of the racist status quo would be challenged by ever-increasing numbers of blacks in the years to come.

Structures and Strictures

Black workers, male and female, blue-collar and white-collar, foreign-born and native-born, had different experiences with employment but shared discrimination, low wages, and lack of economic mobility. The unemployed found it ever more difficult to obtain a job, especially at an appropriate level of skill or experience. Blacks who did work generally found themselves in unskilled jobs, and labored for longer hours at lower pay than whites. As was true all over the country, the barriers to higher-level employment, racial preferences in hiring and firing, and intensified competition at the lowest levels kept black underemployment and unemployment high in New York City, and family income low. Occupational level and age made less difference in terms of earnings than they did in the white community. The evidence for a racially discriminatory job market during the Depression that limited black earnings and opportunities is overwhelming.

Black workers and their families faced a precarious existence. Having steady work was critical. Families managed to make ends meet without resort to either relief or debt only when a large number of family members worked all year long. Non-relief black families also generally had fewer non-working dependents. Any small change in fortune—loss of employment, drop in earnings, or increase in family size—could throw such a family into destitution. Large numbers periodically went into debt or turned to relief to sustain themselves. The New York State Temporary Commission on the Condition of the Urban Colored Population estimated

blacks made up 22 percent of the city's relief load in 1937, four times their proportion in the population. Yet those employed and those receiving aid were not two
separate populations; families moved from one state to the other as their economic
fortunes changed.[59]

Employment opportunities for blacks only improved with the organized efforts
of the black community, as in the case of black nurses. In the private sector, Harlem's inhabitants also used collective pressure when possible to increase opportunities and wages, recognizing that what individuals could not accomplish alone
might be done through mass effort. Given existing power relationships and a system
permeated with racism, few of the fundamental inequalities could be changed even
with vigorous struggle. Nevertheless, small changes for the better could be, and
were, achieved as Harlem became more politically mobilized in the Depression.

Harlem's famous thoroughfare—125th Street. Schomburg Center for Research in Black Culture, The New York Public Library, Astor, Lenox and Tilden Foundations.

Tenement Negro children. Schomburg Center for Research in Black Culture, The New York Public Library, Astor, Lenox and Tilden Foundations.

Divine grocery. Photo by Aaron Siskind. Schomburg Center for Research in Black Culture, The New York Public Library, Astor, Lenox and Tilden Foundations.

Mother and daughter at dinner. Photo by Aaron Siskind. Schomburg Center for Research in Black Culture, The New York Public Library, Astor, Lenox and Tilden Foundations.

A. Philip Randolph, 1937.
Schomburg Center for Research
in Black Culture, The New York
Public Library, Astor, Lenox and
Tilden Foundations.

Frank Crosswaith. Schomburg Center
Research in Black Culture, The New
York Public Library, Astor, Lenox an
Tilden Foundations.

Adam Clayton Powell, Jr.,
ca. 1935. *Amsterdam News.*

...ayor LaGuardia speaking. Seated, from left to right: Ferdinand Smith, National Maritime
...ion; Walter White, NAACP; Jean Muir, actress; Channing Tobias, YMCA. Schomburg Center
...Research in Black Culture, The New York Public Library, Astor, Lenox and Tilden
...undations.

"Harlem, 125th Street, 1938–39, Street Mass Meeting." Morgan and Marvin Smith.

The Citizens' League For Fair Play

requests all self-respecting people of Harlem to

Refuse to Trade with
L. M. BLUMSTEIN
230 West 125th Street

¶ This firm, acknowledging its large proportion of Negro business, has refused to employ Negro Clerks.

Stay out of Blumstein's!
Refuse to buy there!

This Campaign is endorsed and receiving cooperation from the following churches and organizations:

Abyssinian Baptist
Beulah Wesleyan Meth.
Ephesus Seventh Day
  Adventists
Good Samaritan
  Independent Episcopal
Grace Gospel
Hubert Harrison
  Memorial
Mother A.M.E. Zion
Mt. Calvary M.E.
Mt. Olivet Baptist
Refuge Church of God
Shiloh Baptist
St. Martin's Episcopal
St. Mathew's Baptist
St. James Presbyterian
St. Paul's Baptist
Transfiguration Lutheran
United Seventh Day
  Adventists
Union Baptist
African Patriotic League
African Vanguard
Afro-American Voters'
  Coalition
Aster Social and Literary
  Club
Dunbar Literary Club

Business and Professional
  Men's Association
Col. Young Memorial
  Foundation
Central Harlem Medical
  Association
Cosmopolitan Social and
  Tennis Club
Day Worker's League
Dumont Literary Club
Eureka Lodge of
  Oddfellows
Excelsior Lodge, No. 4,
  Preston Unity
Excelsior Literary Club
Garvey Club of N. Y., Inc.
Junior Fellowship,
  St. Philip's
Harlem Women's Ass'n
Keystone Lodge, I.U.O.M.
Ladies & African
  Patriotic League
Manhattan Civic Center
Mills Citizens Voters
  League
New York Age
N. Y. Chapter of Nat.
  Ass'n for College
  Women

N. Y. Chapter, U. N. I. A.
Neptune Lodge Elks.
Negro Youth Progressive
  Ass'n
New York News
Harlem Com. Center
Political Voters
Premier Literary Circle
Progressive Negro Youth
  of America
Progressive Political Ass'n
Charles Romney Fusion
  Rep. Club, 11th A.D.
J. A. Rogers Historical
  Research Society
The Sentinels
Students' Literary Ass'n
  St. Mark's Epis. Church
The Interse Social Club
Undergraduate Chapter of
  Phi Beta Sigma
United Negro Progressive
  Ass'n
Unity Democratic Club
Unique Musical Club
Unison Social Club
Yoruba Literary Club
Young West Indian
  Congress

Don't fail to be in line in the Grand Parade and Demonstration on Saturday, July 28th. All persons are requested to form on 138th Street between Lenox and Seventh Avenues at 10 o'clock.

Handbill of the Citizens' League for Fair Play's "Don't Buy Where You Can't Work" campaign. Schomburg Center for Research in Black Culture, The New York Public Library, Astor, Lenox and Tilden Foundations.

CHAPTER 4

Roots of Organizing

Political activity, long a tradition in black communities, intensified in the 1930s. As the Federal Writers' Project's book on New York City made clear, Harlem was no exception:

> Current events are commonly interpreted as gains or setbacks for the Negro people. This social restlessness results in many public demonstrations. Harlemites in increasing numbers attend street meetings protesting evictions; picket stores to compel the hiring of Negroes, or WPA offices to indicate disapproval of cuts in pay or personnel; parade against the subjugation of colonial peoples, or to celebrate some new civic improvement; and march many miles in May Day demonstrations.[1]

Spurred by earlier mass movements such as Marcus Garvey's Universal Negro Improvement Association, by the increasing public and government receptiveness to political demands in the New Deal period, by the greater difficulty in finding jobs, and by the frustration of educated, middle-class blacks unable to maintain their employment level or their standard of living, grass-roots activism in places like Harlem stretched the limits of existing black organizations and led to the creation of new ones. Traditional vehicles for black political action—the churches; the NAACP and the Urban League; Democratic, Republican, Socialist, and Communist party branches; women's clubs and fraternal organizations—along with new coalitions sought to channel this broad-based political energy into effective challenges to existing power relations, most particularly those pertaining to employment. In Harlem, these efforts focused on access to union and white-collar jobs and on more equitable treatment by relief agencies. Activists employed both new and familiar methods, including marches, protests, mass meetings, and direct negotiations, in pursuit of their goals.

In some ways, the struggle was daunting. Racism, lack of education and training, and the economic hardship of the Depression set limits on black advancement. Furthermore, Harlem in its diversity posed challenges to would-be organizers. Because Harlem was a social and political mecca, its inhabitants varied more in their cultural and national backgrounds than did those in most other black communities. Because it was also a racially segregated ghetto, it had a heterogeneous class population.

Nevertheless, the Depression galvanized a black community that had already developed many of the skills necessary for successful mass action. For two decades

Harlem had been a center for black political organizing. National groups like the Urban League, the NAACP, and later the National Negro Congress had their headquarters there. Local chapters of national and city-wide political parties in Harlem had a tradition of activism. Churches and private women's and fraternal organizations had long goaded the community to efforts of racial uplift. The Depression sped the process of politicization, both because conditions worsened and public officials appeared more responsive to black concerns. The New Deal also politicized the black community. It freed black organizations from the immediate task of providing food and shelter while acknowledging that government had a role to play in ameliorating hardship.

When the government began providing economic services, private groups could at last return to their original tasks. Black churches and political organizations now fought to ensure that blacks received fair and equal opportunities for jobs and relief. In the New Deal period, black groups moved toward an increased use of political strategies (picketing, campaigning, demonstrating) to supplement earlier philanthropic ones (such as running soup kitchens). The goal of these efforts also shifted from the philanthropic to the more overtly political. By mid-decade, for example, black job-placement bureaus moved beyond their mandate of placing unemployed blacks in jobs offered by private industry and began to exert pressure on employers to hire blacks in non-traditional jobs. Groups like the Urban League stopped providing relief funds themselves and demanded more black caseworkers and supervisors in government agencies to ensure fair distribution of benefits.

Black organizations in turn helped politicize the black population, but the process was more interactive than unidirectional. Once Harlemites became active, they pulled their organization with them. Since black leaders did not want to trail their constituents, they moved with the community, seeking to channel the newly released energy by embracing the escalating demands of the people and recasting those demands to further their own goals.

Women and men, members of political parties, unions, and churches, the foreign-born and the native-born, the middle-class and the poor all participated in political activities in Harlem. Mobilization to win jobs in the Depression, known as the "Don't Buy Where You Can't Work" campaign (the subject of the chapter following), perhaps best illustrates such widespread politicization. But that remarkable struggle cannot be understood without first exploring the varied strands of Harlem's political and community history, including organizing in political parties, churches, and trade unions. The broad, grass-roots style characteristic of these Depression-era efforts directly reflected the expansion of black political activity both inside an electoral framework and outside it and helped alter the nature of black protest.

Electoral Politics

The history of black political action and organizing in New York City, which began with its earliest black settlers, gained a strong base with the influx of southern migrants in the early twentieth century. World War I propaganda stressing the fight for democracy abroad encouraged blacks to seek such democracy for themselves. Marcus Garvey's movement of black pride and nationalism encouraged political organizing even among non-nationalists, while the Harlem Renaissance fostered a race consciousness that would imbue these movements with energy and purpose. Because of segregation, blacks created separate institutions: a black press, political forums, and organizations for community betterment. These in turn focused specifically on racial issues. Each of these served over time to politicize Harlem's black community.

In northern cities, segregation also brought blacks together into potentially strong voting blocs, a power that black communities quickly recognized. By the turn of the century, political clubs sprang up in every major black center, and African-American leaders sought to influence local politicians. Often, however, black political clout was limited because of the almost universal tendency for blacks to vote Republican. As the party of the Confederacy, Jim Crow, and white supremacy, the Democratic party represented all that the southern-born migrants had left.

This unwavering commitment to the party of Lincoln did not last long in New York City. Close elections meant both major parties competed for black support, which gave that community a voice in local politics. By the 1920s, New York City blacks had begun voting for Democrats almost as often as for Republicans in local elections because Democratic Tammany Hall appointed African-Americans to municipal posts. For example, after his re-election as mayor in 1921 with close to three-quarters of the black vote, John Hylan appointed a leading black political figure, Ferdinand Q. Morton, chairman of the Civil Service Commission. Republicans, noting this voting shift among blacks, tried to woo them back by promising similar appointments. Mayor James Walker, a Democrat who followed Hylan and held office through the start of the Depression, increased the number of blacks on the city payroll from 247 to 2,275. He won black support also by trying to clean up some of the vice and corruption that went unchecked in the Harlem area, although he ultimately accomplished little. Beginning in the 1920s, most candidates for mayor and governor campaigned in Harlem, including Al Smith, John Hylan, and Fiorello LaGuardia.[2]

Black political groups played a significant role in increasing the number of blacks in civil service and municipal appointments. By 1936, Harlem had a black Tammany district leader, two municipal court judges, two aldermen, two assemblymen, one assistant state attorney general, a civil service commissioner, three assistant district attorneys, and many lower-level city and state personnel. As Gilbert Osofsky noted, "Although the Republican tradition remained the stronger, Harlem became the first Negro community in the nation to lend significant support to the Democratic party." Because election boundaries divided the area between two congressional districts, black Harlem could not put its own candidate in Congress until the redistricting of 1944. In the 1920s, however, six black state assemblymen held office, and several black Democrats served as Harlem's representatives on the Board of Aldermen.[3]

The Great Depression and the New Deal stimulated further political organization because the newly responsive municipal, state, and federal governments provided services best when presented with concrete and organized demands. Since the

New Deal primarily granted benefits to groups (such as youth, unions, or large farmers) it quickly became clear to blacks that it was in their interest to organize. Ideally, New Deal agencies helped the needy regardless of race; in fact, they were often run by discriminatory federal or local administrators. To obtain what they believed they required and deserved, and encouraged by the new government concern for the needs of the poor, blacks organized to demand aid and employment more effectively.

Yet these efforts were not necessarily foreshadowings of the modern civil rights movement. First, to some extent the issues differed. The black community in the 1930s focused primarily on concrete issues of work and relief, while the later civil rights movement began with demands for equal protection under the law and an end to segregation.

Second, in some cases black organizations in the Depression era accepted prevailing racist customs in order to win what they could. For example, the policy of the city's public housing projects was to maintain the "integrity" of the existing neighborhood. That meant blacks could live only in projects built in Harlem. Rather than spend the years deemed necessary to argue for integrated public housing, most black organizations pushed instead for the rapid building of the Harlem River Houses, located in the black neighborhood. This suited the planning board's purposes, as it effectively barred African-Americans from moving into apartments at the other sites, and it also suited most in the black community. The NYUL praised the fact that such buildings were set aside for blacks at all: "Only one municipal Housing Authority in the entire state has had the forthrightness to apply anything approaching equal opportunity to all tenant-applicants without regard to race and color. I refer to the New York City Housing Authority." The houses reinforced segregated residential patterns, but did ensure that blacks would get some public housing.[4] While more radical groups, including the Communist party, protested such "Uncle Tom" tactics, the Urban League believed its best opportunities lay in pragmatism; seeking what it could in desperate times.

The pragmatists and the Communist party did find common ground, however. The NAACP and the Communist party, along with the Consolidated Tenants League, International Labor Defense, and several black churches, urged the use of black professionals in the design and building of the Harlem River Houses. Although the Housing Authority assured them it had appointed the "best qualified" designers, all of whom happened to be white, the Authority did finally appoint a black architect, John Louis Wilson, to the team in August of 1935.[5]

Recognizing the new potential to affect their political future, blacks in Harlem in the New Deal period quickly became a potent force in elections, at least on the local level. Once black party leaders demanded and won more local relief services and more municipal appointments, the number of black registered voters who actually went to the polls jumped. Only 29 percent of the potential Harlem electorate voted in 1932; that proportion rose to 52 percent by 1940. African-Americans could see the possibilities that political action offered. As Nancy Weiss put it: "The New Deal politicized previously mute or poorly organized special interest groups. It encouraged group solidarity among blacks, workers, farmers and others, and it taught them the value of organizing to apply pressure on behalf of their particular goals." It was no coincidence that black political activism grew in the thirties; people struggle for improvements when they believe they can achieve them.

Roosevelt, increasingly popular among blacks as New Deal economic programs reached them, completed the switch of Harlem's black voters to the Democratic party on the national level: 81 percent of Harlem blacks voted for him in 1936. Yet Mayor LaGuardia, a Fusion-Republican who served from 1934 until the end of World War II, also earned a devoted following in Harlem as a result of his clear commitment to helping the needy and opposing racial discrimination. From the 1929 advertisement in *Opportunity* until the end of his tenure in office, LaGuardia enjoyed the endorsements of leading Harlemites. The NAACP's Roy Wilkins praised LaGuardia unstintingly.

Do you want a good public official, industriously, even tirelessly, and conscientiously administering the affairs of government? Here he is. Do you want a shrewd politician . . . a fighter . . . a father and family man? Here he is. Do you want a democrat who believes passionately in the workings of democracy for all the people of the nation? Here is LaGuardia.[6]

As a result of his popularity, Republican clubs flourished in Harlem as well. Thus local black political clubs of both major parties proliferated during the 1930s and enjoyed wide participation. Several claimed over a thousand members. The Appomattox Republican Club, for example, claimed 1,500 members; the Beaver Democrats had 4,000 in 1935, with a quarter of them active; the Citizen's Democratic Club grew to 5,000 members by 1937, three years after its founding. Harlem clubs included Tammany Democrats, Roosevelt Democrats, Fusionists, Fusion-Republicans, and Republicans.

The activism of these party organizations did not end with working for candidates or placing blacks in government jobs. They fought for legislation and programs favorable to their people, such as expansion of civil rights laws and for low-income housing. They further broadened their work during the Depression: smoothing problems with relief bureaus; providing legal assistance, Christmas baskets, and clothing for the needy; and running employment agencies. The growth of these clubs and the increased voter participation in Harlem demonstrated the heightened commitment of Harlem blacks to mainstream political action in the Depression—"mainstream" in that while the New Deal helped blacks, it also kept them dependent on the government for support. This fact limited the kinds of tactics or strategies such groups found acceptable to use.[7]

Non-mainstream parties also sought to harness Harlem's political energy to their goals, and their activities further politicized the community. The Communist party established an Upper Harlem Council of the Unemployed, sponsoring street meetings and rallies to protest unemployment, police brutality, lynching, evictions, inadequate relief, and hunger. Through the efforts of its Harlem Tenants League, the party fought for restoration of rent control laws and protested housing conditions, until the League dissolved over internal rivalries early in the next decade. The party's legal defense of the "Scottsboro boys" (nine southern black youths accused of raping two white women) attracted perhaps the most notice and support from the Harlem community. While in some cases the party worked with other black groups, until 1934 it spent much effort opposing them, which limited its effectiveness in the early years of the Depression.[8]

In 1935 its strategy and rhetoric changed. The Comintern (Communist International) announced a "Popular Front," a new policy of cooperation with progressive forces in local communities to further mutual goals. In a speech at the Abyssinian Baptist Church in 1935, Harlem's black Communist party leader, James Ford, tried to reconcile the party's interest in black problems with its program of working-class unity. In doing so, he stressed the new emphasis on community alliances:

> The interests of the white and black laboring class is the same to an extent . . . but . . . to the Negro people there are conditions that grow out of race discrimination and pile . . . up on those of class discrimination—unemployment, getting inadequate relief, not getting sufficient wages. . . . In order for the Negro to be brought to the level of the whites, both Negroes and whites must fight against these expressions of discrimination against Negroes. And here is where the class issue comes in and the question of uniting blacks and whites. [All organizations must fight together in a] united front. . . . The most efficient way [to fight] is by united action. . . . When I say that I mean the Baptists, Methodists, Communists, Father Divines, Democrats—if all of these can get together on one issue we can back down discrimination.[9]

The Popular Front made the Communists more willing to work with other black organizations, and less likely to employ confrontational tactics. This in turn led other organizations to join in party efforts to protest economic and legal inequalities. The *Amsterdam News* ("mouthpiece of one of the most reactionary reformist groups in Harlem," Ford charged); the Urban League; and the new pastor of the Abyssinian Baptist Church, Adam Clayton Powell, Jr., participated in various cooperative efforts. Communist parades now included members of Father Divine's Peace Mission. As the Commmittee Against Discrimination of Negro Workers on Jobs, the party joined community efforts to place white-collar blacks in Harlem stores. The party joined with the Consolidated Tenants League to move the belongings of dispossessed people back into their homes and hold demonstrations in front of the buildings, often thereby preventing eviction.[10]

Through such efforts, black Harlemites joined the larger group of citizens both within the city and nationwide who became active in the hard times of the Depression and followed Communist and Socialist leadership in protests. Whites and blacks demonstrated and protested in Chicago, Milwaukee, Cleveland, Pittsburgh, and other urban centers. In the Bronx, for example, four thousand rallied in front of one dispossessed tenant's apartment ("Reds Fight Police," the *New York Times* reported) and one thousand in front of another. In both cases, protesters battled with police. The *Times,* not one to favor protesters, commented that the lower turnout at the second ("only about 1,000") was "probably because of the cold." One historian estimated that grass-roots resistance restored 77,000 evicted families to their homes in New York City alone.[11]

While the Consolidated Tenants League (CTL) was not communist, its policies and goals fit in well with the party's agenda:

> Its purpose is to enroll all tenants and to organize apartments in all the five Boroughs of Greater New York, to serve as a clearing house for tenants and employees with grievances against landlords; to furnish legal aid for those unable to do so for themselves; to introduce into the state legislature, bills protecting the tenant and to bring mass pressure to bear upon Municipal, State and Federal Governments for adequate low cost housing.

The CTL had a West Indian president, Donelan Phillips. He and Vernal Williams, a Jamaican follower of Garvey, set up the organization as a dues-paying institution. The CTL first gained press attention when it picketed an eviction trial and the case was thrown out of court. League representatives testified before the Mayor's Commission on Housing. Despite the League's nationalist interests (for example, the organization supported harassment of Italian-American shopkeepers during the Italian invasion of Ethiopia), the Communist party supported and participated in the group's efforts. In part this alliance was due to the successes of the Tenants League. At the same time, Communist party activism spurred the CTL to new heights of organizing. As landlords cut back on services and raised rents, tenants protested, and the CTL occasionally was able to shape those protests into a force for change. It was often less successful in Harlem, however, where renters so desperately needed housing that they feared protest would jeopardize their tenancy. The white tenement-house community proved more active in that regard. As Joel Schwartz discovered, without the threat of homelessness that agitation in a segregated district brought, "radicalism secured a strong foothold in the white projects, which drew from an applicant pool already politicized by the CIO, Workers' Alliance, or tenant leagues."[12]

The Communist party also organized or cooperated in organizing several umbrella organizations, including the Joint Conference Against Discriminatory Practices and the Greater New York Coordinating Committee. Both were attempts to regain the political initiative during this period of activism from the NAACP and Urban League on one side, and black nationalists on the other. The Coordinating Committee in particular helped win Harlem moderates to a Popular Front strategy and became the basis for Adam Clayton Powell's and Benjamin Davis' later electoral successes in the City Council and Congress.

Ford boasted that "there is not a single political group among the Negro masses today that has not at one time or another made gestures of cooperation towards the party." He went on, however, to accuse them of doing so "in order to deceive the masses," and promised that the Communist party would "not fail . . . to expose the leaders of these groups in order to turn the masses to our program."[13] With such an ambivalent partnership, it is no surprise that most other black groups in Harlem maintained their anti-Communist stance and that the party never attracted a large membership. Even Ford claimed the party had only 1,200 Harlem members in 1935, not all of them black.

Still, the party's activities reached far beyond its membership. Thousands participated in at least one of its protests and demonstrations, and some of Harlem's best-known writers and intellectuals, such as Richard Wright, Cyril Briggs, Grace Campbell, and Richard Moore, moved through the party. The party's center for worker education, Harlem Workers' Center, claimed over 2,500 members in 1937. When Communist party leader Benjamin Davis ran for City Council in 1943, the Abyssinian Baptist Church endorsed him. Black minister and educator Olivia Pearl Stokes explained the church's decision:

> They didn't buy his political beliefs but they bought the fact that he was a Harvard-trained man and wanted blacks to go somewhere. So we voted for him to get into the Council because we knew that he couldn't make the Council Communist, he had only one vote. . . . Actually what Ben wanted was basically good . . . equality for all black people. And he thought the only way to get it was through Communism, and some of us didn't agree with that as the only way to get it.[14]

Certainly the party engaged in a wide variety of activities and programs. At one 1937 Harlem branch party meeting, for example, the participants discussed the party's participation in an upcoming conference on Harlem housing conditions, planned a picket line in support of strikers at a department store, discussed fund-raising for a scholarship to the Workers' School and for the National Hunger March on Washington, circulated a petition demanding the release of the Scottsboro boys, and planned an "open air meeting" on neighborhood problems.

Many of the party's protests succeeded, especially when it joined forces with other progressive groups. It helped the black unemployed apply for benefits, and won positions for black workers in skilled, white-collar, and union jobs. Claude McKay, an outspoken anti-Communist, wrote: "It must be admitted that more than any other group the Communists should be credited with the effective organizing of the unemployed and relief workers."

The Popular Front and black support for party tactics continued until the party endorsed the Nazi–Soviet pact of 1939, rejected the strategy of alliances, and advocated the creation of an all-black region within the United States. This shift marked the decline of numerous cooperative programs. The party's efforts lost popular support and several non-Communist organizations, now containing Communist members, essentially self-destructed. For example, anti-Communist Williams moved the Consolidated Tenants League toward a litigation strategy in order to minimize mass action that the Communist party could dominate. Unfortunately these court cases were rarely successful, and ultimately the CTL declined. Similarly, A. Philip Randolph left the presidency of the National Negro Congress in 1940, complaining that Communists dominated that group. The NNC quickly lost its credibility and collapsed.[15]

Nationalists and Integrationists

The political parties in or out of the mainstream had no corner on organizing among blacks. In fact, most often they sought merely to commandeer existing structures and programs, reshaping them to their own ends. Rather, for obvious reasons of inadequate access to organized party power, blacks had traditionally organized outside the confines of the political party system. Harlem was no exception.

Black organizations sought varied goals. Some, like the Urban League and the NAACP, were integrationist and tried to work with like-minded members of the various political parties, while others held ideologies clearly in opposition. Black nationalism, for example, reached deeply into Harlem. Though Garvey himself had been deported from the United States in 1927, his vision and organizational structure remained: the Universal Negro Improvement Association (UNIA) and smaller splinter groups offered a compelling goal and a sense of pride to embattled Harlemites. As Garvey had written, the UNIA's purpose was "to arouse the sleeping consciousness of Negroes everywhere to the point where we will . . . act for our own preservation." The organization's preamble affirmed its commitment "to work for the general uplift of the Negro peoples of the world . . . [and] to conserve the rights of their noble race." Black nationalism encompassed both a desire for a black state in Africa and self-help programs in the diaspora. This drive for group improvement was completely natural, argued Claude McKay:

> No sane Negro believes in or desires legal segregation, in which his racial group will be confined by law to ghettoes. . . . But it is one of the most natural phenomena of human life everywhere that people possessing special and similar traits will agglomerate in groups. . . . wherever a distinct group of people is living together such a people should utilize their collective brains and energy for the intensive cultivation and development of themselves, culturally, politically and economically. . . . In the so-called "melting pot" we have distinguishable [ethnic] groups with special interests, who are none the less American. . . . To these diverse groups must be added the Negro group. . . . Any group-conscious Negro should be interested in the intensive development and advancement of his community.

Light-skinned Adam Clayton Powell, Sr., once remarked that Garvey was "the only man that ever made Negroes who are not black ashamed of their color."[16]

Whatever their political vision, these non-electoral groups also saw an increased activism in their members and took an increasingly militant role in political struggles. Some, like the NAACP and the NUL, escalated their efforts while retaining their unobtrusive methods. These groups worked closely with white businesses and government officials behind the scenes to provide better opportunities for black workers. Others were more visible: churches, unions, and other organizations held outdoor and mass meetings, protests, and marches well attended by Harlemites.

One of the potentially most far-reaching of these organizations was the National Negro Congress. John Davis of the Joint Committee on National Recovery, seeing that the New Deal had not helped blacks until they spoke with a unified and public voice, called a conference in the spring of 1935 of more than 250 black leaders, scholars, and activists to discuss "the position of the Negro in the present economic crisis." Noting the lack of such a united organization in the black community, a second conference created the National Negro Congress to coordinate black political efforts toward equal opportunity. The NNC included among its objectives "decent living wages," the right to vote, equal rights, equal relief, opposition to union discrimination, and "complete equality for Negro women." Only the NAACP refused to participate, preferring quiet diplomacy to mass action, and doubtless fearing the NNC's competition. A broad spectrum of groups, from black nationalists to union organizations, Masons, and Socialists, joined. The well-respected labor leader A. Philip Randolph chaired the group. The Communist party played a major role in its establishment and programming, which led to the group's collapse with the intensification of anti-Communist feeling after 1939. The NNC had distinct limits—its broad base of support meant only minimalist programs could be agreed on by all participants, and battles between church groups and Communists, unionists and anti-union blacks, business leaders and Socialists prevented any real unity. Nevertheless, it did participate in several campaigns to expand job opportunities for blacks in cities around the country, and demonstrated the potential political strength of the black community.[17]

Black mass action to win better economic opportunities also went beyond conventional categories. In 1931, just as blacks found employment most difficult to obtain, the prominent underworld figure "Dutch" Schultz took over the numbers game in Harlem. He wanted to eliminate the local collectors and did so as any good merchant might—by undercutting them, offering his customers lower prices. By opening candy stores as fronts for betting, he enabled players to buy a ticket without having to pay a portion of the winnings to a runner in the traditional way. Black collectors promptly declared a strike. Schultz assumed Harlem players would support him. The exigencies of the Depression and Harlem's new activism, however, led the community to decide otherwise. Even members of the NAACP and the municipal government took a (private) stand. As Assistant Commissioner of Correction Fishman wrote to Walter White:

> The numbers racket was always a bad thing for this poor section but it was at least carried on by colored people, i.e. bankers and runners which resulted in a certain amount of this money staying in Harlem. . . . Under a new arrangement . . . the collection of numbers is being put in the hands of . . . white people and in some instances, aliens, who are not even voters. Under this arrangement, the absolute total of money derived from the numbers racket goes into the hands of white people.

Outraged at the loss of jobs and income that Schultz's plan entailed, Harlemites boycotted the stores until Schultz agreed in 1932 to keep the black runners on at the original rates. The numbers game was still run by whites, but Harlem did get more of the "action" than it otherwise might have.[18]

Such grass-roots politicization provided the energy for a burst of activity by Harlem organizations. Once New Deal agencies took over the immediate tasks of relief in 1933, black groups returned with renewed vigor to fighting the entrenched systemic problems facing blacks. They not only fed the poor, provided health care and shelter, and sought employment for their constituents—no New Deal program provided enough of such help—but also devoted their energies to fighting discrimination in public and private employment. In the new, politically charged atmosphere, existing organizations took on new activist roles. Where they did not, or failed to effect change, Harlem residents created new groups to demand or implement specific policies or programs. Church groups led marches to City Hall, black social clubs joined picket lines in support of jobs for blacks, "mass meetings" sponsored by various groups planned carefully orchestrated actions to improve housing conditions or demand better municipal services. Groups formed coalitions to hasten the attainment of broad goals, such as winning trade union membership or better jobs for blacks. Middle-class blacks, displaced by the ravages of the Depression, provided much of the leadership for these efforts, a "leaven of articulate radicals," to use Joel Schwartz's phrase slightly out of context.[19] Political, social, or religious, socialist or nationalist, black organizations fought to narrow the gap between New Deal promises and Harlem's reality.

The Black Church

Central among the groups working for black equality were Harlem's churches, which had always played a crucial role in the political and social life of the community. As Olivia Pearl Stokes explained:

> The black church has always been three things to the black people. . . . It was the center for all the social life, and launching all the talent in the congregation. . . . It was, secondly, the center for the move for freedom, for civil rights activity . . . [and] it was the spiritual center.[20]

The church provided a forum for blacks to participate in what was denied them in the outside world: it offered community, a sense of common values and commitment, and a nucleus for activism. It served a function similar to that of extended kinship networks for blacks moving to cities or up north. Like many African societies, the African-American community drew few sharp distinctions between the religious and the political spheres; black churches had long been at the forefront of efforts for racial uplift, establishing both philanthropic and political programs. Thus, already organized, churches simply expanded existing programs by drawing on the energies of their members. Certainly they had the best potential for tapping and shaping the new activism of the community, because almost half of all Harlem residents already belonged to church congregations. While lower than membership rates elsewhere in the country (which suggests that in Harlem the churches faced competition from other urban organizations for the loyalty of the community), the rate of church membership still surpassed that of any other single type of organization. More attended churches without becoming members. This high number of church-goers provided a readily available constituency for church-based political action and ensured that a religious leader who took an activist position could reach and persuade large numbers of people. Black community leaders often came from the ministry.[21]

As the community around them became more activist and concerned with secular issues of social welfare and equality of opportunity, the churches followed suit regardless of size or denomination. Ministers used their sermons to educate their congregants politically. William Lloyd Imes of the Saint James Presbyterian Church preached unionism; William Hayes of Mount Olivet Baptist Church praised the Republican party and spoke out against discrimination. Ethelred Brown, pastor at Harlem Community Church, used his pulpit as a vehicle for explaining socialism. Perhaps the two most renowned, the Adam Clayton Powells, senior and junior, pastors of the Abyssinian Baptist Church, preached political sermons ranging from a militant to a social gospel perspective. Louise Meriwether described a sermon by the younger Powell from the youthful vantage point of the fictional Francie Coffin:

> First Adam talked about Haile Selassie [and] . . . the League of Nations. . . . Then he almost wept about that terrible lynching in Florida. . . . His sermon was about Moses leading the Israelites out of Egypt and how the Negro today was in worse bondage and had to free himself. I liked Adam. He talked about things that were happening today and preached such a powerful sermon that the sisters shouting "Hallelujah" and "Amen" kept me from dozing off.

In addition to conducting choirs and other religious activities, churches continued to run the health clinics, day care services, recreation activities, and classes they had begun or expanded in the Depression's early years. They fed and clothed the poor. While the larger churches, such as Abyssinian Baptist, St. James Presbyterian, Bethel AME, and St. Mark's Methodist Episcopal, conducted the largest number of programs, most black Harlem churches registered in the 1935 Manhattan church directory reported that they provided some benevolent and social services.

Once the government took over many of these tasks, though, black churches shifted their primary focus to direct political action. While financial constraints and some lack of cooperation among ministers hampered how much the churches were able to accomplish, they cooperated with labor unions, endorsed candidates, housed WPA projects, held meetings and political forums, organized protests, and posted jobs. Churches supported struggles to place blacks in white-collar and union jobs, many helping to organize these efforts.

Congregants generally responded positively to these calls to action. For example, although conservative voices in the Abyssinian Baptist congregation disapproved of many of the Powells' political programs (some even opposing the younger Powell's ascension to his father's position), the congregation as a whole became increasingly activist over the Depression decade. Adam Clayton Powell, Jr., led delegations of thousands of church members to City Hall with demands such as the reinstatement of five black doctors fired from Harlem Hospital, or a fair proportion of positions for blacks in newly created relief agencies. Often the delegations succeeded. "The Negro church is the foundation of most mass movements among Negroes," wrote contemporaries Roi Ottley and William Weatherby.[22]

Mainstream churches were not the only ones politically active in the New Deal period. Father Divine led and supported numerous political causes. More than merely a religious cult, his community involved itself in issues ranging from the spiritual to the economic and political. Followers ran "Divine" grocery stores, dress shops, garages, laundries, and restaurants. Under his Righteous Government, Divine proposed an election platform and called on his followers to vote, to get off of relief, to oppose unions, and to participate in various political demonstrations. Until 1937 he protested with Communists, but they broke with him after he made his opposition to trade unions clear; his followers battled other groups as often as they joined them.[23]

Gender and Politics

In Harlem women participated in political efforts along with men, in large part because of their strong ties with the black church. As in black communities else-where, in Harlem female church members vastly outnumbered males. For every one hundred women members, there were approximately sixty-four men, varying, of course, among denominations. In each, this proportion far surpassed white.[24] As Ottley and Weatherby wrote, in New York City in 1930, "70,000 Negroes, most of them women, were members of churches." Mary McLeod Bethune added:

> It may be safely said that the chief sustaining force in support of the pulpit . . . has been the feminine element of the membership. Through its [the church's] growth the untiring effort, the unflagging enthusiasm, the sacrificial contribution of time, effort and cash earnings of the black woman have been the most significant factors, without which the modern Negro church would have no history worth the writing.

Richard Wright, echoing this sentiment, tried to explain the gender imbalance:

> In the Black Belts of our northern cities, our women are the most circumscribed and tragic objects to be found in our lives, and it is to the churches that our black women cling for emotional security. . . . Because the orbit of their life is narrow—from their kitchenette to the white folks' kitchen and back home again—they love the church more than do our men, who find a large measure of the expression of their lives in the mills and factories.[25]

Black women had always been involved in political action, through the church, through women's clubs such as the National Association of Colored Women, and through community organizations from the NAACP to the YWCA. They had aided women's causes, including suffrage, support for black women in the professions, and legislation on minimum wages and working conditions for women; while participating in efforts for racial advancement, ranging from lobbying for anti-lynching legislation to raising money for black colleges. For black women, then, struggle was nothing new. It was part of being a good Christian, a good member of the community, a good mother. Yet perhaps at no other time did religion, church, family, community, and racial and political institutions come together for women as they did in this period; women, like men, put their skills to work in the new politicization of the Depression. As black ministers became more involved in community struggles during the New Deal era, their churches became classrooms for the political education of still more churchwomen. According to Olivia Pearl Stokes, black women

> have supported the struggle for keeping the hope of the race alive. [When the church embarked on programs of political or social action] it is the black women who have been there singing, supporting, cooking, hoping, cheering the black ministers as they chose to lead the congregations in support of the struggle for freedom and liberation from inequality and injustice.[26]

Thus in addition to serving in the soup kitchens, leading recreation and social clubs, and providing day care, women spoke out on political issues. Their names and opinions appeared often in meeting minutes; they formed their own subcommittees on behalf of women's issues such as day care, illegitimate motherhood, and improved working conditions for female workers. Women wrote many of the church publications and used this forum to encourage broad political and social action. The February 1936 *Bulletin* of the Mother AME Zion Church, for example, exhorted: "Let us as women" improve Harlem's living standards. It complained about poor working conditions for women and encouraged efforts at reform, while reminding readers to help the needy.

And they marched. In protests and picket lines, demonstrations and parades, black women provided numbers and strength. This combination of political action, protest, and philanthropy was evident among women in the largest congregations, in storefronts, and in less traditional churches. When Father Divine took to the streets protesting housing conditions or advocating an end to discrimination, women in white marched by the hundreds under his banner, chanting, "Peace, it is wonderful. Father Divine is God." Treated by Divine as equals of men, his female lieutenants ("angels") registered voters, cooked food for the poor, and ran dormitories for children without parents. Father Divine's chief assistant, Faithful Mary, oversaw all Divine operations.[27]

These churchwomen blended the rhetoric of political struggle with their commitment to religion and family to create their own language of activism. Thus they spoke of their role as uplifters of their race through proper motherhood and homemaking—"It is you who is Queen of the home and rule there with love, patience, thrift and cleanliness"—and of performing philanthropic and even political acts as their Christian duty. These women continued to use traditionally feminine language in their political efforts. But to say that black women stressed the primacy of the race question over that of gender is to oversimplify. Black women saw themselves as oppressed by gender as well as by race. As Nannie Helen Burroughs viewed it:

> We're a race ready for crusade. . . . We must have a glorified womanhood. . . . Stop making slaves and servants of our women. We've got to stop singing—"Nobody works but father." The Negro mother is doing it all. The women are carrying the burden. The main reason is that the men lack manhood and energy. They sing too much, "I Can't Give You Anything But Love, Baby." The women can't build homes, rear families off

of love alone. The men ought to get down on their knees to Negro women. They've made possible all we have around us—church, home, school, business.

Elise McDougald went further, arguing that "the growing economic independence of Negro working women is causing her [*sic*] to rebel against the domineering family attitude of the cruder working-class Negro man."

Yet the view of most activist black women included a sense of the complementarity of male and female roles and an acceptance of certain traditional norms for the sake of strengthening the black family and the black man against a hostile white society. Politically aggressive and traditionally feminine voices blended. That is, black women participated in struggles not simply for themselves but for all blacks and for all women. As McDougald wrote, "She is measuring up to the needs of her family, community and race." Theirs was a humanist vision, and their voice one of power circumscribed by domesticity.[28]

This political style reflected the options for black women's participation in church-based political action. Despite their increasing activism, the tradition of black women's rarely seeking or attaining top positions in church political programs remained unchanged in the 1930s. Generally the top positions in church efforts were reserved for ministers, and many women still viewed themselves in some sense as religious followers. Still, these women, many of whom may have joined the churches for relief from the double burden of race and sex oppression, found themselves caught up in the new politicization of the churches and became politicized themselves. They tied gender concerns to those of race, family, and community, and in accepting a circumscribed sphere, carved out a powerful place within it from which to participate in political and community action. In a way, then, women's increased involvement in political action can be linked to their greater participation in an increasingly activist church.

This broad community activity of black churchwomen spilled over into the secular realm as well. Women constituted a large majority of the Appomattox Republican Club's 1,500 members, for example, and over two-thirds of the activists in Father Divine's political programs. A black woman was one of six spokespeople in a Communist party–sponsored rally at City Hall. Sarah Pelham Speaks, a "prominent citizen of Harlem," served as secretary in the Twenty-second Assembly District Republican Club and ran for Congress in the 1944 Democratic primary. "Negro political organizations are characterized to an extent not paralleled by white organizations, by their large proportions of female party workers," wrote one contemporary student of black politics. Women as well as men joined anti-eviction demonstrations and marched to demand jobs and services.

The presence of women in turn affected the positions of black politicians. When a black man, Ira Kemp, ran for a Harlem Assembly seat in 1938, two of the three planks he advertised in his handbills pertained to women's issues: a home for "wayward girls" separate from criminals, and "to secure better wages, hours, and working conditions" for domestic service workers. (His third plank promised industrial jobs for blacks.) These issues related to women, but could hardly be considered radical in the sense of altering their status or role in the community. His appeal raised traditional issues of protecting young girls and improving domestic service. He did not argue in his platform for opening better jobs for these women, although he was deeply involved in such a movement. Still, black male leaders were among the most vocal opponents of New Deal restrictions on women's work.[29]

Black women remained active in service efforts as well as in politics. Black women staffed shelters, helped organize workers, and protested inadequate municipal services for Harlem. Some activities they conducted alongside men, others they carried out alone. Harlem's two main day-care centers, a home for unwed mothers, and a residence for single working women were organized and staffed solely by women.

Because they were gainfully employed and were therefore less bound by traditions that kept women in the home, and because most women activists saw racial, not gender, concerns as the first priority and so cooperated easily with the men involved, black women faced fewer obstacles to political participation than their white sisters did. Elise McDougald described these activist black women: "Their feminist efforts are directed chiefly toward the realization of the equality of the races, the sex struggle assuming a subordinate place." Certainly black women were as directly affected as men by the political issues on which Harlem campaigned. Challenging restrictive housing covenants, opposing racism in government agencies, and winning other broad civil rights served the interests of all African-Americans. Additionally, since such a high percentage of black women held or sought jobs, they were as eager as men to improve employment opportunities and working conditions. Both sexes suffered from discrimination based on race, poverty, or lack of skill.

That women were employed and politically active did not mean that they therefore managed to achieve truly egalitarian relationships with men. Such equality was not possible in the 1930s. The failure of women to achieve leadership roles in most churches suggests that black men did not view them as equals. Women presumably accepted this secondary role, since church records reveal little discord over questions of duties and leadership (at least not over gender divisions). Yet the fact that women did often lead non-traditional churches, together with their activism in women's organizations, suggests many wished to lead, given the chance, and therefore that the assumption women would play a subordinate role came primarily from men. As McDougald had written, "True sex equality has not been approximated."[30]

Still, whatever the gender limitations or distinctions, Harlem men and women worked together on political issues of mutual concern. In the Depression, their struggles centered on the improvement of employment opportunities.

"Black and White Workers—Unite!!"

Trade unions stood as one barrier between African-Americans and access to decent jobs. In the Depression the struggle to lift union restrictions intensified, with some success. These efforts built on groundwork laid by earlier black unionists. A. Philip Randolph, the most prominent of such men, came to New York in 1911. A fervent Socialist and trade unionist, Randolph won recognition for the Brotherhood of Sleeping Car Porters and worked for black and union causes all his life. He and

Chandler Owen edited the *Messenger,* a Socialist trade-union journal, and participated in virtually every movement for black self-betterment in his time. He is perhaps most noted for organizing the proposed March on Washington in 1941, which resulted in Executive Order 8802 forbidding racial discrimination by defense contractors.

The post–World War I industrial boom had enabled blacks to enter non-agricultural jobs in unprecedented numbers. This development convinced some in the New York trade unions and in the black community of the need to support Randolph's efforts to unionize the black work force under the auspices of the American Federation of Labor (AFL). The AFL had gained some power as it expanded; the National Urban League and the NAACP saw that organization as their best hope for black economic advancement. To the extent that the AFL fought for better working conditions, fairer wages, and an amelioration of postwar economic dislocation, it could only benefit blacks. Union contracts meant better jobs. Alliance was thus a move born of both pragmatism and idealism.

Randolph hoped to establish an organization that would provide the same bridge between the black community and the labor movement that the United Hebrew Trades provided for Jews and the Women's Trade Union League did for women. In this he had the help of Virgin Islander Frank Crosswaith. Crosswaith had come to the United States as a young man. Like Randolph he was a Socialist, and he participated in the unionizing drives of several black groups, including elevator operators, motion-picture operators, and laundry workers. He then became a labor organizer for the Brotherhood of Sleeping Car Porters and for the International Ladies' Garment Workers Union (ILGWU). He was also politically active, serving on the boards of several organizations, including the American Civil Liberties Union, the American Labor party, and the Young People's Socialist League.

In 1925, with the backing of sixteen unions and the National Urban League, Randolph and Crosswaith established the Trade Union Committee for Organizing Negro Workers (TUC), with an interracial board. It directed interested blacks to appropriate unions for job applications, and tried to persuade unions to accept blacks. The TUC often worked with other groups. The drive to organize laundries, for example ("the greatest fight ever made in this city," the TUC handbill proclaimed), was done with the help of the International Laundry Workers' Union and the Women's Trade Union League.

LAUNDRY WORKERS ORGANIZE, ORGANIZE!

Are you satisfied with your present low wage? . . .
Are you satisfied to be dependent on the whims and wishes of those who control your jobs?
Have you a backbone or a wishbone?
Do you want a voice in regulating your hours, your wages and your working conditions?
THEN ORGANIZE, YES ORGANIZE!
Other workers have bettered their conditions through organization, WHY NOT YOU? . . .
When you are organized, you can increase your wages.
An increased wage means for you increased life, HOW?
Because you live by wages! When wages are high, your life is high, when wages are low, life is low.
THEN ORGANIZE!! YES ORGANIZE!!

The TUC helped win the struggle for the recognition of the Brotherhood of Sleeping Car Porters and leafleted blacks about the advantages of union membership. "Lynching is not the Negro's Greatest Problem," proclaimed one pamphlet:

> Since emancipation about 5,000 Negroes have been lynched. More than 5,000 Negro babies die every year from lack of good food and healthy surroundings because the wages of their fathers and mothers are too low.
> Negro workers join the union of your trade, and reduce the mortality of the race.[31]

In its biggest victory, the TUC convinced Local 306 of the Alliance of Theatrical and Stage Employees and Moving Picture Machine Operators that they should admit black workers in Harlem into full membership, something those workers had requested for five years. It did so by organizing a separate union in eight Harlem theaters: the United Association of Colored Motion Picture Operators. Local 306 finally agreed to accept blacks.

Certainly, many black workers wanted to join unions. Charles Johnson reported that after the longshoremen's union opened its membership, 5,000 of the 5,400 black longshoremen joined. Over half of all black carpenters and musicians became union members.[32] Still, the Trade Union Committee achieved only a few successes. Although New York City union locals enjoyed better race relations than did those in most other cities, prejudice and exclusion remained the rule. Few whites concerned themselves enough with blacks' problems to join the difficult struggle to change entrenched racial traditions. Nor did many in the black community participate. Alienated by earlier union practices, many felt more loyalty to their employers than to unions. Also, most of these unions represented skilled workers, and few African-Americans worked in such fields. Three years after the Trade Union Committee's founding, blacks constituted fewer than 4 percent of all AFL members in New York City although they were 12 percent of its work force. The constitutions of eleven AFL unions and thirteen unaffiliated ones still explicitly barred them. Altogether, twenty-six unions prohibited them in some fashion and five more offered only segregated locals.

Still, the proportion of union members who were black in New York was greater than the national average of under 2 percent. The TUC's most significant contribution to the struggle lay not in direct organizing successes, but in promoting a positive view of unions in the black community and in keeping the question of organizing black workers before the AFL.[33]

Lack of funding and the magnitude of the task drained the TUC, which soon ceased operation. But with the onset of the Depression making the employment situation more desperate, moderate members of the black community joined the effort for better union representation among blacks. In 1934, the Urban League, feeling pressure from organizations farther to the left, proposed creating an organization called a Workers' Council to unionize blacks. Within a year, forty-two councils operated in seventeen states. This effort showed the Urban League's recognition that the problems of black workers were in many ways linked to those of whites. It therefore indicated a slight shift in League policies towards increasing class consciousness. Still, the councils had few concrete successes and did not last.

Those groups more committed to class-based ideologies fared better. In 1933, Crosswaith, convinced that Harlem's problems were "essentially economic," tried again to create an organization to help bring blacks into unions. He and Randolph called a meeting with 110 delegates from over half of all city AFL unions to create the Negro Labor Committee (NLC). Again it had close ties to the Socialists. Immediately the new group launched organizing drives in Harlem.[34]

Progress was slow for the first year or two. One union, the ILGWU, launched a major recruitment drive in 1933 that with Crosswaith's help brought union membership to thousands of blacks, primarily female. The wages of these black workers rose, and they participated in strikes and organizing drives. Before 1933, black women finishers in dress houses earned an average of $10 to $15 for a fifty- to fifty-five-hour week. After unionization with ILGWU Local 22 and a strike, wages began at $22.75 for thirty-five hours. Local 60 (in Harlem) of the ILGWU won a 300 percent increase in wages. Blacks were also elected to local executive boards. In fact, while blacks were less than 6 percent of all ILGWU members, they accounted for 7 percent of its executive board.

But the ILGWU victory was one of the NLC's few early successes. In 1935 the Mayor's Commission on Conditions in Harlem complained that the New York locals of the electrical workers, commercial telegraphers, Railway Express employees, printing pressmen, bill posters, and bartenders contained no blacks. They were "excluded entirely" from clerical unions. African-Americans constituted less than 3 percent of the membership of the building trades locals and under 4 percent of clothing and textile unions. In the latter, almost all the black members belonged to the ILGWU.[35]

Soon thereafter, however, the Negro Labor Committee's organizing picked up speed. After a bitter struggle it succeeded in organizing the *Amsterdam News* staff, who received a union contract in 1936. Its efforts added 4,000 blacks to the ranks of the Building Service Employees Union. When the boot and shoe workers picketed to win union affiliation, the NLC supported it, and persuaded the new organization to include blacks. The admittedly partisan Crosswaith proudly noted in a speech to the NLC, "Practically every trade union within the orbit of Greater New York has had occasion to call upon the Committee for service."[36]

By 1938, the NLC claimed to represent or work closely with seventy-three "bona fide" unions in New York City from both the AFL and the CIO. Charles Franklin wrote that "all the important unions in the city" had representatives on the NLC. Despite criticism from black nationalist organizing groups that the NLC did little to help black workers, the NLC in fact participated actively in union drives all over Manhattan. The committee led strikes, pickets, and boycotts, held seminars and conferences, and wrote articles and pamphlets on behalf of union organizing and the integration of black workers into those unions. When the NLC supported a strike or organizing drive, its members carried picket signs reading, "This strike is indorsed by the Negro Labor Committee. Negro Workers!! Join the union of your trade!! Black and white workers—unite!!" According to articles in the black press in 1937 and 1938, thanks to the committee and its predecessor, black barbers, van drivers, soft-drink workers, salesmen, mechanics, pharmacists, funeral chauffeurs, cafeteria workers, butchers, painters, city employees, and garment workers had successfully unionized. Eager to downplay the fierce competition of nationalist groups also seeking to unionize the community, the NLC boasted, "These have all been organized under legitimate auspices and by honest men, whose reputations are of the highest." It claimed to have organized over half of the Harlemites who belonged to unions. The wealth of good press and the numbers participating in NLC efforts indicate the broad community support the committee enjoyed.[37]

The successes of the Negro Labor Committee came as much from the external political events that affected unions as from black action. The National Recovery Act's Section 7a (1933) and later the National Labor Relations Act (1935) allowed unions to organize aggressively, while the Depression made the need to organize more urgent. As Charles Franklin described it, "There was apparently a slight shift from race consciousness to class consciousness [among unions]." The NLC encouraged blacks to fight for union affiliation, but had union attitudes not changed as well, the struggle would not have enjoyed as much success, as the TUC's experience demonstrates.

Most significant in this regard was the creation of the Congress of Industrial Organizations (CIO). Originally a committee of the AFL, it became a separate body in 1936. Not sharing the craft orientation of most AFL unions, CIO unions were dedicated to organizing workers industry-wide, a more inclusive philosophy that made room for all workers, regardless of race. While the CIO's approach applied to organizing work at all skill levels, its leaders particularly recognized both the necessity and the opportunity to bring union benefits to those in non-skilled and semi-skilled fields. To do so, though, organizers needed new tactics, because unlike skilled workers who could withhold their labor to good effect, unskilled workers could easily be replaced. Traditional craft policies of limiting union membership would be counterproductive. Only if all employees on every level worked together could these inclusive industrial unions succeed. Their only hope rested on the unity of the work force during a strike. So most CIO unions embraced all workers on the job, black and white, as the ILGWU had earlier for similar reasons. Furthermore, because the CIO was more concerned with unskilled workers than the AFL craft unions were, blacks figured more prominently in the ranks of those now deemed organizable. The NLC could draw on a larger pool of potential union members for its protests. Communist party members, deeply involved in many of these unions, urged a policy of racial integration, another reason CIO unions recruited blacks more actively than had those of the AFL. Thus the interracialism of many CIO unions both was a philosophical commitment and made good organizing sense. Even if individual union members or leaders were racist, these newer unions lacked the racist traditions of many AFL unions, rooted in an earlier era's social customs. With the improved race record of many unions, still more black groups moved squarely behind the organizing effort.

So both action from within the black community and changes in parts of the trade union movement, especially the CIO, spurred Negro Labor Committee victories. As the Welfare Council reported, the number of black trade unionists in New York rose from 8,000 in 1930 to 45,000 in 1938. Of 122 strikes reported by city locals, blacks walked off the job with whites in 117. The Federal Writers' Project reported in *New York Panorama:* "Perhaps the strongest of Negro organizations in Harlem are the trade unions. . . . Since the depression and the inception of the

Committee for Industrial Organizations, there is hardly a trade or profession in Harlem that is not organized." Most, it noted, were affiliated with the NLC.[38]

However substantial the growth in black trade union membership, the limits of such efforts were obvious. With the exception of the ILGWU, non-CIO unions remained virtually untouched. In response to a questionnaire from the New York State Commission on the Condition of the Urban Colored Population in 1938, thirteen of the sixteen unions that had explicitly barred blacks said restrictions still applied, and two others had established separate locals. In a few cases New York locals maintained discriminatory policies even though forbidden to do so by the parent body's constitution. As late as 1939 that commission charged:

> That many unions are guilty of . . . unfair practices especially towards the Negro group, is a matter of proven fact. It is openly admitted, even by trade union leaders, that a considerable number of international unions exclude Negroes from membership and privileges, either by provision . . . or by practices . . . or by tacit understanding.[39]

Between 1930 and 1940, black trade union membership increased tenfold in the United States, and the proportion of members who were black more than tripled. Still, in the latter year they constituted only 7 percent of the total trade union membership, less than their percentage in the nation's employed population. Some of the problem lay with training programs, also run by unions, which were often exclusionary and therefore prevented blacks from gaining the skills to be able to join the union in the first place. As the New York State Temporary Commission found, "Negroes have been denied apprenticeship training, particularly in those industries organized and controlled by trade union agreements."

Even when blacks did become union members, they usually did not participate as fully as whites. Within all the unions except the ILGWU, blacks rarely took an active part in union meetings, according to both union officials and members. Franklin speculated that blacks felt out of place in meetings, which were probably social events as well. With the exception of the ILGWU, no unions endeavored to make their black members feel welcome. Many, primarily women, also cared for children and families, and could not spare the time.[40] Thus opportunities for blacks in unions remained circumscribed before and at the point of entry, and even once within them. Integration efforts had begun, but much more time would pass before union leaders cared enough about racism to institute movement-wide reforms.

All this political activity in Harlem by men and women, churches, philanthropic and self-help organizations, nationalists and integrationists, came together around the issue of employment. Sometimes working cooperatively and sometimes at cross purposes, the different Harlem groups sought in their own ways to improve economic opportunities for African-Americans. Trade unionism was only one of the many proposed solutions. One political effort did emerge in Harlem, though, that galvanized almost every group there. Known as the "Don't Buy Where You Can't Work" campaign, its course illustrates the potential strength and the dangers of diverse groups with conflicting ideologies working in concert.

CHAPTER 5

"Don't Buy Where You Can't Work"

Harlem's unionizing efforts coincided with another sort of jobs campaign: one to win clerical positions for qualified blacks in white-owned Harlem businesses. If some unions came to understand the advantages of including blacks and treating them as equals, most employers did not. Hiring blacks for menial tasks or threatening to replace white workers with lower-paid blacks served many private employers well, and the Depression saw no shift in their thinking comparable with that of many unions.

In the absence of laws barring racial discrimination in private industry, black political action became the critical force in securing positions, particularly skilled and white-collar, for qualified black workers. Numerous Harlem organizations devoted their energies to this struggle, relying on the activism of the Harlem community. Many considerations made this an attractive issue. Non-manual employment would grant higher status to the entire community. The displacement of black workers by white all over the city intensified black frustration with the inequality of economic opportunity and generated greater sympathy for a "buy black" or "hire black" solution. The energies of middle-class blacks who had lost their white-collar and skilled jobs to whites galvanized black organizations and the wider community. Perhaps the unskilled also hoped to receive jobs from middle-class blacks once the latter had won white-collar employment and opened businesses. Certainly the absence of blacks in these positions was visible to the entire black community. Thus, challenging discrimination in white-collar work captured the imagination of thousands of blacks, including those who could not benefit from it personally. This effort became known as the "Don't Buy Where You Can't Work" campaign, which used mass protests and boycotts as its most important weapons. The story of this campaign offers an example of how the varied political expressions of the community came together in a broad movement. It also suggests the strengths and limits of such alliances in this era.

With a population already organized in disparate and diverse groups, Harlem needed only a focus to unify protest action. Aldon Morris found in his study of the roots of the modern civil rights movement that political efforts were most successful in communities or "movement centers" that already contained organized groups, generally church-centered. Existing networks could then be used to organize a broad-based and unified campaign in the local community. Harlem in the Depression was such a "movement center." Church-based programs, fraternal and women's groups, and political and social organizations already existed, and many individuals held membership in several simultaneously. Thus Harlem leaders had a network in place and could work (theoretically) in unison when the "Don't Buy Where You Can't Work" campaigns spread across the country to Harlem. The New York effort was aided further by the presence of a charismatic minister, Adam Clayton Powell, Jr., who managed for a time to unify the diverse strands of the movement.[1]

But while this campaign tapped the talents of existing groups and fostered new connections, it also gave voice to those who dissented from the mainstream effort. The community agreed on the broad goal of increased employment for black Harlemites, but disagreed on other goals, and on the means to achieve them. More radical activists, impatient for additional and more dramatic victories, first splintered the moderate movement. Later they moved the mainstream toward more radical positions. If black leaders organized and galvanized the Harlem community, the community in turn pushed black leaders to move farther and more energetically than established organizations are often wont to do.

Black leaders sought to create one coherent movement, but the diversity of Harlem's population proved an obstacle. The problems facing the black community were deep and intractable. To make a significant impact on the practices of white employers, black political efforts had to be both strong in numbers and unified in tactics and goals. Yet the diversity of the backgrounds of the participants often meant conflicting political beliefs and aspirations. Thus, while coalitions of the various black organizations provided numerical strength, they could not always coordinate strategy, since constituent groups viewed the problem of discrimination from different perspectives and often sought different goals. Bitter sectarian battles often raged, focusing energies inward rather than on white employers. At first, therefore, the "Don't Buy" movement was unable to press for change as vigorously as necessary, nor could it maintain a presence effective enough to prevent employers from backsliding once gains had been won.

Ultimately, though, as with most successful political movements, diversity provided the movement's real strength. A coalition allowed for broader community participation because individuals with differing needs and outlooks could find a home within a movement that embraced varied positions. Because the several member organizations served different constituencies, joint efforts spread information to all segments of black society.

Sometimes the programs of one group inadvertently strengthened others. While vocal extremists most dramatically publicized the struggle, for example, their tactics frightened some who, though mobilized by the radicals' exhortations, joined with the more moderate groups within the coalition. Much of the movement's successes can in fact be attributed to the diversity of coalition membership; the agitation of the more radical organizations convinced those at whom the protest efforts were directed of the need to negotiate with centrist groups to forestall the possibility of facing more radical demands. In sum, diversity offered great possibilities and imposed severe limits on the development of political organization and coalition-building in the Harlem community.

An ever-changing coalition, the "Don't Buy" campaign sought to boycott stores in Harlem that refused to hire blacks in white-collar positions. It took almost a decade for Harlem activists to organize a sufficiently wide, yet sufficiently unified campaign to win such jobs. Because it sought to place already trained and educated blacks in white-collar employment in existing white stores rather than to establish training programs or community-owned cooperatives, the movement could be viewed as having primarily middle-class goals, yet it galvanized the poor as well as the middle class to action.

Building a Base

As with unionizing, the drive to place blacks in white stores began in the 1920s. In 1925 the *Amsterdam News* urged the use of consumer pressure to increase the number of local jobs for blacks. The New York Urban League, the NAACP, and the Harlem branch of the State Employment Service had been fighting for such goals for years, albeit through quiet negotiation, not mass action. The NYUL, for example, through its Cooperative Committee on Employment, wrote letters to merchants in 1926 and surveyed 300 Harlem stores on their attitude toward hiring blacks. Little was accomplished. The Negro League for Equal Political and Civic Rights surveyed Harlem businesses the next year with the aim of selecting three or four that refused to hire blacks and trying to "correct this inequality. A peaceful but forceful manner will be carried out to induce the proprietors . . . to change their methods. Failing, the combined strength of the League will be brought to bear to the end that the places under watch will feel the loss of patronage without which they cannot function." It appears the Negro League's "combined strength" was not enough to persuade any owners.[2]

The onset of the Depression impelled some further action. In a 1930 speech to the New York Urban League, Joseph Bibb, the editor of the *Chicago Whip,* described that city's "Don't Buy Where You Can't Work" campaign and suggested that a similar effort be launched in New York. He reminded his listeners that whites owned most of the businesses in Chicago's black neighborhoods, just as they did in Harlem. Through a combination of boycotts, picketing, and meetings with white business leaders, blacks in Chicago had secured jobs—white-collar jobs—in several local businesses. While this proposal had been made before, this time many Harlem political groups and coalitions explicitly endorsed the idea. Still, little progress was made for the first few years.[3]

In the forefront of the early efforts to encourage local stores to hire blacks was "a group of serious and determined women" organized as the Harlem Housewives League. By 1931, less than a year after its inception, the group claimed over a thousand members, meeting every Monday night in the NYUL building. Its leaders, by and large, were better off, prominent in the community, and had long been politically active. A. Philip Randolph's wife Lucille, for example, was the group's vice-president, and Bessaye Bearden, journalist and activist, served as publicity chairman. The women visited the Atlantic and Pacific Tea Company (A&P), Woolworth's, and "other chain stores having branches throughout Harlem," and requested that the management hire blacks as "clerks, messengers, etc. in proportion to the amount of money spent in those stores by Negroes in Harlem." When Blumstein's, a large local department store, hired a black doorman and elevator operator, the Housewives League thanked the owner "for this recognition of the purchasing power of Negroes." The group encouraged all Harlem wives to shop only at stores that belonged to the Colored Merchants' Association or that hired blacks. Even more than the Urban League, which at least urged businesses to allow blacks access to better-quality jobs, the Housewives League accepted the given limits on black occupational mobility. It demanded only that employers hire more blacks; it made no efforts to ensure blacks would be hired for non-menial jobs. The League did not believe it had the resources to wage such a battle.[4]

Adam Clayton Powell, Sr., headed Harlem's Citizen's Committee on More and Better Jobs, which, in addition to collecting food and clothing for the poor, tried to organize a drive to boycott stores refusing to hire black employees. Other churches and political organizations did the same. Through its "New Economic Program," the NAACP negotiated with white merchants in black neighborhoods like Harlem to hire black clerks. Still, these early Depression programs could devote little energy to the cause of white-collar employment. Because of the lack of relief funds, most gave priority to the requirements of the desperately needy.

These efforts indicated a general recognition of the employment discrimination problem, but without a broad base, none posed enough of an economic threat to have any impact on white employers. Nor was there a sufficiently high level of awareness in the community of the potential for black action to establish such a base. As James Allen, president of the local branch of the NAACP, complained, "I don't know any section in New York City that is harder hit by unemployment than Harlem and I don't know of any section that is doing so little about it."[5] Harlemites were devoting their energies to "making do" in the sudden hard times.

Internal differences also slowed the movement's progress, for each group involved in the effort to increase black employment sought different and often contradictory goals. Much of the impetus for the struggle had come from blacks who believed that integration into the larger world of economic opportunities offered the only hope for black workers, but black nationalists joined the effort to further their own cause. Black nationalism cut across class lines. Many middle-class and professional blacks joined with Garveyites in advocating the creation of a separate economy, since a commitment to "buy black" meant more business for them.

Thus, early in the Depression, a few black merchants launched their own version of a jobs campaign. An advertisement for an African-American clothing store in the *American and West Indian News* featured the headline, "American Negroes Competing Against Jews in Haberdashery World." The rest of the advertisement described the black-owned store, its goods, prices, and service, and made no further mention of Jews. Rather, the plea for race solidarity allowed merchants to use the campaign to boost sales, announcing

a drive for more and better business . . . a profit sharing plan that will not only help to reduce expenses but also decrease unemployment. Colored businessmen invariably employ colored help. Each of us CAN and WILL add from 1 to 10 employees, if you will

support us. We are doing our utmost to give you low prices, correct weight, and superior
service, in return for your patronage. Think it over. Trade with Negro stores or only
with those that employ colored help.

These merchants designed a "Race Loyalty" button for blacks "not ashamed of
their Negro ancestry" to be worn by those who agreed to shop only at such stores.
The button proclaimed: "I hereby pledge myself to buy from Race Enterprises
whenever and wherever practicable (or from stores employing Negro help) thereby
helping to create MORE and BETTER jobs right here in Harlem." As August Meier
and Elliott Rudwick point out, for black businessmen the campaign was "essentially petit bourgeois" in nature. It sought to increase their sales and profits rather
than to alter the structure of black employment opportunities.

Not all black leaders supported these "buy black" attempts. E. Franklin Frazier,
for instance, insisted black shopkeepers simply wanted Harlem to "be reserved as
their field of exploitation." Nevertheless, this drive to support black businesses as
the best hope for black employment did enjoy ample and continued support in the
community. The Reverend John Johnson of St. Martin's Protestant Episcopal
Church preached: "If you want to do something for the Negro race today . . . you
can start right here. . . . We must spend our money among our own people."[6]

A further barrier to united action was the disagreement within the community
over whether boycotts (and later, pickets) were an appropriate or effective solution,
especially in light of the ongoing debate over black nationalism versus integration
into the larger work force. The *Amsterdam News* editorialized that even if every
store in Harlem hired black help, thousands more would remain unemployed if
they could not find jobs elsewhere in the city. Why antagonize white employers with
boycotts and protests, and possibly jeopardize that much larger pool of jobs by provoking a white backlash? The *News* feared an intensification of segregation outside
Harlem in retaliation. Most white Harlem stores also advertised heavily in the
Amsterdam News, which may help explain that paper's position.

Black businessmen had their own reservations about a "Don't Buy" campaign.
While they supported the drive to patronize black stores, several felt less happy with
the concurrent effort to persuade white employers to hire black help. They feared
white stores would then woo still more black business away from their own establishments.[7]

The Socialist party and the Negro Labor Committee opposed the jobs campaign
because they believed it conflicted with their primary goal of integrating blacks into
the AFL (and later the CIO). They feared the campaign would antagonize unions
because it ignored union hiring agreements and negotiated directly with employers.
They also worried that employers might seize the opportunity to hire blacks at sub-
union wages or as strikebreakers, and that the effort would generally divert energy
and attention from their trade union struggle. The words of some campaign advocates justified that fear. In a defense of the boycott effort, Vera Johns noted that
white store owners did not hire blacks out of love but rather "because it is found
that the colored worker can do better work and may be paid a lesser wage." Even
in the campaign for economic equality, at least some accepted unequal pay scales
for white and black.[8]

Another group conspicuously absent from the action was Harlem's Communist party. Seeking the solidarity of the working class, black and white, the party feared increased racial antagonism as a result of a campaign that might cause white workers to be fired to make room for black. Instead, it sought to redirect protest energies towards class-oriented problems, such as blue-collar unemployment and inadequate relief—problems local boycotts and pickets could not solve but that required a far broader organizing base. Also, until the Popular Front period, party members were reluctant to work with organizations that sought solutions within the capitalist system. When the jobs campaign did become active after 1933, the party organized a parallel movement called the Committee Against Discrimination of Negro Workers on Jobs. This awkwardly titled group demanded the hiring of blacks in Harlem stores without firing whites. By 1935, the "Don't Buy" campaign was having such success that the party did join the picket line for a time.

Interestingly, the NYUL and NAACP had doubts about the jobs campaign for similar reasons. The Urban League feared the potential for increased racial antagonism in the jobs campaign would jeopardize the tenuous cooperation it had established with white employers elsewhere in the city. Yet rather than stay aloof from the "Don't Buy" effort, the NYUL sponsored letter-writing campaigns and used personal connections to promote black hiring in white-owned shops. For example, in its attempts to place blacks in department stores, white League members sought to persuade white store owners of the advantages of hiring black help. Next, NYUL leaders would "cultivate a top industrialist" and ask him to persuade others. The League also sponsored Vocational Opportunity Campaigns reminding blacks of existing opportunities and urging whites to provide more.[9]

When asked what his organization had done for black employment, James Hubert, executive director of the NYUL, replied:

A. The Urban League has written numerous letters and has had one conference. . . . It has cooperated with other organizations. . . .

Q. What has the league done by way of protesting publicly?

A. That is not the Urban League's method of procedure—not through protest. . . . [That] may be the way to get what you want, but it is not our method.

The NYUL trod a difficult road in the Depression, determined to remain visibly active in black efforts to improve economic opportunity, yet struggling to maintain its good relations with the white business and professional community. The League recognized the growing black activism and sought to use it as leverage but feared it could alienate the League's white allies. The resulting schizophrenia prompted pronouncements such as this one in 1933:

There is no doubt that this prolonged unemployment period has had its effects upon the political and social ideology of the Negro. . . . Throughout the country Negroes are expressing continued dissatisfaction with an industrial system fraught with such dire unemployment. . . . It should not be concluded, however, that the whole Negro group has become "radical." . . . [Negro business and professional leaders are] in the main, very conservative . . . [while Socialists and Communists are followed] largely by sections of the working classes, students and the so-called intellectuals.

Similarly, the NAACP diverged in two important ways from the jobs campaign. First, it sought city-wide opportunities for blacks, focusing on questions of segregation as well as employment. Second, the NAACP preferred different methods than direct street action. The organization challenged the status quo of segregation, for example, by taking discriminatory public facilities to court, since such segregation was illegal in New York. NAACP efforts apparently had an impact on such practices: "Of late, law suits have compelled many . . . to alter their policy," commented the Federal Writers' Project. Still, because the organization's major thrust was litigation, few in the black community had any deep or active involvement with it. In job discrimination cases the NAACP generally became involved when the discrimination was obvious, as in the struggle to integrate the work force on the Eighth Avenue subway or to place black nurses in municipal hospitals, and worked behind the scenes rather than joining in visible public actions.[11]

The majority of black leaders, however, supported the boycott efforts. By 1934 they were able to begin organizing a formal campaign as New Deal programs freed them somewhat from meeting the immediate needs of the hungry. Furthermore, grass-roots community activism had been building, as Harlemites took to the streets in ever-increasing numbers to protest evictions or to demand equal treatment from relief and municipal agencies. Each episode of activism inspired more. The unwillingness of moderate groups like the NAACP to embrace more activist or confrontational tactics left those who clamored for mass action to form their own organizations and thus dominate the early jobs campaign. The impatience of many in the black community, their frustration at the seeming foot-dragging of the NAACP, the Urban League, and others, had helped spur new mass movements for black jobs in Chicago, Baltimore, Detroit, Washington, D.C., and elsewhere, and would do so in Harlem as well.

In February of 1934, Effa Manley called a meeting of "progressive women" to discuss the employment situation on 125th Street. After surveying the problem, she requested help from local black ministers. First to respond was the Reverend John Johnson of Saint Martin's Protestant Episcopal Church. He and Fred Moore, publisher of the *New York Age,* called a mass meeting to form the Citizens' League for Fair Play. As the Reverend William Imes told it:

> The next step was to bring the matter before the group of the Special Citizens' League. It was not . . . [our] desire to form another organization. We were already in too many. [If Johnson would agree to run it] there are some of us in other churches, lodges, labor unions and the like who will be very glad to combat this particular effort to displace colored people or discourage colored people from seeking employment. . . . A great many organizations came in. The thing was rather new and got some publicity. . . . Finally it seemed that nothing short of the actual demonstration in the form of picketing would do.[12]

Participants included eighteen churches and forty-four other Harlem groups, including women's, political, fraternal, and social clubs; and business organizations. Street-corner orators like Ira Kemp, Georgia-born president of the African

Patriotic League, and Arthur Reid from Barbados, both black nationalists from the Garvey movement who had been preaching their versions of black separatism from soapboxes, joined with the more traditional activists of the black churches, the *New York Age,* the Unity Democratic Club, a Fusion-Republican club, the Cosmopolitan Social and Tennis Club, Young West Indian Congress, Premier Literary Circle, and the New York Chapter of the UNIA to promote black employment—evidence of the diversity of the Harlem groups involved in political action.[13]

Sufi Abdul Hamid and his Negro Industrial Clerical Alliance worked alongside the coalition. Hamid, who claimed Egyptian ancestry (but who was actually native-born) and dressed dramatically in flowing robes and turban, had come from the successful Chicago campaign a year before. There he and his followers had won 300 jobs in two months with the use of pickets requesting blacks not to shop at stores that practiced systematic racism in hiring. It was this early success that prompted the *Chicago Whip* and others to join the struggle there. But his anti-white slogans and black separatist arguments alienated many in Chicago, as they would in Harlem, and led the *Whip* to launch a parallel campaign rather than join his efforts. Now, through street corner speeches in Harlem, Sufi Hamid carried on the rhetoric and tactics that had worked in Chicago.

Division on the goals of the jobs campaign had not disappeared with the formation of the Citizens' League for Fair Play. The nationalist political beliefs of Hamid, Kemp, and Reid could not be reconciled easily with the more traditional views of those in the coalition eager to expand the range of opportunities available to blacks in the larger work force. Furthermore, the participants were not always ideologically self-consistent. The fact that the Reverend John Johnson also preached "buy black" sermons and that the *Amsterdam News* first recommended putting pressure on white Harlem store owners but later opposed this strategy indicate that the boundaries between the people who believed in integration and those who sought black nationalist goals were often quite fluid. Personal disagreements played their part in creating internal tensions as well. Clashes between Hamid's group and the UNIA, for example, had become so fierce in 1932 that police temporarily barred both from street speaking.[14]

All agreed on the primary goal of black employment in a period of intense hardship. In an interview with the *Amsterdam News,* Kemp explained his activism: "Harlem in 1932 was in a sorry condition. The depression and discrimination against Negroes and the suffering that was the lot of these people forced me to action." But the consensus between the nationalists and the moderates reached no further. This created severe internal tensions that eventually led to the dissolution of the coalition.

The First Campaign

The Citizens' League for Fair Play chose as its first target Blumstein's on 125th Street, Harlem's largest department store. The Reverend Mr. Johnson preached to his congregants: "I want our meeting this morning to begin a 12 day campaign to persuade Blumstein's department store where 140 persons work (with 16 colored menials) to hire colored girls as sales clerks."[15]

The coalition began with traditional tactics. Approaching Mr. Blumstein, CLFP representatives reminded him of the volume of black patronage and requested that he hire blacks. He replied that he did in fact have several blacks in his employ. All worked in menial positions, however, and Blumstein refused to hire black clerks. He promised to consider the possibility of doing so in the fall, when new positions became available, but insisted that currently he had a sufficient number of workers.

The CLFP found this unacceptable. Churches raised money to print thousands of leaflets advertising a protest parade, and the League set up a picket line in front of the store. The Reverend Mr. Imes testified at a hearing:

> . . . The Reverend Johnson and I were there, just as many other clergymen were there and numbers of men and women from various organizations and leagues. The real demonstration went on for a number of weeks. . . .
>
> *Q.* Is it not a fact that some of our most respected and qualified citizens in Harlem took part? . . . There has been propaganda . . . it is done by the lower element.
>
> *A.* In all these troubles there have been cross sections of people involved. You will find society people, religious people, atheists, you will find cross sections of each community interested in these problems.

Carrying signs that read "Don't Buy Where You Can't Work," picketers pleaded with would-be shoppers to take their business elsewhere. League leaflets requested "all self-respecting people of Harlem to REFUSE TO TRADE WITH L. M. BLUMSTEIN . . . Refuse to Buy There!" At times the pickets became disruptive. Several shoppers reported that picketers seized their bags and destroyed the purchases inside or yelled derogatory remarks. Some picketers pulled patrons' hair. While boycotts were a time-honored tactic for otherwise powerless black communities, pickets were newer, reflecting the shift toward broad-based, visible political strategies. The numbers of participants were impressive. Between 400 and 1,500 attended any given weekly meeting, and the "honor roll" of picketers included 58 men and 83 women who marched regularly.

Blumstein bowed to the pressure and the threat of lost revenue, particularly acute in a depression, and agreed to hire fifteen black women as clerks immediately "to offset any loss of good will," and twenty more in the fall. Yet his difficulties were not over. As he explained to an interviewer in 1935, "the store naturally picked the most attractive personalities among the Negro girls." He meant that Blumstein's selected only light-skinned women. Kemp and Reid, the black nationalists of the picket committee, protested vigorously. They argued that light and mulatto women received employment, "while black ones did all the [picket] work." Again, Blumstein agreed. As he told the story, "This [complaint] was remedied, and Reverend Johnson seemed satisfied." The CLFP called off the picket. Other local stores, fearing pickets and loss of sales themselves, also promised to hire black clerks. Woolworth's, for example, agreed to hire thirty-five.[16]

It is not surprising that Reid, a West Indian and a follower of Garvey, made an issue out of color. In the West Indies color distinctions among blacks determined social status and economic class to a large extent. The lighter one's skin, the higher one's status. This suggests that to Kemp and Reid, the issue was one of class as well as race—lower-class (dark) blacks worked for change, while upper-class (light-skinned) blacks benefited. This charge of class bias was valid, in part. By seeking only to obtain white-collar positions, the campaign mainly helped blacks with middle-class skills, since they were most likely to be qualified for such jobs. Nevertheless, in a sense it was unfair to blame the CLFP for fulfilling its explicitly stated goal of placing white-collar workers in appropriate (middle-class) jobs. Moreover, Kemp and Reid did not acknowledge that, as with other ethnic and minority groups, the potential for unskilled job opportunities would increase once educated and skilled blacks rose in the economic world and established businesses with their own labor needs.

Although the association of lighter skin with higher class had no legal basis in American society, Reid's charge did have resonance for native-born dark-skinned blacks. Historically, many slave masters and, later, white employers demonstrated a bias toward lighter-skinned blacks (as Blumstein had), so economic level, social status, and color did overlap to some extent. Presumably, Reid hoped his charges of bias would win him the allegiance of the dark-skinned, the West Indians, and the poor.

Kemp's and Reid's accusation of color discrimination also represented an attempt to change the jobs campaign into a nationalist movement represented by "true" (dark-skinned) blacks, equating dark skin with race pride. In the spirit of Marcus Garvey, Kemp and Reid told a *New York Age* reporter they were "black people, not Negroes." Ultimately, they hoped blacks would fill all Harlem jobs, creating an all-black, independent economy there. Finally, Kemp and Reid broke from the CLFP to organize a more strongly nationalist Harlem Labor Union, Incorporated. Most members were young and from the West Indies. When Kemp died two years later, Reid continued to run it.

The separation from the Citizens' League was also the result of a more personal power struggle. In part, the color issue was a screen for the struggle to control job allocation. Reid's picket line was sustained by men and women who joined it to gain employment. Since under the terms of the League agreement Blumstein's was not obligated to hire his people, Reid felt his power base was threatened and he left the coalition. Despite the Blumstein's victory, then, the color issue and internal dissension splintered the Citizens' League.[17]

Sufi Abdul Hamid was no more satisfied with the Blumstein's settlement than were Kemp and Reid. He wanted Blumstein's and other white-owned stores to hire more black clerks—and members of his own group—and to guarantee job security. According to Mr. Snyder, manager of the 125th Street store of the W. T. Grant Company chain, he "was approached by Abdul Hamid who wanted the manager to place some of his followers in jobs in the store." The interviewer concluded: "It appears that Hamid was not interested in the employment of Negroes generally but only those who were his 'disciples.'"[18] This claim would be leveled again. Both Kemp's group and the Negro Industrial Clerical Alliance reinstated their picket lines at Blumstein's. Hamid demanded Blumstein hire seventy-five blacks, with a provision against arbitrary firing. The Alliance also picketed Beck's Shoe Store on 125th Street with similar demands. The *New York Age,* until this point a staunch supporter of the jobs campaign, lamented the behavior of the two groups. It described Reid's organization in the article "Renegade 'Boycott Committee' Runs Wild, Assaults Shoppers":

> Intimidating store-keepers, assaulting shoppers and by a campaign of maliciousness with no regard as to the results of their vicious tactics, a group of members of the Citizens' League . . . have broken away from the parent body, constituted themselves a separate group . . . and are demanding complete control of the allocating of jobs to Negroes in 125th street stores. With propaganda against Negroes of light complexion, they are charging that the girls employed by L. M. Blumstein's Department Store are not dark enough to suit them and have even gone so far as to demand of employers that light colored clerks be fired and men and women associated with their organization be hired in their stead. . . . Their tactics are said to be the same as those used by racketeers.

These pickets became disruptive—or effective—enough for the merchants to seek redress from the city government. According to the president of the Board of Aldermen in September of 1934:

> I have had considerable complaint during the last few weeks from merchants throughout the northern end of Harlem in the colored section, complaining that several colored organizations are picketing their places of business.
>
> The first effort is an attempt to compel the employment of colored persons, then, where colored persons are employed, some of the organizations object to the light or dark color of the employees, and attempt to dictate to the storekeepers first as to the kind of colored employees, then the positions in which they are to be placed, and they finally wish to dictate the personnel themselves.

The merchants claimed they were "perfectly willing to employ a fair percentage of colored people provided they are competent to fill the positions, but they do not feel called upon to appoint to positions certain personnel dictated by various groups, nor to create unnecessary positions to which colored help may be employed, nor to discharge one set of colored help and substitute another." This claim is disingenuous, as the merchants demonstrated very little "perfect willingness" to hire black clerks from the Citizens' League picket, either. White store owners complained that black clerks were poorly trained, and that both black and white patronage fell after black clerks were employed. They also admitted, however, that the newly hired clerks "learned readily enough."[19]

Hamid was arrested for disorderly conduct and otherwise hindered by police several times, but he continued the picket until the A. S. Beck Shoe Company received a court injunction. On October 31, 1934, New York's Supreme Court ruled that picketing was illegal because there was no labor dispute. By this time, the Citizens' League had disavowed the increasingly confrontational actions of the pickets, and the black press almost universally condemned it. John Johnson reported he was unhappy with "the uncontrollable forces [the] movement had unleashed." All the opponents of black nationalism rushed to assert the superiority of their approach and heap criticism on Hamid, Kemp, and Reid. James Hubert lambasted the "soapbox orators who . . . heckle and vilify publicly anyone and every other organization that is attempting to deal with the problems at hand . . . a most disgusting scene."[20]

Hamid reorganized his picketers into the AfroAmerican Federation of Labor, reasoning that a union picket would be considered legal. The state Supreme Court ruled otherwise, recognizing that a title did not make a union. Hamid left the business of organizing in 1935 to marry "policy queen" Madame Stephanie St. Claire and found the Temple of Tranquillity on Morningside Drive, which operated a cooperative vegetable market and a garage. He died in a plane crash in 1938 during an attempt to rise (literally) higher than Father Divine, whom he perceived as his foremost rival.[21]

Without the broad-based picket, the hard-won triumphs of the Citizens' League evaporated. Other stores on 125th Street that had agreed to hire blacks never did. Blumstein's kept the first fifteen black women on staff, but never hired the promised twenty in the fall. Without a continuing, visible presence, the League could not force store owners to keep their agreement. Meeting in early 1935, the League found half of the blacks who had won clerical jobs in 1934 had been laid off. Without the legal right to picket, the Citizens' League collapsed. Alternative strategies, such as leafleting or using church pulpits to publicize the boycotts, were certainly still possible, but the League would not or did not adopt them. In view of the large numbers of participants in church activities and the centrality of churches in the campaign, the lack of enthusiasm for continuing the boycott through church efforts is puzzling. Nor did the churches join the ongoing efforts of the NAACP and the Urban League to improve job opportunities by quieter means. Perhaps the Depression gave Harlem activists more than enough else to do. Perhaps the prospects for success were still too discouraging, once the courts took the side of the white merchants. Certainly the Citizens' League was not alone in failing to find viable alternative tactics in the face of the ban. Picket and boycott activities dwindled all over the country as a result of similar court rulings.[22]

In any event, by 1935, conditions were little better for skilled and educated blacks than they had been two years previously.

Q. In regard to the retail stores in New York, could you tell me whether it is a general custom to abstain from employing Negro clerks?

A. Yes, unless the girl is very light in complexion. . . .

Q. Does this apply to Harlem?

Interjection: Yes, even in Harlem

Interjection: Some stores . . .

Interjection: Kress stores

Chairman: Order!

The fact was that any improvements that had come resulted from the pickets. Little hope remained for continued improvement so long as boycotts and pickets were not used, as Cecilia Saunders' testimony before the Mayor's Commission on Conditions in Harlem sugguests:

> *Q.* You are familiar with the employment of Negroes in the stores on 125th Street. When did that begin?
>
> *A.* Less than a year ago.
>
> *Q.* Did the employment of Negroes precede or come after the picketing on 125th Street?
>
> *A.* After the picketing.
>
> *Q.* The merchants to your knowledge, had they done anything before the picketing began in order to give the Negro consideration by way of employment?
>
> *A.* I never heard that they had.[23]

More radical groups in Washington, D.C., Atlanta, and elsewhere defied court orders and continued pickets, despite arrests. Some Harlem groups did so as well. Both the Harlem Labor Union (HLU) and the Negro Industrial Clerical Alliance continued their work after the dissolution of the Citizens' League and turned the drive for black jobs increasingly into an explicitly anti-white campaign, often targeting particular white ethnic groups. Certainly such a tactic was effective in achieving their nationalist political goals; by stirring up the people against a group of whites who were also tradespeople in the area, the two groups encouraged patronage of black-owned stores. Thus, for example, the HLU used the anti-Italian fervor that swept Harlem after Italy invaded Ethiopia to urge a boycott of Italian and white pushcarts in Harlem in favor of black ones. Hundreds of blacks joined these protests and demonstrations.[24]

Their strongest invective, however, was reserved for Jews. Jewish store owners in Harlem, having helped form the Harlem Merchants' Association at the time of the initial pickets, first complained of Hamid's anti-Semitism in 1934. They accused him of repeating Nazi propaganda, and called him "Black Hitler." The *Amsterdam News,* the *New York Age,* and others corroborated these claims, and reported anti-Semitic remarks he had made. He was brought to municipal court in 1935 on charges of disorderly conduct and "instigating a race war." He denied the charges and was released with a warning.

Equally anti-Semitic was the Harlem Labor Union, which, according to the Eighth Avenue merchants, relied to a large extent on Nazi propaganda and some of Garvey's teachings to protest "Jewish control" of black economic life. These merchants reported to the police commissioner that the Harlem Labor Union representatives "used the[ir] platform to vilify the Jewish race and in their addresses have used such expressions as . . .'The Jews are the exploiters of the colored people'. . .'Harlem's worst enemies are the Jews'. . .'Jews and leprosy are synonymous.'" A Federal Writers' Project researcher concluded that the HLU "assumed the character of a 'crusade against Jewish merchants'" and that Sufi Hamid preached anti-Semitism and race hatred. In a rare show of agreement, both the Harlem Merchants' Association and the Communist party protested Hamid's and the HLU's rhetoric.[25] The party opposed the anti-Semitism as divisive and a barrier to the goal of uniting the working class of all races and religions. It opposed such big-otry also because so many party members were Jewish.

While anti-Semitism was only part of the broader anti-white rhetoric, Jews did make the most visible target. The majority of store owners were Jewish, since the Jews had settled in Harlem before the blacks, and remained in their stores after they moved from their apartments. Therefore, anti-white feeling could easily be trans-lated into anti-Semitism. The relationship between blacks and Jews was tense in other economic areas as well (at the Bronx "slave market," for example, most of the housewives hiring domestic workers were Jewish), which undoubtedly encour-aged anti-Jewish sentiment in the jobs campaign.

The issue of anti-Semitism polarized the activist black community, with the groups from the original Citizens' League and black trade unionists protesting such tactics, while supporters of Hamid, Kemp, and Reid denied all charges of anti-Semitism. Claude McKay came to Hamid's defense: "No one was more astonished than the Sufi himself when he was accused of organizing an anti-Semitic move-ment. . . . There was never any anti-Semitism in Harlem and there still is none, in spite of the stupid and vicious propaganda which endeavored to create an anti-Semitic issue out of the legitimate movement of Negroes to improve their social condition. . . . In fact, it is that reactionary attitude that is increasing anti-Jewish feeling." Even this defense, then, conceded the presence of anti-Semitism in Har-lem, but denied that Hamid or Kemp was the source. Other defenders viewed anti-Semitism, or anti-white feeling in general, more benignly as simply part of the strug-gle for black nationalism. Once again, differences in political aspirations prevented the formation of a workable jobs coalition in Harlem.

Questions of corruption and self-interest served to further widen the division between the nationalists and the more moderate, integrationist groups. The remaining members of the League argued that the Harlem Labor Union and the Negro Industrial Clerical Alliance were undermining the campaign for black cler-ical jobs by using political means for personal ends, fighting for the employment only of workers who supported them. Sufi Hamid promised all who joined the Alli-ance a clerical job, but membership dues were $1 each month even if no job was obtained. Store managers like Mr. Snyder of Grant's were not the only ones to charge Hamid with exploiting the situation for his own benefit. Several black employees reported threats of violence from him if they refused to join his "union," even if they already belonged to another. There is also some evidence of bribery of store owners. According to Bernard Deutch, president of the Board of Aldermen: "There has sprung up a racket whereby some of those colored leaders are forcing small storekeepers who employ no help at all to pay a certain sum each week in lieu of employing unnecessary help."[26]

Kemp and Reid's Harlem Labor Union was reported to be equally corrupt. "This organization," reported the *Amsterdam News,* "is racketeering of the most vicious type. It not only lines the pocket of its leader, but plays up the most ancient of prej-udices—race hatred." The HLU's arch-enemy, the Negro Labor Committee, called the HLU "a terroristic campaign in Harlem against Jews, against whites and against the legitimate trade union movement. The leaders of this Incorporated union have literally terrorized many merchants into not only giving employment to members of this alleged union at the expense of both Negro and white union men, but they have also been known to extract money from certain Harlem merchants as insurance against a picket line." Given the NLC's position as competitor, one might suspect it of hyperbole, except that independent investigations by the city and testimony by several merchants corroborated these complaints. The owner of the Owl Shoe Company on 125th Street told Frank Crosswaith that the HLU tried to organize his two black workers in June of 1939. They refused. The HLU picketed and "indulged in dangerous anti-white propaganda." The owner, frightened, signed a contract with the HLU that made no change in work conditions, and agreed to pay $2 a month to the union to prevent another picket. Whether or not the pickets were as "dangerous" as he claimed, certainly they did not win benefits for the staff.

Occasionally these practices flew in the face of the explicitly nationalist commitment of the HLU, calling the sincerity of that position into question. Had the HLU's intent honestly been to promote black employment, it would not have picketed establishments where blacks were already employed, demanding they be fired and that HLU members be hired in their place. In 1933, the owner of Orkin's Dress Shop, fearing that the Blumstein's pickets might soon extend to his store, hired blacks until they made up half his work force. The Harlem Labor Union established a picket line there two years later that demanded a 50 percent black staff. Realizing its error, the HLU quickly changed its signs to 75 percent and demanded that present employees be fired in favor of picketers. The HLU justified its action by arguing that since the clerks had not picketed to win their jobs in the first place, the hardworking HLU members deserved first fruits of the picket committee's success.[27]

Apparently, Reid's organization sometimes seemed more committed to furthering the fortunes of its members and leaders than to furthering the cause of black nationalism. In fact, Reid did not deny that inproprieties occurred. In a defense of Sufi Hamid's racketeering practices and presumably by implication, his own, he explained to an interviewer that while Hamid and his colleagues did use organization money to support themselves,

> [a]n agitator must eat to live, and no matter how noble the cause, petty graft will occur and no one could have grown rich on the amount of money involved. As for the rough tactics which his group employed, such methods were not out of keeping with the necessities of organizing reluctant workers. . . . The fact that Sufi put pressure on employers to fire Negroes and hire members of his own group was a natural corollary to his desire to strengthen the union. . . . Furthermore, many of the Negroes who found employment on 125 Street during the months following the Blumstein affair, were light skinned Negroes who had been employed for the sole purpose of forestalling future boycotts. . . . It was this tactic on the part of the employers which forced Sufi to agitate for the dismissal of the newly hired Negroes.[28]

Accusations of corruption aside, it was clear the Alliance and the HLU had very different organizing styles from that of the League, as Reid's statement hints. Even when anti-white rhetoric was not explicit, the methods used by these groups to integrate white-owned stores also set them apart from the moderate non-nationalists in Harlem. In general, the Harlem Labor Union used more confrontational tactics. It successfully tapped the anger and frustration of black working people who had been consistently denied fair treatment by unions and employers. In an interview, an organizer working for the HLU in 1938 described the strategy used to integrate Harlem's butcher shops. He entered shops when many black women were inside purchasing meat and inquired loudly why no black butchers worked there. The women would murmur assent—their husbands and sons were unemployed. The butcher would reply that the AFL butchers' union already had a contract there. "'I'd say to hell with the AFL, they are downtown and we are in Harlem and they can't help you if we throw a picket line around the place.'. . .We finally put in Negro butchers all over Harlem. . . . You see we could always depend on the Harlem people [to support us] because they were mad, hungry and hemmed-in."[29]

Not surprisingly, Crosswaith's Negro Labor Committee often came into conflict with the HLU. Each group defended its own unionizing efforts, and condemned the other's. "Because of the so-called closed shop contracts with the CIO local 1125," Reid claimed, "several stores on 125th Street cannot put Negro girls to work [because the union denied blacks membership]." He criticized Crosswaith for not fighting such discrimination. Since, as Reid saw it, Harlem's black merchants could not afford to pay the prevailing union wage, the HLU signed contracts to employ blacks at lower pay. When the Moving Van Drivers' Locals 805 and 807 tried to standardize city pay rates by raising prices and wages in Harlem, the HLU organized twenty-eight black van operators into the Harlem Movers' Association, and signed a contract at lower rates. The HLU justified such contracts on grounds that it saved Harlemites money and provided more jobs for black drivers. Crosswaith fired back that it was not enough merely to win employment for blacks: "We worked for 245 years during slavery, but we got nothing for our work." By contrast, he argued, "The NLC has been responsible, not only for much of the increase in employment among Negro workers in this area, but especially in raising the wages and working standards of those workers." With less overt rancor, Crosswaith described his differences with the HLU's approach in his testimony before the Mayor's Commission: "Perhaps the only difference is that others have been putting emphasis on getting jobs for Negroes. That is not the essential solution. I am concerned with what the Negroes will get for work they do."[30]

Part of the antipathy can be accounted for by the opposing goals of the two groups. Since the Harlem Labor Union was committed to black nationalism, it opposed the unionizing drive of the *Amsterdam News* workers; Kemp and Reid believed it inappropriate for blacks to strike against employers of the same color. Here self-interest coincided with nationalism rather than undermining it. The NLC, the HLU's competition, had launched the strike.

The Negro Labor Committee, on the other hand, supported the *Amsterdam News* strike as part of the struggle to improve working conditions. The NLC sought the integration of blacks into the larger work force, both because its socialist leanings led it to seek unity of the working class, and because Harlem could not employ all the blacks who lived there, even were it an all-black economy. Crosswaith believed blacks' economic future lay in a strong, unionized work force that extended beyond the confines of Harlem. Until these sectarian fights could be resolved, the jobs campaign would remain stalled.

The antagonism between the two, of course, came also from competition, as they sought to organize the same workers for their own group. In this, the NLC seemed marginally more successful in winning better contracts for its members. To cite one example: since they were already members of the HLU, the seven black workers at Bishop's Dress Shop could not join with the eight white workers there in a CIO union drive. The white CIO-won salaries rose and their hours declined, but Reid could not win the same concessions for his members. After a prolonged struggle, the black employees succeeded in switching their affiliation and received the higher salaries.[31]

While this bitter infighting plagued the campaign, the NUL and the NAACP continued with their own behind-the-scenes efforts to win better opportunities for black workers. Though the NAACP's most important efforts remained focused on litigation, the organization had become more activist as the Great Depression wore on, pushing government agencies and trade unions to accept qualified blacks, as well as fighting lynching and segregation. Like the NUL it also demanded that employers and unions not only hire qualified blacks, but train them. Both groups' style of letter-writing and quiet pressure did not require or utilize mass movements, but their successes were nonetheless significant.[32]

Black leaders and groups involved in direct action did not find these low-key methods satisfactory. Yet confrontational and often corrupt activities seemed to mainstream black leaders to have dominated the public protests. The Citizens' League, the Negro Alliance, and the HLU had aroused the energies and expectations of many in the Harlem community, but only the nationalists had succeeded in sustaining their momentum. Black leaders supporting non-nationalist solutions watched their control over Harlem's political energies weaken. The HLU's successes challenged them to reclaim the initiative, and the model of several integrationist organizations like the Negro Labor Committee showed them how. Especially as more unions accepted black workers, these black leaders came to agree with the NLC's views. As Adam Clayton Powell, Jr., wrote in 1937, "The HLU can never achieve any success for the Negro worker," as it did not demand union wage levels and actually campaigned against legitimate unions. "For anyone to strive to build a nationalist movement in America among Negroes is to commit racial suicide," he insisted. The NLC's success getting unions throughout the city to accept black members challenged black leaders to think of the jobs campaign more broadly.

The Communist party also inspired centrist black leaders to broaden their goals. During the Popular Front period, the party's new policies resembled those of the Negro Labor Committee and the Citizens' League, but embraced the wider city. Although the party had initially opposed the "Don't Buy Where You Can't Work" campaign, seeing it as disruptive to working-class unity and a tool for capitalists, the Popular Front strategy forced the party to re-evaluate. In order to keep credibility in the community and with liberal black organizations, it had to participate in some fashion.[33]

The Communist party developed a strategy appropriate for its seemingly contradictory position of support for Harlem cooperative action and encouragement of black and white working-class unity. It demanded the hiring of blacks in Harlem establishments without firing whites. It encouraged job actions at large chain stores and public utilities rather than at small family stores where racial antagonism might intensify and undermine class unity. Under the banner of the Committee Against Discrimination of Negro Workers on Jobs, the party led a boycott and picket of the Empire Cafeteria on 125th Street and Lenox Avenue.

Toilers of Harlem! Negro and White
DEMONSTRATE AGAINST DISCRIMINATION!

For jobs for Negroes in Empire Cafeteria and for Unemployment Relief. Wed., September 5, 7 P.M. at 126 Street and Lenox . . .
Negro and White, demonstrate and picket for the following demands:
1. No dismissal of white workers
2. Hiring of additional Negro workers with equal pay
3. No reduction in pay

Again sectarian lines blurred: Sufi Hamid's Alliance and the UNIA participated in this picket because it sought black jobs. The cafeteria hired four black workers without letting any white workers go.

The Joint Conference Against Discriminatory Practices, a Communist-led organization that concentrated primarily on relief policies, also set up (illegal) pickets. At one Saturday demonstration in front of Weisbecker's Market at 125th Street and Eighth Avenue, the Joint Conference was joined by the Elks, the African Patriotic Union, and the Communist party. They demanded (but did not win) a 25 percent reduction in prices as well as the hiring of black clerks. These efforts, confrontational as they were (the Empire picket turned into a mêlée when a protester hurled a rock through the window) did bring both political awareness and jobs to Harlem. As Charles Franklin reluctantly granted: "However illegitimate or racketeering Hamid's organization may have been, it was at least striking at those very frightful conditions in its attempts to get employment for Negroes and to improve working conditions for those already employed." The same could be said for each illegal protest.[34]

Rebuilding: The Second Campaign

The successes of the Communist party and of the Negro Labor Committee made their broad approach realistic and attractive to Harlem's mainstream black leaders disgusted with Hamid's and Kemp's tactics. Ironically, the extremism of Hamid, Kemp, and Reid also strengthened the integrationist organizations. Alerted to the campaign by vocal radicals, many Harlemites joined the struggle for white-collar jobs. The general opposition to confrontational or extreme tactics led many of these newcomers to embrace the more moderate positions in the jobs coalition. Thus, support for the center swelled, as evidenced by rising numbers of participants in the protests and demonstrations led by moderate groups.

All these challenges persuaded black leaders like Powell that they needed to regain the ascendancy in the jobs campaign. The time also seemed appropriate. The Harlem riot of 1935 had raised the specter of further violence if economic changes were not made. As the Mayor's Commission on Conditions in Harlem warned, "The blame [for the riot] belongs to a society that tolerates . . . unemployment, discrimination in industry and the public utilities. . . . As long as these conditions remain, the public order can not and will not be safe." The riot had also heightened municipal officials' awareness of the plight of blacks in the Depression. Meanwhile, the New Deal broadened and legitimized the involvement of government in economic affairs. The blue ribbon commission appointed by Mayor LaGuardia to study Harlem's conditions and recommend policy changes, the speed-up of construction of several schools and low-cost apartment blocks in Harlem, the new responsiveness of city agencies to complaints of discrimination, and the appointment of a statewide panel to investigate conditions of the "urban colored population," all attest to this change in atmosphere. Despite continuing racism, the conscience—or self-interest—of New York's political leaders had been aroused. The opportunity for winning over white store-owners in such a climate appeared far more favorable than in 1933. Even the Urban League apparently reconsidered. James Hubert backed off from earlier positions critical of the boycott efforts, although he still distanced himself from the more confrontational tactics of the HLU.

Q. Do you favor that organizations of Negroes should boycott, especially the 125th Street stores?

A. I favor any method on the part of any group or individual so long as it is lawful. . . .

Q. A newspaper attributes to you the statement that you do not favor such methods. . . .

A. I do not recall making such a statement. . . . I question how far one could go in the use of force . . . you have seen the results obtained. Most of the good has already been lost.

The successes of both nationalist and integrationist efforts, the emergence of a CIO supportive of black issues, and the improvement of the political climate in terms of race relations heightened Harlemites' sense of their community's potential power. They were ready to mobilize. Yet the legal ban on picketing remained a barrier to further effective action by law-abiding groups until 1938. In that year the United States Supreme Court ruled in *New Negro Alliance* vs. *Sanitary Grocery Company* that because blacks suffered employment discrimination solely because of their race, they could in turn make special employment demands based on race and could therefore picket.

The law had always played an important, though not definitive, role in charting the course of the "Don't Buy" coalition. The Citizens' League had won victories with its pickets, victories that evaporated when the courts denied the right to picket on the basis of race. Yet the court decision alone did not destroy the Citizens' League. The end of the picket line did not have to mean an end to the coalition's progress; other solutions could have been tried. The disputes among the constituent groups over League tactics were more to blame for its collapse.

Nor did the right to picket in itself necessarily ensure further gains. The Negro Alliance, the HLU, and the Communist party continued picket activities illegally after 1934. When stopped by police, they tried impromptu sit-ins, persisting despite frequent arrests.[35] Yet these groups only won small isolated victories until joined by a larger coalition.

The importance of the New Negro Alliance case was that it allowed moderate integrationist groups to reassert control over the jobs campaign. In 1935 the Citizens' League had abandoned the effort rather than resort to illegal picketing or new tactics. By doing so, it lost control of the campaign. Its constituent groups soon realized their error. By then, Hamid, Kemp, and Reid had established energetic, visible picket lines that could not be countered by subtle or private maneuvering. The Supreme Court decision restored to the mainstream groups an effective way to unite with like-minded organizations and re-enter (and dominate) the struggle. The Communist party also cooperated in this, hoping both to solidify the legitimacy of its Popular Front strategy and to keep its political vision in the forefront of the jobs campaign.

Adam Clayton Powell, Jr., of the Abyssinian Baptist Church held a mass meeting on March 12, 1938, to form the Greater New York Coordinating Committee for Employment, co-chaired by Powell and William Imes of Saint James Presbyterian Church. Soon after its formation, the committee claimed to enjoy the support of over 200 organizations and 170,000 members—over three times the number in the original Citizens' League. It had the cooperation of the New York Urban League, the NAACP, the Joint Conference Against Discriminatory Practices, the Harlem YMCA, A. Philip Randolph, and the Communist party. As Powell described it, "It was honest because it was poor."[36]

It is likely that the Communist party helped organize and participate in the Coordinating Committee to regain the initiative on fighting job discrimination from the moderate NAACP and NUL on the one side and the nationalists on the other. Communist-organized transport unions continued to discriminate against blacks, another motive for the party to move in this direction. Thus the committee was not simply a non-ideological compromise coalition, which explains why bitter sectarian and turf battles continued even after the committee's founding. Reid, for example, a fervid anti-Communist, refused to associate his group with the committee, which in turn missed no opportunity to criticize the HLU.

Staunch unionist Frank Crosswaith also opposed the Coordinating Committee. Despite the committee's efforts not to conflict with unions, he believed "the legitimate labor movement in this area appears to be the main target. . . . Perhaps the C.P. will get some notoriety out of another race riot in Harlem, but the Negro groups will suffer [;] so will the growing trade union movement up here." The visibility of the Communist party in the committee dismayed anti-Communist Crosswaith, which helps explain his dissatisfaction. Moreover, he took the committee's activities as a personal affront. The whole effort implicitly criticized other groups working for black employment, including the NLC and organized labor. Its successes infuriated him.[37]

Much of the strength of the committee came from black educated and skilled workers, formerly of the middle class, who had lost their jobs in the Depression. Now in menial jobs or unemployed, they helped provide the energy and commitment necessary for political mobilization. Still, this was undeniably a movement of the working class, peopled by domestics, laborers, and service workers. Not only did participants and eyewitnesses make this claim, sheer numbers require it to be true. The black middle class was too small to have generated this size protest alone.

The presence of Adam Clayton Powell, Jr., as leader of the coalition also helped explain the committee's energy and huge numbers. Son of a dynamic and influential minister, minister in his own right of one of the largest and most prestigious churches in Harlem, leader of numerous community efforts on behalf of the poor and the unemployed, and a dynamic and charismatic speaker, Powell symbolized for thousands the noble struggle for equality in Harlem. His presence, like that of Martin Luther King, Jr., in the later civil rights movement, helped unify and direct the campaign.

The Coordinating Committee embraced many of the goals of the Citizens' League, the Negro Labor Committee, and the Communist party; it sought to employ blacks in white-owned stores without displacing whites or undermining legitimate unions, and it worked to integrate public utilities outside Harlem. It tried all of the usual tactics: negotiations, conferences, cooperative agreements. This time, success came much more easily. With such a large constituency, and with the legal right to picket restored, its requests carried clout. The extremism of Hamid and Reid made white store-owners eager to negotiate with the committee, whose demands seemed more reasonable in comparison. In fact, the successes of 1938 might not have been possible earlier, without the conflicts and the extremism that ultimately promoted united action among blacks and put pressure on merchants to negotiate with moderates. Almost immediately the Coordinating Committee won its first victories. The A&P hired a black manager; a local jewelry company hired six black typists.

The committee also employed creative tactics, especially to tackle large public utilities that could not be reached with boycotts and pickets. To persuade the energy companies to hire blacks in non-menial positions, the Coordinating Committee turned Harlem dark once a week by asking families to use candles instead of electricity on Tuesday nights, and it led hundreds in "billpayers' parades" to the gas company offices each month to pay their bills in pennies. Other tactics included asking all Harlemites to request a (legal) out-of-turn gas meter inspection simultaneously and to refuse to pay gas bills until the inspection was completed. Prior to the campaign, at Consolidated Gas, of 10,000 employees, 213 were black, working as porters. New York Edison, also with 10,000, employed just sixty-five blacks, and only as messengers, porters, and janitors. After the campaign, the newly merged Consolidated Edison hired four blacks in non-menial positions, promoted four more, and promised that "an appreciable percentage of all new Consolidated Edison employees would be Negroes." Adam Clayton Powell, Jr., hailed these successes as "the first victory in our campaign for white-collar jobs for Negroes in industry."

The Coordinating Committee then turned to the New York Telephone Company, which had refused to hire black repairmen or operators. Here it employed several strategies at once. Direct negotiations with the company made clear the community's position, while threats of retaliatory action made the company receptive to compromise. For example, the committee threatened that Harlemites would make operator-assisted telephone calls rather than dial directly, which would increase each operator's workload by close to 70 percent, and would jam the phone lines at the moment Wall Street reported its daily figures. The cumulative effects of these pressures compelled the telephone company to re-examine its position. Quickly, it hired black clerical staff. Even these tactics were not enough, however, to force the company to hire black operators. Ultimately it took further pressure from several black groups and government agencies and the exigencies of the war to get black operators on staff.[38]

When necessary, the committee carried out the threat to picket. At the end of April 1938, each firm in Harlem not yet employing blacks received this letter from the committee, signed by Adam Clayton Powell, Jr., and the other officers:

> Dear Sir:
>
> The Coordinating Committee for Employment representing over 200 organizations in Harlem decided unanimously . . . to begin picketing each store in Harlem which does not employ Negroes. . . .
>
> If we do not receive an answer to this letter by Friday at 2:00 your store will be picketed beginning this Saturday and every Saturday thereafter.[39]

After four months of negotiation with the Uptown Chamber of Commerce, the two groups reached an agreement, which stated:

> To effect a fair and equitable settlement of the Negro employment problem as it affects Harlem retail establishments, the Uptown Chamber of Commerce . . . and the Greater New York Coordinating Committee for Employment . . . agree . . .
>
> That stores not already employing between 33 and ⅓ percent and 40 percent colored workers in so-called white collar positions agree to do so as speedily as possible by making replacements with qualified Negroes as white employees resign or are discharged for cause. . . .
>
> [In family-owned stores] the owners agree to engage a qualified Negro for the first new job created in their establishment.
>
> That the stores agree not to limit the opportunities of Negro workers for advancement, . . . nor shall colored workers be discriminated against in the matter of wages.
>
> That when stores operate under a closed shop agreement with a recognized union the owners or managers agree to use their influence with union officials to the end that Negroes may be admitted to membership. In short, there will be no pretense at denying Negroes employment in union stores on the subterfuge that to hire them would be in violation of existing union contracts. . . .
>
> [Chain stores] will not adopt a policy of discrimination against Negroes employed in their stores located out of Harlem.

The "Memorandum of Agreement," as it was called, further required employers not to discriminate in the event of forced layoffs, and to submit all disputes to a joint arbitration committee made up of the two organizations.

For its part, the Coordinating Committee agreed that:

> at no time will it demand the replacement of a white worker with a Negro except [when that worker was hired in direct violation of the agreement]. . . .

That resort to picketing, boycotts and other mass demonstrations against stores shall not be made [unless the store violates an Arbitration Committee decision].

The Coordinating Committee agrees to encourage campaigns among the masses to increase the colored trade of all cooperating stores. . . .

The Coordinating Committee agrees to use every possible means to prevent independent action against stores subscribing to this agreement by colored groups not associated with the Coordinating Committee.[40]

Within two months of the memorandum, 300 blacks had white-collar jobs in Harlem. Every large store on 125th Street had at least one black employee. The Chamber of Commerce reported higher sales by 1940, although this was probably due to the increased prosperity brought about by war preparations.

As for the "colored groups not associated with the Coordinating Committee," that is, the Harlem Labor Union, trouble with that organization finally eased after an agreement that Reid would join the Coordinating Committee and cease picketing stores already unionized by the AFL or CIO. He violated that agreement numerous times until District Attorney Thomas E. Dewey prosecuted him as a racketeer in 1939. Although the charges were ultimately dropped, he left the Union, and it lost its militant and nationalist character soon thereafter. (Kemp had left the group to run for New York Assembly in 1938 on a more mainstream platform. He lost by only a few votes, and died a few days later.)[41]

Powell and the Coordinating Committee turned next to the World's Fair, which was to be held in New York City in 1939. He asked the World's Fair Corporation to ensure the availability of non-menial jobs for blacks. When polite requests failed, blacks moved their pickets downtown for the first time, to the Fair's headquarters in the Empire State Building. Bill Robinson and chorus girls from Ethel Waters' shows joined the hundreds of lower-class and middle-class demonstrators. After two months of such efforts, Fair organizers yielded, promising positions for several hundred black clerks and other workers.[42]

The Lessons of the Campaigns

The jobs campaign had meant different things to different segments of the Harlem community. To middle-class black leaders it represented an opportunity for white-collar blacks to acquire appropriate jobs. To black merchants it meant an increase in black business; to black nationalists it was a step toward a black state; to others it offered an opportunity to build a power base among the unemployed. To Socialists, Communists, and black trade unionists it diverted attention from the struggle of black workers to integrate existing unions unless the two efforts went hand in hand. This disunity of purpose and internal competition hampered the campaign and divided public opinion. Not until the members of the coalition agreed on both tactics (legal pickets, support for unions, and negotiations) and goals (the hiring of blacks without the firing of whites) did the campaign achieve success.

The 1935 riot in Harlem alerted the white community to the economic discrimination practiced against blacks and the need for some response, however small, to avert further violence. This new willingness to cooperate helped contribute to the jobs campaign's success, but any success would have been impossible without the activist participation of Harlem blacks. The campaign allowed them to take whatever control they could of their economic future through political action and the forging of alliances in the community. In the "Don't Buy" campaign, every individual in Harlem made real choices about whether and how to become involved in the efforts to bring better employment opportunities—an empowering experience. The struggle to gain white-collar employment could not have solved Harlem's economic problems even if all the movement's programs had been implemented. Its real contribution was the political mobilization of Harlem. The campaign allowed the black community to test its strengths, refine its arguments, and try out its struggle for equal opportunity in a narrow setting that offered African-Americans some hope of having an impact.

The success of the Coordinating Committee and the jobs campaign brought new goals. Having black clerks in Harlem stores did not solve the unemployment problem, as there were not enough jobs in that community for everyone. Nor were enough Harlem men and women sufficiently educated or skilled to take advantage of such employment opportunities had they been offered. The problems were more deeply rooted. By 1944, the majority of salespeople in Harlem were black, yet Harlem's economic troubles persisted. The huge number of unemployed black workers willing to accept lower wages in order to obtain a job challenged unions to join with blacks rather than to exclude them. In this case blacks may have been unemployed because of their race, but unemployment was the issue that had to be addressed.

Furthermore, the campaign, by picketing exclusively in Harlem, did not persuade stores not located there to end their discriminatory policies. That would require new, broader, and bolder strategies—cooperation between black groups and organized labor, a recognition of working-class needs, and the expansion of the campaign beyond Harlem's boundaries.

In recognition of this, the Coordinating Committee, the Communist party, the Urban League, the NAACP, and the Negro Labor Committee had begun to move out of the black community to integrate the public utilities, working with the trade union movement and focusing on training and apprenticeship programs as well as on white-collar and skilled jobs. Cooperating this way had brought success with New York Telephone, Consolidated Edison, and the World's Fair; these groups went on in the next decade to use the techniques of the "Don't Buy" campaign to integrate more of the transit system's labor force, several large insurance companies, and department stores.[43]

While black nationalism retained some community support, its strength had diminished with the victories of the churches and the unions, and it would not rise again with such popular force until the late 1950s. On the other hand, the Communist party, having strengthened its base in the black community with its staunch support for black economic opportunity, then lost it with the Nazi–Soviet pact, the end of the Popular Front, and the increased virulence of Red-baiting in the 1940s. This left the moderates in the dominant position, something demonstrated by their most popular spokesperson, the younger Powell, as he swept into city office in 1941 and Congress shortly thereafter.

The Depression saw an expansion of black political action in Harlem that had begun earlier, instigated by changes both internal and external to the black community. African-Americans had undertaken numerous efforts in earlier years to gain improvements for their race. But the economic desperation of the Depression and the new willingness of government, unions, and employers to respond to organized grievances and to threats of violence or riot marked this period as a particularly active one for political organizing. This expansion brought thousands into the political process who had not participated before, and activism essentially burst the confines of traditional politics. While existing party organizations and black groups participated actively in these political efforts, many people also sought different political vehicles. Thus, the new energy had many outlets: the reinvigorated traditional parties, mass rallies, union drives, black nationalist and integrationist organizations, churches, and newly formed political groups. The boundaries between these new and ongoing structures were remarkably fluid. Not only did much of the leadership of these organizations overlap, but individual Harlemites joined with different groups, depending on the issue at hand. Class and race intersected with and reinforced each other, as did black nationalism and a commitment to improve Harlem's economic opportunity structure.

Yet conflicts among and within groups at times weakened these efforts, as when self-interest overwhelmed a commitment to nationalism, or sectarian battles vitiated programs and actions to bring about jointly supported goals. Internal struggles over class and nationalist visions and between moderate and radical perspectives provided a spectrum of opportunity for involvement, but also worked against farther-reaching structural change. Even if these internal conflicts had disappeared, the external limits on black economic advancement: racism, lack of training, the Depression, and entrenched economic and political practices preferential to white or middle-class groups, were still too great to be overcome at that time.

Despite its limitations, however, black mass action in the Depression also revealed the tremendous potential of such efforts. Harlemites struggled in this decade to alter the power relations of society, and while they did not succeed in that, they solidified a political base and experimented with tactics that would prove critical in the years to come.

While certainly not all the problems of coalition-building in a diverse population had been resolved, these political programs set the stage for more dramatic and sweeping efforts, such as the 1941 March on Washington Movement led by A. Philip Randolph, and ultimately the modern civil rights movement. All over the country, black efforts had produced improved job opportunities for the black middle class, and helped galvanize mass action on other fronts, such as housing and the distribution of relief. They also furthered the involvement of blacks in organized party politics, making possible the ascendancy of such elected leaders as Adam Powell in New York and William Dawson in Chicago.[44]

There were significant differences between this campaign and the modern civil rights movement, however. The efforts of the 1930s sought primarily to improve black employment opportunities. Black organizations used racial equality and nondiscriminatory legislation as the tools for pursuing better opportunities, but the jobs themselves were the goal. For the modern civil rights movement, equality was the central focus.

The tactics of the two eras also differed. In the 1930s the moderates obeyed the law and ceased all activities when they saw that continued action would violate a legal court injunction. In the 1950s and 1960s, however, intentional civil disobedience was the centerpiece of moderate efforts. The reason for these opposing approaches reflects the two movements' different goals. While a jobs campaign fought for opportunities within an existing structure, civil rights was by definition a struggle against unjust laws. The civil rights movement's moral force came from actively challenging the legal basis of racist social structures. Finally, unlike the civil rights movement, the jobs campaign did not persuade many whites to actively pursue black equality.[45]

Yet the victories of the civil rights movement could not have been won without the groundwork laid by these earlier efforts. The New Deal decade made the value of political organizing particularly visible. The Depression alerted the white public to the plight of those who suffered, bringing black problems into the open and ensuring that they received a sympathetic hearing. The political struggles for equal opportunity that emerged in such an environment laid an indispensable foundation for future efforts. When the time was right, new coalitions would draw on tactics first employed in unionizing and "Don't Buy" campaigns in Harlem and elsewhere, thereby fighting more effectively for equality in the decades following the Great Depression.

CHAPTER 6

Harlem on Relief

New Deal programs made the difference between starvation and survival for the thousands of New Yorkers who had no jobs or who could not afford to live on the meager wages they earned. The previous programs of the Emergency Work and Relief Bureau, the New York City Department of Public Welfare, and private philanthropy did not have the funds to maintain the high levels of aid required. By 1935, the state and federal government bore three-fourths of all of New York's relief costs.[1] The New Deal consisted of a series of programs instituted by the Roosevelt administration that relieved the suffering of millions across the country through financial grants, public works projects, loans, and similar means. These programs, administered on a local level, however, often provided grants inadequate to live on, and the needy often found themselves hampered by bureaucracy and the arbitrary application of byzantine rules.

Both the positive and negative aspects of relief had a greater impact on Harlem than on the rest of the city, since a larger proportion of its population relied on government aid. Furthermore, blacks endured unique forms of discrimination: rent and food in Harlem generally cost more than elsewhere, although relief grants did not reflect this; and many agencies practiced overt racial discrimination in the granting of work relief, the placement of workers, and the provision of services.

Despite these limitations, the vast amounts of federal money from New Deal programs freed private social service agencies from the responsibility of economically supporting the unemployed and allowed them to proffer other non-financial services. Private groups had given monetary help to 85,000 New Yorkers in 1931. This figure declined to 17,000 in 1934, and steadied at between 6,000 and 10,000 for the rest of the decade.[2] While private philanthropies like the Association for Improving the Condition of the Poor continued their financial assistance programs, other organizations such as the Children's Aid Society and the New York Urban League returned to providing the services they had been established to offer. Local groups in Harlem also supplemented other relief efforts. While small budgets limited their impact, these groups offered services that city-wide public and private agencies did not provide sufficiently, and they fought for equality of treatment and aid in those agencies.

The Relief Population

Unemployment rates remained stunningly high throughout the Depression. Having no other financial resources, most of the unemployed turned to relief. In 1937, employable adults made up 70 percent of the home relief rolls in New York. Those lowest on the occupational ladder, a population that included much of the African-American community, needed relief most often. The impact of the Depression on different occupational classes is revealed in the proportion of each on relief (though the number on relief is less than the number unemployed). (See Table 6.1.)

The fact that blacks worked primarily in fields with exceptionally high unemployment was not the sole reason blacks required relief more often. They were also more likely than whites to be on relief in every occupation and at every age. Education also seemed to make little difference. Levels of schooling of black relief recipients virtually mirrored those of the black population statewide, and the proportion of high-school–educated blacks on relief and those with only one to four years of education was the same. As the Mayor's Commission on Conditions in Harlem put it, the city paid the price for job discrimination in the high numbers of blacks on the relief rolls.[4]

Both discrimination and the concentration of blacks at the lowest occupational levels meant that blacks usually lived closer to subsistence even when employed. Therefore, they went on relief rolls several months sooner than whites after losing their jobs. Nor did they find it easy to return to work. Even as the decade ended, and employment in war-related industries brought white relief rolls down, blacks saw little change in their job opportunities. The proportion of those on New York's relief rolls who were black rose in 1940. "It is estimated that for every two Negro clients dropped from relief rolls, three are added," the NYUL reported gloomily. In that year, one black moved to private industry from the Work Projects Administration for every four whites. The black proportion on relief increased, therefore, both because whites found work more quickly, and because the number of black cases themselves rose, according to the Urban League. Twice as many blacks as whites were on relief because of such factors as unemployment (as opposed to illness, for example), so their greater presence cannot be accounted for because of greater ill health, age, or number of widows.[5]

Some family types, of course, found economic problems particularly difficult to

TABLE 6.1
Relief Recipients: Percent Usually Employed at Specified
Occupation and Class, Manhattan, May 1934[3]

Field	Percent	Occupation Level	Percent
Manufacturing & mechanical	42.2	Professional	4.3
Transportation & communications	10.9	Proprietary, managerial, official	3.1
Trade	14.3	Clerical	8.1
Public service	0.6	Sales	4.3
Professional service	5.1	Semi-professional	0.6
Domestic & personal	25.3	Skilled	14.6
Illegal & unknown	0.4	Semi-skilled	30.2
All others	1.2	Unskilled	13.2
		Servants & allied	21.6

overcome. Single-parent families often lived closer to subsistence than two-parent households; not surprisingly, a higher proportion of relief families had a widowed, separated, or divorced head than did the general population. While this was true for both races, the number of single-headed black families on relief was strikingly high, reflecting both their greater poverty and the higher frequency of such family arrangements in the black community. In 1939, for example, in a poor area in Harlem (Health Area 20) almost 34 percent of all white family heads on relief were widowed, deserted, or divorced. For blacks, the comparable figure was 46 percent.[6]

Larger families also needed relief more often than smaller; with a low income a large number of mouths to feed could easily push a family into destitution. Of non-relief black families, the Bureau of Labor Statistics study found almost half had just two members, less than a fifth had over four. Black relief families were generally larger. This tendency was most pronounced, of course, at the lowest income levels. For families earning $500 a year, those not on relief had just under three people on average, compared with four to five people in relief families. The larger the family, black or white, the more likely it would need external help. White relief families also had more children on average than non-relief white families. Black relief families, however, were generally smaller than white; blacks earned so little or were so often unemployed that they qualified for relief even with fewer family members to support.

Family size did not reflect only the number of children. Many families, white and black, included additional adults, usually relatives. Yet white families with extra adults were slightly less likely to go on relief, blacks slightly more so; apparently blacks more often took in indigent relatives or friends.[7]

The System

Once families went on relief, they did not receive ample help. The new system of public aid had grave limitations for everyone receiving it. Relief grants were low and services generally poor. For example, in regard to city lodging houses for the homeless, the Mayor's Commission on Conditions in Harlem noted in 1935:

> The present facilities are inadequate, unhealthy, . . . and consequently difficult and extravagant to service and administer. Lodgings are in scattered public and private lodging houses, including inferior hotels and private agencies. There is complaint about the quality and quantity of the food served and the meal ticket is abused by those on relief and by the accredited commercial restaurants.[8]

Public relief, though, was not a monolith. It consisted of several different programs, each of which changed its policies and practices over time. Eligibility requirements, numbers accepted for aid, the distribution of cases among the several relief agencies, and the funds received by the needy all varied over the Depression decade. These policy changes often had more to do with changes in who could receive relief than with unemployment rates. Relief rolls depended on many factors, of which unemployment was only one.

The city and state had long provided some financial support programs through the Board of Child Welfare and the Department of Public Welfare. The number receiving relief from the two sources rose dramatically as the effects of the Depression intensified and the New Deal made additional funds available, and it continued to rise slowly throughout the decade. Primarily, the growth in these programs ("categorical relief") after the New Deal began resulted from the periodic easing of eligibility requirements, as the federal government assumed a larger share of the costs. In 1934, for example, single people became eligible for city relief. By 1937, the Board of Child Welfare (BCW) had, among other changes, made fathers with children and unmarried mothers eligible for aid for the first time. Between 1932 and 1937, the number receiving BCW aid doubled, to over 19,000 families, or almost 37,000 children. The Department of Public Welfare's rolls increased similarly.[9]

Originally private, the Emergency Work and Relief Bureau became public with its rescue from the brink of bankruptcy by the 1931 State Temporary Emergency Relief Act. In 1932 it joined with the Home Relief Bureau of the Department of Public Welfare. It provided public funds for direct relief payments and surplus commodities, and some public works jobs. When federal money became available through New Deal agencies such as the Federal Emergency Relief Administration (FERA), Mayor LaGuardia created a separate structure, the Emergency Relief Bureau (ERB). Subsuming the Home Relief Bureau (HRB), it provided financial aid to unemployed adults and their families. Its rolls grew quickly and remained high; in 1935 it alone supported 8 percent of all city families.[10]

Those who could work could also turn to another public alternative: work relief. First administered by the ERB, it was subsequently provided by the Civil Works Administration (1933–34), the Temporary (later Federal) Emergency Relief Administration (1931, 1933), and later, the Works Progress Administration (1935). The Civilian Conservation Corps (1933) and the National Youth Administration (1935) provided income support and jobs for students and unemployed young people.[11]

While the unemployed generally preferred work relief to home relief, and political leaders remained committed to the ideal of work relief for all potentially employable adults, in practice the high cost of such programs meant the majority of relief recipients in New York received home relief allowances. While work relief rolls rose and fell during the period, the changes were more a product of budget concerns than of the economic climate or clients' preferences. Still, even at its lowest level, more than 100,000 men and women participated in work relief projects in New York City, building roads, bridges, playgrounds, and airports; writing stories, dramas, and guidebooks; doing research projects; performing dances and plays; keeping house for the families of sick mothers; and serving in various social work, charitable, and educational positions.

Overall, with a few exceptions, the number of New Yorkers on the city relief rolls rose steadily to a peak in 1936. By the end of that year, almost a fifth of all New Yorkers received some sort of direct aid. All told, over a million New Yorkers benefited from government relief, not including those who received health and other non-monetary government benefits.[12]

Blacks, the poorest group in the city, relied heavily on public relief. The proportion of blacks on relief rolls was more than double the proportion of whites. In 1933, within nine months of the opening of the Home Relief Bureau offices, 25,000 black Harlem families were granted aid. While 14 percent of the white population received relief from the city in 1935, fully 44 percent of blacks did. Some studies put the figure even higher. By 1936, blacks constituted 21 percent of the city's relief rolls, well above their proportion in the city's population. That figure was also higher than the nationwide rate of 18 percent, close to double the rate for whites. In every northern city with a substantial black population, African-Americans had greater representation on relief rolls than they did in the general population.[13]

Aggregate relief figures, however, mask the tremendous turnover in the agency caseloads and say nothing about the experiences of individual families. In the year beginning May 1934, over 225,000 families and individuals joined the rolls, but the rolls themselves rose by a net of only 67,000. Families moved on and off relief in sizable numbers. Those leaving, however, did not necessarily do so for jobs in the private sector. In 1936, for example, of the 256,000 home relief cases closed, only a fifth moved to private employment. Two-thirds went to WPA jobs, and the rest found relatives or friends willing to support them. The proportion of blacks moving to private employment was even lower than that of whites.[15] The employment market was not improving.

Almost two-thirds on relief (home or work) in 1937 had been on some form of relief continuously since first joining the rolls. While for the majority this meant two or three years, some had required aid since as early as 1930. Much of the relief fluctuation, then, came simply from shifts among agencies.[16]

All this led critics to question whether relief agencies in fact met the city's full needs. Although hundreds of thousands received relief, such aid did not reach all who required it. All told, well under half of New York City's unemployed received public aid at any given time. The City Affairs Committee estimated thousands more worked only part-time and needed income supplements. In 1934, the Russell Sage

TABLE 6.2
Number Receiving Public Relief on January 1,
New York City, 1930–1940[14]

Year	Total on Public Relief	Direct (Home) Relief	Categorical Relief	Work Relief
1930	15,715	2,100	13,615	—
1931	30,677	4,409	26,268	—
1932	120,627	50,079	40,546	30,002
1933	179,913	96,636	43,950	39,127
1934	358,985	127,720	43,265	188,000
1935	399,128	250,858	43,676	104,594
1936	476,599	196,620	46,101	233,878
1937	421,071	190,275	52,319	178,477
1938	407,792	206,402	68,640	130,750
1939*	394,164	186,283	76,739	138,856
1940*	341,829	167,401	79,959	105,047

*Monthly averages.

Foundation estimated that the one million unemployed lived in 660,000 family units consisting of approximately four members each. This meant over two and a half million people, or 37 percent of the city's population, presumably needed some sort of financial help. Assuming the 350,000 families getting relief also contained four members, less than one and a half million received it. As late as 1940 the New York State Employment Service estimated that for every relief recipient, two jobless individuals went without aid.[17]

Despite appearances of race-blind distribution of aid suggested by the large numbers of blacks on relief, in most areas around the country relief agencies accepted an even lower proportion of black needy than white. This practice belied the expressed policy of public relief agencies that race should play no part in the distribution of aid. Alfred Smith of the FERA announced to the Joint Committee on National Recovery in 1934:

> It is intended as expressed in the rules and regulations of the FERA that "relief be given to needy unemployed persons without discrimination because of race, religion, marital status, political affiliation, citizenship or non-citizenship, or membership in any special or selected group."[18]

"Stingy Starvation Relief": The Home Relief Bureau

In New York City, however, these promises were for the most part upheld, at least in the granting of home relief. Several organizations investigated this question. The Communist party estimated 80 percent of Harlem household heads were unemployed in 1935. The usually more restrained New York Urban League estimated the figure at 60 percent. If that was so, the number on relief, approximately 40 percent of Harlem, is lower than the presumed need but approximates the relative rate of white unemployed receiving relief. Though complaints of being denied relief because of race reached relief bureaus, the mayor's office, and various black agencies, several investigations, including one by the Mayor's Commission on Conditions in Harlem, concluded that little overt discrimination occurred in the granting of home relief.[19]

That did not, of course, preclude racism in personal dealings. Given the attitudes of most whites in this period, it is hardly surprising to discover episodes of racial insults and other racist behavior in Home Relief Bureau offices. As Fred Benedikt, a former HRB employee, testified:

> Miss Camille White was called "black ape" by Mrs. Bryan. But Mr. Courtney when it was brought to his attention said that there had been no fuss in his precinct. A little later when he saw that we were in conference with Miss White . . . he said to us, "Oh yes, that thing is very trivial. I do not remember it . . . yes that happened." In other words, when people are called "black apes," it is too slight for Mr. Courtney to remember. . . . Miss Brown . . . [who] used to call people "spicks," once asked a woman whom she did not know was part Negro blood whether she would like to work next to "those God-damn niggers.". . . Andrew Perner . . . consistently transferred Negroes out of his department whenever he could . . . I recall in 1934 . . . he was standing outside the door of his office

. . . [and] very leisurely drawled out, "There are too many shines working over there."
This is a man who is now office supervisor.

What is more surprising is that despite pervasive racism, the allocation of aid was
as non-discriminatory as it was. Certainly some caseworkers were racist, but the
high proportion of blacks on the rolls, announced rules against racial discrimination, standardized procedures, and the presence of black investigators suggest that
in most cases the Bureau judged applicants strictly on their economic need. The
Mayor's Commission noted that Harlem's Relief Bureau offices overspent their
budgets as often and to the same extent as others did. The amounts of relief granted
per person in Harlem were no lower than elsewhere. What is notable is how little
open racial discrimination there was in an era when that was the norm. The proportion of blacks receiving relief in the South, for example, was notoriously low.
Since southern blacks were no less needy, Smith's high-sounding pronouncements
can be called into question. In New York, such obvious discrimination rarely
occurred.

Still, the Mayor's Commission conceded, Harlemites' complaints of delays in
checks or investigations, or unfair denials of relief, similar in type but more frequent
in number than elsewhere, usually seemed legitimate. The Home Relief Bureau
admitted that complaints from the Harlem area far exceeded those from other city
neighborhoods. The commission concluded that although they were judged by the
same criteria, Harlemites did not receive the benefit of the doubt in investigations
as often as white applicants. Blacks who could not document their past earnings or
verify their two-year residency, for example, were more often rejected than were
whites with the same difficulties.[20] Discrimination in relief did exist but it was subtler and less pervasive than in most other places.

When discrimination did occur, black organizations and individuals were quick
to act. While the philosophies of the various organizations in Harlem led each to
approach the problem from a different angle, groups ranging from the UNIA and
the Urban League to the Communist party protested unfair treatment of blacks by
relief agencies. Demonstrations, letter-writing campaigns, testimony at state and
municipal hearings, news stories, and other organized efforts documented claims
of discrimination, often to good effect.

The Universal Negro Improvement Association's New York branch set up a program to aid Harlem residents who believed relief agencies had treated them
unfairly. The UNIA gathered all the relevant data and contacted the appropriate
agency on the client's behalf. Often this intervention resolved the problem, as the
agency explained what the application lacked and the UNIA helped correct it. By
and large, the UNIA reported, the difficulty lay in the client's inability or unwillingness to supply required information. The UNIA helped track down information
on pensions, missing persons, medical records, and so forth. Whenever the UNIA
brought a case, the relevant agency gave the client another hearing. The UNIA
claimed to have helped 10,000 Harlemites through its programs.[21]

In part, the UNIA's success depended on the responsiveness of agency leadership.
William Hodson, commissioner of the Department of Public Welfare, forthrightly
affirmed: "As you know I will not tolerate any discrimination in the administration

of relief in this city. If you have any specific cases where there was discrimination or intimidation, please bring them to my attention so that I might make investigation." He kept his word.[22]

Agency personnel behaved in this way largely because of Mayor LaGuardia's commitment to equal treatment of blacks and whites. Unlike earlier mayors, he responded to black appeals in concrete and far-reaching ways. He made his commitment to equal access and opportunity clear with agency regulations, the appointment of decent men, careful oversight of departments, the appointment of highly respected civic leaders and scholars to study the conditions leading to the Harlem riot of 1935, and his general willingness to speak out clearly in support of black interests.

If other groups relied on mayoral goodwill, the Communist party did not. More apt than these other organizations to rely on mass action, the party encouraged its Harlem Unemployed Councils to protest inadequate relief through pickets and demonstrations in front of Harlem relief offices, and sit-ins inside them. If police arrested the protesters, the party provided legal defense. Its frequent clashes with police, and its visible activism in the community, won the Communist party respect in Harlem, if not large numbers of members.[23]

Their disagreement with other groups was not just tactical, but philosophical. While the UNIA accepted the terms that agencies set, for example, the Communist party refused to do so. In some cases the HRB maintained that an applicant it had rejected had no financial need. While the UNIA generally accepted relief guidelines in setting need standards, the party did not. One of the party's earliest protests, in front of the HRB office on East 125th Street in 1933, demanded that the Bureau "provide adequate relief for the starving working people in Harlem." The Communist party charged that home relief allowances in Harlem provided less than the minimum amount necessary to maintain a family, and furthermore, that blacks found it harder to obtain relief. According to Harlem party leader James Ford: "I say that if you send a Negro to a Relief bureau . . . and send a white person there is a difference. If you go among the unemployed today you will find . . . there is one form of relief for Negroes and another for white."

Other conflicts between blacks and the relief agency centered on unprovable claims of discrimination, statements only the black client or worker heard or saw. The agency investigated each protest but did not consider one person's word sufficient evidence to act on. The Communist party generally took the side of the complainant, rejecting the agency's position that undocumented racism could not be remedied. This activism on behalf of individuals, which included securing rent for the dispossessed and higher relief grants for several needy families, demonstrated the party's commitment to concrete action as well as to large-scale propaganda efforts.[24]

The party also concentrated on organizing and on building alliances in its United Front period. One of the first coalitions, the Joint Conference Against Discriminatory Practices, fought to end relief discrimination and to open Relief Bureau jobs to blacks in 1934. It successfully organized many of the HRB employees and encouraged them to fight racism wherever they saw it in the agency. The Joint Conference, led by black Cuban Arnold Johnson of the party, brought together over sixty organizations, including the Unemployed Councils, the Elks, several black Protestant and Catholic churches, Democratic clubs, the NAACP, the UNIA, Harlem's YWCA and YMCA, Father Divine's Peace Mission, and several unions. The HRB Employees' Association (the newly organized union) reported that over 2,000 people attended its mass meeting on December 14, 1934, to protest the alleged Jim Crow practices of the Relief Administration.

While many black groups struggled for the same ends, unity was far from total. The Communist party and the UNIA still fought each other on the streets. Sectarian battles were no less bitter on these issues than on that of white-collar employment. Still, these activities ensured that, in general, the policies of equal access were maintained. James Ford of the Communist party noted the results in 1935. In 1933 Harlem had one relief office. Two years later it had three. "We see more getting relief, more Negroes employed in bureaus as clerks, administrators etc. How was this gotten? How was this discrimination overcome? It was overcome by this struggle of the people and by people belonging to organizations like this."[25]

While covert and unintentional racism did block some blacks from access to relief, the central reason so many needy could not get public aid was the difficulty all applicants had in qualifying for relief and remaining qualified. Criteria for acceptance were rigorous and rigorously enforced, and for several reasons many blacks found it more difficult to meet these requirements than whites. At the Emergency Relief Bureau in 1935, for example, even after eligibility requirements had eased, clients had to have resided in New York State for two years, and in the city for one. These residence requirements hurt blacks not only because they were relative newcomers but also because the poor state of their housing necessitated frequent moves, making long-term residency harder to prove. Also, lodgers found it difficult to establish proof of residency because they lacked such evidence as gas bills. James Ford claimed "insufficient residential verification" was the cause of most Harlem relief denials.[26]

The agency's thorough investigation included a visit to the applicant's home, former employer(s), and bank. Caseworkers also checked with a central Registration Bureau to make sure no other relief agencies, public or private, were helping support the family.

If a family could not account satisfactorily for its previous source of livelihood, it was rejected as well. Charles Battles, an unemployed black man, applied for aid. Until that time he had been managing only by going to a market and helping unload trucks for tips. The relief agency rejected this explanation. The caseworker claimed Battles could not have survived on such low earnings, and demanded documentation of employment. As he had none, he could not qualify for relief. The ERB reported in 1937 that in four years of operation it had rejected 45 percent of all applicants as ineligible. As it admitted, many of these were needy.[27]

Even after clients were accepted, caseworkers periodically rechecked their files for any new or unreported income. Furthermore, if employable relief recipients refused to accept "suitable employment" when found for them, relief was "promptly withdrawn." This rule applied to women as well as men. According to the Commissioner of Welfare, "suitable employment" meant "jobs [that] meet reasonable minimum standards of wages, hours and working conditions." A caseworker's estimation of "reasonable minimum standards," however, did not always coincide with that of the relief recipient. Since live-in or poorly paid domestic work was considered "suitable employment," this requirement hurt blacks more than whites. Women of both races were understandably reluctant to take live-in positions that would take them from their families, or to accept intolerably low wages. Thus they often refused such jobs and were subsequently dropped from home relief. Sarah Wilson, with six children, refused a domestic position paying $3 for a thirty-hour week, and on that basis, she was denied public aid. But because agencies offered such jobs more often to black women than white (because so many blacks could not qualify for other work, and because some caseworkers only offered domestic work to black women regardless of their training), this penalty of losing relief was imposed more often on black women than on white.[28]

Even ERB officials admitted their agency's scrutiny of clients was "grueling," demonstrating the "absolute need" of applicants willing to endure it. During congressional testimony, a New York City settlement worker had the following interchange with Senator Robert Wagner of New York:

Sen. Wagner: Is it your experience that families accept charity as a last resort?

Mrs. M.: Absolutely. I had a teacher in New York City tell me children came to school with dresses which finally came apart and then they stayed at home for lack of clothing, no underwear and no shoes. Then as a last resort the mother goes to work and a woman will work at cleaning offices for as little as 8 cents a room, night after night from 6 to 12, and then come home and take care of a large family and sometimes take in boarders or take in washing. Then finally they give up the home. . . .[29]

A follower of Father Divine told him of her pre-conversion experiences with caseworkers:

The investigators they were all like detectives, Father, acting like I had committed a crime. They acted as if I didn't even birth myself my two children, as if I had killed my husband perhaps or had him in hiding some place, when he had runned off with a cat of a gal. . . . Dear Father, the investigator searched my ice box and examined the toilet. Father I felt as if I was stripped of all my clothes. . . . I was ashamed of my life.

Other rules and limits also affected blacks more than other groups. The new Social Security Act, designed to provide the elderly (among others) with a secure pension, excluded farm workers and domestic workers from coverage. Blacks were disproportionately hurt nationwide, as 65 percent worked at these two occupations. Harlem women, so many of whom worked as domestics, could anticipate no government help in their old age. This affected not only the women but also their families, who divided meager incomes or relief allocations among still more family members. Nor did relief agencies take the different lifestyle of many Harlem residents into consideration. The BCW's refusal to provide relief for illegitimate children had a more adverse effect on the black community, where illegitimacy was more widespread—or at least more openly admitted. This restriction remained on the books until 1937.[30]

Not only was home relief difficult to obtain or keep, payments were, as a rule, inadequate. Relief may have saved the lives of many New Yorkers but it hardly made their lives pleasant. Once granted, family allowances covered only the barest of necessities. Over the decade, the relative dollar level of the family grant remained fairly constant, at a minimum level of subsistence. The Board of Survey on Transfer of Relief Administration offered a table of food budget increases over time, and noted: "All changes in food allowances since 1934 have been due to increases in prices."[31]

Home relief budgets varied according to the size of the family, the type of lodging, and whether any family member worked. Based on city-wide costs for shelter, food, light, fuel, household necessities, medicine and medical care, and occasionally clothing, relief manuals provided charts of the amount and type of food necessary for infants, children, adolescents, men, women, and pregnant and nursing women, along with the cost of each item. The manual even listed the amount of milk required, by age. In some agencies, adults' food and clothing allowances varied according to whether they were "at home" or "at work." The Communist party urged the needy to demand all the "stingy starvation relief that the law allows, . . . the miserly aid which Home Relief bureaus will give you." The party was correct. The Mayor's Committee on Unemployment Relief believed the city agencies' family relief budgets fell 40 percent short of the "minimum standard of living." In 1934, a family of two parents and two children received $54.86 a month on home relief (excluding the ever-fluctuating clothing allowance). The allowance rose only to keep pace with prices. Thus this family's 1937 allowance, $61.16, remained well below the minimum "emergency" subsistence level, which the WPA estimated to be $83.31. Food allotments plus commodities brought the total up to the emergency standard but not to the minimum "maintenance" level. Over half a million children lived in these families.[32]

The Department of Agriculture estimated that an "inexpensive but adequate diet" in the Northeast cost $11.70 per person, per month. Due to the higher costs of food in Harlem, non-relief families living there spent slightly more than this amount. Yet when setting its allotment levels the HRB did not consider neighborhood differences and based its figures on borough-wide price averages. Although this policy was not intentionally discriminatory, it did penalize Harlemites. Harlem residents on relief received, on average, $7.85 a month for food. Such relief grants could not adequately meet need. Women studied in a home relief investigation in 1935 reported that because their $2.50 weekly food allotment was so inadequate, they often took advantage of free meals at shelters and soup kitchens. The Women's Emergency Shelter, for example, housed approximately 175 women, but fed between 500 and 600 a day.[33]

Nor were housing costs better met. Before 1933 the HRB paid rent only if the family was threatened with eviction. That year, the agency began including rent in the relief budget. Still, not until 1937 did the agency raise its rent allowances enough so that most families did not have to dip into food money for rent.

Again, racism made the situation worse in Harlem. The HRB set one borough-wide housing payment despite substantially higher rents in Harlem. According to the Home Relief Manual, "The rent allowance shall be the actual rent paid, provided that it falls within the rents [approved as maximums]." If the family paid a higher rent, their relief budget was to be increased only if the family was "unable to procure suitable living quarters according to the rent schedule within the area in which they are accustomed to live." This humane provision, however, was usually honored only in the breach if Harlem clients' complaints are any indication. As the study for the mayor pointed out: "In the district of Harlem this problem [of a fixed amount for the rent budget] is accentuated since the tenant is forced to pay higher rent than he would in any other section of the city for the same type of apartment."[34]

Catherine Pond, on relief when her husband went into the hospital, had to pay $42 for rent. Despite this, the relief agency allocated only $21 for her housing costs. The roomer she had taken in to make up the difference brought in white women, so she made him leave. Her new lodger, rather more decorous, could only afford to pay $10 a month, so Mrs. Pond had to use virtually all her relief to pay her rent. Her case was one of many the UNIA heard in which more than half the family's relief income went to cover housing. Clara King, sick with rheumatic fever and on relief since 1930, received $15.20 every two weeks. She paid $20 a month for rent, $11.25 for food and $2.50 for utilities. Because her relief check did not go far enough, she took in a lodger. Still unable to pay her bills, she appealed to the HRB for more help. Workers there told her she was receiving the maximum allotment for a cold-water flat. She had no money to move, however, and could not find a heated apartment for less than the rental payment maximum. She needed clothing as well, but the HRB had no allocation for it. As a final blow she learned she could not qualify for any additional relief because she had a lodger.

The limited allotment for personal items such as clothing also had a dramatic impact on people's lives. Dorothy Perry was told she could not receive relief unless she attended WPA household training classes. But she could not go because she had no suitable clothes, and no money to buy any.

As Mayor LaGuardia's Committee on Unemployment Relief reported in 1935, "interviews with the administrators of the 34 precincts throughout the City showed that in only one precinct was the food allowance adequate for maintaining health standards. . . . The precinct administrators with one exception reported unanimously that the home relief rental allowance was not sufficient to meet the average rentals in their districts." The committee concluded: "The Home Relief Bureaus have never been able to allow sufficient funds to cover even the barest necessities of clothing for either adults or children."

As late as 1940, relief grants still fell below recognized minimum subsistence levels. According to the 1940 Department of Welfare relief manual, an unemployed family of husband, wife, and two children could receive up to $28.60 a month for food, $8.90 for clothing, and $5.60 for household supplies, including fuel. In a centrally heated apartment with private toilet, they could receive a maximum rent allowance of $27.50, for a maximum total relief income of $70.60. To put this in perspective, the average white non-relief family in New York spent three times as much on food, twice as much on housing, four times as much on household operation, two and a half times as much on clothing, and still had money left for other items such as recreation and medical care. Relief rates approached but did not match spending by Harlemites not on relief.

Home relief rules also affected family composition. Because relief budgets subtracted money earned by any family member, young people left home if they found work, so as not to decrease the family's relief allowance. Poor, they often moved into substandard housing, much to the distress of both parents and social workers. At the same time the Department of Welfare refused to allow unmarried children to apply for relief separately. Thus children with income left, and adult children without it were forced to move back home. Hallie Brummage, twenty-three, worked at a dress shop for six years until it closed in 1937. She earned $16 a week. She then joined the relief rolls until a caseworker discovered her mother worked on a WPA project. Home relief dropped her from the rolls despite her objections that she had not lived at home since she was sixteen, and her mother's income could not support her as well as her fifteen-year-old sister.[35]

Overall, then, relief grants were generally decided without regard to race. This gave blacks greater access to aid than they enjoyed elsewhere in the country. On the other hand, family budget grants, also prepared without regard to race, were not only low but also had inequitable consequences in a segregated city.

At first blush it is surprising to discover how few Harlemites complained about the inadequacy of low home relief grants. Nor did those on work relief object, although they earned little more than those on home relief. Unskilled workers on WPA projects in 1938 earned between $50 and $60 a month, the skilled earned between $75 and $95, and professionals $90 to $100. In general, the WPA set the prevailing wage as its maximum. In comparison, non-relief workers made significantly more. Unskilled WPA workers at $60 a month earned $720 a year, and the skilled earned $1,140, compared with $1,671 for non-relief wage earners as a group. For professionals the $1,200 annual WPA salary did not come close to the $3,700 earned on average by non-WPA businessmen and professionals.[36]

In fact, most Harlem home or work relief recipients who criticized relief agencies did not object to the low allotments. In the public testimony before the Mayor's Commission and in the UNIA investigations, some complained that relief did not pay enough, but most often, blacks objected to being denied relief or dropped from the rolls unfairly, or to being classified inappropriately for work relief placements.[37] Perhaps African-Americans, unused to government help, appreciated any amount they received, or feared that complaining would result in the loss of what little they were receiving.

But an analysis of the earnings of employed blacks in this period suggests a different explanation. Although home relief allowances fell below official minimum standards, and the WPA set its wages at the minimum prevailing rate, in many cases both were at least as high as average black earnings in the private sector. The Bureau of Labor Statistics study's data on Harlem showed unskilled workers earning $630 a year ($820 if only men are considered), while WPA workers at that level earned $720. Semi-skilled workers in the study earned $771 ($985 for men), and skilled, $1,000, less than comparable WPA workers. A home relief family of four in 1937 received $734 in a year. These figures suggest that for blacks, home relief grants and work relief wages were no worse, and in some cases better, than other opportunities. Robert McElvaine has pointed out that the WPA's minimum wage often came to twice previous black wages. A study of thirty-nine non-relief families in Harlem and Brooklyn found only twelve of the fifty-nine employed black adults earned over $20 a week. Most, then, did not do as well as did a skilled WPA worker.[38] Considering how close to destitution black families hovered, relief offered no less than employment did. Accustomed to making do on extremely low earnings, blacks experienced little decline in financial status when on home or work relief, but actually saw an improvement in the number of services newly available from relief agencies.

Hiring Discrimination

From the perspective of the black community, then—or at least of those who spoke out—the allocation of home relief was evenhanded and the work and home relief grants small but acceptable and only indirectly discriminatory. Much more objectionable were overtly discriminatory hiring practices of relief agencies. Home relief grants may have been granted without regard to race, but that agency's hiring and work placement practices revealed open racism. Inequality and discrimination troubled activist Harlemites far more than low grants themselves.

The Mayor's Commission, the Urban League, the Communist party, and the UNIA all accused the Home Relief Bureau of regularly denying positions to qualified blacks and of relegating black workers to low-level jobs. Fred Benedikt, formerly active in the Communist-organized union of HRB workers, testified:

> Discrimination against the Negroes on the [HRB] staff became an issue at the beginning of 1934. At that time we started to organize our union. . . . We saw . . . that our Negro fellow employees had a very special problem. Discrimination against them because they were Negroes. . . . At that time there were 25 precincts. No Negro supervisors. There was one case supervisor, Mr. Mason. No Negro office manager, no occupational clerk. . . . They are very careful that the Negro must stay out of white collar projects. Out of 242 projects, there are no Negroes on 178 of them.

Organized black protests, particularly when coupled with union support, produced several victories. In 1933 the Urban League called upon state and local officials to explain why so few blacks with college degrees obtained employment with the Home Relief Bureau when that agency regularly hired white high-school graduates. After protracted arguments and the replacement of Mayor Walker by newly elected Mayor LaGuardia, more blacks were hired. Benedikt described eight cases of black workers who appealed their dismissals or demotions to the HRB's union grievance committee. Of them, "the majority were reinstated to their old positions or remployed." While he complained that "this meant the administrator had been forced to reinstate people who never should have been fired in the first place," he might also have acknowledged that the reinstatement demonstrated a willingness to reverse racist practice when confronted about it.[39] The combination of vocal black protest and an effective union grievance procedure proved a potent weapon for obtaining justice.

When the civil service came to the ERB, many black workers, not part of that system, lost their jobs. The Urban League and the Citizens' Coordinating Council, a coalition the Urban League had helped establish, persuaded Commissioner Hodson to re-employ 126 of them: one-third of the total number of reappointments. The Urban League also argued for black counselors and more black participants in CCC (Civilian Conservation Corps) camps.[40] In other words, vigilance was necessary to remedy racist practices, but protest usually did prove effective.

Probably the most persuasive call for change came from the Mayor's Commission on Conditions in Harlem. Its 1935 report found little evidence of widespread discrimination in the distribution of relief, but concentrated its criticism on what it viewed as the discriminatory hiring practices of the HRB. The report noted that as of July 1935, less than 9 percent of the staff and only thirteen of 244 supervisors were black. Predictably, most worked in the Harlem office. While even the 1,063 employed (of over 12,000) was a dramatic improvement over the thirty-one there in 1931, it remained woefully low. While the department argued that the figures exceeded the black proportion in the population, the Mayor's Commission responded that the number employed at the HRB should reflect the proportion of the relief rolls that were black—over 20 percent. Nor was the concentration of African-Americans in low-paying jobs in the agency the result of chance or lack of training. The commission found that trained black social workers received positions inferior to those of their white colleagues.[41] In other words, the Urban League's complaints had been valid.

The job placement bureau of the ERB also discriminated against qualified blacks, according to the Mayor's Commission. Mary Irvin, a qualified dressmaker, testified before the commission that she asked for work every day from the Relief Bureau's job placement service. The service officer informed her he had only domestic service positions available, even though every day white dressmakers received dressmaking placements from the same agency. The NUL reported:

> In New York City, for instance, Negroes comprise 21 percent of the City's relief load during the summer of 1936 and 18 percent of those placed on private jobs through the Work Referral Division of the ERB. This 18 percent, however, amounted to only 82 men . . . a pitiful number in view of the more than 60,000 Negro employables receiving relief. In Toledo, Ohio, Negroes comprise 8 percent of the total population, 16 percent of the State Employment Office registrations, and only 4 percent of the placements made in October 1935.[42]

All this first generated vehement defense and denials by the ERB's secretary, Edmund Butler, followed by concrete changes in the running of the Bureau. Butler argued that since the proportion of blacks on the staff surpassed their proportion in the general population, he could see no evidence of discrimination. He claimed that the 8 percent figure (the proportion of blacks in the agency) represented the upper brackets above the grade of investigator, not all black employees. Finally, he argued that according to the commission report, these complaints were investigated by the Bureau, which demonstrated that body's commitment to fairness. Although "discriminating against the Negro by reason of race exists everywhere . . . [and therefore there might be isolated cases in the ERB] I deny absolutely that the discrimination existed to any substantial extent in the ERB." In fact, he maintained, relief distribution *was* discriminatory—"in favor of the Negro."[43]

Despite the denials, the director established an Advisory Committee on Negro Problems in June of 1935, whose members included clergy, Urban League representatives, and YMCA officers. Mandated to "assist the Emergency Relief Bureau in handling the problems of the Harlemite's situation," this committee transformed the Bureau. It successfully persuaded the ERB to raise the number of blacks in "responsible positions" from nine to sixty-three in one year. The Bureau corrected cases in which black supervisors earned less than white. As director Oswald Knauth admitted: "There is no blinking the fact that there have been abuses in Harlem as elsewhere. Equally, there is no blinking the fact that we are correcting these conditions as fast as is humanly possible."[44]

Even James Ford acknowledged the central importance of the Mayor's Commission in bringing about change. Predictably, he claimed credit for leading a reluctant commission down the correct path: "The Mayor's Commission has been forced to . . . agree to many of the things brought forward by the people of the community." By the summer of 1935, relief workers constituted the largest group of black professionals on the city payroll.

Discrimination did not cease immediately, of course. As late as 1938, the NYUL reported that the ERB refused to train black Dictaphone operators. The League had to arrange its own training for them at the Harlem YWCA, after which the ERB placed them and accepted a second group for training at ERB offices.[45] Yet active protest had done much to improve employment opportunities for blacks in home relief agencies. Despite the good intentions of many in city government, and clear regulations against it, discrimination certainly occurred. While black protest, and municipal responses, did not erase the problem completely, the frequency of discrimination in home relief hirings appears to have declined. In this respect as well as in home relief grants, New York City's ERB discriminated less than did similar agencies in most areas around the country, and responded more readily to organized black objections.

The ERB's readiness to rectify errors and concrete instances of discrimination against clients or employees revealed a willingness to abide by the color-blind rules of fairness its guidelines demanded. In some cases, changes were made reluctantly, as with hiring practices. Still, they were made. Other city agencies had a much less enviable record.

Simply examining where public services were located demonstrates the general neglect of Harlem by many relief agencies. Of the nineteen temporary shelters for homeless and transient individuals in Manhattan, only one, the Salvation Army Colored Annex, was located in or near Harlem (although most others did accept blacks). A study of "unattached" black women in the same year noted the same phenomenon; the Women's Emergency Shelter was far from Harlem and could not accommodate everyone needing shelter. The Salvation Army Working Women's home rarely accepted blacks; the Harlem YWCA offered only temporary facilities, and those at 25 cents a day.

These unfair practices were frequently challenged by black monitoring groups. The NAACP, for example, protested a Home Owners Loan Corporation decision denying a loan to Andrew Morton, an elderly Harlemite. The HOLC, claimed the NAACP, "is making some unfair distinctions and discriminations in considering applications of colored people." In this case, the assistant chairman of the HOLC had written: "it seems that the applicant is a Negro and is 81 years of age . . ." suggesting both race and age were factors in evaluating his ability to repay the loan. "The Association [NAACP] considers this case of great importance because of the precedent being set for dealing with the applications of Negro homeowners on relief." The NAACP further claimed that the New York HOLC office routinely classified homes in Harlem as rooming houses and refused all applications of homeowners on that ground.[46]

The most overt discrimination, however, occurred in work relief. Like the HRB, WPA hiring practices discriminated against blacks, especially in the agency's reluctance to hire blacks in supervisory positions. Because the administrator, Victor Ridder, was willing to support a policy of non-discrimination once the matter was brought to his attention, however, the WPA made direct efforts to rectify the situation. After an open hearing on discrimination in November of 1935, Ridder agreed to promote black staff to administrative positions. The *Amsterdam News* reported his promise to place "20 Negroes in key WPA positions before he resigns on July 1." As Ridder explained, "I shall do this because Negroes are discriminated against, and never get a chance to prove their worth." The *News* story continued: "He declared that despite opposition in his own organization he had increased the number of Negro workers from 8 to 12 percent, an increase of 5,000 jobs." Yet what he gave with one hand, he took away with the other. "The 20 Negroes selected for the key positions cannot afford to fail in their jobs, he said, because many local WPA officials are opposed to the advancement of colored workers and would seize upon any failure to bolster the illusion that Negroes are inefficient and unreliable." Blacks received better positions, but it became their burden to disprove white racism.[47]

Ridder established an advisory board to help root out discrimination: the "Race Relations Unit." The final WPA report in 1943 described the unit's history and significance:

> Outstanding among complaints received in the early days of the Administration [WPA] were those received from Negro organizations, which asserted on many occasions that members of their group were victims of discrimination. The Race Relations Unit under a Race Relations Officer was established for the adjustment of complaints of Negroes and to secure a clearer and more definite understanding of problems concerning them. This Unit maintained liaison between WPA and Negro organizations and acted in an advisory capacity on many matters affecting them.
>
> Prompt handling of complaints resulted in the elimination of many of the causes of complaints about discrimination.

In 1936 Ridder reported that the WPA employed two black managers, four supervisors, a senior engineer, and a black staff physician.[48] Progress was real, but again depended on the commitment of individuals to enforce non-discrimination rules. Harry Hopkins, who directed the WPA, held generally enlightened views on racial issues, and took care to establish non-discriminatory and even-handed policies from the central office. While those rules were routinely ignored in local bureaus across the country, Ridder in New York proved a supporter of racial equality. Thus the WPA's record in New York City was better than it was in most other cities.

The commitment to equal access, however, often did not extend to less visible practices. Much in the operation of the works programs proved intractably and blatantly discriminatory. Lamented Alain Locke: "One of the fatal gaps between good intentions and good performance [in government] is in this matter of local administrators, where often an executive policy officially promulgated gets short circuited into discrimination at the point of practical application." The FERA admitted that blacks had "much less chance for work relief." This problem was widespread; all over the country, blacks faced greater employment discrimination, which placed them disproportionately in need. Then they faced similar discrimination from work relief agencies.[49]

The WPA and Public Works Administration (PWA) generally subcontracted work, and subcontractors often resisted pressure to hire blacks. The subcontractor for the Triborough Bridge project (under the PWA) and another for the Post Office project refused to take any blacks. Nor, despite vociferous black protest, did either agency exert pressure on contractors to do so. In response to NAACP complaints and despite the strong stand of federal agency head Harold Ickes on racial equality, PWA officials wrote, "The bulk of workers are handled by subcontractors, therefore, we do not in any way interfere or dictate in the selection of workers."[50] The Mayor's Commission on Conditions in Harlem found "systematic discrimination has been carried on against the Negro in work relief." On twelve major public works building projects surveyed by the NAACP, only forty-one blacks found employment. As James Allen of the NAACP noted, "There is some indication of the smallest number of men employed belonging to a racial group."

These discrimination patterns occurred also under the WPA. Foremen on WPA bridge construction projects told black applicants that no blacks were ever employed there. Frank Crosswaith testified:

> You have the matter of discrimination on Federal and State jobs. . . . let me take a Federal job for example: the United States Courthouse on Pearl and Center Streets. . . . On that job you have one thousand men employed. There are no Negroes there. The United States Post office building is being erected at 34th Street and Eighth Avenue. . . . About seven hundred men are employed there. Couldn't find a single Negro on the job. The Department of Health on the corner of North and Center Streets, . . . five hundred men and one Negro.[51]

The hiring problem cut two ways. Some subcontractors simply refused to hire blacks. Others sought to hire workers only of their own ethnic group. Both policies hurt blacks because there were no black contractors. Jews, Italians, or Irish excluded from one firm could hope to receive preferential treatment from another. Blacks had no such opportunities. Of course, this pattern of public discrimination through private subcontracting was not unique to New York City. As Allen testified, "Being the type of organization we are [NAACP] we carried these protests to Washington [and] laid the information before the President of the United States, with the Senator of the State, with [the] Governor of the State, with the State Superintendent of Public Buildings. Most of the letters came back with the same excuse."

All in all, the work relief agencies had an unimpressive record of black placements. A December 1934 Temporary Emergency Relief Administration (TERA) report on discrimination against blacks on work relief in New York City listed five complaints about racial discrimination at the work place: segregation of work locations, the maintaining of superior black workers in subordinate positions, the assignment of less desirable tasks to blacks, intimidation and overly critical attitudes of supervisors. The report found black workers routinely receiving incorrect work classifications, generally that of "laborer." One clerk refused to assign blacks to any jobs at all; several WPA project leaders also refused to do so. TERA investigators discovered WPA memos stating "quota for colored filled."[52]

Albert Dillard, an interior designer for eight years, complained in a letter to Mayor LaGuardia that he had received a WPA ticket stating that his trade was "painter."

> Despite the fact that I can prove my qualifications and eight years' experience as an interior decorator, I was offered a laborer's job. On the other hand, a number of white painters who reported for work were not questioned. . . . All Negroes who reported for skilled work while I was there were sent to work as laborers.

William Dammond leveled a similar charge. He was told the civil engineering work relief job he had applied for had been filled. He later discovered it had not. When he objected, the agency told him that although it had been advertised as a civil engineering job (for which he was trained), it was in fact another sort of engineering job. Yet, another civil engineer received the position.

The TERA report also found a disproportionate number of blacks let go and dismissal of qualified and efficient black workers and those with large numbers of dependents. With no systematic scheme for layoffs, prejudiced foremen found it simple to select blacks for the first round.[53]

Aggregate statistics bolster the evidence of discrimination. Blacks made up 8 percent of the WPA's work force (higher than their proportion in the population) but over a fifth of the home relief population in 1936. Looking at it a different way, the Race Relations Unit found, of those on relief before the WPA, two-thirds of the white group was absorbed into the WPA by November of 1935, compared with just over a third of blacks. Approximately half of all WPA jobs were classified as unskilled; five-sixths of all blacks worked in jobs at this level, though many of them claimed to have skills. Certainly such discrimination was common to jobs in which white supervisors had the responsibility for judging, assigning, and promoting black workers. Garfield Freeman, assigned to the Parks Department as a laborer in 1932, requested a promotion. Although he had been on the job for two years, the department denied the request. The Mayor's Commission on Conditions in Harlem asked him why he thought his supervisor would not promote him.

> *A.* Because . . . he doesn't wish to make a colored man foreman.
>
> *Q.* Have you any reason to believe that your present foreman would discriminate against you because you are colored?

A. Only from his ways and actions. . . . He has jobs he knows I am capable of doing and he picks over me and puts white men to doing it.

Q. Do you believe when you are skipped over . . . because of your inability to do the job or is it your belief that you are skipped over because of your color?

A. He knows I know how to do the job but it's my honest belief I am skipped over because of my color.

As the Race Relations Unit noted, the fact that so many more whites than blacks entered WPA rolls showed discrimination "in work referral or placement or both." Commissioner of Accounts Paul Blanshard wrote to E. Franklin Frazier in 1935 that a survey of work relief referrals in Harlem

> seems to establish clearly some discrimination against Negro workers. . . . Two kinds of discrimination are revealed, general and local. . . . 1. The sections predominantly Negro in their composition did not receive their proportionate share of allotments of work relief jobs. 2. Within predominantly white precincts Negro home relief clients were not given a proportionate share of referral assignments to work relief jobs.

The director of the Race Relations Unit explained the unequal treatment as the result of a poorly planned start-up. With money suddenly available, 200,000 workers were hired in sixty days, with no rational planning. "To the average worker, it was ruthless, unjust, cold blooded governmental regimentation. To the Negro worker it was rank discrimination."[54] Because of the lack of careful oversight, even without intent, racist conventions flourished.

As with HRB discrimination, the black community brought these incidents to agency attention, often successfully. Again, once the public focused attention on racism, agency officials responded. For example, black protest moved the WPA to investigate the racist remarks and activities of a Mrs. Hutchinson, director of the city's Historical Records Survey. The result of the investigation, described in a memorandum to the federal project head, indicates that protest did have some impact on conditions for African-Americans:

> This is to inform you of an unpleasant situation which has arisen on the Historical Records Survey in New York City. [Mrs. Hutchinson has made several remarks to co-workers indicating] a prejudice on her part against having Jews or Negroes on her project. . . . Although the charges of specific acts of discrimination all seemed to break down under investigation nevertheless there was no doubt that Mrs. Hutchinson did have a personal prejudice, which was known to her workers. It was [the investigator's] opinion that she had made a conscientious effort to avoid discrimination in administering the project but . . . [she] lost the confidence of many of her workers [because of what she said]. . . . The project cannot continue successfully under her direction.

The investigator suggested the WPA urge her to take a leave and look elsewhere for employment. A second memorandum reported that she had requested such a leave, and added, "I wish to assure all supervisors and workers on the project that the National office does not permit discrimination against its employees because of race, religion, or union activities." This episode is significant as well for its implied counter-argument to those employers who insisted that integration in the work place would be impossible because of the opposition of the existing work force. The first memorandum reported the receipt of numerous telegrams demanding she be fired. This, and the fact that she "lost the confidence of many of her workers" with her racist remarks, suggests an unexpectedly progressive attitude on the part of white employees.[55]

The New York Urban League claimed responsibility for some improvement in relief hirings. As the League described its perception of racial discrimination in work relief:

> Relief has been inadequate all over the city. It has been a serious question whether we have received our share here in this section [Harlem]. Our office has been flooded with complaints. . . . Some are not valid. But there are some complaints that we are compelled to recognize. One of these is the placing of skilled colored mechanics as day laborers. [We complained and were told there were not enough skilled jobs.] But the question is still unanswered when colored mechanics are taken off the skilled trade jobs and assigned to work as day laborers when the white workers are continued on skilled work.[56]

The Urban League agitated for better treatment of black workers and the hiring of more blacks on WPA and PWA projects throughout the New Deal period. It also urged more work projects for Harlem, such as an expansion of Harlem Hospital and an additional health facility in the area. The Urban League also investigated specific complaints of discrimination and helped organize alternative training programs for blacks who were refused such training in government or private agencies. More radical organizations maintained just as active a profile. The Communist party, in its "united front" with other groups, sponsored rallies, marches, and delegation visits to demand that blacks receive a fair share of work relief jobs, including skilled ones.[57]

Part of the controversy over discrimination that raged both in New York and in the federal government centered on what proportion of work relief jobs blacks should receive. Most agency heads on both the federal and local levels argued that blacks should appear on work relief rolls in the same proportion as they appeared in the general population. Harold Ickes stipulated that all PWA contracts include a clause requiring that blacks be hired in proportion to their representation in the particular trade. He did so to ensure that blacks would receive an adequate share of the jobs. Certainly this concern was justified, especially in the South, which routinely provided less relief for blacks than for whites, despite the former group's greater need.

In New York City, however, where the proportion of blacks in the population was fairly low, and where relief agencies more often could be pressured into applying objective standards, federal rules based on general population figures did not further the struggle. There, black organizations and the Communist party urged agencies to apportion relief jobs according to the makeup of the relief population. They argued that work relief existed to help the needy specifically, so it was meaningless to consider any other population as the base from which to draw the pool. By this standard, the city's work relief programs fell far short. James Hubert made exactly that argument:

During the month of February [1935] there were employed in the Works Division a total of 119,914 people. Now it is interesting to note that of that number Negroes constituted only 8,091 of the total number employed. In other words, only 6.8 percent of the total. . . . Now you might say that is pretty fair according to population. The Negro constitutes 4.7 percent in New York City. However when you take it in the light of the number of Negroes unemployed, it does not look so good. Almost 14 percent unemployed Negroes in New York City. Another fact is that Negroes are restricted very largely to the poorer paying jobs . . . which means that although the Negro constitutes six percent of the employed, he is earning less than about two percent of the money that is being paid out, so that in my opinion, there is absolutely discrimination in Public Works. It is almost impossible, in my opinion, for Negroes to get consideration at all on most of the projects.[58]

This debate became explicit over the question of black labor in constructing the Harlem River Houses. Ickes announced in 1936 that blacks would receive 3 percent of the skilled work in the construction of the Harlem River and Williamsburg Houses. According to the *Amsterdam News,* although it sounded like "planned discrimination," Ickes had intended the opposite. Based on the proportion of blacks in New York City's skilled trades, the 3 percent ensured a fair proportion of spots for qualified blacks. Furthermore, Ickes ordered that, because the project used only organized labor, unions provide all blacks with membership cards. This "will force entry of Negroes to certain unions from which they have been barred. . . . Once [in] . . . they should immediately begain to clamor for permanent membership and fight for that right."

Some black leaders argued that more than 3 percent of the skilled positions should go to blacks because a higher proportion of skilled blacks than whites was unemployed. Others believed the Harlem housing projects should hire only blacks. In response, the *Amsterdam News* employed the same argument it had raised against the "Don't Buy" campaign: projects elsewhere would then hire only whites. In this case the paper's fears were based on existing practice. When blacks did receive work placements, they often found themselves on Harlem jobs, regardless of where they lived. Many Harlem work relief projects only used blacks, and many jobs outside Harlem did not employ any.[59]

Ickes used quotas to increase black representation on PWA projects; Ridder used similar methods with WPA work placements. Conveniently, by 1935, federal policy and local agitation by black groups coincided. In May of that year President Roosevelt issued Executive Order 7046 mandating that in the WPA all those "qualified by training and experience to be assigned to work projects shall not be discriminated against on any grounds whatsoever." Locally, Ridder sent a more detailed memorandum on the subject to WPA personnel:

NOTE: TO BE POSTED AND KEPT POSTED
ON ALL SPECIAL BULLETIN BOARDS

Special Notice #8

Absolutely no discrimination should prevail in the selection or assignment of workers at any point in the U.S. Works Progress Administration.

No requisition for personnel which, as a prerequisite, discriminates against any group, or which is based on any other qualification than that of ability to perform the work specified, shall be considered, unless approved by the Administrator.

Any request violating this rule must be referred immediately to the Administrator personally.

The earnest cooperation of all workers, in whatever capacity, is asked to bring about good relationships and to end any unfair or unjust practice.

                                                            Victor F. Ridder, Administrator.

Such efforts paid off. The Race Relations Unit's 1935 investigations resulted not only in increased black staff hiring but also in a promise of more work projects in Harlem and of moving more blacks into the WPA from home relief. By January of 1936, 27,154 blacks held WPA jobs (of 245,568 total jobs), a tremendous jump both in number and in percent of the total WPA work force. The Race Relations Unit investigated and adjusted 250 discrimination cases.[60]

As with other agencies, though, progress here was tempered by fear of radicalism. Ridder, one of the strongest supporters of equal opportunity in the city, took great pains to distance himself from the Communist party, which was also fighting for black rights. According to the *Amsterdam News:*

Because of the population increase in Harlem and the exploitation of that section by both white and colored, . . . discrimination has increased in New York City. The Works Progress Administrator declared that Communists had capitalized on this discrimination to commit "subversive acts" in the WPA. "The Negro Communists in the WPA are in the same proportion as the white," he said, "and I will treat them all alike. No one else, however, will suffer because of the destructive activities of the Communists who have only themselves to blame for whatever happens to them."

Since the Communists had had such singular success organizing worker and client grievances into one coherent voice for change, it is hardly surprising Ridder saw the party as a threat. Nevertheless, working at cross purposes meant slower progress than cooperation would have brought.

The Race Relations Unit also held this anti-Communist position. While it castigated the WPA for its rushed and discriminatory initial hiring, it went on to complain that the intervention at that point of "agitators, organizers, and *professional defenders of the Negro"* (the unit's emphasis) intensified the crisis. Edmund Butler of the ERB suggested that the large number of black complaints about his agency was due, not to greater abuses, but to the huge numbers of "pressure groups" in Harlem.[61] This distaste for all black protest, and the tendency to see it as the product of irresponsible outsiders, allowed agency officials to go less far than they otherwise might have in addressing problems of inequality in their organizations.

Through the end of the decade, the proportion of blacks in WPA jobs exceeded their proportion in the population, but still remained lower than their proportion on home relief. Furthermore, blacks remained primarily in the unskilled ranks. While many of these unskilled placements reflected the black applicants' lack of training, agencies continued to receive complaints that skilled blacks were receiving menial jobs.

The black proportion on WPA rolls did not increase substantially until the early 1940s, when war-related industries expanded. At that time, because whites found private jobs more quickly, the proportion of blacks on relief climbed even as their numbers decreased.[62] While sympathetic agency officials and strong public protest had made work relief opportunities for blacks better than they might have been, war in Europe would bring the greatest changes.

Blacks worked in other work relief agencies as well, of course. The National Youth Administration (NYA) and the CCC, for example, provided jobs for young people out of school, and the former also offered financial support to students still enrolled, often enabling them to continue their schooling. In 1938–39, some 3,083 black adolescents, 18 percent of the total, received aid from the city's NYA. Again, the personal beliefs of the director affected black placements. The national head of the NYA, Aubrey Williams, and Mary McLeod Bethune, head of a special Negro Division, insisted that local administrators consider black candidates equally with whites. Nationwide in the NYA, 40 percent of black work-study students held professional or semi-professional positions. Until external needs for labor proved irresistible, equal opportunity for blacks in work relief seemed to depend on the outspokenness of blacks and the sympathy of those with administrative control.

The federal government certainly proved itself more responsive to the interests of the black community than it had ever been before. The creation of a Civil Rights Section in the Justice Department by the Attorney General in 1939 and the appointment in 1937 of the first black federal judge, William Hastie, are two examples. By 1941, blacks were a higher proportion of government workers (excluding the WPA) than they were of the general population.[63] Still, local custom and the widespread belief in black inferiority ensured that well-intentioned rules would by no means eliminate discriminatory practices.

"Rescued Thousands . . . from Despair"

Despite the undisputed fact that not all eligible black home relief clients received WPA placement and that the placements were generally menial, Harlemites as a group did benefit tremendously from work relief programs. Relief jobs, however inappropriate to their skill level, restored to many some sense of self-sufficiency that had been lacking in the years of fruitless searching for work.

Not only did the WPA and the PWA provide jobs and income, the projects themselves improved the lives of Harlem residents. PWA workers erected a four and a half million dollar public housing project: the Harlem River Houses, which accommodated 574 families, with a nursery, playground, and health facilities. The city's 1937 school budget included two new school buildings for Harlem to be built by relief workers. According to the yearly WPA reports, workers in Harlem fixed sewers, renovated bathhouses, built a new health clinic, cleaned parks and riverfront areas, and built a new wing for Harlem Hospital, which doubled its capacity.[64] The WPA brought the unemployed and the needy together in its housekeeping program (taken over from the NYUL), which paid approximately 2,000 unemployed women, mostly black, to help poor, ill, elderly, and working families. These women received a one-week training course in marketing, nutrition, and basic nursing, and earned $70 a month. The WPA sought not to retrain women but to bolster existing skills, so it did not prepare them for the higher-status or better-paying jobs that might come in the future. Yet the unemployed received work and thousands of families got needed help.[65]

The Federal Writers' Project's study of Harlem, not surprisingly, praised WPA efforts. While it acknowledged Harlem's "extreme poverty . . . overcrowding, illiteracy, malnutrition, disease and social dislocation," the project said of the WPA's contributions: "It provides assistance to the health centers, operates the Lower Harlem Chest Clinic for Tubercular Diseases, and assigns teachers and recreational directors to church community centers. The WPA Federal Arts Projects conduct various cultural activities," including a Theater Project that ran shows with all-black casts, offering many black actors their first opportunity to play traditionally white roles. Perhaps the most famous of these transferred *Macbeth* to a Haitian setting and starred Jack Carter, Edna Thomas, and Canada Lee. The Arts Project also sponsored performances of plays written by black playwrights, including *Walk Together Chillun* by Frank Wilson, and Rudolph Fisher's *The Conjure Man Dies*. The Federal Writers' Project launched a massive study of the black community in New York and employed dozens of black scholars, students, and writers to investigate such topics as black art; black Jews; the black press; Harlem's economic and religious life; education, housing, and health in the black community; and the impact of relief on blacks. The WPA adult education programs in Harlem employed 127 teachers offering forty-five subjects, from biology to stenography.

Harlemites took full advantage of these opportunities. The WPA estimated that 30,000 participated regularly in at least one of its arts or educational programs. Over 10,000 adults attended classes in English, history, vocational education, or literacy. Another 3,500 children and adults took art classes.

The history of Harlem's WPA art and education programs reveals the deep interest and involvement of the community. As one Federal Writers' Project researcher of Harlem described it:

> Professional workers, artists and laborers united against Harlem's poverty have recognized the relationship of the cultural and economic problems which are a part of its everyday life. With the establishment of the Federal Art Project of the Works Progress Administration, the needs of the Harlem community in this direction were recognized, and free art classes similar to those in other communities throughout the city were established for those unable to pay for private tuition.[66]

The first free art class in Harlem was held in 1934. Immediately popular, classes opened at fifteen centers, mostly in space donated by churches, community centers, the YWCA and YMCA, the New York Urban League building, and schools. At first black artists donated their time; later, the WPA program paid them. The Federal Art and Music Project established a Music and Art Center at 123rd Street and Mt. Morris Park West using "mostly Harlem residents" as teachers. It quickly grew too large for its space and split into the Harlem Community Art Center and the Harlem

Music Center. The Art Center conducted classes for children, teens, and adults, days and evenings. Jacob Lawrence got his start there. In the first year, over a thousand people attended classes in painting, drawing, etching, sculpting, costume design, weaving, and block prints. By 1936, the programs had become so popular that the community-organized Harlem Art Festival at St. Mark's Church and the Uptown Art Laboratory (321 West 136th Street) overflowed those spaces and spilled out onto the street.

That same year Mayor LaGuardia appointed a committee to study art and educational activities in Harlem and to plan programs to meet community needs. The Municipal Art Committee called a meeting of representatives from Harlem institutions and from the departments of Parks, Education, and Housing, from Harlem's libraries and churches, and the YWCA and YMCA. As a result of this and earlier efforts, by 1937 the WPA conducted adult education, recreation, nursery, art, and drama programs at eighty Harlem centers in daily operation. As the chairperson of the committee wrote to the mayor, "I believe that through such cultural activities greater happiness can be brought into the lives of the people . . . and even a great financial saving . . . through occupying the minds and time of the children and adults." "No section of New York City has given greater support to the culture, recreational and vocational projects of the WPA and cooperating agencies than has the district of upper Manhattan," commented the WPA.[67]

Even in art, blacks had to fight for equality; but in this case the issue was satisfactorily resolved:

It was the Emergency Work Bureau artists who brought a real problem to the congregation of the Church of St. Benedict the Moor, colored. They painted a new ceiling for the church. The congregation wanted a decoration of angels, and a dispute arose as to whether they should be white or colored. After some feeling and many arguments, the question was happily settled and now there is a ceiling filled with clusters of colored and white angels.

It would be interesting to discover whether the angels were in separate (but equal) or integrated clusters.

The WPA supported and staffed not only art and education projects, but other local service programs as well. Nine recreational centers offered organized play in areas off the busy streets for Harlem children after school and during the summers, while several WPA nurseries cared for younger children for up to six hours a day. Several of these programs provided lunch and snacks for their charges, as did the public schools.[68] This not only provided nutrition for hungry youngsters, but helped parents stretch meager budgets a bit farther. The WPA also provided staff to private agencies, many of which served Harlem. In this the WPA made perhaps its greatest contribution to the poor, because it allowed those agencies to expand their programs without additional expense.

Public relief also contributed to Harlem in a subtler but nonetheless crucial way. Evidence suggests that however meager the payments, relief helped keep families together. The number of children with living parents who were accepted by the state for care in orphanages or foster-care programs declined once the New Deal began.

Perhaps facilities were already at capacity and the Department of Public Welfare (DPW) therefore became more stringent in evaluating applications. More likely, however, relief provided the funds for needy families to remain intact. In 1929 and 1930, the department accepted approximately 40 percent of all applications to place children under state care. By 1933, with the onset of the New Deal, and no announced change in orphanage policy, both the number applying and the proportion accepted dropped.

The number of applications declined because of relief, according to the DPW. Of course, declining applications might also have been due to the increasing difficulty of acceptance. This seems unlikely, as the proportion accepted did not fluctuate that drastically, and parents using this as a last resort would be too desperate to be deterred by odds. The DPW itself reported "no further institutions for the general care of dependent children are needed," and in fact some could be closed. Of those who did apply, the department rejected a higher proportion than before 1933 because the increased availability of home relief made it possible for parents to keep their children with them. In fact, it became departmental policy not to accept children for institutionalization if the family was eligible for home relief unless the home situation warranted it. Thus New Deal funds enabled more families to remain intact and not turn to the DPW. It also prompted the agency to accept fewer of those who did apply. As a result of both factors, commitment numbers remained at lower levels throughout the remainder of the decade. The proportion of non-orphaned children committed because of the family's "unemployment" or "insufficient funds" fell by half after 1934. As a New York State Department of Welfare report put it:

> The small ratio of increase in child dependency during the year [up 3.2 percent from 1931–32] suggests, when considered in connection with the rapid development of relief measures, that these measures have been largely successful in forestalling the break-up of families and the consequent necessity of caring for a largely increased number of children in institutions or foster homes.

Aid from the various welfare programs "has kept destitute families together," the Governor's Commission on Unemployment Relief claimed. The WPA Advisory Council credited the WPA with having "rescued thousands of persons from despair, . . . it has made the continuation of some kind of home life possible for them."[69] Of course the DPW had in some sense mandated that "rescue" by denying relief families the option of commitment.

Private Agencies

Voluntarism as well as public relief played a large role in the lives of poor blacks and whites. For Harlem these private agency services proved especially crucial, yet it was in their dealings with racial questions that most private groups showed their limitations. First, not all charities operated in Harlem, or served blacks. This meant that the neediest community actually received less help than the others. Second, except for the Charity Organization Society, where blacks made up almost a third of all cases, most organizations served blacks far less actively than whites, the former constituting perhaps a tenth of their caseloads. Third, most private agencies preferred to maintain the racial status quo rather than challenge segregation and discrimination openly. The real limits to their services came from an unthinking racism. Hiring practices and governance structures illuminate the point. The Colored Orphan Asylum noted in 1944 that "until the past few years there have been no Negro women on the [all-female] board" and that "prior to 1937 all professional jobs were held by white workers." The Children's Aid Society permitted its black workers and its sole black supervisor to work only with black charges. Its board was also completely white during the Depression.[70]

The city-wide charities that served Harlem did meet a multitude of needs as they had before the New Deal. Some, like the Association for Improving the Condition of the Poor (AICP) and the Charity Organization Society (COS), continued to provide financial aid to the city's needy (though public relief had brought the size of their caseloads down). The proportion of clients who were black rose, as it did on public relief rolls. The grants of these agencies were little more generous than public aid: in 1940 the Community Service Society (the newly merged AICP and COS) paid an average of $26 per month, per family, to those receiving no other aid. New York Catholic Charities paid $30. Agencies operating under the auspices of the Russell Sage Foundation paid $24. The Jewish Social Service Association offered up to $43, but few blacks claimed that religious affiliation.

Most private agencies, though, stopped their economic support programs, leaving it to public relief, and instead expanded their non-financial services, including visiting nurses, clinics, homeless shelters, orphanages, and inexpensive rooms in "respectable" buildings for working women. As the AICP put it, in 1933,

> government assumed the main responsibility for unemployment relief. This "encouraged" in New York City a close integration of public and private services and at the same time enabled private agencies to resume their special, intensive and individualized work.[71]

Perhaps because private citizens now expected government to bear the welfare burden, the number of philanthropic organizations did not increase. Except for the number of day nurseries in Manhattan, which grew from sixty-one in 1927 to eighty-two a decade later (falling to seventy-seven in 1940), as many agencies of each type closed as opened in the 1930s. Three fewer tuberculosis hospitals and sanitaria operated in 1937 than did a decade earlier. The number of agencies for dependent children fell in the same period from seventy-six to sixty-six.

Even the AICP and the COS, because of their sharply lowered number of financial support cases, turned more of their efforts toward service programs. They provided medical services and convalescent care, ran homes for the elderly, offered preschool programs and health education, and provided shelters for the homeless. The Community Service Society, committed to serving people's "physical, emotional, and social needs," ran an employment service, a nursing service, and a medical clinic, sent children to summer camp, and counseled troubled families. The total number "under care" (that is, receiving some sort of aid) hovered around 19,000 throughout the decade.[72]

Many of these organizations had already established branches in Harlem, including the AICP and the COS, the Children's Aid Society, the New York Tuberculosis and Health Association, the YMCA and YWCA, and the Henry Street Visiting Nurses. They simply continued or expanded their services. In 1940 the Community Service Society, for example, boasted ten case workers for Harlem alone, and organized twenty-five black women to study the needs of Harlem families so the organization could better serve them. Club Caroline, a Phelps-Stokes Fund residence, housed "50 colored girls." Catholic charities served blacks and whites of all faiths, and "discrimination is not obviously significant anywhere," as a WPA Writers' Program researcher concluded. The New York City Colored Mission continued its programs of day care, vocational education, and shelter.[73] Nearby churches such as the Cathedral of Saint John the Divine (on 110th Street) and Riverside Church hosted meetings and provided services to the community, from job placement bureaus to food kitchens. The YMCA and YWCA offered vocational courses and other social services.

Black groups continued to supplement these services with aid of their own. The NYUL, Katy Ferguson House, and White Rose Mission managed still to offer vocational training, temporary lodgings, and other services that were provided inadequately by public or white private agencies. The Abyssinian Baptist and St. Philip's churches built homes for the aged. And of course black churches, some with new WPA-funded staff, continued their social programs, providing food, shelter, day care, help in obtaining relief, job referrals, and so on.

Thus, in addition to eleven Home Relief Bureau offices, thirty-three public schools and libraries, and other municipal agency branches, Harlem also had privately run health clinics, child care centers, temporary lodgings, educational, vocational and art programs, and children's shelters.[74] Staffed in many cases by WPA workers as well as volunteers, these private agencies offered opportunities and services that met needs of both a financial and a non-financial nature.

Perhaps the most dramatic contributions of private relief agencies in Harlem involved children. Examining the largest programs reveals both the magnitude of these services and their ultimate limitations. It also illuminates the impact of the relief programs on needy black children in the Depression and the importance of government funding for such private efforts.

Harlem's youth had a variety of needs. The lack of parks made safe play areas a necessity. Working parents needed supervision for their children. Many youngsters, like their parents, did not get enough to eat. Children whose parents had died or who could no longer support them needed institutional or foster care, but most such programs in the city refused to accept blacks.

Traditional programs of shelter and recreation reached thousands of needy black children. Day nurseries, though small, operated widely in Harlem. Many were run by community members who received money both from local donors and from government agencies, and whose staff consisted primarily of black female volunteers and WPA workers.

Nurseries and child care facilities varied in services, price, and size. The Hope Day Nursery on West 133rd Street served children as young as four months and up to age six. It accepted thirty-four children at a time, who paid 25 cents a day and received care from volunteers and WPA and NYA workers. St. Benedict's Nursery, though Catholic, was open to all black children, and cost $1.50 a week in 1935. Slightly more expensive, the Gleener Club and Nursery charged $2 a week, but served the children two meals a day. The black women who ran Utopia Children's House on West 130th Street offered their services free of charge because they believed poor families could not afford private day care. Only four workers there received a salary, contributed by the WPA, the Board of Education, and the NYA. To give some sense of its scope, in 1937 the UCH served approximately 150 children a day, offering preschoolers all-day care, and children aged six to twelve before-school and after-school care. The House served 85,000 lunches a year, paid for with federal and municipal funds; offered art, singing, dancing, and crafts classes; and gave away shoes and clothing.[75] Government aid proved crucial to these small programs' ability to sustain a high level of community assistance.

Other, larger organizations, usually run by whites, offered child care along with other services. The largest private institution serving Harlem youth, the Children's Aid Society (CAS), had renovated four buildings in that neighborhood by 1935, two for the Boys Club use, two for the Girls'. Facilities included a medical and dental clinic. Nurseries and kindergartens looked after young children of working parents. A visiting housekeeper service sent women into the homes of ill mothers to cook and clean. If this did not succeed in keeping a family intact, the CAS provided temporary foster care for the children until the home situation stabilized.

Each year approximately 2,500 boys and girls used these Harlem clubs (which offered not only recreation but nutritious lunches), and almost the same number received medical and dental exams. Over 3,000 youngsters took advantage of the playground facilities each year, while older children studied trades there. In 1940 the CAS announced plans to open a new, larger Boys Club on 134th Street, with the same medical, dental, vocational, and recreational services.[76]

The CAS recognized the problems facing Harlem's children: "Incomes are low, living conditions are wretched, and it is no wonder that many young boys especially are committed to temporary shelters because their homes are not fit and there are few institutions to which they may go." Yet despite its real contributions to Harlem, the CAS's response to these problems remained traditional. "Realizing full well that Harlem's basic problem is economic," its counseling service advised young men to pursue time-honored black employment opportunities. Therefore its new Boys Clubs taught "useful trades" such as auto repair, building maintenance, pressing, tailoring, cooking, waiting tables, and carpentry.[77]

The CAS explained its policies in terms of practicality. Its counseling and employment center, established in 1936, advised black youths to train for traditionally black jobs since they would be more likely to find employment:

> Because of racial and educational handicaps from which the Negro has suffered, many of the present generation of young people are training for fields in which there are still few openings for members of their race. Understandable as is their ambition to compete

on an equal basis in all fields, it must be guided by the practical aspects of the case or it will result in heartbreak for many. . . . There is little correlation between the types of training selected by Negro boys and the types of positions open to them in the commercial field.

The CAS preferred to consider the immediate financial interest of its charges rather than assist in the struggle to break down racial barriers in employment. When it did offer training in non-traditional skills, it reported: "It has been found practically impossible . . . to place any number of these boys in the jobs for which they are trained." The CAS examined figures from the New York State Employment Service for Juniors, Harlem Branch, and found that "90 percent of the junior placements in Harlem are in messenger work and service jobs such as dish washing, boot blacking, domestic help, etc."[78] By setting policy based on the findings of an organization that refused to demand equal hiring opportunities for white and black, the CAS helped perpetuate the segregated labor market under the guise of being realistic.

The CAS did this, not as an unexamined act of discrimination, but in recognition of economic relations in a crisis. Certainly it was not the only organization to rely on traditional assumptions about African-Americans' economic role. For example, local WPA officials urged black women to consider household service, "a field which is uncrowded and wherein greater material rewards than many suspect are available to the trained worker."

These CAS programs met an important need. Still, for an organization to determine, as the CAS did, that "there is ample proof that the likes and dislikes of the Negro lad, his tastes, his ambitions, normal virtues, weaknesses, susceptibility to temptation and delinquency, are practically identical with boys of other racial groups" and yet to provide non-identical opportunities, was to do the children an injustice. To the thousands of boys and girls finding shelter, food, and safe recreation there, the CAS provided an invaluable service. What it did not do was struggle to break down the social conditions that created such hardship to begin with.

The correct balance between short-term pragmatism and longer-term equality of opportunity was difficult for many welfare agencies to strike. The Mayor's Official Committee for the Relief of the Unemployed and the Mayor's Committee on Welfare, for example, donated some of the funds they had privately raised in 1938 to "camps for children—colored." Rather than come up with ways to compel all-white camps to accept blacks, these groups chose to support black camps, perpetuating existing racial divisions. While this allowed more black children to go to camp in the short run (if the city had fought a protracted battle to get black children to white camps perhaps none would have gone for several years), still, it meant black children would never enjoy the better-endowed facilities of the white camps.

Similarly, the Children's Aid Society, rather than integrating its summer camps, bought land upstate in New Paltz for a camp for black children. The society argued that the camp, Walkill, was "one of the few organizations for summer vacations for Negro boys and girls," but it did not explain why it would not place black and white children together. Most of its services were segregated, in fact. For black dependent children (orphans and others whose parents could not care for them), the CAS ran a cottage within a larger CAS institution in Valhalla, New York, and placed black children in foster homes "in neighborhoods where they will be accepted." Certainly such services were critically important. In 1932, its first year of providing help for black dependent children, forty-five came to the Valhalla cottage and fourteen entered foster homes. Five year later, sixty-five lived in Valhalla and forty-one received foster care. The CAS's strength and that of groups like it lay more in fully utilizing existing community potential than in remodeling structures or rethinking traditional assumptions. These groups had the ability to make a significant difference in the provision and allocation of services, so long as such services did not challenge the prevailing assumptions about racial segregation.[79]

The burdens of the Depression pushed most agencies into short-term solutions, especially those caring for black children dependent on state support. The pressing problem of where to place black dependent children was not new, but the number of homeless and temporarily homeless children had escalated dramatically after the onset of the Depression. The CAS reported it had its hands full meeting the "unprecedented demand for help."[80] The problem was that the city did not run services of its own, argued a Children's Court report, and therefore could not mandate more places for black children:

> Neither the State nor the City maintains any institution or placing-out agency for the care of normal dependent and neglected children of any race, creed or color. Such children are boarded by the City in institutions or with agencies operating under religious auspices.

Although "the facilities for the care of Protestant neglected and dependent Negro children have more than doubled in the past seven years, chiefly in the direction of foster home placement," the facilities remained unequal to the task, and the Children's Court cited figures from the emergency children's shelters, the Society for the Prevention of Cruelty to Children, to support its accusation. In 1933, a white child placed in the SPCC could expect placement in a more permanent setting in just over two weeks. Black children had to wait close to four weeks for a place to become available. The Valhalla cottage accepted "dependent Negro boys between the ages of 12 and 16" because virtually no other private institutions served black boys of that age. Black Protestant non-delinquent girls over age twelve had absolutely nowhere to go, and had to be sent to Catholic institutions or to those for delinquents. Of thirty-four Protestant agencies for dependent and neglected children, only seven took blacks. None for delinquents took blacks under the age of twelve. The Colored Orphan Asylum, the largest organization accepting black dependent children, had doubled its pre-Depression capacity in response to rising demand for space, but this was still not enough.[81] The Children's Court continued to protest the lack of facilities throughout the decade. The Welfare Council echoed these sentiments: "The facilities for care in the Negro group fall far short of those provided for the white and far short of what is needed in relation to the size of the problem."

The desperate need for facilities was due solely to discrimination. As the Department of Public Welfare pointed out in 1936: "Some plan must . . . be devised for improving both the quantity and the quality of existing institutional work for Negro children. As now carried on, this work is inadequate and unsatisfactory." Such a plan was obviously not devised; as the following year the department repeated itself, adding that while "the facilities for institutional and boarding care for Negro children are very inadequate," for children city-wide no further institutional expansion was necessary. That year, the COA was forced to stop accepting new admissions because of overcrowding. In other words, space existed for any child who required it, so long as the child was white.[82]

The need for an outside solution was pressing because the black community could not afford to establish its own services: "The impossibility of any financial reserves within the Negro group itself . . . [prohibits any] provision of privately financed social services," argued the Welfare Council. In fact, it continued, this poverty created the need for those institutions in the first place. In other words, if the community were wealthy enough to afford private care for all its dependent children, fewer children would need such services.

The characteristics of children committed to state care attest to the validity of this conclusion about the poverty of Harlem residents, but they also suggest some of the benefits of relief. The family status of African-American children remanded to the Colored Orphan Asylum did not change in the 1930s. Both in 1925 and a decade later, approximately one-fifth of the residents actually had no known parents living. Just over a third still had one parent ("half-orphans"), while half came to the COA with two living parents.[83] If relief had not provided minimal family maintenance, presumably the proportion of non-orphans committed to state care would have risen.

What did worsen during the Depression was the physical and mental condition of the children committed. "The depression increased the number of children coming to the Asylum from homes where they had been in contact with cases of tuberculosis. Many of them were undernourished. . . . The children invariably come from broken or insecure homes and therefore have many serious emotional and mental handicaps."

The speed at which the COA returned children to families or found foster placements declined as hardship continued to spread in the black community. The average child at the start of the Depression stayed with the COA for just over two and a half years. This figure rose by about four months annually. The increasing length of stay suggests a worsening of conditions in the black community during the Depression. It may also have reflected families' greater ability to remain intact once they received relief money. Only the most desperate cases (who would therefore remain longer) needed state care.[84]

Despite the increased poverty of African-American families and the rising demand for space in child care agencies for black children, no other private organizations opened their doors to blacks during the Depression. In 1939 the Domestic Relations Court reported that conditions were no better than those it had complained of a decade earlier. None of the agencies accepting blacks had vacancies, including the Colored Orphan Asylum. The New York City black population had more than doubled since 1920, yet few new agencies since that year had agreed to accept blacks. The same was true for delinquents: the first institution for delinquent black children between ages eight and twelve opened only in 1937.[85]

This crisis prompted a group of concerned citizens to ask the Children's Aid Society in 1938 to supervise a new city-wide program of foster care for dependent black children, modeled on its own smaller program. The Service Bureau for Negro Children opened in May of 1939. Although the existing government-sponsored agency, the State Charities Aid Association Child Placing and Adoption Committee, had succeeded in finding only eighteen to twenty black foster homes a year, the Service Bureau found places for seventy-seven in its first twelve months. By 1940, it served 209 black children. "The Bureau has shown that economically stable homes with intelligent and understanding Negro foster parents can be found," reported the CAS in its annual report.[86]

This did not solve the problem of institutional care. The courts and the CAS relied on moral appeals to persuade other white institutions to accept black children, and they were rarely successful. Meanwhile, the need continued to rise: from 1938 to 1940, as the numbers of white children under public care declined, the number of black children needing care rose slightly.

The COA also consistently argued for other private agencies to extend service to blacks, but to no avail. As late as 1940 the COA's executive secretary complained:

> During the past year at the Colored Orphan Asylum we have been continuously conscious of the insufficient community resources for the care of Protestant Negro children who must be removed from their own homes either by the Children's Court or by the Department of Welfare. This Association has exerted its best efforts to perform its share of the task, to the extent of making heavy financial sacrifices. This has not been enough. The foster care needs of the largest Negro community in the world are too great for the financial resources available for this work. The need can be met only through wider public support.
>
> Our position as the oldest and largest voluntary agency in this field of service imposes a challenging responsibility to dramatize this need to those able to help. Further, we must apply what we have learned in more than a century of experience toward the development of a coordinated program for the future.

Not until 1942 did anyone seek to use legal means to compel a change in the racial policies of these agencies.[87]

The COA's statement reveals a clear recognition of the needs of the community, yet demonstrates the limits of voluntarism. Private relief agencies provided crucial services for the community, yet they were limited not only by lack of funds but by traditional views that left them incapable of initiating deep or meaningful changes in the larger social order.

Public and private relief agencies served a population in desperate need. Yet their good intentions were often limited by both internal and external constraints. Confronted with a huge demand but limited by finances, agencies imposed strict rules for eligibility and provided the most meager of allotments. Private organizations expanded their programs and fund-raising, but in their pursuit of solutions to the Depression's economic hardships most continued to rely on traditional assumptions about the role of relief and the place of the relief recipient.

Because the black community was the worst-off economically, it needed relief services the most desperately, and therefore suffered from these limitations the most acutely. Furthermore, the question of race brought additional problems. Many private agencies flatly refused to serve the black community at all. Others perpetuated the racist structure of the existing social and economic order. Despite agitation in the black community, for example, job placement and vocational training for Harlem continued to stress traditionally black jobs in domestic service. Despite a dramatic rise in the need for facilities for dependent black children, no one sought to compel reluctant agencies to accept them, only to persuade them by appeal.

Even in public relief agencies, which had explicit rules proscribing discrimination, blacks often received unequal and inferior treatment. Neither regulations nor well-intentioned administrators could prevent the circumventing of the rules by those practicing discrimination, whether intentionally or not. Thus blacks were less often given the benefit of the doubt in relief investigations and found it more difficult to secure appropriate employment either within these agencies or on work relief jobs. Even the standardization of relief practices actually penalized blacks. Home relief, under the guise of objectivity, provided blacks and whites with the same stipends, when racial prejudice had locked blacks into higher-priced neighborhoods.

Black agencies responded to these problems both by addressing the community's most pressing needs themselves and by protesting unfairness whenever it occurred. Thus these groups provided funding and facilities for day care, health, and educational services, while black activists demanded more jobs and better services from public programs and worked with private ones to achieve the same ends.

In part because of the periodic successes of these groups in obtaining more resources, in part because any help was better than nothing, and in part because the black community had had so little to start with, Harlem in fact received tremendous benefits from relief services, public and private. Over half of all blacks in New York received money at some point in the Depression. Relief saved from starvation and eviction those with no other recourse. Since relief recipients usually had families and often took in relatives who also faced hard times, this aid provided for far more people than relief statistics alone suggest. The income made it easier for many families to stay together and for children to remain in school (the lack of employment prospects, of course, also helped this decision). Relief brought new roads, buildings, and parks to Harlem. Residents took classes, saw plays, and sent their children for special programs, all funded by relief agencies. Public works jobs, however low-paying, offered some sense of self-reliance and financial stability.

Although discrimination did mar the equitable distribution of public relief, New York City proved a surprisingly hospitable place for blacks, particularly because of Mayor LaGuardia and generally fair-minded relief administrators. Here the non-discriminatory pronouncements of men like Harold Ickes and Harry Hopkins were generally obeyed. When they were not, a unified and outspoken community intervened. In the provision of services and in their attempts to minimize racial discrimination, New York's relief agencies compared favorably with agencies elsewhere. Despite both intentional and unintentional discrimination, relief saved lives and provided important services to Harlem.

CHAPTER 7

Mean Streets

Whether on relief or employed in private industry (and most black families experienced both at some point in the Depression), few managed to make ends meet without some sort of extra income. People with little helped those with less; ties of family and community proved strong and durable. Men and women picked up temporary work whenever possible. Families took in lodgers or boarders or moved into the homes of relatives. Many borrowed money from friends or kin or bought groceries on credit from local merchants. Some engaged in illegal activities. A large proportion of Harlem arrests during the Depression were for possession of policy slips, prostitution, and illegal distilling, all income-producing rather than violent crimes. These activities were certainly not new to the 1930s; blacks had been poor before this. But more families resorted to them in the years of the Depression.

One woman's experiences illustrate the available choices—and their limitations. Thirza Johnson was twenty-one years old with three young children. Her husband had worked for the WPA for eighteen months. Despite that income the family could not pay its bills, and Mr. Johnson "tampered with the gas meter." For this he received sixty days in jail. The family had been receiving $5.40 every two weeks to supplement Mr. Johnson's paycheck, but without the WPA income that amount was completely inadequate. The utility companies cut off the gas and the electricity and Mrs. Johnson fell a month behind in paying the rent. When all three children fell ill, she asked her mother to come in from New Jersey to help. Her mother told her employer she needed a few days off to tend to her grandchildren. He fired her. This brought the number in the house to five, but the relief agency refused to increase the family's relief allotment because Mrs. Johnson's mother was not a New York resident. The grocery store gave her no more credit. Completely desperate, Mrs. Johnson turned to the UNIA for aid, and the Home Relief Bureau at last agreed to help.

Families like the Johnsons were so poor they were often forced to choose among necessities. Consumption patterns of Harlem families reveal both their real poverty and the constraints of living in a segregated community. Because of low incomes, African-Americans lived in poor, overcrowded housing, with high disease and death rates, and high crime. Yet, as the preceding chapter showed, the New Deal programs had brought some progress to Harlem as well: health care, for example, improved in the Depression decade, and for a few, new public housing became available.

Certainly black Harlem was not one homogeneous neighborhood. Within it lived population clusters divided by income and nativity. On some blocks only a few families received relief; on others, a majority did. Particular streets hosted the grocery stores, benefit societies, or restaurants of different national groups. As Vernal Williams, lawyer for the Consolidated Tenants League, explained:

> Why, every one of us have our own standards of living. We don't all live together. Just as you have Riverside, West End and Park Avenues, we have the same standard among our people, and you won't find that doctors [are] willing to go to the cheaper quarters along where the longshoremen live. . . . [To live in the Dunbar apartments, for example] you had to be a doctor or a wealthy business man or work in the Post Office.

Nevertheless, virtually no family was immune from the Depression's ravages, and all shared both the burdens of life in a discriminatory society and the strengths found in networks of support within the black community.[1]

Making Ends Meet

The most important first step for impoverished Harlem families was to supplement their earnings. Many families in the New Deal era turned to the long-standing practice in black communities of taking in lodgers. Perhaps because everyone was poor, the number of lodgers in black families in this period did not appear to bear a relation to any economic consideration. In the Harlem sample of the 1935 Bureau of Labor Statistics study, neither the family's earnings nor its expenditures provided a reliable predictor of whether or not that family would take in lodgers. The decision did depend on family size to some extent; families with many children seldom had lodgers.

Almost half of all black families surveyed by the BLS had one or two lodgers, whose rent provided, on average, an extra $199 a year to the host family's income. Blacks took lodgers far more often than did whites. While 6 percent of all white families took in at least one lodger, 29 percent of the city's black families did, and this income constituted a larger portion of total black families' earnings. Both black and white figures exceeded pre-Depression rates. Even in the sections of Harlem where the wealthiest lived—"Striver's Row" (136th to 139th streets between Seventh and Eighth avenues) and "Sugar Hill" (145th to 155th streets along Edgecombe Avenue and St. Nicholas Place and Avenue)—many families had to take in lodgers to help pay the rent.[2] The taking in of lodgers was thus a widespread tactic for supplementing wages.

Black families in Harlem as elsewhere also turned to non-financial solutions, such as swapping and borrowing, and relied on the generosity of those temporarily better off. Evidence of these sorts of alternative economic strategies comes from many sources. Relief agencies, for example, demanded from applicants an accounting of expenses and income for the previous twelve months. Other agencies, such as the Bureau of Labor Statistics, investigated current earnings of non-relief families. Private organizations conducted their own studies. Of the eighty-one Harlem families in the BLS sample, sixteen reported receiving gifts, and one a loan, from friends or relatives. Three others had picked up odd jobs and thirteen received "other income" from interest, "pool game," or sickness benefits from a lodge. If the number of families receiving money from gifts, loans, insurance, winnings, odd jobs, and lodgers are added together, over half of the BLS survey families supplemented their earnings over the year, with an average of $153 per family with such added income.[3] Families turning to the Unemployed Unit of the Universal Negro Improvement Association (UNIA) for help in obtaining relief also reported a heavy reliance on such means of supplementing their incomes.

Several families told of moving in with friends or relatives or receiving economic help from them. Both Nathan Campbell and Sarah Johnson told the UNIA that their family received money from friends. Minnie Jones complained she had to borrow money from her employer for food. In every income category, almost twice as many blacks as whites in New York City reported contributing to the support of relatives in 1935. Many men and women worked in exchange for free rent. Madeline Bright served as superintendent of an apartment building in return for lodgings. This, too, was common practice; one-fifth of single black women not living with families surveyed in Philadelphia, and two-fifths of such women in Chicago, engaged in this sort of exchange as well.[4]

The proportion of all black families relying on these practices cannot be precisely documented. But impressionistic evidence suggests such interactions were commonplace. Francie, the protagonist of Louise Meriwether's Harlem-based novel, *Daddy Was a Number Runner,* borrows from her neighbor:

[Mother] gave me a weak cup of tea.
"We got any sugar?"
"Borrow some from Mrs. Caldwell."
I got a chipped cup from the cupboard and going to the dining-room window, I knocked at our neighbor's window-pane. The Caldwells lived in the apartment next door and our dining rooms faced each other. . . . Maude came to the window.
"Can I borrow a half cup of sugar?" I asked.
She took the cup and disappeared, returning in a few minutes with it almost full.
"Y'all got any bread?" she asked. "I need one more piece to make a sandwich."
"Maude wants to borrow a piece of bread," I told Mother.
"Give her two slices," Mother said.

Loften Mitchell remembered: "In this climate [Harlem] the cooking of chitterlings brought a curious neighbor to the door. 'Mrs. Mitchell, you cooking chitterlings? I thought you might need a little cornbread to go with 'em.' A moment later a West Indian neighbor appeared with rice and beans. Another neighbor followed with some beer to wash down the meal. What started as a family supper developed into a building party." As another contemporary wrote, "The people [of Harlem] are the kindest and most sympathetic people that can be found. They will take one into the home and share everything there except the mate or sweetheart."[5]

Some turned to illegal activities such as bootlegging and numbers running. Between 1931 and 1935, over half of all black arrests in Harlem were for "possession of policy slips," and police charged three-quarters of all black females arrested with vagrancy and prostitution. One woman included in a Welfare Council study explained that she earned money from "rent parties and home brew sales" and rented out rooms in her apartment for "immoral" purposes. The investigator suspected another family of earning money in this fashion as well, but that family did not admit it. Several people reported altering gas pipes and electrical wiring to avoid paying utilities; arrests for "tampering with gas meter" or similar offenses dotted the Harlem precinct records.

> Our electricity had been cut off for months for nonpayment . . . [explained Francie] so Daddy had made the jumper. . . . I took the metal wire from behind the box where we hid it, and opening the box, I inserted the two prongs behind the fuse the way Daddy had showed me. . . . Daddy said almost everybody in Harlem used a jumper.

Lillian Holmes, to document her need for relief, told the UNIA how she earned money in the past. For several years, she reported, she had been "engaged in the illegitimate business of *manufacturing liquor*" (UNIA's emphasis): six gallons of 100-proof alcohol a week. Her living costs, including manufacturing, came to $199.90 a month, while she earned approximately $208. In April 1937, however, there was a *"RAID"* (UNIA emphasis), at which time she applied for relief but was rejected. Paroled, the UNIA record concludes, she "return[ed] to making 'hot stuff.'" The record does not reveal whether the UNIA persuaded the relief agency in question to accept Ms. Holmes or whether she continued her life of crime.[6]

Income-producing strategies did not add enough income for most families to live comfortably. They had to budget carefully and often deprive themselves of one necessity to afford another. The widespread poverty of Harlem and its character as a segregated community were reflected in consumption decisions made by black families. High rents required large portions of family earnings, and family size determined the amount spent on food and other household goods. The amount families set aside for such items as recreation and personal care, by contrast, varied according to personal decision. Consumption decisions therefore depended on many factors, some beyond the control of the family. How Harlemites chose to spend their money reflected all of these considerations and demonstrates the extreme poverty of the area.

The average family in the Harlem sample of the Bureau of Labor Statistics study spent $548 per person for the year. Both income and the size of the family, of course, affected this figure. Not unexpectedly, the poorer the family, the more per-person expenditures depended on the number of members; as more people sit down to eat a small pie, each slice becomes smaller. At higher income levels, families spent with fewer constraints; a larger family could spend as much per person as a smaller family and simply save less.

The typical blue-collar and clerical non-relief black family earned $1,446 and spent $1,459, compared with white earnings of $1,745 and expenditures of $1,839. On average, black families spent just under a third of their total expenditures, $450, on food and almost as much, $417, on rent. White families, by contrast, spent approximately 40 percent of their budget on food and 20 percent on rent. Controlling for income yields similar results. Black families at each economic and occupational level spent a lower proportion of their total income on food, and a higher proportion on rent, than did comparable whites. Blacks at each level spent more than whites on other housing costs, personal care, and clothing, but less on medical care.[7]

Rent was influenced less strongly by family size than were other items, presumably because rent was high everywhere in Harlem. In fact, although black families spent less per person than did whites of the same family size (because they earned less), they paid more for housing. On the other hand, rental costs did vary within the black community. In absolute terms, the poorer the family, the less it spent on rent. On average, black families from each income level, whether foreign-born or native-born, spent the same proportion of their income on housing. The Mayor's Commission on Conditions in Harlem reported that in a study it conducted of 675 black families on two Central Harlem blocks most paid close to half their total income for rent. On the better-off block, the average family brought in $88 a month (or $1,059 a year) and paid $36.69 for rent. On the poorer block, families earned, on average, $70 a month and paid $25 for rent. Though rents everywhere in Harlem were high, families moved frequently in the Depression in search of lower housing costs. The average family applying to the UNIA for help in 1937 had moved between four and seven times since 1929.[8]

Blacks spent less of their total income on food than whites at the same economic level, in part because their families were smaller and in part because so much of their income was used for rent. But food was costly; food prices did rise during the Depression, and they were higher in Harlem. Between 1934 and 1935, for example, food prices rose 11 percent. In the later year, a dozen eggs cost approximately 40 cents in most city neighborhoods, and 42 cents in Harlem. Flour cost 6 cents a pound; cornmeal 7 cents; again slightly higher in Harlem. Milk cost 13 cents a quart, potatoes 2 cents a pound, and carrots 6 cents a bunch. Meat was more expensive. Bacon cost 37 cents a pound; ham 29 cents city-wide, and more in Harlem. *Amsterdam News* columnist Roi Ottley noted that food prices in Harlem were "considerably higher" than elsewhere in the city during the Depression. "For every dollar spent on food the Negro housewife has to spend at least six cents in excess of what the housewife in any other comparable section is required to pay." Adam Clayton Powell, Jr., claimed "foodstuffs were 17 percent above the general level." The Reverend Mr. Garner of Grace Church complained: "Our food in Harlem is higher than the food we can get elsewhere. Food on the east side is much cheaper than food in the immediate neighborhood." The Department of Markets received more complaints from Harlem than from anywhere else about unfair costs and "shortweight practices."[9]

Black families spent slightly more on clothing, household furnishings, and personal care than comparably impoverished whites possibly because, poor for a longer time, they could not continue to defer those needs. For medical care, white spending exceeded black in both amount and percentage of income. For both races, families with lower incomes were less likely to have annual medical exams or to go to a private doctor rather than a free clinic. Many poor families deferred dental visits.

The poorest spent less on every item in the budget than the general pool of blacks did. In fact, in the Harlem sample the poorest blacks had so little disposable income that the amount allotted for food did not change, regardless of family size. With more members a family might vary the quality of food it bought (less meat, for example, and more vegetables), but it could not afford to increase its overall food budget.[10]

A British West Indian family of six in the BLS survey typifies this frugality. The mother worked intermittently as a general helper in a laundry for $3 a day. The father, a painter's helper, worked all fifty-two weeks that year but earned $22 per week for six months, and only $19 a week during the next six months. The two adult sons living at home worked only sporadically, one as a porter in a tailor shop and the other as a helper in the meat market. Two other sons attended high school. This family reported monthly expenditures of $40 for rent, $10.87 for "household operation," $14.72 for clothing, and $54.08 for food. They held their other expenses to a minimum: less than $15 for "furnishings and equipment" for the entire year, $39 for recreation, and the same amount for "personal care." Six dollars that year went for medical care, $4 for education, and $4 for "community welfare"—even in poverty, the family helped others in need. Despite their best efforts and a $15 gift or loan, the family reported debts of $55 at the end of the year.[11]

This family was by no means unique. Most of the Harlem families in the survey did not break even; fully three-quarters of them ended the year with some small deficit. Interestingly, the percentage of families with deficits did not decline as income rose. Rather, most families appeared to live at a level slightly above their actual income. Presumably, these families had all suffered a decline in their usual earnings and had not yet adjusted completely.

Still, for each income level, the average deficit of white families far exceeded that of black. Ninety-five percent of all Harlem black families in the survey either overspent by less than 5 percent of their total income or actually saved money. Only two families exceeded their income by more than 10 percent. The average debt for whites who had debts was $265, or 15 percent of their total expenditures, according to the BLS city-wide study of wage earners; while for blacks it was $115, or 8 percent. Either whites were even less accustomed to a low income, or they viewed their economic reversals as temporary and planned to rely on credit until the crisis passed. Presumably, black families also found it more difficult to obtain credit, which kept their average deficits lower. This may help account for the greater proportion of blacks on relief, and the fact that they had to turn to it more quickly than whites did after losing their jobs. Gunnar Myrdal suggested that blacks were able to live closer to their incomes because more often than whites they made their own clothes and food and did their own laundry. This, he noted, made more work for black women, who were also more likely than white women to work outside the home.

Poverty alone could not account for indebtedness, since, according to the Harlem sample, black families at all income levels were equally likely to fall into debt. Nor could family size: among non-relief families, those with deficits were no larger than those without. In other words, families of all types used debt as one way to stretch tight budgets. This did not imply extravagance, however, since those families with surpluses and those with debts spent approximately the same amount for food, rent, and all other items. In practical terms, then, any wage-earning family could find itself in the red. An emergency need would probably force a family into debt since virtually all lived close to the edge of their income level. As Myrtle Pollard explained, impoverished Harlemites got along by buying one thing at a time. If someone needed a new coat, the rent would have to go unpaid that month.[12] When this strategy failed, a family could find itself forced to turn to relief.

The Bennett family illustrates the preceding discussion: the all-too-common pattern of economic decline, a cut in consumption, debt, and finally application for relief. David Bennett, a thirty-three-year-old laborer, and his wife and two children lived on his WPA wages until January of 1937, when he received his last $14.46 check. He had found work as a longshoreman and earned $88 that month. He also supplemented this with $32 in tips he received as a "helper" at the Washington Market. That month, despite $15 in medical bills, the family met all its obligations, paying $24 in rent, $37 on food, and an $8 insurance premium. After these costs, plus clothing, utilities, and carfare, there was still something left over for cigarettes and "entertainment." The following month David earned only $66 at the docks and $14 at the market, but the family still managed by cutting food purchases down to $30, paying only half the insurance, and foregoing clothing and "entertainment." The family struggled on this way for a while; David earning between $80 and $110 a month, and everyone spending less.

The third week in August, however, David lost his longshoreman's job, and his wife hired herself out as a domestic worker to two families. One paid her $7 a week, the other $4. By skimping on food they managed again, but September was much worse. With only Mrs. Bennett's wages of $44 and the $12 David earned shining shoes, they eliminated all spending but rent and food (which they had cut again). In October they decided to take in a lodger who paid $3.50 a week. They broke even only by pawning a watch and eight pairs of shoes.

In November, David's wife lost her previous jobs and hired on with two new families. She now earned $4 from one, and $3 from the other. That month the Bennetts went into debt. Food, rent, and utilities cost $65, while David's $12 from shoeshining, his wife's $28, and the lodger's $14 came to only $54. They withdrew money from their Christmas fund in December, but still could only pay half their rent that month. By the new year, they had to accept a loan of $10 and a gift of $3.50 from friends because Mrs. Bennett had again lost her jobs. Now able to afford only $22 for food, and paying no rent or utilities, they applied for public relief. Rejected with no explanation, they took another loan of $15, and turned to the UNIA for help. The file ended with the notation "no food."[13]

Consequences

The constant choosing between necessities or going without, the struggle to maintain a livable income, and the weight of discrimination and segregation resulted in poor housing and health, high crime, and inadequate public facilities in Harlem.

Neither the Depression nor the New Deal lessened the segregation that trapped black families in substandard housing. Rental costs for Harlem residents remained high in the Depression, although absolute costs fell slightly. In 1933, the City Affairs

Committee reported Harlem to have "the worst housing conditions in the city. . . . Negro tenants pay from one percent to twenty percent more of their income for rent than any other group, despite the fact that the income of the Negro family is about 17 percent lower than that of the typical family in any other section of the city." This committee in fact understated the problem. The Neighborhood Health Committee surveyed rental costs in Manhattan in the Depression's early years. It found that while the average Manhattan apartment rented for $44 a month, most in poor areas paid significantly less. In East Harlem, for example, where poor Italians and Puerto Ricans lived, rents averaged $30. In Central Harlem, however, rents never fell below $31 a month, and often ran as high as $70. The average resident of Central Harlem paid $52. The League of Mothers' Clubs found tenement-house blacks paid almost $1 more per room, per month, than comparably poor whites. Thus, for most Harlem residents, rents had not declined much; they were in some cases even higher than pre-Depression rates. Even the Brotherhood of Sleeping Car Porters was forced to resort to rent parties to pay for its offices.[14]

The policies of relief agencies aggravated housing problems. The enormous demand on their limited funds led several to provide no rent payments until eviction was threatened. Landlords learned that the sooner they made such threats the sooner they received overdue rent. Families who did not qualify for aid therefore faced eviction earlier than they otherwise might have. The Communist party, which fought eviction notices in the courts and carried the furniture of evicted families back into their apartments in an effort to stop the process, reported that hundreds of successful evictions occurred each week.[15]

Yet, inexpensive lodgings of good quality remained difficult to find. The interracial, city-wide Association to Promote Proper Housing for Girls, in conjunction with the Phelps-Stokes Fund, had established an inexpensive boarding house in Harlem for "colored working girls of good character" in 1928. It was the third such residence in the city; the first for blacks. The women who set it up did so explicitly because Harlem "girls, and in fact all tenants, have been exploited on account of their color." Harlem women helped plan and staff Club Caroline, named for the Phelps-Stokes Fund's founder. It could not solve the housing shortage. By 1931, this residence, filled to capacity, served only eighty Harlem working women.[16]

Some black families economized by moving to smaller apartments of lesser quality or by moving in with relatives. The biggest problem in Harlem, the Welfare Council reported, was "the changes . . . in living conditions. . . .'Doubling up' of families was common." Previously independent children returned to their parents' homes. The Charity Organization Society reported that, of families receiving care, twice as many families lived with relatives in 1931 as two years earlier; three times as many took in lodgers. A study of city slums found the average number of persons per room had risen in Harlem since the beginning of the Depression because of such changes in household composition.[17]

All this was due not only to poverty but also to segregation. As the New York State Temporary Commission on the Condition of the Urban Colored Population pointed out, blacks gained access to apartments only when conditions there deteriorated and white tenants could not be found. In other words, blacks inherited bad conditions that simply got worse. Landlords neglected these apartments, but charged high rents because blacks could not find housing elsewhere. Mrs. S. Jecter of 16 West 136th Street, who supported her three children on her part-time earnings, complained that her landlord refused to make any repairs. She reminded him often of the fact that her gas stove was broken and she had no doorknobs, making the apartment impossible to lock. She paid her rent every month, nonetheless. She came home one day to find an eviction notice. Her landlord had grown tired of her complaints, and she was left without recourse.

Vacancy rates also demonstrate this enforced segregation. A Housing Department survey of 333 Harlem blocks revealed a far lower vacancy rate there than for New York City as a whole. In 1937, on average, four apartments per block in Harlem were vacant, and fewer than half of all available apartments rented for less than $25, the maximum allocated for rent by the ERB. In the equally poor Lower East Side, by comparison, thirteen apartments were available per block, twelve for under $25. Though most blacks could not afford high-quality apartments anywhere, the same rents they paid in Harlem would have bought better housing elsewhere in the city. According to a Bureau of Labor Statistics study of black "self-sufficient" (nonrelief) families in the city in 1936: "Their dwellings are small and rents are unduly high in comparison with the facilities furnished. . . . Living quarters for Negroes . . . are limited to a few small sections of New York City."[18]

Apartments on Amsterdam Avenue rented for $60 to white families in January of 1935. In July of that year, blacks moved in. The landlord cut the building staff from seven to four and raised the rent to $75. The 8,300 families in New York City helped by the Charity Organization Society that year paid a median monthly rent of $24. The 1,285 Harlem families' median rent topped $30. These same white families earned an average weekly wage of $17 (down from $25 in 1929), while black median earnings had declined in the same period from $22 to $14.

Every study had similar findings. The Health Department found in 1935 that average monthly rentals in Central Harlem came to $52, while for the rest of Manhattan the figure was $44. The NAACP reported that "90 percent of the Negro families in Harlem pay from $30 to $60 per month rent." According to an Emergency Relief Bureau study of the housing of relief recipients: "The Harlem population pays the highest rents in the City for accommodations that are inferior to those in areas with better housing." The study found that of apartments rented by relief families, 10 percent in Harlem and 36 percent elsewhere in Manhattan cost less than $5 per room, per month. At the highest rental levels, over half of all Harlem apartments rented for more than $8 per room, while only a fifth of all other Manhattan apartments did. So blacks, poorer than whites, had to pay more for rent, thus spending a higher proportion of their income for housing. Harlem families on relief paid their rents by borrowing, dipping into their food allowance, or simply going into debt to their landlords. The ERB suspected that over 10,000 families in this area alone needed additional relief money for rent.[19]

The cost of the housing did not reflect its quality. Of the thirty-one inhabited buildings on two blocks studied by the Housing Commission, nine had been officially condemned. The Housing Authority concluded after a survey of Harlem that "due to circumstances over which they have no control, many families are compelled to accept the old law tenement accommodations [buildings erected before

1901 and therefore not subject to the health and safety codes passed that year]. These houses are usually without heat, hot water and bathrooms together with improper plumbing, inadequate light and air, and have hall party lavatories." The Citywide Citizens' Committee on Harlem found that of 2,191 occupied Class B buildings they examined in West Harlem in 1941, 1,979 had major violations. Over 29,000 people lived in them. (Housing was classified by the type and number of facilities—heat, hot water, toilet, bath—provided, with A as the best and F as the worst.) The Mayor's Commission estimated that 10,000 blacks lived in cellars and basements with no toilets or running water. A former manager of Harlem apartments, an "agent for one of Harlem's largest real estate concerns," the New York Life Insurance Company, informed the Mayor's Commission:

> Do you know that apartments in my houses reeked with filth through no fault of the tenant? Bad plumbing—rats—mice—bugs—no dumbwaiters—no paint—heat— water and would you believe it I have been in apartments where young children lived and the toilet of the floor above flushed upon them. In fact things were so bad that I even appropriated money from the rents to help make the dumps livable much to the chagrin of my superiors.[20]

Because Harlem had been built more recently than many areas in Manhattan, some of the housing there did provide modern conveniences. A higher proportion of Harlem apartments had private bathrooms, hot water, and heat than did apartments elsewhere in Manhattan, the ERB study found, although these amenities did not always work. It listed approximately the same proportion of Harlem as non-Harlem Manhattan apartments in "good," "fair," and "poor" condition. That these newer apartments did not receive a "good" rating more often than the rest of the borough supports the conclusion that landlords in Harlem did less to maintain properties than they did elsewhere. A WPA study revealed that, while better-maintained apartments did not rent for more in Harlem than in other Manhattan neighborhoods, poor apartments cost substantially more. A Class A new-law tenement rented for $33 in Harlem, and between $30 and $35 elsewhere, but the rent for a Class F tenement ranged from $13 to $17, except in Harlem, where its average rental came to $23. Fewer apartments in Harlem received "unacceptable" ratings than in Manhattan as a whole, but a third rather than a fifth of old-law tenements there were classified "high rental."[21] These findings, then, suggest that many Manhattan families lived in poor housing during the Depression, but that Harlemites paid more for it.

The Harlem River Houses on Seventh Avenue between 151st and 155th streets, built by the PWA in 1937, offered modern, clean, spacious apartments at rents of $19 to $31 a month. The Houses also provided playgrounds, a nursery school, a health clinic, and laundry facilities. The United Tenants' League of Greater New York chose it as "the cleanest and most beautifully kept project in the city." But 20,000 families applied for the 574 spots.[22]

As a result, more people lived in a smaller area in Harlem than anywhere else in the city. As Langdon Post, Commissioner of Housing, testified:

A recent survey of . . . Harlem . . . [revealed] the average family income is $17.14. Forty percent of that went for rent. . . . In other parts of the city it is 20 to 25 percent for rent. . . . There are of course violations . . . but the problem of Harlem is not so much the bad housing, although there are plenty of them, it is the congestion to which they are forced through high rents.

On the block of 133rd and 134th streets between Seventh and Lenox avenues, 671 people per acre crowded together, the highest density in the city. The block of 138th and 139th streets between the same avenues held 620 per acre. The Mayor's Commission on City Planning found 3,871 people living between Lenox and Seventh avenues on 142nd and 143rd streets in 1935: "the city's most crowded tenement block." As the *Herald Tribune* reported, this block

is tenanted exclusively by Negroes. On its four sides the area presents a front of gray and red brick fire escapes broken only by dingy areaway entrances to the littered backyard about which the rectangle of tenements had been built. . . . Half of all the tenants are on relief and pass their days and nights lolling in the dreary entrances of the 40 apartments which house them or sitting in the ten by fifteen foot rooms which many of them share with a luckless friend or two. Unless they are fortunate their single windows face on narrow courts or into a neighbor's kitchen and the smell of cooking and the jangle of a dozen radios is always in the air.

The Citywide Citizens' Committee on Harlem noted that while Manhattan enjoyed 1.3 acres of parks and playgrounds per thousand people, or 17 percent of the borough's area, such greenery made up less than 9 percent of Harlem, or 0.4 acres per thousand people. The presence of modern conveniences in many apartments, then, did not make the difference between misery and comfort. As Thomas Sancton characterized it, "a Harlem tenement is a hundred delta cabins, plus tuberculosis." The Housing Authority report of 1937 concluded:

The position of the negro in Harlem is the most distressing of all. There is more crowding there than anywhere else in the city. The area in which negroes may reside is rigidly circumscribed and he is obliged to pay exorbitant rentals because the number of apartments available to him is so limited. Judge Watson of the Municipal court testified that the situation in Harlem is already as bad as it was in the post-war period. He said that while 90 percent of the dispossess proceedings before him were for non-payment of rent, this was caused by his dissatisfaction with the conditions of the premises or with the service rather than by inability to pay. . . . The mortality and tuberculosis statistics show the effects of overcrowding and other slum evils on life and health to be worse there than anywhere else in the city.[23]

In response to the Mayor's Commission report on Harlem housing, Langdon Post of the Housing Authority sadly reported to Mayor LaGuardia: "The facts and conclusions arrived at are, I am sorry to say, only too true, and the conditions described are, in my opinion, not in the least exaggerated. . . . I wish I were able to qualify the facts contained in the report and modify the conclusions, but in all honesty I cannot do so." The Slum Clearance Committee reported to the Municipal Housing Authority:

> The statistics . . . show that the Negro section of Harlem which is a slum area, has all the evils of a slum area in even a greater degree. . . . On the other hand, the Negro section of Harlem has none of the alleviating factors present in connection with other slum areas of New York City, for: it has fewer social service agencies . . . ; it has the greatest congestion of population . . . and it has higher rents than any [other] slum area of New York City.[24]

Black nationalists and the Communist and Socialist parties all tried to mobilize tenants to protest these inexcusable conditions, and occasionally took landlords to court. While they won some victories, segregation proved stronger than activism in Harlem. At the Harlem River Houses, for example, the long waiting list proved too great an intimidation to those lucky enough to have an apartment there. There was nowhere else to move. In any building, tenants who made trouble could be evicted, but in Harlem there were low vacancy rates, and outside of Harlem, few would rent to blacks. Thus, blacks expelled from their apartments faced homelessness as their most likely fate. Segregation, then, inhibited the emergence of black activism on housing, despite efforts of the Consolidated Tenants League and others.

Every housing report of the period linked Harlem's poor housing to other social ills, especially poor health. The existing situation, argued the Housing Authority, "spells many evils the most salient of which are disease, immorality, crime and high mortality. But the vast amount of unemployment is the greatest of all evils for that and that alone is the propelling force which drives the populace to seek cheaper rentals and into dilapidated homes." Harlem housing conditions constituted a "serious menace . . . not only to the health of the residents but to the welfare of the whole city," argued the Mayor's Committee on City Planning. It concluded that "large areas are so deteriorated and so unsuited to present needs that there is no adequate solution but demolition."[25]

Certainly health statistics in Harlem did not compare favorably with those in the rest of the city, because of both substandard housing and inadequate incomes. In 1934 in Central Harlem, fourteen people died per thousand, compared with ten per thousand in the city as a whole. The area's tuberculosis rate was over four times higher. Of every one thousand live births, ninety-four Central Harlem babies died, almost double the city's rate. Black women died in childbirth twice as often as whites; in part because over one-third of the black deaths compared with one-seventh of the white came as a result of an illegal abortion. For every cause of death, and virtually all health problems, Central Harlem had the highest rate of all Manhattan Health Districts. Of 1,921 students registered in P.S. 157 at 327 St. Nicholas Avenue, only 248 had no "observable" health defects in 1934. With the exception of bad teeth (942 with dental problems), the largest problem was "nutrition," with 641 students suffering from inadequate diets. While city-wide rates of malnutrition among school children ranged between 17 and 20 percent in the years after 1929, a 1936 study claimed that fully 63 percent of Harlem school children "suffer[ed] from malnutrition."[26]

On the other hand, these mortality and morbidity rates, though worse than those for the rest of the city, had declined since the 1920s and the pre–New Deal years. A comparison of health statistics for these earlier periods suggests that both races had seen dramatic improvement in the quality of health care. While medical advances contributed to the mortality decline, of course, the improvement also resulted from the increased availability of free health clinics. Clinic use had risen, especially for blacks. The number of prenatal care clinics operated by the Department of Health rose from seventeen in 1928 to twenty-three in 1935. The number of tuberculosis patients in Central Harlem using clinics rose from one percent of the total in 1930 to 22 percent in 1940, while the overall Manhattan rate rose from 6 to 23 percent. In 1937, a large new facility at Fifth Avenue between 136th and 137th streets became the Central Harlem Health Center. In New York City as a whole, a fifth of all native-born blacks and almost a tenth of all native-born whites in 1935–36 reported receiving some free medical care. At all income levels but one, black reliance on free clinics exceeded white. (For both races these rates were comparable to those of other cities.) In many cases this meant a lessening of the gap between black and white because of a substantial improvement in black access to health care and a slowing of improvements in white health as Depression conditions worsened.[27]

Mortality statistics continued to drop during the rest of the decade. In 1940, the general death rate in Central Harlem had dropped to 12.4 per thousand, the Manhattan rate to 11.5, and, for the first time, the mortality rate in another health dis-

TABLE 7.1
Mortality, General and from Certain Causes,
Central Harlem and Manhattan, 1925, 1937[28]

	1925		1937	
	Harlem	*Manhattan*	*Harlem*	*Manhattan*
General (deaths per 1,000 population)	16.2	14.3	14.5	12.5
Tuberculosis (deaths per 100,000)	247.0	111.8	234.3	90.3
Pneumonia (deaths per 100,000)	244.0	164.0	109.0	97.0
Infant mortality (deaths of children under one year per 1,000 live births)	114.4	72.9	75.0	54.0
Maternal mortality (deaths per 1,000 women giving birth)	8.2	4.8	7.9	4.6
Stillbirths (per 1,000 births)	71.8	55.0	76.0	53.0
Homicide (per 100,000)	18.7	11.0	24.1	3.6

trict surpassed Harlem's. Harlem's tuberculosis deaths and infant mortality rates declined. Because the black community had been so destitute before the Depression, in some ways conditions for them had improved with the advent of New Deal programs.

Relief programs correlated with some health improvements as well. While those on relief—the poorest—had a higher overall death rate, according to E. Franklin Frazier, they had lower rates of infant mortality. Probably relief babies were healthier because caseworkers advised their parents about prenatal and child care, and because of the medical care available to them. Pregnant women also received higher home relief food allotments.[29] Thus, in terms of public services, the Depression worsened conditions in Harlem while the New Deal improved them.

Poverty, poor housing, and poor health intensified other problems in Harlem. The Citywide Citizens' Committee on Harlem argued that "the poverty, the difficulties of home life and overcrowding, and the suffering of the adult population as a result of the unemployment in [Harlem] have . . . made educational needs greater than that of the average neighborhood of the city." Yet old buildings, scarce playgrounds, and overcrowded schools worsened the educational situation, demoralizing both teachers and students.[30] The Mayor's Commission heard testimony from the executive secretary of the Central Committee of the Harlem Parents' Associations expressing her "great distress" about overcrowding and the poor facilities in Harlem. She politely "beg[ged] and petition[ed]" the commission to "do something about this because we, the parents of the children, are suffering because our children are involved." Mrs. William Burroughs of the Harlem Teachers' and Students' Association echoed these remarks, demanding that the city

> . . . remedy overcrowding . . . safeguard life and health of pupils—immediate abandonment of old unsanitary firetraps, four in . . . Harlem . . . clinics in schools. . . . Retardation . . . is a vital problem in Harlem. . . . Many pupils come from an area with small educational facilities. In addition to this, the scandalous conditions here, inadequate staff, crowded classes, outmoded buildings, skimpy supplies, frequent lack of sympathy, lifeless curriculum, do not help; but hinder a slow pupil.

Ira Kemp forthrightly tied these conditions to racial discrimination and advocated the nationalist position he had articulated in the "Don't Buy" campaign.

> . . . We believe that the various school institutions in Harlem are overpopulated with teachers who aren't our people. . . . We feel a considerable percentage of teachers [in Harlem] should be colored.
>
> *Q.* Do you mean to insinuate that there is discrimination?
>
> *A.* I do. . . .
>
> *Q.* The specific question is whether you know of any instances where there is a violation of the law. Do you know of any girl [teacher] that has been discriminated against?
>
> *A.* My answer is that the system of keeping colored girls off the rolls who are on the eligible lists is so systematic that you can't get at it.

Q. We are asking for proof. . . .

A. I explained before that it is impossible to get facts from the authorities. We have had many complaints.

Ultimately, the Mayor's Commission on Conditions in Harlem concluded:

The school plant as a whole is old, shabby . . . in many instances not even sanitary or well-kept and the fire hazards . . . are great. The lack of playgrounds and recreational centers . . . is all the more serious when it is considered that some of the schools are surrounded by . . . corrupt and immoral resorts of which the police seem blissfully unaware. Four of the schools lack auditoriums: one endeavors to serve luncheons to 1,000 children when there are seats for only 175. Most of all, no elementary school has been constructed in Harlem in 10 years. . . .

Prejudicial discrimination appears from the fact that the Board of Education, asking funds from the federal government for 168 school buildings, asked for but one annex for Harlem.[31]

Although general test scores are not available for Harlem pupils, the IQ tests of Harlem youngsters at the Colored Orphan Asylum attest to their tragically poor education. Over half the children scored "dull normal" or lower. Only thirty-five children of 183 scored anywhere above "normal." Since it is unlikely that parents gave up less intelligent children more readily than brighter ones, this sample probably represented a cross section of poor and orphaned black children. If one accepts the widely held argument that IQ tests primarily reflect education and training levels and familiarity with mainstream norms and culture, particularly for non-white, lower-class students, one must conclude that the educational system in the Depression failed these children horribly.

The Teachers Union, Local 5 of the American Federation of Teachers, endorsed the Mayor's Commission's findings of poor school facilities in Harlem and cited "overcrowded classes, dangerous lack of adequate recreational facilities, antiquated and unsanitary school plant, 'horrifying' moral conditions, inadequate handling of the over-age child, and shortage of teaching staff." It concluded: "The conditions described . . . make proper teaching and proper receptivity to the teaching process impossible." The union's proposals—reducing class size, funding new school buildings, modernizing the old, hiring unemployed teachers to take children to nearby parks for recreation, staffing school playgrounds until six o'clock, and providing free lunches and winter clothing to the children of the unemployed—were endorsed by, among others, the Mayor's Committee on Harlem Schools, Father Divine's Peace Mission, the Joint Conference Against Discriminatory Practices, the Adam Clayton Powells, William Lloyd Imes and other ministers, YWCA and YMCA representatives, and Countee Cullen. To spur government action, the union reminded the mayor of the link between these problems and the 1935 riot: "The unhealthful and inadequate school buildings in Harlem had much to do with the unrest which led to the disorders of March 19."

Harlem residents added their voices, circulating petitions to the Board of Education:

Public education in Harlem has been . . . long and grossly neglected. The facts are notorious.

Dirt and filth and slovenliness have no more educational value for our children than for yours. . . . New school-houses with ample grounds and appropriate modern facilities are urgently needed to supplement or replace overcrowded and outmoded structures, to provide for the large increase in our population during the past decade or more. . . .

Teachers, principals and superintendents are needed who have abiding faith in our children and genuine respect for the loins and traditions from which they have sprung. . . .

So far as public education is concerned, we beg you to dispel by concrete action the widespread conviction that this region is neglected because its people are comparatively poor in this world's goods and in social and political influence, because many of them are of African descent.[32]

In March of 1936, Harlem organizations, including the Communist party and several black churches, created a Permanent Committee for Better Schools in Harlem, meeting in the New York Urban League building "with 400 delegates representing every phase of social, political, religious, cultural and civic activity in Harlem." These efforts, the commission report, and the memory of the Harlem riot brought some improvements within the year: the city budget included appropriations for four new school buildings, some repairs were made at most Harlem schools, and "many individual cases of discriminatory zoning have been satisfactorily settled." That year for the first time students could take a course in black history.[33]

Of course Harlem's educational problems were by no means solved. In 1941, the Citizens' Committee reported that overcrowding forced many Harlem schools to run on a three-shift school day. From West 114th Street to West 191st, there was not a single public vocational or secondary school. One junior high school served the entire area from 125th Street to 155th, between the Harlem River and St. Nicholas Avenue. In one elementary school, ten classes lacked classrooms; in another, six did.

Still, educational levels among blacks did rise in the 1930s. Whether because Harlem's schools provided a better education than those of the South, because jobs were scarce in the Depression, or because relief eased families' desperation, black children from both relief and non-relief families attended school for longer during the Depression than they had before. The proportion of black children aged fourteen to twenty-four remaining in school rose through the 1930s until it approached the figure for whites.[34]

Education problems, aggravated by low incomes and high living costs, led to continued high juvenile delinquency rates in Harlem in the 1930s. Miss Hill, assistant housing director at the YWCA, told a *Herald Tribune* reporter: "It's a vicious circle in a city of such color segregation. . . . The Negroes can't pay these rents without help so they jam the houses. Juvenile delinquency is terrible under such conditions. Many mothers . . . have to go out to work and the children come to school with the keys of their houses around their necks. There is no one there when they go home and so they simply play around in the alleys."

As Walter White of the NAACP wrote to Mayor LaGuardia in 1936:

There is no question . . . that the Negro aspect of the problem of delinquency is an exceedingly grave one. The percentage of Negro boys in [Warwick, an institution for delinquent boys] . . . has risen steadily. But what are the reasons for this disproportionate rise? It is an inevitable development of the economic and other conditions in Harlem. . . . You know, of course, that the percentage of unemployment is very high [there] today . . . [and] the wages paid in private industry are usually so low as to necessitate both mother and father being away from home from early morning until late at night and thus unable to give proper home training and care to their children. . . .

This lower economic status inevitably causes more Negro children to be brought into the Children's Court than otherwise . . . and here again do they suffer . . . from a lack of sympathetic and interested assistance. . . . Contributory in large measure to this is the fact that the Protestant welfare agencies do not have the same attitude towards Negro children as towards white ones. . . .

Many if not most of these children, both white and colored, are not really delinquent but are the victims of under privilege. But as you know, New York [does not] provide for proper foster home placement. . . . The inevitable result is the disproportionate percentage of Negroes at Warwick. This is accentuated by the fact that when these boys are ready to be released and should be returned to normal society . . . they are not able to find jobs . . . and their home environment has not improved sufficiently to justify their return there.[35]

Despite the high numbers of black children adjudged delinquent in the Depression, the type of criminal behavior did not change from earlier years. In fact, numbers of delinquents (or at least, arrests for delinquency) actually declined slightly over the decade for both blacks and whites. While theft (including burglary, larceny, holdups, and pickpocketing) remained boys' most frequent crime, hitching rides on various forms of public transportation, and peddling without a license followed directly after. As noted earlier, these crimes primarily indicated the depth of economic need in the community.[36]

As in previous years, the problem of high rates of conviction for delinquency did not necessarily lie in an overtly racist court system, although doubtless racist judgments were given. The story was more complex; the courts were able to act only to ameliorate existing difficulties and provide a sort of bandage. When Benedict Lucy, twelve, came before the Children's Court, it was his third appearance. A year earlier he had received six months' probation for deserting home. The next time, he was charged with stealing his mother's purse. The judge again placed him on probation. Finally his mother asked that, since he kept running away, he be sent to Warwick. The court-appointed psychologist concurred, hoping the institution would help him "[stop his] bedwetting [and provide] regular schooling, church attendance, trade training. . . ." Obviously Benedict's thefts and desertions reflected far deeper problems, which city services had not or could not address. And so he ended up in court and in juvenile detention, the court having few other alternatives, even though his difficulties cried out for other solutions. As Agnes Sullivan of the Welfare Council commented about several such cases, it "indicates that it was handled on the basis of the offense rather than in terms of his needs."

Gene Wooley stole letters from a mailbox at age nine, "ladies hose valued at $14.41" at eleven and a half, and a "box of ladies vests valued at $9" a year later. For this the judge remanded him to Warwick. Yet, while punishment may have been the court's only option for Gene as well as for Benedict, the real problem lay elsewhere. "From his early childhood there has been economic stress in the home due to Mr. Wooley's irregular employment. In 1926, when Gene was five years old, the economic situation became acute when his father was committed to a State Hospital with a diagnosis of dementia praecox." The economic instability of many Harlem families bred emotional upheaval as well as pecuniary need, perhaps felt most acutely by youths. Thus black children were more often found delinquent. But incarceration did not address the problems these children faced.

Unlike delinquency, adult crimes rose. While most death rates declined in Harlem during the Depression, homicides rose from nineteen per 100,000 in 1925 to twenty-four in 1937, while city rates fell. A 1931 investigation of the relationship between housing and crime found, not unexpectedly, that Manhattan's slum areas had higher rates of arrests of all types and a higher rate of convictions than the borough's average. The top two areas were both in Central Harlem. The same held for later years. Still, like delinquency, by and large, Harlem crimes by adults were more often income-producing than violent. As already noted, arrests for prostitution, operating illegal stills, and playing the numbers rose. Of a random sample of Harlem arrests in the first six months of 1935, all types of theft, from shoplifting to grand larceny, constituted only an eighth of the total, despite the fact that the period surveyed included the riot, with its many burglary arrests. Possession of policy slips, by contrast, accounted for about a third of all Harlem arrests. Except for the rise of arrests for policy slips and the decline for other gambling offenses since the early years of the Depression, the rates for the different sorts of crimes remained fairly constant.

Of those arrested statewide, a smaller proportion of blacks than whites were charged with homicide or with theft of any sort, which suggests that whites were less often arrested for minor crimes than blacks were. The black rate for these more serious crimes proportional to their population, however, was greater than the white. Statewide, the ratio of whites arrested to their total population was 140 to 100,000, compared with 853 for blacks.[37]

As we have seen, crime statistics are not foolproof indicators of community behavior. As with delinquency, discrimination or racism may have led to selective arrest, prosecution, and conviction. Perhaps police cared less about black crime and therefore acted less vigorously on Harlem cases. This would mean that arrest rates were lower than actual criminal behavior. Similarly, the rise in Harlem homicide deaths may have been due to a new vigilance by police rather than a real rise in the number of murders. An alternative possibility is that racism provoked officers to arrest blacks more readily than whites. The greater poverty of blacks might further skew their arrest rates, since the rich are generally more able to avoid arrest for minor crimes such as disturbing the peace than the poor are. Racist juries and judges might be similarly disposed to distrust blacks. Thus high black arrest and conviction rates may reflect factors other than strictly higher rates of criminality. Nevertheless, whatever the actual rates, criminal behavior in Harlem offers hints of the problems faced by a poor black community. Criminality reflected not only black behavior, but white as well.

Police corruption led to selective and discriminatory enforcement of the laws in

Harlem. An NAACP memorandum argued that Harlem's high rate of arrests for prostitution and illegal sale of alcohol was attributable to police corruption: "We are made to look more immoral, less decent than anyone else and the environment of prostitution is being fostered [*sic*] on our women and young girls by the Harlem police officials in their scheme and business of tribute." A second memorandum estimated "perhaps forty to fifty percent of [prostitutes] . . . (colored) are forced or semi-forced and the rest act voluntarily." This memorandum cited the Cotton Club and several Italian-owned saloons as central "clearing house[s]" for these women. While the memo noted that the NAACP did not advocate illegal activity, it pointed out that it hardly seemed fair that black women were arrested for prostitution more often than white. The NAACP was convinced police arrested black women more often because they feared public outcry if they arrested too many whites.

Police similarly enforced gambling and liquor laws selectively, to the detriment of blacks and the benefit of whites. The memo claimed that police permitted numbers-running in white stores but enforced the law for black-owned stores. It estimated that in 1932 Harlemites lost $50,000 a day to the white operators of the numbers game; adding, "this racket would not go on one minute if the police were on their job. . . . It is common knowledge that [a recent meeting of ten white] club and cabaret owners . . . decided to pay $30 per place per week to Sergeant Miller for protection for such as open gambling, selling liquor, taking numbers, etc." Harlem's black saloonkeepers were more often arrested than white for serving after the legal 3:00 A.M. closing, although both white and black bar owners stayed open late. To make matters worse, lamented the NAACP, "a canvass of them [white saloons] showed they did not have a colored man working for them other than a porter here and there." In sum, the effect of discrimination was to "leave the field of money making in Harlem entirely in the hands of the white police and the white racketeer."[38]

The police were known in Harlem not only for their corruption, but for their readiness to harass local residents. A draft of the Mayor's Commission's report on the Harlem riot noted: "The police themselves admit that they entered the homes of Negro citizens WITHOUT A WARRANT AND SEARCHED THEM AT WILL . . . [they admit to] interference in the association of white and colored people; searching of homes without a warrant, detention of innocent men in jail, and even the MUTILATION AND KILLING of persons upon slight provocation!!! . . . [but Commissioner Valentine] maintained that there was NO REASON FOR DISCIPLINARY ACTION" [Emphasis theirs]. William Patterson, a black man, was falsely accused of a crime and subsequently released. When he complained about his arrest, the Mayor's Commission on Conditions in Harlem discovered, "detectives threatened Patterson if he did not withdraw his complaint. . . . There were other cases similar to this case in which Negro citizens' homes were entered and searched by officers of the law without warrants to take such action." The commission's investigations not only provided information, but moved some of the victims to action: the commission reported that as a result of its findings, "Patterson instituted Civil action against the officers responsible for his arrest."

Many different black organizations reported incidents of police brutality involving black citizens. Walter White of the NAACP sent a telegram to Mayor LaGuardia and Police Commissioner Lewis Valentine in 1939:

ROOKIE POLICEMAN BEATING UP NEGRO IN NEW YORK CITY WITHOUT CAUSE . . . 40TH
AND BROADWAY . . . WHEN POLICEMAN, SHIELD # 8589 BEAT UNMERCIFULLY NEGRO
BOOTBLACK HE STOPPED ONLY BECAUSE CROWD INTERVENED. BOY WAS LATER
RELEASED BUT HAD BEEN BEATEN SO BADLY HE REQUIRED MEDICAL TREATMENT. WE
ASK IMMEDIATE SUSPENSION OF OFFENDING OFFICER PENDING INVESTIGATION AND
ISSUANCE OF DRASTIC ORDER BY YOU AND COMMISSIONER VALENTINE . . . WITH
RESPECT TO SUCH VIOLENCE.

Valentine reported to the mayor: "Investigation disclosed that only sufficient force
necessary to effect arrest was used . . . and that there is no cause for disciplinary
action. Complainant interviewed and now requests matter be dropped."[39]

Adam Clayton Powell, Jr., reported another incident. Tommie Aiken, standing
on the bread line at 142nd Street and Lenox Avenue since morning, was pushed
out of line. A policeman (Officer #9761) told him to move to the end of the line.
When he explained that he was simply trying to get back to his original place, the
officer hit him in the face. He "beat him over the head with a blackjack and after
he was knocked down unconscious [the officer] struck him in the face and especially
in the eyes. . . . [Aiken was] rushed to Harlem hospital . . . [and] operated on in an
attempt to save his sight. The operation was unsuccessful."

According to the police report, Aiken was arrested for "wilfully and wrongly
striking [an] officer . . . with clenched fist while officer was attempting to arrest him
for causing a disturbance, using loud and boisterous language, tending to excite several hundred men . . . possibly thereby tending to cause a riot." Commissioner Valentine supported the officer's report. Aiken told a different story.

> I was arrested for felonious assault. I was in 142nd Street Armory [where it was] said
> there were free meals. . . . The officer tried to shift me out of line. I told him I was there
> a long time so he pushed me and hit me with a night stick in the eye and knocked me
> out. I was unconscious and I was taken to Harlem Hospital. I woke up, I think, 45 min-
> utes later.

A witness supported Aiken's story. "The officer came through one door and two
white fellows got in back of Aiken. The officer thought Aiken was with those two
fellows. He said get in the back of the line. Aiken said, 'This is my original place
and I am here since early this morning' . . . Officer Redcliff said to him, 'You black
son of a bitch' and struck him over the head. Aiken fell to the floor, another officer
ran from the front side with a blackjack and Redcliff kicked him."

At Harlem Hospital, Dr. Epstein reported Aiken was suffering "from possible
fracture sustained when officer struck prisoner with baton." According to the doctor, this caused a "rupture of [his] left eyeball." After Aiken gave his statement the
doctor reported him "clear and orientated. Well behaved and quiet."[40]

All the elements of the Harlem crime scene came together in the 1932 murder of
a white saloon owner by a black man. As Ferdinand Morton described it:

> Tuesday April 26 a murder occurred at a saloon 2249 Seventh Avenue. A colored man
> killed an Italian [saloon proprietor]. The murderer was the man [pimp] of a colored
> prostitute. . . . The colored fellow being drunk, also his girl, got into an argument, the

colored man hit his girl, the Italian in turn hit the colored man, the colored man then cut the Italian who died today at one o'clock. The point is this—with proper police supervision the thing could not have happened. . . . There is a white cop on that beat name Pete, shield number 7726, who rumor and common talk have it, is so wrapped up in chiseling that he'd take milk from a baby. . . . It is common knowledge that he did not like the Italian that was killed. . . . From all reports the murder was partly an accident. . . . The plan was to just beat the Italian up. . . . The general talk of the neighborhood is that the white officer Pete gave one of the mob his blackjack to beat the Italian with, but during the fight, the little fellow, Pee Wee, who the Italian had previously hit, slipped in and cut the Italian to death. . . . That will give you an idea of the collusion of the police and the evil doer of Harlem.[41]

Harlem crime rates documented police bigotry and corruption as much as they revealed Harlem's poverty and unsatisfactory conditions.

Community

Yet while blacks in Harlem recognized the harsh conditions they lived under and the pernicious effects of their poverty, few believed the solution was wholesale abandonment of the area. Living together offered resources and strengths unavailable to dispersed individuals. Rather, African-Americans demanded better services where they lived, recognizing the positive power of community. The Reverend Mr. Garner, minister of the Grace Congregational Church, testified before the Mayor's Commission: "We find that our rents are higher than anywhere else in the city in proportion to what we get. Our food in Harlem is higher." But he refused to consider the suggestion that blacks move elsewhere to find less expensive housing:

> Our industrial life and social and economic and religious lives are centered in Harlem at the present time. We object to the breaking up of our community on those grounds. . . . To break up the community in small segregated groups gives no opportunity for the friends to develop themselves on and among themselves [*sic*].

Street surveys of the Mayor's Commission and the "Negroes in New York" study of the Federal Writers' Project documented the large numbers of storefront churches, billiard halls, social clubs, dance halls, and mutual welfare lodges that provided social space throughout the Depression decade. Over two thousand social, political, and mutual aid societies flourished in Harlem, including the United Aid for Peoples of African Descent, the Tuskeegee Alumni Association, Iota Phi Lambda (a sorority for business women), the King of Clubs (half of whose members were black police officers), the Hampton Alumni Club, the Bermuda Benevolent Organization, the Southern Aristocrats, the Trinidad Benevolent Association, the Anguilla Benevolent Society, the St. Lucia United Association, California #1, the New Englanders, the Hyacinths Social Club, the Montserrat Progressive Society, St. Helena's League and Benefit Club, and hundreds of others.[42]

Both poverty and community, then, shaped Harlem family and social life. As Loften Mitchell recalled,

[t]he child of Harlem had the will to survive, to "make it." . . . This Harlem child learned to laugh in the face of adversity, to cry in the midst of plentifulness, to fight quickly and reconcile easily. He became a "backcapping" signifying slicker and a suave, sentimental gentleman. From his African, Southern Negro and West Indian heritage, he knew the value of gregariousness and he held group consultations on street corners to review problems of race economics, or politics.

He was poor but proud. He hid his impoverishment with clothes, pseudo-good living, or sheer laughter.

. . . In the nineteen thirties we had our own language, sung openly, defiantly. . . .

We celebrated, too—our biggest celebrations were on nights when Joe Louis fought. . . . When he won a fight I went into the streets with other Negroes and I hollered until I was hoarse. . . . We had culture too. The Schomburg Collection, a mighty fortress . . . three theaters, Louis Armstrong, Cab Calloway . . . Bill "Bojangles" Robinson . . . Bessie Smith . . . Langston Hughes . . . Romare Bearden . . . Augusta Savage. . . .

Richard Wright explained the energy and joy in black culture as rooted in poverty and anger:

Our music makes the whole world dance. . . . But only a few of those who dance and sing with us suspect the rawness of life out of which our laughing-crying tunes and quick dance steps come; they do not know that our songs and dances are our banner of hope flung desperately up in the face of a world that has pushed us to the wall.[43]

Others offered even less sanguine pictures. Alfred Smith of the FERA, a black man, discussed the African-American family in terms that today might be viewed as racist, but that nonetheless raised important questions about the impact of dire poverty on family life:

The comparatively unstable family life of the Negro in urban areas may be ascribed to poor living conditions. Illegitimacy, illiteracy and a lack of a sense of responsibility or obligation all have their roots in the Negroes' unfortunate past, but are nurtured and fostered in city slums. Negroes are required to pay a larger proportion of their income for rent than any other group and they get less for their expenditure. The landlord who rents to the Negro mass in urban areas has no sense of responsibility to his renters. Negroes are forced to live in proscribed areas of the city, and in quarters where their health and morals suffer. They get little attention, little notice (other than being occasionally photographed in his slums as examples of need for "better housing") and much sympathy.

One part of his equation, "unstable family life," deserves some attention. Black and white leaders lamented the frequency of female-headed households. Clayton Cook of the Children's Aid Society reported 20 percent of Harlem black children "come from 'broken homes'—that is—families that have only a woman at the head. At one school in 699 families out of 1,600 . . . the father was either dead or had deserted." Certainly the high number of widows attests to the evil effects of poverty on adult (particularly male) longevity. Some social problems such as juvenile delinquency occurred more often in families without fathers according to contemporary studies (although, interestingly, the effects were more pronounced for girls than for boys). Yet other measures of "social disorganization," such as reliance on relief, seemed to bear no relationship to whether or not a man was present at home.

Many feared an absent male would ensure that these families would live in poverty, since black women had even lower earning potential that black men did. In fact, ironically, these economic liabilities were mitigated by the Depression. While black working women did earn less, on average, than working men, female-headed families more often had additional earners. Thus, in the BLS sample, for example, families without a husband present earned no less per person than those with both husband and wife. Nor were black families with women at the head more likely than others to be on relief: the figure for black female-headed families on relief, 20 percent in New York City, was no higher than the proportion of female-headed families in the black population. A study of 675 Harlem families done by the Mayor's Commission found families on different blocks had very different average incomes. But in both high-income and low-income blocks, the proportion of female-headed families was identical.[44]

Thus, while the likelihood of some social problems (such as juvenile delinquency) seemed correlated with the presence or absence of a father, other measures of "social disorganization" (such as reliance on relief) seemed to bear no relationship to that question. It may be that the Depression threw so many men out of work that their absence made little economic difference to the family. When employment opportunities improved in the next decade, two-headed families would fare better than single-parent households, on the whole. But in an era of high unemployment and highly fluid household structures in which a family's income came from a variety of contributors, the presence of a male mattered less economically than one might expect.

Making ends meet was a difficult business in Depression Harlem, and families used a variety of financial and non-financial, legal and illegal methods to do so. No one starved, but few in Harlem prospered, and the consequences of such grinding poverty reached into all areas of life. Housing and health were poor, mortality and crime rates high. Strong kin and community networks prevented much of the worst from occurring, and New Deal programs provided some help. Harlem itself, though, remained a ghetto and a slum and its people trapped in the conditions brought on by poverty and discrimination. As the New York State Temporary Commission on the Condition of the Urban Colored Population concluded in 1939:

> While the Commission has no desire to indulge in dramatic over-statement it does earnestly wish to impress upon your honorable bodies the extreme seriousness of the conditions which it has studied. The conditions often seem almost incredible in so advanced a commonwealth as the State of New York, and they cannot remain uncorrected without general danger to the public welfare of the State as a whole.[45]

CHAPTER 8

Been Down So Long

If the Depression had caused government spending to skyrocket, fears of Axis aggression spurred further increases by the end of the 1930s. The United States joined the Allied powers as a major armaments supplier and poured funds into war-related industries. Training programs expanded. Millions of the unemployed and the never-before-employed found jobs; living standards and prices began an upward climb. The process accelerated once the United States entered World War II at the end of 1941.

African-Americans, arguably the population most in need of employment, training, and a better living standard, looked forward to sharing in the new economic boom. Hundreds of thousands applied for training programs and industrial jobs and enlisted in the armed forces. They quickly discovered that their opportunities were sharply limited by the familiar forces of racism and inertia. With its long experience in political organization, and with the newer experience of a government responsive to that organizing, the black community mobilized again to demand a fair share of new opportunities, using the nation's war needs to its advantage. Often such strategies succeeded. With the perceived need for unity in wartime, the rising demand for workers, and the increased public sensitivity to racism brought about by a reaction against Nazism, government officials and white leaders yielded to some limited black demands. Thus preparation for war and the war itself brought some change to the black community.

Ultimately, though, it brought the frustration of raised hopes with little concrete improvement. Political efforts by blacks and sympathetic whites won some victories, both nationally and in local communities: jobs, access to training programs and union membership, government services like day care, and rent control laws. The slow pace of even these limited improvements and the continuation of racial discrimination led to riots on army bases and in several cities, including New York. Those, in turn, brought further changes and increases in government services. Yet, for all this, most of the problems of the black ghetto remained. As in the Depression, the improvements simply did not challenge the power structure in any fundamental way.

Gains and Limits

The arming of the Allies, often cited as bringing the United States economy out of the Depression, did not improve black employment opportunities as much as white. It took both growing demand for labor (especially after so many men joined the armed forces) and increasingly militant black political pressure to bring about an improvement in black employment possibilities.[1]

New Yorkers, whether black or white, did not benefit much from early war preparations, in part because the city had little defense industry. Among the ten leading industrial states, New York was seventh in the per-capita value of military contracts in 1940–41. The city contained more consumer industries than it did industries related to war production. In the first six months of 1941, more than 10 percent of the population still received some form of relief. Approximately 159,000 families remained on home relief rolls, only 27,000 fewer than in 1937. Over half of them had at least one employable member. Almost the same number held WPA jobs. Of the home relief cases that did close between 1940 and 1941, only a third did so because the recipient obtained private employment. The rest switched to other public aid or received help from relatives. Unemployment in New York City was higher in 1942 than in 1939, and it was higher than the national unemployment rate. Not until 1943, when the city began receiving more defense work (the city received 12 percent of all Navy contracts, for example), did unemployment fall substantially.[2]

Even taking New York's general employment difficulties into account, blacks there still fared worse than whites. In 1940, 40 percent of New York's black population continued to receive some sort of relief, even though the white rate had fallen. In 1942, 10,000 fewer African-Americans received home relief than had done so six years earlier, but their proportion in the total home relief group rose from 22 to 26 percent because whites left the rolls more quickly. The Community Service Society reported a similar shift in its relief caseload.[3] Work relief figures revealed the same facts. Thirty percent of the labor force in Central Harlem received work relief or were completely unemployed in 1940. In the nearby (primarily white) Washington Heights Health District, by contrast, 16 percent listed themselves as on work relief or unemployed. In April of 1941, blacks held 22 percent of the city's WPA jobs, higher than their proportion in Depression years, testifying to their greater difficulty obtaining private jobs. That proportion rose to almost a third by October 1942, and remained at that high level until the agency shut down in February 1943.[4]

William Hodson of the Department of Welfare explained that the WPA ended because employable workers no longer required its services, citing as evidence the simultaneous decline of home relief and WPA cases. But he added that those remaining on the rolls included not only the unemployable but "a considerable number of employable Negroes and aliens who find it . . . difficult to obtain employment."[5]

Defense needs helped break down the gender-segregated job market of earlier years, as many white women moved from the service sector into previously male jobs in industry. But black workers of both sexes faced the familiar walls of a racially segregated labor market. With better opportunities available, white men and women left the traditionally black jobs they had taken in the Depression, but still allowed few blacks to compete for the better jobs. The Urban League claimed that war industry hirings began with white men, moved then to white women, then to black men, and finally to black women.[6] Black men and women still worked at different jobs, and both regained sole possession of their place at the bottom. Neither group succeeded in rising as quickly as whites had.

In the long run, neither the gender nor the racial shift in occupations endured. To the detriment of the newly risen women workers, men returning home from war wanted their jobs back, and their wives and girlfriends at home. While some women managed to retain their positions after the war, the widespread wartime breakdown in the gender-segregated market proved only temporary. Racial segregation, on the other hand, did eventually decline, beginning with Executive Order 8802 and the establishment of a Fair Employment Practices Committee. That change proved more permanent.

In the short run, however, blacks continued to work at the bottom rungs of the employment ladder. Military production did help more blacks escape dependence on relief, but they did not find jobs as quickly as whites. Those who did secure employment often found it only in traditional fields, now open again as whites moved to defense work. Higher-level employment by and large remained closed to blacks. In manufacturing, the Urban League reported in 1941,"Negroes perform chiefly the unskilled labor work." As late as 1942, 80 percent of black New York State Employment Service placements were in service jobs, mostly household employment. As African-American tax commissioner Hubert Delany commented: "The masses of New York City's Negro workers . . . have been limited because of economic restrictions and prevailing attitudes in the community largely to traditional types of jobs of a menial nature." Only in the civil service, with its "competitive examinations and merit" system, did African-Americans achieve positions as administrators, supervisors, and investigators, positions still for the most part closed to them in private industry.[7]

Black workers remained trapped by the vicious circle of system-wide racism. Private employers used the now-familiar rationalization that their workers would protest black hirings or promotions, or that unions would not admit them. Both they and unions argued that blacks lacked appropriate skills, but rarely did either accept blacks for training or apprenticeship programs. Charles Collier, the New York Urban League's Industrial Secretary, wrote: "We are having a hard time making employers throughout the city realize that they have a definite social responsibility in the matter of providing job opportunities for Negro youth. We are also finding it difficult to secure the full cooperation of those in the labor movement." Only 5 percent of all trainees in war production training programs were black in 1941; of over 4,500 U.S. training courses, only 194 accepted blacks. Vocational schools refused to accept them because they claimed black graduates could not find jobs. In 1941 the United States Employment Service reported it placed only one of every fifty black training school graduates. When the Bureau of Employment Security of the Social Security Board asked employers in defense industries across the country if they would hire blacks, over half said no, even for unskilled work. Blacks held only 142 of the 29,215 positions in ten New York–area war plants. The *Nation* concluded: "the problems of the Negroes in Harlem have been increased rather than lightened by the war boom."[8]

The Reverend John Johnson of St. Martin's Episcopal Church, a founding member of the Citizens' League, feared that continued discrimination and poverty in the midst of seeming opportunity were producing black defeatism and a loss of religious faith. In a 1941 sermon on crime he preached: "Unemployment, the ever-threatening notice of dispossess, the fearful specter of starvation, have combined to destroy morale. These people are too often desperate in their need, and they have the further feeling that they are forgotten and nobody cares. . . . [The] extreme economic disadvantage [of the African-American is] . . . the result of race prejudice that denies to him the same rights and opportunities as other citizens." Following the long tradition in the black community of blending political activism and religious commitment, he argued:

> The apathy of decent citizens in Harlem is something frightening. . . . Yet the strongest force there is to combat this apathy lies within the hands of the colored people themselves. The religious life of our community must become more militant. . . . The decent law-abiding citizens must become better organized behind the efforts of their churches and social agencies. The basis of . . . criminal acts . . . is a breakdown of religious faith. Religious faith will help us combat . . . poverty . . . to overcome it. [It] will give us the stamina to survive in spite of the worst that race prejudice can do. . . . The arms we must take up are ever-increasing self-discipline and a never wavering faith in a good, just God.[9]

Throughout the country, "decent citizens" did organize in churches and social agencies, as black leaders and their white allies raised their voices for equal opportunity both in the armed forces and in defense industries. As Robert Weaver of the National Defense Advisory Commission argued, "We cannot stop tanks with squads of janitors. We cannot blast the enemy with buckets of charwomen." Representatives from the National Urban League and the New York Urban League met with federal agencies in October of 1940 and again in January of 1941 to demand that black war workers be fully integrated into industries and unions. They appealed to an argument of social utility:

> Unless employers and white workers are willing to share the available jobs among qualified workers of all groups, then they must pay the social costs. They must pay for the relief, crime, juvenile delinquency and disease which are relatively high among Negroes because of their economic disabilities and lack of opportunities.

Many agencies promised to improve; some did. Most unions involved in defense work agreed to lift bans against blacks. Four unions previously closed to blacks opened separate locals, and one removed the racial prohibition from its ritual. Although eight AFL unions and seven non-AFL unions still excluded blacks, the number of black union members nationally rose from 180,000 in 1935, to 600,000 five years later, and 1,250,000 by 1945. In Harlem, change came more slowly, in part because of the earlier successes of the Negro Labor Committee and the Harlem Labor Union. By 1944 in census tract 230 (138th to 142nd streets between Lenox and Eighth avenues) one-fourth of the 426 black workers interviewed were union members, slightly higher than the Depression rate. Fifty-four percent of the black union members belonged to the CIO, 39 percent to the AFL, and 7 percent to independents.[10]

Such efforts encouraged further activism among African-Americans. Most dra-

202   *"Or Does It Explode?"*

matic was A. Philip Randolph's threat in 1941 to lead thousands of blacks in a march on Washington to protest hiring discrimination. On April 1, 1941, Lester Granger of the NUL, Walter White of the NAACP, Channing Tobias of the YMCA, Mary McLeod Bethune of the National Youth Administration, and A. Philip Randolph of the Brotherhood of Sleeping Car Porters asked President Roosevelt to forbid discrimination in the armed forces and defense industries. Secretary of War Henry Stimson and Secretary of the Navy Frank Knox refused to desegregate the armed forces. The President did not insist. Instead, he issued a statement condemning discrimination. The black delegation argued that this was not enough, but Roosevelt feared angry employers and an intransigent South and hesitated to go farther. These black leaders promptly proposed a March on Washington at a meeting of the NUL, NAACP, and other black organizations in Chicago, and Randolph agreed to lead it. The decision to march revealed the dramatic change that had come over the black community during the Depression, as this proposal for confrontational, direct action enjoyed rapid and broad support even among moderate groups.

The formal call for a march on Washington went out from a strategy meeting at the Hotel Theresa in Harlem over the signatures of Granger, Layle Lane of the American Federation of Teachers, White, Crosswaith, Randolph, Tobias, Adam Clayton Powell, Jr., and Henry Pope. Roosevelt sent his wife Eleanor and Mayor LaGuardia to dissuade them, but to no avail. Desperate to avoid anything that could divert the war effort by undermining unity—or the appearance of unity— FDR signed Executive Order 8802 in June of 1941 requiring all defense industries and training programs receiving government contracts to "provide for the full and equitable participation of all workers . . . without discrimination because of race, creed, color or national origin." Randolph called off the march despite the President's failure to desegregate the armed forces.[11]

The order had a dramatic effect on black employment. More blacks found jobs, and more acquired training. Industrial work saw the sharpest increase in the proportion of black employees between 1940 and 1944: a rise of 13 percent in four years. In the United States as a whole, the proportion of black males in the total male work force rose between 1940 and 1944 from 8.6 percent to 9.8 percent. For the first time large numbers of blacks obtained skilled work.[12] The percentage of war production training program enrollees who were black more than doubled between 1941 and 1943, and these trainees had more success obtaining jobs; from 3 percent of all war workers in 1942, African-Americans grew to 8 percent by September of 1944. A tenth of the black youngsters trained in NYA programs in April of 1942 moved to industrial employment, a 40 percent increase from the start of that year. Employment opportunities for blacks in New York likewise improved as the impact of the executive order and the increase in defense contracts reached the city. The proportion of blacks obtaining skilled and semi-skilled jobs there doubled between 1940 and 1944. Accordingly, the proportion of black placements by the NYSES in service jobs declined from 88 percent in 1939 to 73 percent by 1943.[13]

When industries did not provide equal access to jobs, the newly established Committee on Fair Employment Practice (FEPC), created by the executive order, ruled on the complaints. In its first year, the committee received over 6,000 complaints of racial discrimination. The New York City office received the most complaints of any in the country: 1,162 in eighteen months, or 20 percent of the national total. Blacks filed 78 percent of the complaints nationally; of these, a third came from black women (who made 86 percent of all complaints by women). In New York City, where religious discrimination, mostly against Jews, constituted the most frequent complaint (43 percent), race came second, with 19 percent of the total.[14]

The success of Randolph's March on Washington Movement in turn inspired new efforts to win equal opportunities for African-Americans. Many public and private organizations not directly associated with the war effort complied with the non-discrimination order on their own, and blacks and sympathetic whites used the momentum created by the executive order to establish new advocacy groups and pass new laws supporting equal opportunity.

New York City was one center of such activism by both the black community and black and white officials. Adam Clayton Powell, Jr., elected to the City Council in November of 1941 and to Congress in 1944, used his position to publicize black concerns and his experience in mass political organizing to win concessions from businesses and government agencies. When he ran for Congress he urged black Communist party member Benjamin Davis to replace him on the City Council. Davis won, and continued Powell's struggle to bring about an end to discrimination. Powell's People's Committee (which he had created from the Greater New York Coordinating Committee to support his efforts in the City Council race), with its headquarters at the Abyssinian Baptist Church, continued to use "mass pressure and picketing" to improve conditions for blacks.

Mayor LaGuardia, long an advocate of non-discriminatory hiring policies (it was he who convinced President Roosevelt that Randolph would not be deterred without his taking action against discrimination), first tried moral suasion to change white employers' attitudes about hiring blacks, then ordered private companies doing business with the municipal government not to discriminate. He supported the efforts of black organizations to end racist practices in industry, at public utilities, and in the provision of social services.[15]

The governor fell into step as well, appointing a committee "to deal with the problem of discrimination in employment." Predating the executive order by a few months, the Governor's Committee on Discrimination in Employment operated under the aegis of the State Council on Defense. Neither confrontational nor devoted to mass action, it stressed study and persuasion by example. In a letter sent to "leaders in the fields of social service and public opinion," the council argued that "public opinion is the weapon which will rule out discrimination practices where they occur" and requested supporting statements from these leaders for publication. As black leaders had done, the council's plea linked social change with a more effective national defense effort. Activists working for decades to alter social and economic practice had now found a persuasive argument for such change.

Public opinion proved easier to move than before, not only because of increased demand for workers and patriotic fervor to strengthen national defense, but for subtler reasons as well. Mussolini invaded Ethiopia in 1935, and Hitler snubbed a black U.S. Olympic team athlete, Jesse Owens, at the 1936 Berlin Olympics. These events linked Nazism and Fascism with racism in American thought, a link intensified by rumors (and later evidence) of Nazi ill-treatment of Jews. While many whites lived easily with the contradiction of opposing racism abroad while accepting it at home, others made the connection and began, however slowly, to support changes in the way whites treated blacks. This small opening in the wall of racism allowed the black community to win some long-sought changes in discriminatory practices of private agencies and employers and of city government.[16]

The NAACP finally succeeded in placing blacks in several city departments previously closed to them. In 1942, Dr. Edward Bernecker, Commissioner of Hospitals in New York City, announced that all city nursing schools would accept qualified black student nurses. By 1943, over 300 black nurses served in the city's Department of Health, and 1,250 more worked on hospital staffs as nurses, administrators, and supervisors. In this, New York City held the best record of black hiring in the country. Sydenham Hospital integrated its staff, the first voluntary hospital in the city to do so. The New York Urban League persuaded most convalescent homes to accept black patients. In conjunction with Harlem newspapers, the NYUL opened a school to train blacks for the police examinations. When New York City took over the private subway lines in 1940, the NAACP persuaded LaGuardia to forbid discrimination in the hiring of mechanics and motormen.[17]

Despite this victory, the transportation labor force proved difficult to integrate, in part because the struggle involved many separate groups, including the municipal government, unions, and private employers. Ultimately a multiracial coalition emerged, but almost a decade passed before that goal was accomplished. Throughout the Depression, black organizations had struggled against racism in subway and bus jobs. The city, which owned all the subway lines by 1940, proved fairly responsive. The private bus companies, on the other hand, resisted such pressures, and the white head of the Transport Workers Union (TWU), Mike Quill, offered only sporadic help to the cause until the end of the decade. In 1934, for example, of 10,000 employees, the then-privately owned IRT included only 580 blacks, who worked as messengers, porters, and cleaners. The BMT had two hundred, in comparable jobs. Quill did join the NAACP and the Coordinating Committee for Employment at about that time in persuading the IRT to hire blacks in high-level positions. Yet when blacks lost their jobs a few months later, Quill and the union remained silent. As a result, when the IRT joined the municipal system, blacks fought to institute civil service rather than have union affiliation.

By the time the TWU went on strike against the bus companies over wages in 1941, Quill had become more outspoken on behalf of blacks. The Negro Labor Committee, the Coordinating Committee, the NAACP, the Harlem Labor Union, and the National Negro Congress launched a boycott of the Fifth Avenue Bus Company and the New York Omnibus Company at the same time as the TWU strike. The HLU originated the idea of a black bus boycott, but Adam Powell quickly moved to lead the struggle.

Once the union won its strike, the black organizations requested that the union help them lift the ban on black drivers and mechanics. As Powell pointed out, blacks stayed off the buses so whites could win a higher living standard. Now blacks asked whites to do the same for them. For nearly a month, the United Bus Strike Committee set up pickets at bus stops in Harlem and held rallies. Although the

TWU claimed to support black efforts, its actions throughout the picketing were ambivalent. But the Communist party, which had organized the union and which participated actively in the black boycott through the National Negro Congress and the Coordinating Committee, pushed Quill hard. Some Harlemites picketed TWU headquarters. The three parties—the TWU, the Bus Strike Committee, and the bus companies—finally began to negotiate. First, the TWU proposed a hiring scheme that alternated between the races as new jobs opened. The company, seeking to divide the TWU and the Bus Strike Committee, offered to hire only blacks for the next 180 available positions if the TWU would suspend the seniority rule for white workers currently laid off. The union balked, and Quill was caught in the middle. The final agreement placed 91 laid-off workers first, then 170 blacks, then agreed to alternate white and black hirings until the black proportion of the total work force reached 17 percent. In 1944 (by which time the city ran all the Manhattan bus and subway lines), more blacks were employed in this field in New York City than anywhere else in the country. Only with a strong black voice and the cooperation of management and union leadership did private industry change its practices.[18]

Another new multiracial coalition that emerged in the early 1940s also won several important victories. In November 1941, Magistrate Anna Kross, presiding in a Harlem court and confronted daily with Harlem's problems, called a meeting of social agencies. This gathering of more than 250 black and white "leading citizens," including Adam Clayton Powell, Sr., Algernon Black of the Ethical Culture Society, Lester Granger of the Urban League, Walter White of the NAACP, A. Philip Randolph, three state assemblymen, Father George Ford (a white Catholic priest), Robert Wagner, Jr., and Rabbi David Pool of the Spanish-Portuguese Synagogue, gave birth to the Citywide Citizens' Committee on Harlem. It took as its mandate "To relieve the suffering and the tensions, to fulfill the promise of equality of opportunity . . . to try to make up for the neglects and mistakes of the past in the relations between Negro and white communities." Its efforts won places for blacks in jobs both in Harlem, and in private companies and public utilities elsewhere in the city. Delegations met with managers and consumer groups to gain their cooperation in hiring blacks for non-menial positions. Though it was in many ways a continuation of earlier coalitions such as the Greater New York Coordinating Committee, the Citizens' Committee had an advantage. The executive order provided a model for laws and regulations against racial discrimination, and the governor and mayor supported state and municipal efforts to extend its provisions to all employers. The Governor's Committee on Discrimination in Employment and the Committee on Fair Employment Practice committed the two levels of government to combat racism in defense industries, and in 1945, New York State became the first state to establish an agency empowered to "eliminate and prevent discrimination in [all] employment because of race, color or national origin either by employers, labor organizations, employment agencies or other persons."[19]

The Citywide Citizens' Committee had clout, given its members and government support for its goals, and had several important triumphs. Although New York Telephone had agreed in theory to hire black operators, it did not actually do so until pressured by the Citizens' Committee and the FEPC. By 1944 it had finally hired six. Two years later, 200 blacks held such jobs, "and they are distributed throughout the various exchanges of the city." This victory gave New York the most integrated telephone system in the nation. In 1946, only 230 blacks worked as operators in the entire country.[20]

The Citizens' Committee seemed proudest, though, of its victory against child care agencies that discriminated against blacks. Of twenty-four agencies that served neglected children dependent on the state, only five accepted blacks before 1942. The numbers of such black children had declined a bit since the 1930s, but their proportion in the dependent juvenile population rose because of the larger drop in the number of white dependent children. Of all youths committed to the Children's Aid Society by the Department of Welfare, 30 percent were black in 1940, rising to 55 percent in 1942. The Domestic Relations Court noted in 1942 that for this group, "there are no facilities whatsoever except boarding homes. The Colored Orphan Asylum has closed intake to girls," and boarding homes had proven harder to find in wartime. As Roi Ottley explained, "What makes Negroes in Harlem especially indignant is that a large number of the private institutions—openly barring Negro juvenile delinquents and neglected children—are supported mainly by city taxes." The Citizens' Committee persuaded the New York City Board of Estimate to pass a resolution in May of 1942—the Race Discrimination Amendment—that withheld city funds from any institution for children that discriminated on the basis of race.[21] Again, blacks won in wartime what they could not achieve in peace.

The first to comply with the new rule was the Colored Orphan Asylum, which changed its name to the Riverdale Children's Association. That agency received no applications from white children for two years. Jewish and Catholic agencies also agreed immediately, though at little cost since most black children were Protestant. Of Protestant groups, nine institutions with places for 626 children flatly refused and lost municipal funding by 1945. Seven agreed to accept blacks and had taken 100 by 1945, while three others that had agreed still had not taken any by that date. Despite this slow start, black children eventually received service everywhere.[22] The Race Discrimination Amendment took the city a long way toward better accommodating the needs of these children.

Another organization also won a long-sought victory. The Committee on Street Corner Markets, which included members from the Urban League, NAACP, Rabbinical Assembly, Domestic Workers Union, Women's Trade Union League, Harlem branch of the YWCA, and State Department of Labor, finally persuaded the city to provide a hiring hall to replace the Bronx "slave markets." Still, the victory was far less than what was needed. Cara Cook, chairperson of the committee, explained that the hiring hall was only to provide "comfortable quarters off the streets. . . . We will not supervise [hiring] . . . arrangements or interfere with them in any way." The sanctity of private contracts took precedence over the enforcement of decent minimum standards for employment.

Another wartime benefit for Harlem, albeit related more to expediency than to politics, was additional public day-care facilities. While Central Harlem, with nineteen such agencies, received a less than equitable share of Manhattan's 199, still, this marked an increase from the number open in the 1930s. All but two provided care all day long. If the surrounding Health Areas (East Harlem, Riverside, Washington Heights) are included, the area had 113 facilities, two-thirds licensed or inspected by a municipal agency. The thirty-seven Board of Education nursery schools, previously open only to relief children, now accepted children of all working mothers. Approximately 800 to 1,000 children received day care in Central Harlem alone. The Children's Aid Society reported that in the early 1940s more children participated in its Harlem clubs, kindergartens, recreation, and daily lunch programs than had in the 1930s.[23]

Despite these improvements, Harlem's economic and social life saw little substantial change in the early 1940s. While economic opportunities expanded, discrimination remained widespread, and blacks still did not improve their economic standing as quickly as whites did. The changes that had come failed to fundamentally alter the underlying racism of the system. The 1942 report of the Citizens' Committee on Harlem charged:

> The lack of equitable job opportunities, together with other restrictions, constitute the main causes of the deplorable housing problem, the high incidence of illness, family disorganization, disproportionate rate of delinquency, and the high incidence of . . . crime.

Even after the establishment of the Fair Employment Practices Committee and other wartime measures, blacks in Harlem still found it more difficult than whites to obtain employment and relied more often on public relief. Those who had work still had difficulty rising to skilled positions. While the Association to Promote Proper Housing for Girls complained that its houses for working-class women in the city could not attract tenants in 1944 because "unemployment and very low wage working girls are almost non-existent," its house in Harlem, Club Caroline, was full, meeting "a very definite need in the community."[24]

In 1943, Assemblyman William Andrews charged: "There is still a vast surplus of available able-bodied men and women who deserve but cannot find compensatory work and consequently must remain on public relief rolls. Of these the Negro has suffered most acutely—and primarily because of his color. . . . Many employers and also many workers refuse to permit Negroes to work on equal terms with others and they are either entirely excluded, or regardless of capabilities, are kept in the most menial and unskilled jobs."

This remained true for black women as well as men. The NUL played on patriotic sentiments to encourage the employment of black women, adopting as its 1943 Vocational Opportunity Campaign slogan: "Womanpower is vital to victory." It argued that of 1,900 war occupations over 1,400 were "suitable to women." Many women in the city in fact already worked in these jobs. "Yet in spite of the progress women workers have made in the overall picture of war production there is a definite lag in the full employment of Negro women." Almost two-thirds of all black women still worked in domestic and personal service in 1943.

As late as 1944, whites still moved to higher jobs more often than blacks. Nationally, for example, the proportion of blacks in the ranks of laborers, personal service, and domestic workers rose (although the absolute numbers of blacks in those fields declined), because whites left these jobs before blacks could.[25] Blacks did have better opportunities than before, but still fared worse than whites.

Thus black family income remained below white, although the expenditure gap was smaller than it had been in the Depression. In 1943, the average New York City family spent $2,740, slightly more in Manhattan. In Harlem, the figure was $2,395. This continued poverty meant living conditions in Harlem remained worse than elsewhere. The Federation of Protestant Welfare Agencies found 40 percent of the black elderly it studied in 1945 (whom it defined as those over fifty-five) living "in the very poorest of circumstances" with only 20 percent receiving some sort of public aid. Of those over sixty-five, only a third received Social Security (although those who did, received as much aid as whites). A quarter had to be supported by relatives, and almost as many had to continue working to survive.

A further illustration of the greater poverty of the black community comes from the Children's Aid Society's Service Bureau for Negro Children. In 1943 it accepted for care one-quarter of all black applicants, but only 8 percent of white applicants. It is doubtful that white families gave up their children more readily and so were rejected by the CAS as less needy. Rather, these figures reveal the greater resources the CAS knew were available to the white community both to avoid destitution and to provide alternative services for children whose parents could not afford to keep them.[26]

Black mortality rates still exceeded white. In 1943 the city reported 12.8 deaths per thousand blacks, compared with 10.7 for whites (excluding the armed forces). Infant mortality rates explained much of the discrepancy: 62 deaths of children under one year for every thousand live black births, compared with 38 per thousand for white. While Central Harlem's mortality rates had improved somewhat since the thirties, its health problems remained severe. The Central Harlem infant mortality rate was the highest in the borough. Its tuberculosis death rate, while lower than during the Depression, remained more than twice the borough's average and over four times the city's. The Citizens' Committee blamed much of this on poor health facilities: "Harlem Hospital as a physical unit is inadequate to meet the needs of the community it serves." It was overcrowded, while the two private hospitals nearby rarely accepted black patients. As a result, although the city considered five beds per thousand inhabitants the desired ratio, the Harlem area provided two.[27]

The war years also did nothing to destroy residential segregation, and blacks continued to endure its liabilities. Harlem residents still faced higher costs than other city residents. The Citizens' Committee reported that "food costs are so steep in the immediate Harlem area that Negroes who work in other sections buy away from Harlem to save money." The New York City Department of Markets reported Harlem prices were 15 to 20 percent higher than in other city areas.

The NAACP surveyed small grocery and large chain stores, and examined shoppers' receipts in several poor city neighborhoods in 1942. The same shopping list of basic food items that cost $3.88 in Harlem cost 5 to 15 percent less in the Lower East Side, Hell's Kitchen, Bedford-Stuyvesant, or Greenwich Village. For each $25 spent on food downtown, it cost $1.50 more to buy the same food in Harlem. A pound of bacon cost 34¢ at a Lower East Side chain store, and 42¢ in Harlem. Lettuce was 8¢ a head on the Lower East Side and 12¢ in Harlem. "It would seem she [the Harlem housewife] pays more for products inferior even to those that cost considerably less in other sections of New York." A survey by *PM* magazine in 1942 of twelve Harlem grocery stores found prices 15 to 25 percent higher than elsewhere. A three-and-a-half-pound bag of flour bought at an independently owned store on the Lower East Side cost 22¢, but 26¢ in Harlem. A dozen eggs came to 55¢ in Harlem, a nickel higher than downtown. A followup a year later revealed no change. Chain stores, though offering goods at a lower price, in fact made even more of a profit: "The chain stores literally exploit in Harlem to a greater extent."

Perhaps white control of these stores helps explain the apparent exploitation; a black owned only one of the forty-three independent stores investigated. Of the other forty-two, half employed blacks. No chain groceries did. Still, the black-owned store also charged high prices. More likely, the exploitation came from a deeper cause, the systemic racism that nourished segregation throughout the city. Much of Harlem's high food prices did reflect real costs. The *PM* survey determined that store rents were 20 to 50 percent higher in Harlem than in other poor neighborhoods and found that most store owners extended credit to their customers, which also increased expenses. The NAACP reached the same conclusion. Some Harlemites did create an alternative to such high prices, with two cooperatives at 479 West 150th Street and 202 West 136th Street, which offered food at a lower cost.

If higher prices were partly out of store owners' control, quality and availability of items were not. Quality was lower in Harlem, and storekeepers cheated their customers more often. The *PM* investigator found the meat quality poorer, and grade A eggs difficult to find. Moreover, the posted price often did not tally with the price actually charged. The Department of Markets reported it still received more complaints about short weights from Harlem than from any other city neighborhood.[28]

Other long-standing discriminatory practices also remained unchanged. Despite some progress in sheltering neglected black children, facilities for delinquent black youngsters were still inadequate. In 1942 the Domestic Relations Court warned: "The situation . . . is indeed grave." Few private agencies accepted blacks, and state agencies had no more space available. Despite the fact that the numbers of delinquents did not rise substantially for either race, spaces had become difficult to find for both black and white delinquents because so many institutions had closed. In 1940 the court committed 887 delinquent children to institutions; over half went to agencies not in operation two years later. Shelters were filled to capacity with more children awaiting placement. Furthermore, according to the court, "the average stay of Negroes [in those shelters] is longer than Whites." In a study of this problem, the New York City Department of Investigation and Accounts found that, of sixteen children staying in temporary shelters longer than a week, only one was white. Of the 212 staying less than five days, 134 were white.[29]

Some of these children needed foster care, which proved no easier to find. Again, the situation was worse for blacks than for whites. "For some children, particularly in the Protestant Negro group, no such treatment is provided by the State, City or private institutions." As the court reminded the mayor:

> The situation in regard to Protestant Negro children is not new. . . . [We] have repeatedly called attention to the lack of institutional facilities for these children. For years it has been necessary to turn back into the community children who were a menace to themselves or others, because no facilities or inadequate facilities existed for them. One might speculate just how much this situation contributed to the recently publicized crimes of violence in the Harlem area.

A 1942 memo from the Domestic Relations Court stated that black Protestant delinquent boys over twelve were either sent to the Society for the Prevention of Cruelty to Children (a temporary shelter) or back home, as there was no place available for them. Placement services for black Protestant delinquent girls, as with neglected girls, "are even more limited than for boys," consisting of seven beds at the Brooklyn Training School and fifteen at the Walkill Cottage of the CAS (and the latter had had no vacancies since September of the year before). The New York State Training School for Girls had been full "for some time."[30]

Thus, many of the fundamental problems black Harlemites had faced in the Depression remained essentially unchanged in the war years. While many in Harlem found employment, and often better employment, and while some improvements came as a result, many adverse conditions persisted. Harlem moved out of the Depression more slowly than other areas; for blacks, racism, segregation, and discrimination limited the wartime opportunities others enjoyed. Many in the black community anticipated real changes because of the executive order and other promising developments, but their hopes were not borne out. This fostered a certain ambivalence in the black community about the war effort. As Claude McKay found:

> Many step-ladder personalities . . . agitate the common crowd [in Harlem]. . . . While not altogether pro-Nazi they do gloat about the Nazis upsetting the international apple-cart, and they are not pro-British. Many of them declare that a Nazi victory might be better for the black people. . . . Often words such as these are tossed into the crowd: "The white folks don't care a damn about you." And the people argue, wondering how close the soap-boxers are to the truth. . . . There are no indications that the black people are pro-Nazi. But there may be a dangerous feeling that life cannot be worse for them even if the Nazis should win.

A black soldier wrote a letter to the *New York Age*. His patriotism could not be in question as he was serving his country, but his ambivalence was plain:

> Hope with me that I shall see . . . a second Emancipation Proclamation from prejudice . . . by these part-time Americans who . . . are . . . ripping to rags the American flag's meaning of equality. . . .
> I wish this was a mixed army. Then we Americans could actually be fighting side by side. . . . Then I could easily glare at the Japs and grit: this is my country, my native land.[31]

Or Does It Explode?

The gap between anticipated change and the much more limited actual improvements in the early 1940s aggravated underlying tensions of economic and social hardship in Harlem. In 1943 these tensions exploded into Harlem's second riot in a decade.

According to the police report of August 1, 1943, a police officer named Collins arrested a woman for disorderly conduct at the Braddock Hotel on 272 West 126th Street at about 7:00 P.M. A Mrs. Roberts interfered with the arrest. Her son, Robert Bandy, a soldier in uniform whom she was visiting, threatened the officer and punched him. The policeman placed him under arrest as well. By this point a small crowd had gathered, and when an unidentified man hit the police officer from behind, Bandy ran. The officer threw his nightstick at Bandy, who caught it. The policeman then drew his gun and fired, wounding the soldier. Bandy was then brought to the hospital, still under arrest.

The rumor rapidly spread (promoted by "agitators," claimed the police report) that a white policeman had killed a black soldier who had been protecting his mother.[32] Crowds gathered and smashed windows from 110th Street to 145th, but riot activity centered on 125th Street between Lenox and Eighth avenues. Looting came later in a "second wave." Mayor LaGuardia spent the night riding the streets in a police car trying to calm the rioters and restore order, while police arrested hundreds, mostly for disorderly conduct, unlawful entry, and burglary. The mayor closed the streets to traffic, ordered the bars and nightclubs shut, and persuaded several black ministers to join him in his pleas for calm. All in all, these actions helped minimize property damage and loss of life. Still, 1,469 stores were vandalized, 606 people arrested, and 189 injured. Six blacks were killed, four by police and two by other blacks. Damages and losses totaled between three and five million dollars.

Not unexpectedly, many in the following months sought to understand the nature and causes of the riot, especially because community participation in it had been widespread. As in the riot of 1935, rioters came from all classes and ages and both sexes, according to witnesses. Even the police acknowledged this: "Those actually committing malicious acts of violence were irresponsible, ignorant individuals. [But] the probability is that many decent citizens were in the various groups, who in the most instances are intelligent and law abiding, and while not actually taking part in the physical disturbances, aided and abetted, indirectly, in said disturbances, by their presence."[33]

Adam Clayton Powell, Sr., argued that the riot merely expressed overtly the anger and frustration that had long been present in Harlem:

When Bandy hit Collins over the head with that club, he was not mad with him only for arresting a colored woman, but he was mad with every white policeman throughout the United States who had consistently beaten, wounded, and often killed colored men and women without provocation. Those window smashers were not mad with the windows, they were mad with all the white men living or dead who had heaped every insult and indignity upon them for centuries. When they were smashing windows they thought they were breaking the skulls of . . . race haters and race baiters. They were wrong, terribly wrong, but they were mad and mad men are always abnormal.

Powell argued that the "first wave" of the riot was not vandalism, or greed born of economic deprivation, but a race riot. "These window-smashers were . . . race rioters expressing their pent-up hatred of the white man's pagan civilization, called Christian."

His son agreed. He too believed it was a race riot because the causes came out of the oppression of one race by another: from "blind, smoldering and unorganized . . . resentment against jim crow treatment of Negro men in the Armed Forces and the unusual high rents and cost of living forced upon Negroes in Harlem."[34]

Both men believed few of these rioters participated in the later wave of "wholesale looting, thieving and robbing." Powell Senior claimed the looters were a different group, "criminal subhuman savages" who cared not at all about social wrongs. Although not all were criminals, they all came from the "criminal class. They all want something for nothing. They never work except when they are forced and that is only for a short while." This analysis fit well with Powell's political position. By distinguishing between two sorts of black rioters, those with legitimate grievances and those simply out to loot, he made two important points. First, he warned white Americans of the danger of ignoring black frustrations. The "criminal class" always lurked, ready to strike using any pretext. Second, he reminded whites that not all protestors fit the stereotyped image of violent blacks seeking to gratify immediate desires. Whites could, and should, work with these "responsible" black people. The riot and the looting were a reality; Powell found a way to communicate the message of black anger while calming white fears of black violence.

A *Nation* editorial disagreed with Powell's claim that the looters were merely vandals. In its analysis of the root causes of the riot, the *Nation* referred to the economic hardship of Harlem, as Powell had, but argued that the looters, too, acted in response to economic frustrations, "protesting in their own way."

Sociologist Harold Orlansky agreed that the riot was fundamentally about race. Rioters did not vandalize black stores or harass black police. Black passersby were not attacked, but whites were. The object of attack that night was whites; perhaps not white people, but certainly white power. The riot began with the shooting of a black man by a white policeman. Would a black policeman in the same situation have sparked a riot? Thousands of blacks joined the riot, from all classes. Plenty of well-dressed middle-class blacks joined the fray. Orlansky concluded from all this that the focus was not economic need per se, but race.[35] Like the others, he tied the behavior of the rioters—all the rioters—to the economic frustration born of heightened expectations and dashed hopes, and saw in the riot a general protest against power and authority. He argued that each group in the riot took what it wanted: children took food and toys; men, clothing and liquor; and women, clothing and household goods. The riot was an attempt to seize what had been unfairly denied: as poor, the rioters protested against property; as blacks, they protested against whites. In each case, participants protested against authority that had been used systematically to oppress them.

Store owners in Harlem agreed it had been a race riot and that their white-owned stores had been the explicit targets. In a statement issued by the Harlem Chamber of Commerce, they argued that the police and government needed a tighter grip on Harlem, or store owners, fearful of another riot, would leave. That, they threatened, would "mean loss of jobs for Negroes." While the police's restraint "unquestionably spare[d] the lives of many rioters and looters . . . it sacrificed property . . . and immeasurably injured the prestige of the police with the lawless element in Harlem." Not unexpectedly, they denied that economics caused the riot: "Does anybody seriously believe that those gangsters are concerned over Harlem's economic problems?" Ignoring the fact that economic improvement had not come to Harlem as quickly as promised, or as quickly as it did to the white community, the Harlem Chamber of Commerce focused simply on the changes since the 1930s. "Harlem's purchasing power has never been greater." To prevent a recurrence, then, Harlem must look forward rather than backward. "Well meaning but misguided theorists have failed . . . because they insist on injecting into their investigations every ill from which Negroes have suffered for the past 75 years. This is no time to theorize. This is not time for ancient history. This is a job for the thinking people of Harlem, not for carpetbaggers." It would be hard to imagine a time when "ancient history" played more of a role than during the riot, but store owners naturally viewed the situation differently.

In a more conciliatory tone, the Harlem Chamber of Commerce went on to acknowledge the same ills they had just denied. It urged Harlem businesses to "lean over backwards" to obey price ceilings, to hire blacks, and not to raise rents, so residents would have no cause for frustration or rioting. Again, the fear of extremist activity, this time in the form of a riot, brought whites in power closer to an acceptance of the black moderates' position.[36]

The rioters' focus on white property and, by extension, white privilege, and the participation of black men and women of all ages and classes, certainly points to frustration shared throughout the black community. Social and economic conditions in Harlem had improved by 1943, thanks to New Deal programs and the wartime industrial boom. Yet, despite the New Deal, despite Executive Order 8802, despite local, state, and federal agency rules barring discrimination, blacks' income and occupational opportunities had not kept pace with whites'. Racism still prevailed. Housing, schools, and hospitals in Harlem remained in worse condition than those elsewhere in the city. A black soldier, fighting for America and against Nazi racism, had been shot by a white police officer. The imbalance in power relations that restricted African-Americans to those areas of least opportunity remained unchanged in 1943. Such unfulfilled expectations produced frustration and anger, which rumors of a racial killing channeled into violence. In spontaneous as in organized political action, inequality more than poverty provoked Harlemites.

Harlem's problems in the Depression and early war years—indeed, the problems of African-American communities in general—resulted from a complex combination of economic, demographic, and social factors that created oppression based on both race and economic class. Already severe before the Depression, these problems intensified with economic catastrophe. In response came the activism of an African-American community that continued to see discrimination at a time of both intense need and general government responsiveness to the plight of the poor. These struggles brought real victories. In the New Deal era and during wartime, black political action brought more financial support, better health care, and stricter rules against discrimination in government, unions, and industry. Change was possible; this awareness renewed and reinvigorated protest, both organized and spontaneous. Yet for all their successes, Harlem blacks gained significantly fewer benefits than whites did. It was this disjunction between the possibility of change and the meagerness of actual improvements that made Harlem riot twice. And each riot in turn reflected the community's at least half-conscious recognition that government would respond to its protest.

What brought riot rather than choreographed protest in 1943 may have been the failure of the external community to address black grievances adequately. In 1935 the "Don't Buy" coalition had collapsed, leaving no broadly accessible channel for protest in its wake, so black grievances had no outlet save riot. In 1943, black organizations like the Citizens' Committee continued to operate. What was missing at that time was the attention of the white world. The war preoccupied government officials, and black Harlemites may have sensed that little more could be accomplished through decorous behavior. Skeptical of the effectiveness of existing organizations, then, Harlemites saw no clear and promising method to redress grievances peacefully. If organized groups could not channel that protest energy, a riot is hardly a surprising result. In short, Harlemites responded to discrimination and prejudice with anger and violence when organized protest seemed useless. In that sense, the riots represented, not a rejection of political activity, but rather extensions of it.

Crisis brings change impossible to achieve in calmer times. The riot seemed no less a crisis to New Yorkers than the war, and Harlem received some real benefits as a result of both. LaGuardia promised to fight residential segregation in privately owned housing projects such as Stuyvesant Town and he argued for more postwar public housing projects for blacks. He increased funding for juvenile delinquency prevention programs. The Office of Price Administration announced one week after the riot its intention to open an office in Harlem. The mayor persuaded the Commissioner of Markets to crack down on price-ceiling violations in Harlem. In two weeks, that office issued 65 summonses and 51 warnings to Harlem merchants. Although not motivated by the riot, the city instituted rent control by the end of that year—the last major city in the country to do so.[37] Neither wartime improvements nor these new developments brought rapid or dramatic change to Harlem. Neither fundamentally altered the system of racism and class bias that trapped blacks. Yet each step forward brought more of the black poor out from the bottom, and fueled further community activism to win yet more improvements.

The Past Is Prologue

In 1929, the rest of the country plunged into the Depression already familiar to Harlem blacks. Wages and employment rates plummeted. Private charities gallantly struggled to aid the thousands of new needy; government did far less. At the bottom of the heap economically even in good times, blacks as a group suffered more than whites. Many had moved north in search of a better life and, generally, considered their new situation an improvement over the old. Yet they still found themselves struggling for the barest subsistence in the early Depression years.

It is hardly startling to conclude that as a group blacks suffered more than whites in the Depression because they were generally poorer and because they faced the additional burden of racial discrimination. Yet the nature of the black experience in this era is not easily reduced to such generalizations. The Depression did not lower black living standards as much as it did those of whites, because blacks had less distance to fall. In fact, because hardship was so widespread in the 1930s, government turned its full attention to the poor, and therefore to blacks, for the first time. This brought real benefits to a community long in need of them. With the election of Roosevelt and the installation of New Deal programs, outside aid became available to the city and its black community on an unprecedented scale. Public works and home relief agencies made millions of dollars and hundreds of thousands of jobs available to the needy.

Not that Harlemites did not suffer from a desperate, grinding poverty in the Depression. They did. Though no one found it easy to get or keep a job, for blacks it was more difficult than for whites. Employed black men and women lost their jobs before their white colleagues. When they did find work, it was generally menial and low-paying, in part because of lack of skills, and in part because of the intensified job competition of the Depression, which strengthened existing racial barriers to advancement. Even those blacks who managed to keep their white-collar, professional, or business positions found their earnings had plummeted.

The labor market in the Depression was divided not only by race but also by gender. Black women and men, both relegated to unskilled fields, did not do the same things. Furthermore, although black women found employment more quickly than men in the Depression, their jobs generally paid less and were more often temporary; they worked for fewer hours and for fewer weeks a year than black men did.

Before the Depression, at least blacks at the bottom were secure there—they held jobs whites did not want. After the Crash, black men and women both suddenly found themselves competing with whites for these worst jobs. In the desperation of the 1930s, white men were now willing—even eager—to compete for "Negro" men's jobs, such as porter or waiter. Similarly, white women moved into traditionally black women's jobs in domestic service. Thus the foothold blacks had gained in steady, if marginal and poorly paid, work was lost. At the same time, increased competition drove wages down still further and black unemployment leapt. Black family income, never high in prosperity, declined still further in the Depression, until average Harlem earnings totaled less than the "emergency standard" estimated by local and federal officials.

Relief grants amounted to almost as much as most blacks earned from private employment, and in that sense, to restate the point, going on relief did not bring about a decline in living standards for blacks to the same extent it did for whites. On the other hand, if there was little or no decline, this only demonstrates the absolute inadequacy of black earnings, because relief was universally acknowledged to be below what was considered a minimum standard of living.

This issue was not simply an academic one for Harlemites. Low relief payments had a significant impact on the quality of life in Harlem, since so many there relied on public aid. Underemployed, underskilled, undereducated, closer to destitution even in good times than were their white neighbors, blacks turned to outside help more often than did whites.

Even this aid was not equally distributed to blacks and whites. Most New York relief agencies discriminated against blacks in some way. Home relief was generally granted without regard to color, but questionable applications by blacks were less likely to receive the benefit of the doubt than those of whites. The Home Relief Bureau's job placement service often refused to place skilled blacks in appropriate jobs. Less obvious but still devastating in its impact, blacks in fact received less aid because the higher costs Harlemites incurred living in a segregated community were not reflected in their relief grants. African-Americans also suffered because they were less able, as a group, to demonstrate eligibility under the rules. The preponderance in Harlem of lodgers and others with no proof of residence meant more of Harlem's needy failed to qualify for aid.

Work relief, especially that provided through private subcontracting, often overtly excluded qualified blacks from employment. While many blacks did work on public projects, far fewer of them received jobs than their proportion among the unemployed warranted. Most work relief projects segregated black workers, assigning them jobs only in Harlem or placing all blacks in menial jobs, regardless of skill level. All this may have been at least in part due to the lack of black staff in the responsible agencies; qualified blacks found it significantly harder than whites to find employment there. Although Mayor LaGuardia and the administrators of several agencies tried to rectify inequalities as the black community brought them to public attention, discrimination continued to mar public relief programs.

But the New Deal also brought real improvement to Harlem. Whatever its limits, blacks did benefit tremendously from relief programs. Perhaps the financial help was not as plentiful as it might have been, or as generous as it was to whites, but it did keep thousands from starvation and eviction. In many cases the aid received was no worse than the meager earnings families had managed on in times of national prosperity, and certainly was more than blacks had ever before received from government. Employment programs provided jobs and skills to men and women who often had neither. Work relief projects in Harlem not only provided employment, they improved the community. Projects built better roads and drainage systems, new housing and other facilities, and brought day care, health, educational, and similar services to local residents.

Health care, public employment, family relief, child care—in many ways these made Harlemites better off than before the Depression. In the 1930s Harlem had more clinics, playgrounds, day nurseries, and art, vocational, and academic classes than it did in the previous decade. A far higher proportion of blacks received relief than whites, both in New York City and in other urban centers, north and south. Municipal governments, particularly in northern cities, seemed more responsive to black needs. As their dramatic swing to the Democratic party demonstrates, blacks believed the New Deal relief agencies had made a tremendously beneficial difference in their lives.[38]

In part, the New Deal served blacks as well as it did because of an activist black and leftist political community that protested inequality at every point. Already organized through their churches and service agencies and long involved in local politics, blacks had the experience necessary to mobilize successfully on their own behalf. The Depression fostered this culture of political activism. Harlem residents took the skills they had developed and fought for better job opportunities in both private and public employment, and for fairer treatment by relief agencies. Harlemites flocked to picket lines and demonstrations in support of dozens of causes, led by integrationists, nationalists, Communists, and trade unionists.

These protests brought black issues into the public eye, as did the 1935 riot. Political leaders and private employers implemented changes in response. Thus, by the end of the Depression, African-Americans worked as clerks in white-owned stores and public utilities, more often belonged to unions, and held responsible jobs in civil service, in relief agencies, and in government, all the result of black mass action.

The relationship between protest and change was not one-way. The possibility of change, the evidence of change, inspired action. Blacks in Harlem and other northern urban communities protested more often and more overtly than did rural southern blacks. A tradition of visible, large-scale protest had emerged in places like Harlem (where violent retaliation was less likely) and was reinforced every time the political system responded. Victories, however minor, helped many blacks do better than they otherwise might have.

Despite these protests, public aid often still failed blacks. Where that occurred, private agencies, both white and black, tried to fill the gaps. With home and work relief programs in place, private philanthropy no longer had to sustain the destitute singlehandedly, and many organizations expanded their non-financial services. In serving the black community, the record of white-sponsored private relief efforts resembled that of the New Deal agencies. Some made real efforts not to discriminate, taking pains to hire black staff and to locate offices in the Harlem area. Many others, however, expressly limited their clientele to whites or made only restricted services or funds available to blacks. While they may have provided critically needed services, such as health care, meals, recreation programs, nurseries, and temporary shelter, to Harlem residents, they also acted to uphold the racial status quo rather than to challenge it. Thus, vocational training programs and job placement bureaus advocated traditionally black jobs for their Harlem clients. Workers at these agencies placed black children in all-black camps, orphanages, and foster homes. Those who opposed the racial discrimination of other agencies relied on moral suasion to bring change, rather than seeking legislation as they would in the next decade.

Black organizations provided services as well. Theoretically, they operated without the access limitations and problematic methods of the white organizations. Their effective reach, however, was sharply limited by small budgets and staffs.

Both the poverty of the Depression and these anti-poverty programs shaped people's lives in Harlem. Deflation brought prices down, although this did not help the unemployed. The pump-priming of the New Deal brought prices back up a bit, creating more jobs and more income, but making it more difficult to make ends meet on low earnings or aid grants. The most desperate, unable to meet their family's financial needs, placed their children in institutions that were ostensibly for orphans. Desertion and crime rates rose. Yet many believed that relief minimized the number of families driven to such extremes. Fluid black household structures also helped mitigate the devastating effects of unemployment and family separation.

The Depression brought deterioration of city housing because landlords could not afford to maintain their properties. Loss of income also forced families to move into cheaper, smaller, and more dilapidated apartments. In Harlem, blacks still in the grip of segregation could not threaten to move to other neighborhoods if landlords kept rents high or did not maintain the building. As a result they had to pay more for housing and often brought in lodgers to defray the cost. Overcrowding intensified. Building conditions worsened. New, publicly funded low-income housing offered an alternative to some who were living in the worst quarters, but the supply of such apartments fell far short of the need.

Mortality rates, especially for contagious diseases like tuberculosis, remained high in Harlem during the Depression as a result of the generally poor living conditions. Poor nutrition resulting from meager food budgets heightened the problem. The new availability of clinics in the New Deal years made regular health care available to many Harlemites for the first time, however, so while black death rates stayed higher than white throughout the decade, they did decline once New Deal programs were in place.

Other advances came as well. Education levels rose and political participation increased in the Depression decade. New social services provided children with constructive activities off the streets when no parent was at home. The thoroughly mixed record of those trying years was pointed up by the Urban League's findings: as a result of the Depression, black professionals served their communities with greater commitment than before, children remained in school longer, blacks received better medical care, and government aid was easier to obtain; but there was more overcrowding and more husbands deserted their wives.[39]

There was a similar mix of improvement and inequity in the early war years. The expansion of American defense industries brought the country as a whole out of the Depression. It brought blacks out as well, but to a much lesser extent than whites, and more slowly. As war industries received new orders, they threw open the doors to workers desperate for a job. Yet blacks did not receive a fair share, nor did most skilled blacks find jobs commensurate with their abilities. Training and apprenticeship programs refused black applicants, or accepted very few. Not until A. Philip Randolph threatened a march on Washington in 1941 did President Roosevelt agree to issue Executive Order 8802 prohibiting discrimination by companies receiving government contracts. At this point things improved noticeably for Harlem blacks, not only in terms of employment and training, but in the responsiveness of local government to many manifestations of racial discrimination. Again, black political protest had succeeded.

In the first few years, however, mobilization for war brought relatively little real improvement in the basic opportunities available to Harlem blacks. Economic hardship caused by discrimination continued to plague Harlem, which in turn perpetuated that area's poor housing, health, and social conditions. More laws existed in 1943 prohibiting discrimination, but many public agencies and private organizations ignored them. A dismaying number of unions and training programs still excluded blacks. African-Americans continued to face discrimination in hiring and promotions. The limited nature of the wartime changes, and their slowness in arriving, caused Harlem to riot in 1943 over the shooting of a black soldier in uniform by a white police officer.

As a 1944 article in *Collier's* described it, Harlem, with the "largest concentration of Negroes in the world" had "obscene living conditions" in which 300,000 blacks lived in housing designed for 75,000. Lacking adequate day care, jobs, or police protection, and afraid wartime gains would be taken away after peace was won, Harlem "as a whole [remains] very inflammable, dynamically race conscious, emotionally on the hair trigger, doggedly resentful of its Jim Crow estate. It doesn't ignite, it explodes."[40] If the desperate poverty of the Depression meant the nation was too involved with economic issues to pay much attention to racial ones, now the war in Europe overrode all other concerns. As earlier, then, blacks in the war-preparation years made some real gains, but the continuing impact of racism ensured that they lagged behind those of whites.

The testimony, stories, and statistics presented here illuminate and detail the experience of African-Americans in the Depression. Harlem provides example after example of the complex workings of social and political change within the existing system. In the microcosm of Harlem, divergent groups and issues met—national policies and local interests, black and white, integrationist and nationalist, public and private, political and philanthropic. Not always in opposition, these groups alternately merged and split in a complex reflection of race, class, and gender dynamics in the shadow of poverty and powerlessness. The imperfect progress of Harlem blacks in the 1930s mirrors the ambivalence in American society regarding questions of race, poverty, and power.

Harlem struggled inside an interlocking structure of racist institutions and assumptions from which it did not escape. Yet, within these limits much change did occur—short of what should have been, but far beyond what had been before. Though Harlem did not do well compared with white communities, it did far better compared with its earlier self. United effort by Harlemites and the commitment of some government officials enlarged opportunities. This contradiction of change within fixed boundaries defined the African-American experience during the Depression.

The New Deal period did see a shift in the attitudes of some whites about blacks. Several federal officials, in acknowledging government's obligation to help the poor, also recognized that the aid ought to be distributed solely on the basis of need. They therefore opposed discrimination. While in many places such high-minded pronouncements fell on deaf ears, in New York, LaGuardia and his appointees proved sensitive to questions of racial equality, as did many local administrators of federal agencies.

Seeing this receptiveness, Harlemites could mobilize to ensure the promised fair treatment and illuminate the areas of continued discrimination. While black political efforts in this period did not fundamentally alter the power relations of American society, they did accomplish a great deal. In the short run, blacks won white-collar jobs, union membership, more equitable treatment by some relief agencies, and other benefits. In the longer run, the movement of some blacks into higher-level jobs (and the downward movement of whites into "Negro" jobs) began to break down traditional assumptions about occupational segregation by race.

But certain conditions present in the black community and in the larger society tended to work against more permanent or far-reaching change. Internal struggles over class versus nationalist goals or between moderate and radical perspectives divided an otherwise potent effort. At the same time, contradictions in the white community over the relationship of race to class limited progress from that direction.

Poverty and scarcity were not new to blacks; inequality rather than poverty per se stirred Harlemites to action in the New Deal era. How to fight it became the over-riding question. Members of the community differed, proposing solutions that worked at times in concert but occasionally at cross-purposes. The range of available choices illuminated the possibilities and the limits of black opportunity in the Depression. Groups differed in strategy and style. The NAACP and Urban League worked quietly, behind the scenes, while Powell and the Communist party stirred masses of people to march. The Harlem Labor Union advocated still more confrontational methods. Ideology varied as well. Some in the community believed that since whites held power, integrationist policies were blacks' only hope. Others, arguing that blacks ought to strengthen their own community since whites would not, advocated nationalist policies. Yet these distinctions did not represent separate constituencies. While black leaders generally supported one view or the other, and preferred one type of strategy, most Harlemites shifted their support back and forth during the Depression. What seemed appropriate for one situation made less sense in others. Thus most of the black community supported both a "buy black" campaign and the drive to unionize black workers in existing white labor organizations. They petitioned in support of NAACP efforts, and picketed with the Communist party and the Citizens' League.

More than any other determinant, pragmatism seemed to be the compelling force behind Harlemites' choices of allegiance. Few advocated revolution; few quarreled with the successes of black political action. Most attached themselves to programs or movements that seemed to offer improvement in the opportunity structure of Depression-era New York. Certainly professional and well-to-do blacks made up the core membership of the Urban League and the NAACP, and they generally preferred quiet methods that did not involve taking to the streets. Better connected in the white community, they were concerned about jeopardizing white support, and at the same time more confident of gaining direct access to white leaders. All-black organizations and those made up of poorer and less-educated blacks had neither such concerns nor such confidence. Yet the well-to-do supported nationalist programs if those suited their self-interest, as when black businessmen advocated a "buy black" campaign; and many younger professionals and intellectuals embraced more confrontational tactics than did their seemingly staid elders.

The tactics employed in Harlem and elsewhere during the 1930s and early 1940s taught important lessons for future political struggles. Victories proved elusive when only one group pursued them, or the community let its attention flag. A combination of strategies seemed to be most effective. When extremists and moderates sought the same goal, progress usually resulted.

Any lapse of vigilance allowed whites to undo what blacks had achieved. Thus the Citizens' League's collapse set back the placement of white-collar blacks in Harlem stores. Civil rights–era struggles in Harlem to place black clerks and bus drivers testify to the continued reality of that political truth. White racism endured; black political victories often did not.

Success was also difficult for organizations working alone. The lack of broad backing limited the effectiveness of the Harlem Labor Union and the Communist party in winning positions for black clerks, and of the NAACP in integrating nursing programs. Successful political organizing depended on shaping and coordinating diverse approaches into a pointed, unified thrust. The Coordinating Committee enjoyed its victories only because all the elements of the struggle coincided: the HLU threatened shop owners from one side, while the sheer numbers in the coalition prevented the normal operation of business. At the same time, the riot reminded whites of what could happen if they ignored black demands, and the Mayor's Commission lent intellectual legitimacy to black grievances.

Overall, though, moderate strategies did tend to draw more support in the black community than more radical efforts, whether nationalist or Communist. Harlemites participated in rallies and demonstrations sponsored by whatever group championed causes they sympathized with: the Harlem Labor Union, the Communist party, and the AfroAmerican Federation of Labor received broader support for their programs than their membership rolls might suggest. Nevertheless, regardless of whether communism or black nationalism were feasible options for the period, the community simply did not support either position in a deep and sustained way. Most politically active Harlemites supported the efforts of those seeking integration with the wider world of economic and political opportunity, and participated in actions of other groups only insofar as they furthered these goals. Radicals did often help force concessions from the white community, but those concessions usually met the demands of the moderate groups. Even the successes of radical groups, then, seemed to strengthen the moderates.

Violence also played a part in improving conditions in Harlem. When formal means for redressing grievances broke down with the Citizens' League's collapse, when nothing as forceful emerged to take its place, anger and resentment exploded into violence. The riot of 1935 demonstrated in a dramatic and frightening way that blacks were unwilling to accept inequality passively. The riot's destructiveness and the implicit threat of further violence persuaded private citizens and public officials alike to respond to black complaints. That this response did not go far enough is evidenced by continued protest and a second riot eight years later. Nevertheless what changes did come resulted in large measure from the riot of 1935.

Government support also proved critical to the success of black efforts. FDR and his appointees in several New Deal agencies did make rules against discrimination in many New Deal programs. In New York the strong commitment of LaGuardia provided a standard of fairness to which black groups could then hold agencies and individuals. The community had to keep after government officials before they would act. Nevertheless, had the officials not been responsive, few black protests would have had any effect. Even in New York, racist administrators managed to circumvent rules against discrimination. Thus both black activism and the receptiveness of white officials contributed to the improvement in conditions.

But government support also limited the scope of black successes. Municipal agencies made no attempts to control decisions of private organizations or employers. Every battle won in one agency had to be repeated in the next. And other concerns like patronage or seniority affected LaGuardia's appointments as much as did the candidate's political views on race. Some departments operated virtually autonomously, such as the hospitals and the police, and there was little LaGuardia could do to challenge the racism there. Commitments to maintain the status quo also limited government's will to bring about change. It was Public Works Administration policy, for example, to build housing projects that would reflect the racial composition of existing neighborhoods—in other words, maintain segregation.

Furthermore, the theories underlying the government's decisions limited the help it could give to blacks. Since economic need was the overwhelming issue in the Depression, in theory, race was irrelevant. Therefore, in the name of fairness, agencies were to provide equal amounts of aid to whites and blacks. This by no means always translated into actual practice. But even when it did, as was generally the case in New York, the assumptions of the underlying theory were flawed. In reality race determined economic opportunity to an extent generally unacknowledged by liberal whites of the period. Race-blind policies therefore often hurt the race that was farther behind to begin with. Segregation and discrimination meant Harlem had different and greater needs, needs not acknowledged by a bureaucracy committed to balance sheets, budgets, and other administrative standards. Therefore, national and local government policies aided blacks on one hand, yet worked against any real change on the other. Blacks received needed monetary aid and services, and occasionally argued successfully for anti-discriminatory agency rules, but the government made little effort to challenge those racist assumptions and institutions that trapped blacks at the lowest socio-economic levels.

If the African-American community that lived with these interlocking social, political, and economic limitations was a "culture of poverty," then it was a culture very different from the one many sociologists and historians have suggested. Instead of passively accepting their fate, Harlemites fought vigorously and effectively for improved opportunities and living conditions. Certainly community and family life adapted to conditions of poverty and racial oppression. Household structure remained fluid so that most could find some kind of economic support in hard times and had somewhere to live in a segregated city. Sharing, swapping, and borrowing within extended networks of kin, friends, and social groups were familiar in Harlem life, supplemented with occasional "economic misdemeanors." But the apathetic unemployed, the school dropouts, the irresponsible families unwilling to leave welfare painted by theorists of a "culture of poverty" (and lately of an "underclass") simply were not the norm there. Individuals looked constantly for work and took the most unpleasant jobs rather than accept unemployment. Families chose debt, unremitting labor, and overcrowding before they resorted to relief. Children remained in school longer than ever before and adults returned to school once classes became available to them. Harlemites took to the streets in both violent and non-violent protests. While female-headed families and illegitimacy were more common in black communities (or at least, more openly admitted to), neither bore any relation to the economic well-being of that family during the Depression. The community simply was not the self-destructive, lethargic, dependent one described by some scholars and policy makers.

Nor is there any evidence welfare destroyed the black family. Desertion rates rose in the Depression, but not among relief families. In fact, the opposite appears to be true: during the Depression, relief helped keep families together. Only after World War II, when welfare agencies denied aid to families with unemployed males present, did it make economic sense for husbands in poverty-stricken families to desert their wives. Then, the best way a man could support his family was to leave it. Depression-era agencies recognized that employment was difficult to find, and gave aid to couples and two-parent families, thus actually decreasing the likelihood a couple would be forced to separate for economic reasons.

Unquestionably, Harlem blacks were better off in 1943 than they had been before the Depression. With war industries in full gear and numerous antidiscrimination laws in place, black employment opportunities had improved and the strength of an organized community would soon send a black man to Congress. African-Americans enjoyed a wider range of public and private services and benefited from rent control and better education and training programs. These years had provided the black community with the heady experience of a government more responsive to its needs than ever before, and most important, perhaps, with the exhilaration of political success.

Yet the limits of these improvements and successes remained glaring. Blacks certainly did not have the opportunities that whites had. In many ways, life for blacks had not changed; Harlem's root problems were too great to be remedied without dramatically altering the economic and social structure of the country. Harlemites remained trapped by the intersection of racial discrimination and poverty. Both the promise of improvement and the continued discrimination were real; it was the combination of the two, or the disjunction between them, that would soon renew and intensify the struggle for equal rights and equal opportunities.

Appendices

I. POPULATION

I have called black Harlem that part of upper Manhattan where the proportion of the population that is black exceeds Manhattan's average of 12 percent. There are two basic statistical divisions used for New York City: census tracts and Health Areas (approximately 10 block units). The former are smaller and more precise than the latter, but most municipal statistics are provided for Health Areas only. (Larger groupings of Health Areas are called Health Districts.)

Census tracts I use: 184, 186, 190, 201, 202, 204, 206, 207, 208, 210, 212, 213, 214, 216, 217, 218, 220, 221, 222, 226, 227, 228, 230, 231, 232, 234, 235, 236.

Health Areas (and their Health Districts):
Central Harlem (all): 8, 10, 12, 13, 15, 16, 19, 24
East Harlem: 20
Riverside: 11, 18
Washington Heights: 7, 9

Either way, the black population of Harlem is almost identical: 185,553 in the census tracts above, and 187,165 in the Health Areas. Using data on the whole area of Harlem, even where blacks were fewer than 12 percent, the black population totals 189,257.

Because so much of black Harlem is not completely black, if available data do not provide race breakdowns, I use only Central Harlem for determining black characteristics. (Central Harlem Health District contains all four Health Areas over 95 percent black, and overall, was 70 percent black. Furthermore, 63 percent of all Manhattan blacks lived in Central Harlem.) The population in Central Harlem differs in some ways from the black population on the outskirts of the area, such as in family structure and income level. Unfortunately, Central Harlem statistics are the only ones that can be assumed reliably to refer mainly to blacks. Of course, these data will be supplemented by Harlem and Manhattan data when available by race.

New York Population Figures, 1930

	Population	Percent Black
New York City	6,930,446	4.7
New York City black	327,706	
New York City foreign-born black	54,754	
New York City "other races"	15,515	
Manhattan	1,867,312	12.0
Manhattan black	224,670	
Manhattan foreign-born black	39,833	
Manhattan "other races"	10,886	

New York Population Figures, 1930 (*Continued*)

	Population	Percent Black
Harlem (H.A.s over 12% black)	342,790	54.6
Harlem (by census tract)	277,881	
Harlem black (H.A.s over 12% black)	187,165	
Harlem black (by census tract)	185,553	
Harlem "other races" (H.A.s)	1,396	

Data for Harlem Health Areas

	Population 1930			Population 1940			Percent
H.A.	Total	"Colored"	Percent	Total	"Colored"	Percent	Unemployed*
7	33,691	21,863	64.9	37,532	32,788	87.4	22.7
8	30,412	29,892	98.3	32,314	32,246	99.8	28.1
9	24,853	4,418	17.8	28,894	5,193	18.0	19.3
10	28,593	28,401	99.3	28,203	28,085	99.6	28.9
11	22,673	6,721	29.6	24,192	6,968	28.8	23.9
12	23,863	22,717	95.2	22,590	22,500	99.6	27.7
13	24,359	23,548	96.7	25,087	24,711	98.5	34.3
15	22,068	11,855	53.7	23,999	22,584	94.1	29.7
16	27,252	8,753	32.1	26,166	12,462	47.6	31.4
18	25,048	4,123	16.5	28,538	13,424	47.0	17.8
19	24,810	12,008	48.4	26,436	24,595	93.1	31.7
20	30,696	8,478	27.6	28,833	12,973	43.3	37.0
24	24,472	5,784	23.6	24,904	21,239	85.3	27.8

*Percent of labor force, 1940. Includes those on public work.

Because 1940 provides only "colored" (black and "other races"), I used "colored" for both decades. The difference between black and "colored" in 1930 was less than 1 percent for every Health Area except #24, where the difference was 1.4 percent.

All above data from: Welfare Council Research Bureau, *Population in Health Areas, New York City, 1930* (New York, 1931), pp. 3–4; Department of Health and Neighborhood Health Development, "Health Center Districts, New York Handbook of Statistical Reference Data: 10-Year Period, 1931–1940," 1944, pp. 70, 74, 94, 98, Public Health Library, New York City.

The Puerto Rican population is problematical. In 1930 the U.S. Census classified 77.4 percent of Puerto Ricans in New York City as white. The black Puerto Ricans, 10,152 in number, are sometimes included with other blacks in statistical tables and sometimes not. Few tables say specifically. Evidence also suggests many black Puerto Ricans resisted the label of "Negro." Thus different tables may be referring to different-sized base populations. Since Puerto Ricans constituted only 3 percent of the total non-white population, however, this ambiguity should not significantly affect the conclusions. Similarly, some tables specify "Negro," while others use "non-white" or "colored." The non-white, non-Negro population of New York City, Manhattan, and Harlem was tiny, as noted above. Again, therefore, differing base populations should not alter the validity of the findings for the black population. ("Colored" refers sometimes to the Negro population, and sometimes to the total non-white.) Welfare Council, *Population in Health Areas: New York City, 1930* (New York, 1930), p. 1.

Harlem's patterns of black settlement defy precise description. Moving outward from Central Harlem, the proportion of each Health Area's population that was black decreased by sudden drops rather than gradually. From 158th Street south to 126th, between Fifth and Eighth avenues, blacks constituted over 95 percent of the population. Yet the next-highest black concentration was 64 percent, in Health Area 7 between Eighth and Amsterdam avenues, from 141st Street to 158th. Below 126th Street (to 114th) blacks were half the population, but just south of Health Area 7, they were only 17 percent. These distinct levels may be due to black choices among several types of housing, or to different levels of resistance to black encroachment, or both.

Although E. Franklin Frazier argued that poverty and its related problems intensified as one approached the center of Harlem, an examination of mortality, unemployment, and death rates by Health Area in 1940 reveal no such relationship. The area worst off in most categories, Health Area 13, ranked fourth in the proportion of its population that was black. Health Area 12, the geographic center of Harlem, had the lowest unemployment rate. The Health Area with the highest proportion of blacks, Area 8, ranked second lowest in overall and tuberculosis death rates, and only third highest in infant mortality. The area with the lowest proportion of blacks (that is, the more integrated area, and better-off according to Frazier) ranked in the top three for unemployment and general mortality.

Ranking of Harlem Health Areas
Four Highest and Two Lowest for Each Category

Percent Black	Unemployment	Death Rate	Infant Mortality	TB
8 (highest)	13	13	13	13
10 (next)	19	16	15	12
12	16	12	8	19
13	15	15	12	10
16 (least)	12	24	16	24
24 (next)	24	8	19	8

Robert Weaver, *The Negro Ghetto* (New York, 1948), pp. 69–70; E. Franklin Frazier, "Negro Harlem, an Ecological Study," *American Journal of Sociology* 43 (July 1937): 72–88.

II. EMPLOYMENT, UNEMPLOYMENT, RELIEF

Black Employed Workers in the United States
by Socio-Economic Group, 1920–1940:
Percent Distribution

	1920	1930	1940
Professional	1.6	2.1	2.6
Proprietary, managerial, official	20.2	16.9	16.1
farmers, tenants	19.3	15.9	14.9
wholesale, retail	0.5	0.5	0.6
other	0.4	0.5	0.6
Clerk and kindred	1.3	1.5	2.2
Skilled, foremen	3.1	3.2	2.9
Semi-skilled	7.7	9.4	12.3

Black Employed Workers in the United States
by Socio-Economic Group, 1920–1940:
Percent Distribution (*Continued*)

	1920	1930	1940
Unskilled	66.1	66.9	63.9
farm labor	24.8	20.2	17.8
non-farm labor	21.7	21.6	15.3
servant	19.6	25.1	30.8
TOTAL	100.0	100.0	100.0

Committee on Fair Employment Practice, *First Report, July 1943 to December 1944* (Washington, D.C., 1945), p. 139.

Whites and Non-whites, Total and Male, in the Labor Force,
in Private Industry, on Public Work, and Seeking Work,
1940, for Manhattan and Harlem Health Areas

Manhattan		8	10	12	13	15	16	19	24
Population over 13 years old:									
Non-white	256,629	26,092	24,818	19,176	20,008	19,253	9,339	19,229	17,653
White	1,355,646	64	106	81	358	1,309	11,757	1,444	2,921
N.W. male	118,365	11,437	11,120	8,434	8,407	8,627	4,090	8,537	8,174
W. male	667,694	31	37	37	190	737	6,895	757	1,481
Percent in labor force including WPA:									
Non-white	66.4	64.4	72.1	67.5	63.8	72.0	55.1	66.2	68.1
White	60.7	68.8	63.2	55.6	77.1	66.1	62.2	59.6	58.2
N.W. male	82.9	82.7	85.8	82.7	81.7	87.1	74.5	81.7	85.9
W. male	81.2	80.7	75.7	83.8	88.4	80.5	78.7	78.9	79.3
Percent in labor force employed in private industry:									
Non-white	71.8	71.9	71.0	72.3	65.3	70.1	63.3	68.5	72.2
White	80.3	93.2	79.1	80.0	84.1	73.3	72.3	64.1	72.4
N.W. male	69.7	71.1	68.3	66.5	60.1	65.2	58.8	65.6	70.3
W. male	78.3	96.0	85.7	80.6	83.3	70.5	69.9	65.2	70.5
Percent in labor force employed at WPA and other public work:									
Non-white	8.3	8.6	8.9	9.9	11.4	8.1	13.3	7.8	6.9
White	3.0	0.0	3.0	13.3	1.8	6.1	5.8	7.3	8.8
N.W. male	10.9	10.7	12.0	15.3	16.7	11.9	18.5	11.0	8.9
W. male	3.8	0.0	0.0	9.7	1.8	7.9	7.0	8.4	11.7
Percent in labor force unemployed and seeking work:									
Non-white	19.8	19.6	20.1	17.8	23.3	21.8	23.4	23.6	20.9
White	16.7	6.8	17.9	6.7	14.1	20.6	21.9	28.6	18.8
N.W. male	19.4	18.2	19.7	18.2	23.3	22.9	22.7	23.8	20.9
W. male	17.9	4.0	14.3	9.7	14.9	21.6	23.2	26.5	17.9

U.S. Department of Commerce, Bureau of the Census, *Sixteenth Census of the United States, 1940: Population and Housing: Statistics for Health Areas, New York City* (Washington, D.C., 1942), pp. 125–27, 138–39.

Harlem Household Incomes by Occupational Class, 1932:
Percent of Each Class Earning at Specified Level

Occupations	Under $600	$600–$1,199	$1,200–$1,999	$2,000–$2,999	$3,000 or More	Median
			Income Levels			
All classes	24.4%	35.1%	26.1%	11.1%	3.4%	$1,019
Professional	14.3	27.1	20.0	24.3	14.3	$1,440
Proprietary	17.2	31.3	21.9	17.2	12.5	$1,250
Clerical	15.2	26.9	32.4	17.9	7.6	$1,364
Skilled	25.5	32.8	27.3	12.3	2.1	$1,003
Semi-skilled	20.8	35.0	31.2	10.4	2.5	$1,100
Unskilled	28.2	37.9	23.9	8.0	2.1	$907

Clyde Kiser, "Diminishing Family Income in Harlem: A Possible Cause of the Harlem Riot," *Opportunity* 13 (June 1935): 172.

Reasons for Not Being in the Labor Force, 1940, Manhattan,
Numbers and Percent

	Total		Women		Men	
	No.	Percent	No.	Percent	No.	Percent
Total not in labor force:						
Negro	83,692	100	64,789	100	18,903	100
Native white	318,442	100	241,045	100	77,397	100
Foreign-born white	214,130	100	166,330	100	47,800	100
Other races	2,466	100	1,068	100	1,398	100
TOTAL	618,730	100	473,232	100	145,498	100
Own housework:						
Negro	37,894	45.3	37,319	57.6	575	3.0
Native white	164,805	51.8	162,745	67.6	2,060	2.7
Foreign-born white	136,903	63.9	134,976	81.1	1,927	4.0
Other races	829	33.6	780	73.0	49	3.5
TOTAL	340,431	55.0	335,820	80.0	4,611	3.2
In school:						
Negro	17,390	20.8	9,182	14.2	8,208	43.4
Native white	79,730	25.0	38,594	16.0	41,136	53.1
Foreign-born white	7,436	3.5	3,536	2.1	3,900	8.2
Other races	663	26.9	202	18.9	461	33.0
TOTAL	105,219	17.0	51,514	10.9	53,705	36.9
Can't work:						
Negro	21,366	25.5	14,484	22.4	6,882	36.4
Native white	31,322	9.8	16,167	6.7	15,155	19.6
Foreign-born white	43,466	20.3	17,136	10.3	26,330	55.1
Other races	585	23.7	42	3.9	543	38.8
TOTAL	96,739	15.6	47,829	10.1	48,910	33.6

Reasons for Not Being in the Labor Force, 1940, Manhattan,
Numbers and Percent (*Continued*)

	Total		Women		Men	
	No.	*Percent*	*No.*	*Percent*	*No.*	*Percent*
In institution:						
Negro	925	1.1	659	1.0	266	1.4
Native white	4,853	1.5	2,500	1.0	2,353	3.0
Foreign-born white	5,800	2.7	2,858	1.7	2,942	6.2
Other races	66	2.7	5	0.5	61	4.4
TOTAL	11,644	1.9	6,022	1.3	5,622	3.9
Other and unknown:						
Negro	6,117	0.7	3,145	4.9	2,972	15.7
Native white	37,732	11.8	21,039	8.7	16,693	21.6
Foreign-born white	20,525	9.6	7,824	4.7	12,701	26.6
Other races	323	13.1	39	3.7	284	20.3
TOTAL	64,697	10.5	32,047	6.8	32,650	22.4

U.S. Department of Commerce, Bureau of the Census, *Sixteenth Census of the United States, 1940: Population,* vol. 2: *Characteristics of the Population,* Part 5 (Washington, D.C., 1943), pp. 138–39.

III. EXPENDITURES AND DEFICITS

Expenditures

For each race, occupational class played only a very small part in consumption decisions. Rather, the proportion of income spent for different items by both black and white families varied primarily with income level and family size. Perhaps the types of food, clothing, or recreational materials differed among the classes, but class differences in overall consumption patterns do not emerge from the data. Black figures resemble each other more closely than they do whites from the same occupational class. For example, in the $1,500 to $1,749 income category (black professional families in this survey were larger than others, which affects the figures), one sees the following percentages:

	Wage-earning		Clerical		Professional	
	Black	*White*	*Black*	*White*	*Black*	*White*
Food	32.3	39.6	29.5	36.8	30.9	36.6
Rent	23.9	23.3	32.2	24.7	25.9	23.4
Household, furn.	12.8	10.7	9.5	9.2	12.7	10.0
Clothing	10.9	7.2	9.8	7.0	11.0	10.0
Transportation	4.5	4.6	3.3	4.0	6.0	5.0
Personal care	2.7	2.1	3.9	1.9	2.5	2.2
Medical	3.7	3.6	3.0	6.7	1.7	3.0
Recreation	3.1	2.1	2.7	3.2	2.7	3.0

	Wage-earning		Clerical		Professional	
	Black	White	Black	White	Black	White
Reading	1.0	1.1	1.1	1.3	1.3	1.1
Formal education	0.1	0.1	0.0	0.5	0.1	0.0
Other	5.0	5.6	5.0	4.7	5.2	5.7
Avg. family size	2.9	3.3	2.1	3.2	2.9	3.2

U.S. Department of Labor, Bureau of Labor Statistics, *Family Income and Expenditure in New York City, 1935–1936,* vol. 2: *Family Expenditure, New York City* (Washington, D.C., 1939), pp. 114, 116, 155–57, for this and other income levels. Based on 1,703 white families, 294 black.

Deficits

In the survey of New York City households from every occupation level, the BLS found that for families earning less than $750, expenditures exceeded income in white families by an average 62 percent and in black by 2 percent. Unlike the BLS study of blue-collar and low-salaried clerical workers, this broader study found that the more families earned, the more likely they were to have savings (the average black family breaking even at $2,000, white at $2,250), but both studies agreed that at every economic level white families spent more than black families. U.S. Department of Labor, Bureau of Labor Statistics, *Family Income and Expenditure in New York City 1935–1936,* vol. 1: *Family Income* (Washington, D.C., 1941), p. 5. For example, at the income level of $500 to $750, white families owed an average of $408; black, $18. For a full list of deficits and surpluses by income level, see U.S. Department of Labor, Bureau of Labor Statistics, *Family Income and Expenditure in New York City, 1935–1936,* vol. 2: *Family Expenditure* (Washington, D.C., 1939), pp. 107, 151.

IV. HEALTH

Free Health Clinics, 1927: New York City, Manhattan, and Harlem

	N.Y.C.	Manhattan		Harlem	
Clinic Type	No.	No.	per 100,000 Manhattan pop.	No.	per 100,000 Harlem pop.
Maternity	91	52	2.9	7	2.6
Tuberculosis	41	22*	1.2	2	0.7
Mental health	67	37*	2.0	5	1.9
Cardiac	54	32	1.8	2	0.7
Cancer	9	5*	0.3	2	0.7
Health exam	29	16*	0.9	1	0.4
Venereal disease	141	100	5.5	3	1.1
Dental	152	84*	4.6	9	3.3
Eye	79	46	2.5	4	1.5

Free Health Clinics, 1927: New York City, Manhattan, and Harlem
(*Continued*)

	N.Y.C.	Manhattan		Harlem	
Clinic Type	No.	No.	per 100,000 Manhattan pop.	No.	per 100,000 Harlem pop.
Baby health	121	63	3.5	9	3.3
Child health	34	61	3.4	5	1.9
TOTAL	818	526	29.0	49	18.1

*Estimates

This table refers to municipal and private clinics and hospitals providing free clinics open to the public. Harlem's figures are based on total Harlem population, not its black population. It is here estimated at 270,000, slightly over the 1925 figure. (Estimated totals vary from 210,000 to 340,000: I rely on Cities Census Committee, *Population of the City of New York, 1890–1930* (New York, 1932), p. 73, which provides data by census tract for 1925 and 1930.) For each type, Manhattan clinics were between 52 percent and 70 percent of New York City's total. When no separate figure for Manhattan was given, I used 55 percent as a conservative estimate. Those estimates have asterisks. This underestimates the number of Manhattan clinics, as seen by the fact that adding the estimates and the known figures does not quite equal the actual total of 526. Thus the contrast between Harlem and Manhattan rates is greater than the chart suggests.

New York City and Manhattan figures from Welfare Council, *Health Inventory for New York City* (New York, 1929), pp. xi, xii, 7, 17, 301, 306, 308, 311, 316–18, 320, Public Health Library, New York City. Harlem: pp. 321–28. 1927 N.Y.C. population: 6,450,819. Manhattan: 1,814,710 (extrapolated): Health Department, *Annual Report, 1927* (New York, 1927).

V. BUREAU OF LABOR STATISTICS SURVEY: DATA AND ANALYSIS OF THE HARLEM SAMPLE

From data collected in 1934 and 1935 by the U.S. Department of Labor, Bureau of Labor Statistics, in the Bureau of Labor Statistics papers, RG 257, BLS #807, National Archives, Washington, D.C. The N.Y.C. black families sampled are scattered through boxes 31–51. I selected all cases in which the family was labeled "Negro" and had an address in Harlem: 81 cases. Aggregate data can be found in the published study: U.S. Department of Labor, Bureau of Labor Statistics, *Money Disbursements of Wage Earners and Clerical Workers in the North Atlantic Region 1934–36,* vol. 1: *New York City* (Washington, D.C., 1939).

Correlations for 81 cases are considered significant (that is, that there can be assumed to be a relationship between the two variables in question) if the figure is greater than 0.3 or less than -0.3.

"Husband" and "Wife" refer to household heads. "Men" and "Women" refer to all adults present in the household.

Family Structure

(Total sample. For foreign-born/native-born breakdowns, see below.)

1. Family size

No. in Family	No. of Families	Percent
2	34	42.0
3	26	32.1
4	9	11.1
5	7	8.6
6	1	1.2
7	3	3.7
10	1	1.2
Total families	81	

Mean (average) family size: 3.14
Standard deviation: 1.48

2. Family composition (members in economic family): Number of families

	Child(ren) of the Household Head			
Other Relatives	None	Under Age 17	17 or Older	Both
Husband and wife present:				
No non-nuclear relatives	28	12	5	5
Relative(s) under age 17	3	0	0	1
Adult relative(s)	11	1	3	1
Only wife present:				
No non-nuclear relatives	0	0	4	1
Adult relative(s)	5	0	1	0

3. Adults (16 or older)—composition of potentially employable members of sample

	Number	Percent
Nuclear family:		
Husbands	70	32.1
Wives	81	37.2
Daughters	11	5.0
Sons	21	9.6
Relatives and friends:		
Sibling of couple	11	5.0
Parent of couple	11	5.0
Other relative	8	3.7
Non-relative in economic family	2	3.7
Not in family:		
Boarder, lodger (for whom there was economic information)	3	1.4

4. Children in the household

	Ages 14–17	Age 18
At work	0	2
Unemployed	0	1
Students	8	0
Unknown, probably student (grade completed is one year off age, no occupation stated)	0	1
Unknown, probably not student (grade completed is well below age)	0	0

5. (Total sample) education, age

	Average	No. of Cases	Standard Deviation
Age	36.1	219	12.4
Husband's age	39.9	70	9.5
Wife's age	37.7	81	10.2
Education (highest grade completed)	7.8	214	3.0
Husband's education	7.3	69	2.9
Wife's education	7.4	79	3.0
Education of those over 18	7.8	208	3.0
Male's education	7.8	104	2.9
Female's education	7.8	110	3.1

6. Average education by age (number of years of education)

	Average	No. of Cases	Standard Deviation
16 to 21 years of age	9.7	25	1.8
22 to 30 years of age	8.2	62	3.1
Over 30	7.2	127	3.0

7. Percent age 16–21 in school

	No.	Percent	No. Unspecified, Not Employed	Percent
Total	5	20.8	3	25.0
Female	3	25.0	3	25.0
Male	2	16.7	1	8.3

Employment

1. Distribution of the number of workers (earners) in family

Number of Earners	Number of Families	Percent
1	26	32.1
2	42	51.9
3	7	8.6
4	6	7.4

Average number employed in the family: 1.92
Standard deviation: 0.84

2. Earnings at employment

	Average	No. of Cases	Standard Deviation
Average weeks worked:			
Husbands	49.1	70	7.5
Wives	34.6	44	15.5
All males	44.4	95	14.2
All females	37.3	58	15.3
TOTAL	41.7	153	15.0
Average earnings:			
Husbands	$1,007.47	70	372.9
Wives	$421.28	46	321.8
All males	$878.36	95	438.0
All females	$459.53	60	336.9
TOTAL	$716.23	155	449.9
Average weekly wage:			
Husbands	$20.56	70	7.4
Wives	$12.04	44	5.2
All males	$19.06	95	7.3
All females	$12.14	58	5.4
TOTAL	$16.44	153	7.4
Average family income	$1,528.60	81	632.6

3. Employment status and occupation (by level and category)

	Total		Husbands		Wives	
	No.	Percent	No.	Percent	No.	Percent
Employment status:						
At work 52 weeks	72	33.8	45	64.2	10	12.7
At work 27–51 weeks	50	23.5	22	31.4	20	25.3

	Total		Husbands		Wives	
	No.	*Percent*	*No.*	*Percent*	*No.*	*Percent*
Employment status: (cont.)						
At work 1–26 weeks	31	14.6	3	4.3	14	17.7
Unemployed, seeking work	5	2.3	0	0.0	0	0.0
In school	5	2.3	0	0.0	0	0.0
At home (not seeking work)	50	23.5	0	0.0	35	44.3
TOTAL	213		70		79	
Occupational level:						
At home	60	28.0	0	0.0	35	43.8
Laborer	5	2.3	5	7.4	0	0.0
Unskilled factory	6	2.8	1	1.5	3	3.7
Domestic service	21	9.8	0	0.0	14	17.5
Unskilled service	62	29.0	33	48.5	9	11.2
Semi-skilled factory	16	7.5	2	2.9	12	15.0
Semi-skilled other	19	8.9	16	23.5	2	2.5
Skilled	2	0.9	2	2.9	0	0.0
Clerical	23	10.7	9	13.2	5	6.3
TOTAL	214		68		80	

	All Men		All Age 16–21	
	No.	*Percent*	*No.*	*Percent*
Employment status:				
At work 52 weeks	52	51.0	5	20.8
At work 27–51 weeks	28	27.5	4	16.7
At work 1–27 weeks	15	14.7	4	16.7
Unemployed, seeking work	4	3.9	2	8.3
In school	2	2.0	5	20.8
At home (not seeking work)	1	1.0	4	16.7

	All Men		All Women	
	No.	*Percent*	*No.*	*Percent*
Occupation category:				
At home	7	6.9	53	46.9
Labor	5	5.0	0	0.0
Unskilled factory	2	2.0	4	3.5
Domestic service	0	0.0	21	18.6
Unskilled service	52	51.5	10	8.8
Semi-skilled factory	2	2.0	14	12.4
Semi-skilled other	17	16.8	2	1.8
Skilled	2	2.0	0	0.0
Clerical	14	13.9	9	8.0
TOTAL	101		113	

4. Earnings by occupation category and level

	Total Earnings	Weekly Wage	No. Weeks Worked
A. TOTAL SAMPLE			
Occupation category:			
Laborer	$1,146.20	$23.15	50.4
No. cases	5	5	5
standard dev.	466.6	10.5	3.6
Unskilled factory	$508.33	$13.38	37.8
No. cases	6	6	6
standard dev.	208.3	2.1	13.0
Domestic service	$219.80	$7.97	30.0
No. cases	20	20	20
standard dev.	176.2	4.1	17.3
Unskilled service	$735.65	$17.32	41.1
No. cases	60	59	59
standard dev.	427.6	6.8	16.1
Semi-skilled factory	$607.88	$14.64	41.4
No. cases	16	16	16
standard dev.	207.4	3.0	10.0
Semi-skilled other	$908.16	$19.81	47.6
No. cases	19	18	18
standard dev.	526.3	9.0	10.4
Skilled	$1,000.00	$20.00	50.0
No. cases	2	2	2
standard dev.	353.6	7.1	0
Clerical	$1,018.91	$20.08	49.1
No. cases	22	22	22
standard dev.	382.9	6.6	10.7
Occupation level:			
All unskilled	$629.85	$15.31	38.9
No. cases	91	90	90
standard dev.	446.2	7.6	16.5
All semi-skilled	$770.89	$17.38	44.7
No. cases	35	34	34
standard dev.	434.3	7.2	10.5
Skilled	$1,000.00	$20.00	50.0
No. cases	2	2	2
standard dev.	353.6	7.1	0
Clerical	$1,018.91	$20.08	49.1
No. cases	22	22	22
standard dev.	382.9	6.6	10.7
B. ALL MEN			
Occupation category:			
Laborer	$1,146.20	$23.15	50.4
No. cases	5	5	5
standard dev.	466.6	10.5	3.6
Unskilled factory	$710.50	$15.25	46.5
No. cases	2	2	2
standard dev.	135.1	0.4	7.8

	Total Earnings	Weekly Wage	No. Weeks Worked
B. ALL MEN (*cont.*)			
Occupation category:			
Domestic service	0	0	0
No. cases	0	0	0
standard dev.	0	0	0
Unskilled service	$791.80	$18.28	40.84
No. cases	50	50	50
standard dev.	436.1	6.9	16.7
Semi-skilled factory	$969.50	$19.99	48.5
No. cases	2	2	2
standard dev.	201.5	2.3	5.0
Semi-skilled other	$987.35	$20.25	48.2
No. cases	17	17	17
standard dev.	492.5	9.1	10.3
Skilled	$1,000.00	$20.00	50.0
No. cases	2	2	2
standard dev.	353.6	7.1	0.0
Clerical	$1,077.77	$21.08	50.9
No. cases	13	13	19
standard dev.	327.8	6.1	2.8
Occupation level:			
All unskilled	$820.04	$18.60	41.88
No. cases	57	57	57
standard dev.	439.3	7.2	15.97
All semi-skilled	$985.47	$20.22	48.26
No. cases	19	19	19
standard dev.	466.8	8.6	9.8
Skilled	$1,000.00	$20.00	50.0
No. cases	2	2	2
standard dev.	353.6	7.1	0.0
Clerical	$1,077.77	$21.08	50.9
No. cases	13	13	19
standard dev.	327.8	6.1	2.8
C. ALL WOMEN			
Occupation category:			
Laborer	0	0	0
No. cases	0	0	0
standard dev.	0	0	0
Unskilled factory	$407.25	$12.45	33.5
No. cases	4	4	4
standard dev.	159.3	2.0	13.6
Domestic service	$219.80	$7.97	30.0
No. cases	20	20	20
standard dev.	176.2	4.1	17.3
Unskilled service	$454.90	$12.01	43.3
No. cases	10	9	9
standard dev.	240.2	2.8	12.9
Semi-skilled factory	$556.21	$13.88	40.4
No. cases	14	14	14
standard dev.	153.3	2.3	10.2

	Total Earnings	Weekly Wage	No. Weeks Worked
C. ALL WOMEN (cont.)			
Occupation category:			
Semi-skilled other	$235.00	$12.50	36.0
No. cases	2	1	1
standard dev.	304.1	0.0	0.0
Skilled	0	0	0
No. cases	0	0	0
standard dev.	0	0	0
Clerical	$933.89	$18.63	46.3
No. cases	9	9	9
standard dev.	458.1	7.5	16.6
Occupation level:			
All unskilled	$311.00	$9.62	33.8
No. cases	34	33	33
standard dev.	219.9	4.1	16.3
All semi-skilled	$516.06	$13.79	40.1
No. cases	16	15	15
standard dev.	196.4	2.2	9.9
Skilled	0	0	0
No. cases	0	0	0
standard dev.	0	0	0
Clerical	$933.89	$18.63	46.3
No. cases	9	9	9
standard dev.	458.1	7.5	16.6

5. Correlations

Between family income (excluding wife's wages) and if wife is at home or at work: 0.0 (45 cases)

Between family income and either that wife is at home or her job level (unskilled, semi-skilled, skilled work): −0.07 (45 cases)

Between family income and either that wife is at home or her job level for all occupation categories: −0.12 (45 cases)

Between education and occupation for entire sample: 0.07 (208 cases)

None is statistically significant.

	Correlation	No. Cases
Correlation for all but husband:		
Between family income and whether employed	0.01	142
Between education and whether employed	0.10	138
Between age and whether employed	−0.19	192

	Wife	No.	Husband	No.
Correlation between:				
Family income and employment of self	−0.15	80		
Education and whether employed	0.16	78		

	Wife	No.	Husband	No.
Correlation between: (cont.)				
Educ. and occupation (all categories)	0.05	78	0.12	67
Education and occupational level	0.01	80	0.01	67
Age and whether employed	−0.24	80		
Age and occupation (all)	−0.23	80	−0.29	68
Age and occupation level	−0.20	80	−0.25	68
Age and weekly wage	−0.07	57	0.33*	70
Education and weekly wage	0.14	55	0.16	69
Weekly wage and occupation (all)	0.53*	43	0.03	68
Weekly wage and occupation level	0.52*	43	0.07	68

*Statistically significant

Savings and Deficits

	Average	*Standard deviation*
Savings (deficit)	−$30.31	65.0

1. Correlations

Correlation between savings and:	
Income	−0.11
Expenditures per person	−0.22

2. Percent of total income owed (−) or saved

% of Income Owed	No. Families	% of All Families	% of Income Saved	No. Families	% of All Families
−40	1	1.2	0	5	6.2
−12	1	1.2	1	4	4.9
−6	2	2.5	2	2	2.5
−5	13	16.0	3	6	7.4
−4	9	11.1	4	4	4.9
−3	11	13.6	12	1	1.2
−2	16	19.8			
−1	6	7.4			

3. Comparisons of families with savings and families with deficits at the end of the survey year

	Families with Savings	*Families with Debts*
Number of familes	20	61
percent of total	24.7	75.3
Average family size	3.1	3.2
standard deviation	1.2	1.6

	Families with Savings	Families with Debts
Average saved (owed)	$40.90	−$53.66
standard deviation	33.1	55.2
Avg. earnings	$1,381.55	$1,366.97
standard deviation	325.0	650.0
Avg. income	$1,503.95	$1,536.69
standard deviation	382.0	698.0
Expenditure per person	$524.25	$555.21
standard deviation	163.1	206.7
Avg. exp. on food	$414.75	$460.38
standard deviation	111.0	221.0
Avg. exp. on rent	$420.15	$439.75
standard deviation	142.0	164.0
Avg. exp. on all other	$628.15	$687.92
standard deviation	292.0	424.0
Avg. number of lodgers	0.6	0.6
standard deviation	0.8	0.8

None of the differences between savers and debtors is significant.

Lodgers

1. Distribution of lodgers per family

No. of Lodgers	No. of Families	Families with Savings	Families with Debts
0	47 (58.0%)	11 (55%)	36 (59%)
1	21 (25.9%)	6 (30%)	15 (25%)
2	13 (16.0%)	3 (15%)	10 (16%)
TOTAL	81	20	61

2. Average rent from lodgers (for families with lodgers): $199. Standard deviation: 148.9.

3. Correlations

Correlation between lodgers and:	
Number in family	−0.06
Number children under 17 present in family	−0.02
Total family earnings*	−0.02
Total family expenditures	0.17
Expenditures per person	0.22
Number employed in family	0.10

None are statistically significant.

*As opposed to income. The question here is whether families, seeing their low earnings, took in lodgers to increase their total income. Income is determined by adding earnings and non-wage income, including money from lodgers.

Family Expenditures

	Average	Standard Deviation
Family expenditures on food	$449.11	200
Family expenditures on rent	$434.91	158
Family expenditures on all other	$673.16	394
Expenditures per person	$547.57	196
Rent per family member	$153.45	62
Food per family member	$153.38	56
All other per member	$233.32	121

Correlation between expenditures per person and:	
Number in family	−0.47*
Income	0.46*
Savings	−0.22
Correlation between income and:	
Food expenditures	0.84*
Rent	0.64*
All other expenditures	0.94*
Food per family member	0.33*
Rent per family member	0.00
All other per family member	0.49*
Correlation between number in family and:	
Food expenditures	0.60*
Rent	0.14
All other expenditures	0.94*

*Statistically significant

Food: Food costs were affected directly by both family size and income. For two families earning the same amount, the family with one more member would spend $81 more on food annually. In terms of income, for each dollar increase the family would spend an additional 26¢ on food. These adjustments were not as marked in foreign-born black families as in native-born ones.

Food = 195 + (81 × family size) with a correlation of .60.

Food = 44 + (0.265 × income) with a correlation of .84.

Food = −8.75 + (36.25 × family size) + (0.225 × income).

Foreign-born versus Native-born Blacks

24 families were foreign-born (29.6%)

57 families were native-born (70.4%)

42 families were native-born and earned less than $1,855 (the highest foreign-born income). These families can be compared with the foreign-born to test whether national differences in consumption were in fact income or family-size differences.

1. Earnings and expenditures

	Native-born	Foreign-born	Native-born earning less than $1,855
Avg. family size	3.16	3.08	2.69
standard deviation	1.51	1.44	
Avg. no. workers	1.93	1.88	1.57
standard deviation	0.90	0.68	0.59
Avg. earnings	$1,458.39	$1,162.00	$1,155.74
standard deviation	651.79	301.0	282.0
Avg. earnings per person	$755.64	$618.09	$736.14
Avg. no. lodgers	0.6	0.5	0.6
standard deviation	0.8	0.7	
Total lodger rent (for families with lodgers only)	$216.88	$156.00	$209.94
standard deviation	168.68	75.35	
Avg. income	$1,633.16	$1,280.29	$1,309.00
standard deviation	707.6	285.9	291.4
Avg. exp. on food	$469.40	$400.92	$376.81
standard deviation	223.76	117.5	
Avg. exp. on rent	$456.75	$383.04	$424.91
standard deviation	174.15	96.12	
Avg. exp. all other	$736.65	522.38	$536.74
standard deviation	442.64	173.38	
Avg. exp. per person	$570.95	$492.04	$541.00
standard deviation	197.0	186.9	179.4
Avg. savings	−$30.67	−$29.46	−$29.24
standard deviation	75.28	30.00	
Percent families with savings	26.3	12.5	26.2
Avg. percent of income saved	−2.1	−2.5	−2.5
Percent owing over 5% of income	17.5	29.2	21.4

2. Family size

No. in Family	Native-born		Foreign-born		Native-born < $1,855	
	No.	Percent	No.	Percent	No.	Percent
2	22	38.6	12	50.0	21	50.0
3	21	36.8	5	20.8	16	38.1
4	6	10.5	3	12.5	4	9.5
5	5	8.8	2	8.3	0	0.0
6	0	0.0	1	4.2	0	0.0
7	2	3.5	1	4.2	1	2.4
10	1	1.8	0	0.0	0	0.0
TOTAL	57		24		42	
No. adult women	83	52.5	28	50.9	55	56.7

3. Number with children under age 18

No. Children	Native-born No.	Native-born Percent	Foreign-born No.	Foreign-born Percent	Native-born <$1,855 No.	Native-born <$1,855 Percent
0	42	73.7	15	62.5	31	73.8
1	11	19.3	4	16.7	8	19.0
2	2	3.5	3	12.5	2	4.8
3	1	1.8	1	4.2	1	2.4
4	1	1.8	0	0.0	0	0.0
5	0	0.0	1	4.2	0	0.0
TOTAL	57		24		42	

4. Number of lodgers by nativity of family

No. of Lodgers	Native-born No.	Native-born Percent	Foreign-born No.	Foreign-born Percent	Native-born <$1,855 No.	Native-born <$1,855 Percent
0	33	57.9	14	58.3	25	59.6
1	13	22.8	8	33.3	9	21.4
2	11	19.3	2	8.3	8	19.0

5. Correlations

	Native-born	Foreign-born
Correlation between lodgers and:		
Earnings	.05	.01
Number of children under 17	−.01	.00
Family size	−.02	−.18
Expenditure per person	.2	.23

None is significant

	Native-born	Foreign-born	Native-born <$1,855
Correlation between expenditures per person and:			
Income	.47	.31	.59
Number in family	−.35	−.82	−.63
Savings	−.20	−.39	
Correlation between food expenditures and:			
Income	.84	.82	.55
Number in family	.69	.27	

	Native-born	Foreign-born	Native-born < $1,855
Correlation between rent and:			
Income	.64	.41	.65
Number in family	.19	.08	
Correlation between all expenditures on other items and:			
Income	.94	.83	.76
Number in family	.46	−.02	

Given the small number in each population, the correlations are probably not strong unless they exceed 0.3 for the total native-born group and 0.4 for the other two groups. Obviously, family size correlated with per-person expenditures. In terms of overall spending, however, the number in the family seems to bear a relationship to consumption decisions only for American families (excluding rent). Income plays a part in each consumption decision, according to the data, but less so in the case of rent. In virtually every case, the relationship between income and expenditure is slightly weaker for the two poorer groups than for the general American black population. Presumably this finding is due to the lower income of the two poorer groups. If minimum requirements are fixed (minimum dietary needs), and neither group earned much more than this minimum, income would not determine spending patterns as much as if these families had excess income which they could choose to spend on additional amounts of some item.

6. Employment and occupation

	Native-born		Foreign-born		Native-born < $1,855	
	No.	Percent	No.	Percent	No.	Percent
Employment status:						
At work 52 weeks	55	35.0	17	31.5	31	32.3
At work 27–51 weeks	33	21.0	17	31.5	23	24.0
At work 1–26 weeks	21	13.4	10	18.5	11	11.5
Unemployed, seeking work	5	3.2	0	0.0	3	3.1
In school	3	1.9	2	3.7	1	1.0
At home (not seeking work)	40	25.5	8	14.8	27	28.1
TOTAL	157		54		96	
Occupation level:						
At home	48	31.4	10	18.2	31	32.3
Labor	3	2.0	2	3.6	3	3.1
Unskilled factory	5	3.3	1	1.8	3	3.1
Domestic service	13	8.5	7	12.7	8	8.3
Unskilled service	42	27.5	18	32.7	25	26.0
Semi-skilled factory	11	7.2	5	9.1	10	10.4
Semi-skilled other	14	9.2	5	9.1	9	9.4
Skilled	1	0.7	1	1.8	0	0.0
Clerical	16	10.5	6	10.9	7	7.3
TOTAL	153		55		96	

	Native-born		Foreign-born		Native-born < $1,855	
	No.	Percent	No.	Percent	No.	Percent
Home:	48	31.4	10	18.2	31	32.3
All unskilled	63	41.2	28	50.9	39	40.6
All semi-skilled	25	16.3	10	18.2	19	19.8
Skilled	1	0.7	1	1.8	0	0.0
Clerical	16	10.5	6	10.9	7	7.3
Status of employed only:						
At work 52 weeks	55	50.5	17	38.6	31	47.7
At work 27–51 weeks	33	30.3	17	38.6	23	35.4
At work 1–27 weeks	21	19.3	10	22.7	11	16.9
TOTAL	157		54		96	
Occupation level:						
Laborer	3	2.9	2	4.4	3	4.6
Unskilled factory	5	4.8	1	2.2	3	4.6
Domestic service	13	12.4	7	15.6	8	12.3
Unskilled service	42	40.0	18	40.0	25	38.5
Semi-skilled factory	11	10.5	5	11.1	10	15.4
Semi-skilled other	14	13.3	5	11.1	9	13.8
Skilled	1	1.0	1	2.2	0	0.0
Clerical	16	15.2	6	13.3	7	10.8
All unskilled	63	60.0	28	62.2	39	60.0
All semi-skilled	25	23.8	10	22.2	19	29.2

Notes

In the midst of my research, New York City's Municipal Archives reorganized Mayor LaGuardia's papers. All research conducted after the reorganization is labeled "new box." Please note that unless otherwise specified, all references to departments and Mayoral Committees are for New York City. The Russell-Sage collection has been divided between Columbia University and the City College of New York. At Columbia the items are integrated into the general collection at the Social Work Library, and are listed here without the Russell-Sage notation. That library often collected the works of an agency and bound them together; when I cite such material I list the specific title and the title of the bound volume. The Russell-Sage Collection remains separate within the CCNY library, and those works are named here with their Russell-Sage classification.

Introduction

1. Both pamphlets from Police Department, Sixth Division, "Memo to Police Commissioner. Sub.: Report of Disorder," 20 March 1935, Mayor LaGuardia papers, box 41, Municipal Archives, New York City. Mr. Minor of the Young Liberators refused to apologize for the misleading pamphlet. In testimony before the Mayor's Commission appointed to investigate the riot, he explained: "I would like . . . for the one who got out the circular to have been 100 percent in their knowledge but the strong evidence justified them in believing that such a crime was committed." Mr. Minor, Testimony before Mayor's Commission on Conditions in Harlem, 22 May 1935, LaGuardia papers, new box 3770. In the police report the boy's age was given as fifteen, and his name as Lini.

2. The details of the riot come from "Report of Disorder," p. 1. The Mayor's Commission agreed with the police description of the events. Mayor's Commission on Conditions in Harlem, notes, 1935, pp. 3–5, LaGuardia papers, box 755. Rivera later testified that although no one had struck him, he bit his captor because he heard one of the men holding him propose, "'Let us take him in the cellar and beat the hell out of him.'" Lino Rivera, Testimony before Mayor's Commission on Conditions in Harlem, 22 May 1935, LaGuardia papers, new box 3770. Ralph Ellison, *Invisible Man* (New York, 1952; reprint ed., 1972), pp. 542–43.

3. Mayor's Commission on Conditions in Harlem, "Report of the Subcommittee Which Investigated the Disturbances of March 19th," 29 May 1935, pp. 1, 5, 8–10, 12–13, 15, LaGuardia papers, box 755; Mayor's Commission, "The Negro in Harlem: A Report on Social and Economic Conditions Responsible for the Outbreak of March 19, 1935," Report, 1935, p. 5, LaGuardia papers, box 2550. "The distinguishing feature of this outbreak was that it was an attack on property and not upon persons," the commission reported: p. 5. Alain Locke, "Harlem: Dark Weather-Vane," *Survey Graphic* 25 (August 1936): 460. The police

reported that only white stores were vandalized, but this seems not to have been the case. "Report of Disorder," p. 2. The Mayor's Commission included Dr. Charles Roberts (chairman); publisher Oswald Villard; lawyers Eunice Carter (secretary), Morris Ernst, and Arthur Garfield Hays; Countee Cullen, Hubert Delany, Dr. John Grimley, William McCann, A. Philip Randolph, John Robinson, Tuskeegee trustee William Schieffelin, Judge Charles Toney, and Dr. E. Franklin Frazier ("technical expert").

4. Adam Clayton Powell, Sr., "Riots and Ruins," Manuscript, n.d. [preface dated 1945], p. 30, typescript collection, box 33, Schomburg Center for Research in Black Culture (hereafter, Schomburg Archives), New York City; Mayor's Commission, "The Negro in Harlem," p. 108; Mayor's Commission, "Report of the Subcommittee," pp. 1, 2, 8; Nannie Helen Burroughs, "Declaration of 1776 Is Cause of Harlem Riot," quoted in Gerda Lerner, ed., *Black Women in White America* (New York, 1972), pp. 408–10.

5. Puerto Ricans also lived in Harlem, primarily in East Harlem. This group usually tried to distinguish itself from blacks; not always successfully. Sometimes Puerto Ricans were included under the heading "Negro"; other times they were counted with whites. Rarely do the reports specify. The numbers of Puerto Ricans were small in this period, however, so this ambiguity has virtually no impact on the data. See appendix for further discussion of this point.

6. Gilbert Osofsky, *Harlem: The Making of a Ghetto*, 2nd ed. (New York, 1971); Nathan Huggins, *Harlem Renaissance* (New York, 1971); David Lewis, *When Harlem Was in Vogue* (New York, 1981); Jervis Anderson, *This Was Harlem* (New York, 1982); Harvard Sitkoff, *A New Deal for Blacks* (New York, 1978); Raymond Wolters, *Negroes and the Great Depression* (Westport, Conn., 1970); Nancy Weiss, *Farewell to the Party of Lincoln* (Princeton, 1983); John Kirby, *Black Americans in the Roosevelt Era* (Knoxville, 1980); Horace Cayton and St. Clair Drake, *Black Metropolis* (New York, 1945); Julia Kirk Blackwelder, *Women of the Depression: Caste and Culture in San Antonio* (College Station, Tex., 1984); Mark Naison, *Communists in Harlem During the Depression* (Urbana, Ill., 1983); Larry Greene, "Harlem in the Great Depression" (Ph.D. dissertation, Columbia University, 1979). Dominic Capeci, Jr., *The Harlem Riot of 1943* (Philadelphia, 1977) provides a brief but solid overview of Harlem in the Depression, and an excellent discussion of the 1943 riot.

7. The commission had subcommittees on health, housing, relief, employment, crime, and education, and believed that "all elements in the population were represented" in the hearings: Mayor's Commission, "The Negro in Harlem," p. 17. These reports were never published because of their highly critical tone, but the *Amsterdam News* printed them all in its 18 July 1936 issue. Mayor LaGuardia did circulate copies of the report to all department heads, though, and asked for responses. The commission held 21 public and 4 closed hearings, and conducted a year of investigations.

8. Mayor's Commission, "The Negro in Harlem," pp. 6, 107; Mayor's Commission, "Report of the Subcommittee," p. 8. Locke, p. 459. Not everyone was as progressive as the mayor and the commission, of course. The mayor received a letter from a white Harlem resident, 21 March 1935, asking how long the mayor expected whites to "support this colored rabble, over 50 percent of whom are on Home Relief? [They are] a wild, seething, race-mad populace. . . . Really, this has ceased to be a joke." Anonymous to Mayor LaGuardia, 21 March 1935, LaGuardia papers, box 2550.

Chapter 1

1. Commonly used descriptions of Harlem and Harlem blacks in contemporary white newspapers. See, for example, a series called "Hot Harlem" in the *New York Daily Mirror*: "Harlem Sets the Pace for Broadway Dances," 23 July 1930, p. 3; "To Laugh or Sob with

Harlem, Read Its Papers," 24 July 1930, p. 3; "Happy-Go-Lucky Harlem Life as Told in 'Briefs' Thriller," 25 July 1930, p. 3, Mayor LaGuardia papers, box 755, Municipal Archives, New York City.

2. Nathan Huggins, *Harlem Renaissance* (New York, 1971), p. 25. Population data: Ira Rosenwaike, *Population History of New York City* (Syracuse, N.Y., 1972), p. 121; New York State Temporary Commission on the Condition of the Urban Colored Population, *Second Report,* Legislative Document #69 (Albany, 1939), p. 20. Foreign-born: Ira de Augustine Reid, *The Negro Immigrant: His Background Characteristics and Social Adjustment 1899–1937* (New York, 1939), p. 233. Loften Mitchell, "Harlem Reconsidered," *Freedomways* 4 (Fall 1964): 468–69.

3. James Weldon Johnson, "The Making of Harlem," *Survey [Graphic]* 53 (1 March 1925): 635, 639; Claude McKay, *Harlem: Negro Metropolis* (New York, 1940), p. 16; Mitchell, "Harlem Reconsidered," p. 469.

4. James Weldon Johnson, *Black Manhattan* (New York, 1930; reprint ed., New York, 1975), pp. 282–84; Johnson, "Making of Harlem," p. 639. Anti-segregation laws had been on the New York State statute books since 1918; some civil rights laws, since 1909.

5. Johnson, "Making of Harlem," pp. 637–38; Gilbert Osofsky, *Harlem: The Making of a Ghetto,* 2nd ed. (New York, 1971), pp. 93–94, 119–20. The black real-estate ownership figure comes from John Nail, of Nail and Parker Real Estate, and is quoted in the President's Conference on Home Building and Home Ownership, *Negro Housing* (Washington, D.C., 1932), p. 216.

6. Osofsky, *Harlem,* p. 130; Winfred Nathan, *Health Conditions in North Harlem, 1923–1927,* National Tuberculosis Association Social Research Series #2 (New York, 1932), p. 16. E. Franklin Frazier did perhaps the best-known study of black population distribution in Harlem in "Negro Harlem, an Ecological Study," *American Journal of Sociology* 43 (July 1937): 72–88. He divided Harlem into five concentric zones corresponding to successive waves of expansion and demonstrated that the percentage of the population that was black decreased as one moved farther from Central Harlem. Although he was correct in that, he was incorrect that concentric circles best described the pattern of black Harlem's expansion. (See appendix.) His zone chart appears in Frazier, *The Negro in the United States,* rev. ed. (New York, 1957), p. 263. For general theories on urban expansion, see, for example, Robert Park and Ernest Burgess, eds., *The City* (Chicago, 1967); Sam Bass Warner, *Streetcar Suburbs* (New York, 1976); and for blacks: Louise Kennedy, *The Negro Peasant Turns Cityward: Effects of Recent Migrations to Northern Centers* (New York, 1930); Frazier; Allan Spear, *Black Chicago* (Chicago, 1967).

7. See appendix for figures, boundaries, census tract, and Health Area data. Welfare Council, *Population in Health Areas: New York City, 1930* (New York, 1930), pp. 2–6; Godias Drolet and Anthony Lowell, New York Tuberculosis and Health Association, "A Half Century's Progress against Tuberculosis in New York City, 1900–1950," Report, 1952, p. 4, Columbia University Social Work Library, New York City. According to the 1905 state census, 3,500 blacks lived north of 125th Street. Mayor's Commission on Conditions in Harlem, "Character of the Negro Community," Report, n.d., p. 6, LaGuardia papers, box 755; Mayor's Commission, "The Negro in Harlem," Report, 1935, p. 20, LaGuardia papers, box 2250. Between 1910 and 1920, Harlem's black population increased from 28,690 to 83,597. Between 1920 and 1930 it rose to 189,257. (Frazier, *Negro in United States,* p. 264, and Osofsky, pp. 122–23, reported different figures, but similar population jumps.)

8. Kelly Miller, "The Causes of Segregation," *Current History* 25 (March 1927): 827–31. Counter-argument: Herbert Seligman, "The Negro Protest Against Ghetto Conditions," *Current History* 25 (March 1927): 831–33. Study: Louise Kennedy, pp. 143–52; Willis Weatherford and Charles Johnson, *Race Relations: Adjustment of Whites and Negroes in the United States* (Boston, 1934), p. 343 (general findings about northern cities).

9. Frazier, *Negro in the United States,* p. 262.

10. Mitchell, "Harlem Reconsidered," pp. 473–74. See also *New York Herald, The New York Market* (New York, 1922), p. 78 ("Harlem: Negro Section"); "Harlem Sets the Pace." Greater New York Federation of Churches, *The Negro Churches of Manhattan* (New York, 1930), pp. 6–7, 9; Jervis Anderson, *This Was Harlem* (New York, 1981), p. 238 et passim; Nathan, p. 65; New York Housing Authority, *Harlem, 1934: A Study of Real Property and Negro Population* (New York, n.d.), pp. 2, 4; Mayor's Commission on Conditions in Harlem, "Recreational Institutions: Theaters, Playland, Ball Rooms and Halls, Social and Athletic Clubs, Parks and Playgrounds, Billiard Parlors and Bowling Alleys," list, 1935, no page, LaGuardia papers, box 33; Municipal Art Committee to LaGuardia, 7 December 1936, Neighborhood file, Manuscript Reference and Resource Center, New York; Welfare Council, *A Health Inventory for New York City* (New York, 1929), pp. 323–28. NYUL and others on blocks bounded by Eighth Avenue and Lenox, between 134th and 138th Streets. Harlem Hospital: Lenox and 136th Street. East Harlem Health Center: 345 East 116th Street. Community Hospital: 8 St. Nicholas Place. St. Luke's: 113th Street and Amsterdam Avenue. Sydenham: 565 Manhattan Avenue. Harlem Hospital was completely open to blacks; the other three made at least some clinic services available to them. The Department of Health ran two maternity centers in Harlem, and five baby health stations. Harlem Tuberculosis and Health Committee: 202 West 136th Street.

11. City black population in 1910: 91,709; in 1920: 152,467; in 1930: 327,706. Native-born blacks in 1920: 122,031; in 1930: 272,952. Osofsky, p. 128; Robert Weaver, *The Negro Ghetto* (New York, 1948), p. 26; Rosenwaike, p. 121; New York State Temporary Commission, p. 20; Mayor's Commission, "The Negro in Harlem," p. 41; *New York Herald,* p. 63. For the birthplace of New York City blacks, 1930, see Osofsky, pp. 128–29. Also U.S. Department of Commerce, Bureau of the Census, *Population Trends in the United States, 1900–1960,* by Irene Taeuber, Technical Paper #10 (Washington, D.C., 1964), p. 199. Southernborn: Mayor's Commission on Conditions in Harlem, "Character of the Negro Community," p. 7. Of 224,670 blacks in Manhattan in 1930, 47,642 were born in New York State, 124,087 others were native-born non–New Yorkers, and 39,833 were foreign-born blacks. United States Department of Commerce, Bureau of the Census, *Negroes in the United States, 1920–1932* (Washington, D.C., 1935), p. 32.

12. Alain Locke, "Harlem," *Survey* [*Graphic*] 53 (1 March 1925): 629–30.

13. Powell: Adam Clayton Powell, Sr., *Against the Tide* (New York, 1938), p. 71. South Carolinian: in Clyde Kiser, *Sea Island to City: A Study of St. Helena Islanders in Harlem and Other Urban Centers* (New York, 1932; reprint ed., New York, 1969), p. 122 (case study # 5). Also see John Van Deusen, *The Black Man in White America* (Washington, D.C., 1938), pp. 29–31; Kennedy, pp. 41–50; Locke, "Harlem," p. 629. Migration study: C. Warren Thornthwaite, *Internal Migration in the United States,* Bulletin #1 of the Study of Population Redistribution, Wharton School, University of Pennsylvania (Philadelphia, 1934), p. 30. Low rate of return: Kiser, p. 221.

14. There were 98,620 foreign-born blacks in the U.S., 54,754 in N.Y.C. 39,833 in Manhattan. Osofsky, p. 131; Reid, p. 233. They constituted 17.7 percent of Manhattan's black population, 16.7 percent of the city's: Reid, p. 248. Charles Johnson, "Black Workers in the City," *Survey* [*Graphic*] 53 (1 March 1925): 641–42; Kennedy, p. 222.

15. W. A. Domingo, "The Tropics in New York," *Survey* [*Graphic*] 53 (1 March 1925): 648–50; Osofsky, pp. 131–35; Margaret Brenman, "Some Aspects of Personality Development in a Group of Urban Lower-class Negro Girls: A Research Memorandum," 20 April 1940, p. 3, Carnegie-Myrdal study, Schomburg Archives, New York City. Family structure: Frazier, *The Negro in the United States,* pp. 326–28.

16. Eugene Knickle Jones, "The Problems of the Colored Child," *Annals of the American Academy of Political and Social Science* 98 (November 1921): 142.

17. Poor education and training: James Hubert, "Harlem, Its Social Problems," *Hospital Social Service* 21 (1930): 45. In 1910, for example, in southern areas only approximately 60 percent of black children ages 7 to 13 were able to attend school—and it was primarily that generation that migrated North in the 1920s. The number in school rose by 1920 with the South's new compulsory education laws. Dean Dutcher, *The Negro in Modern Industrial Society* (Lancaster, Pa., 1930), p. 35. For children, though, the move north improved their educational opportunities. In 1920 well over 90 percent of black children 7 to 13 in the North and West attended school, higher than in the South. On economic disadvantage of education for southern blacks: see Stanley Lieberson, *A Piece of the Pie: Blacks and White Immigrants Since 1880* (Berkeley, 1980), pp. 354–55. Split labor market: see, for example, Edna Bonacich, "A Theory of Ethnic Antagonism: The Split Labor Market," *American Sociological Review* 37 (October 1972): 547–59.

18. Ira de Augustine Reid, New York Urban League (NYUL), "Twenty-four Hundred Negro Families in Harlem," Report, May 1927, p. 25, Microfilm Sc R3612, Schomburg Archives. He also reported more girls than boys were enrolled in vocational schools. The National Tuberculosis Association found in 1927 that 12 percent of Harlem's black youth were so enrolled. Nathan, p. 18. Adult education: Charlotte Morgan, "Finding a Way Out: Adult Education in Harlem During the Great Depression," *Afro-Americans in New York Life and History* 8 (January 1984): 17.

19. Kennedy, pp. 80, 84; Charles Johnson, p. 643; Claude McKay, *Home to Harlem* (New York, 1928), pp. 45, 49; Arthur Todd, Welfare Council, "New York City as a Community," Memorandum, April 1932, p. 62, in *New York City Welfare Council Publications,* vol. 4, Columbia University Social Work Library. Longshoremen: Sterling Spero and Abram Harris, *The Black Worker* (New York, 1931; reprint ed., New York, 1974), pp. 198–200. That is why a few unions like the International Ladies' Garment Workers) Union made such efforts to recruit blacks, so as not to be undercut by them.

20. Charles Johnson, pp. 643, 718; Jones, p. 1; Kennedy, p. 74. In the U.S. more black men were in the labor market than native-born whites (81 percent and 75 percent, respectively) but fewer than foreign-born whites (89 percent). Dutcher, p. 33. The black rate though, had declined since 1910, primarily because of improved educational opportunities.

21. Dutcher, pp. 90 (U.S. black), 102 (U.S. white), 105 (U.S. foreign-born), 97 (N.Y.C. black), 106 (N.Y.C. foreign-born). N.Y.C. white (actually total population): National Industrial Conference Board, *The Cost of Living in New York City, 1926* (New York, 1926), p. 4. Manhattan blacks mirrored the city's black pattern, but had a slightly higher rate for public service and a slightly lower one for clerical. Domingo, p. 21.

22. Illiterate in any language. Approximately 2 percent of New York City blacks over ten years old were completely illiterate, compared with 12 percent of foreign-born whites and less than 1 percent of native-born whites. Bureau of the Census, *Negroes in the United States,* pp. 237, 252; Todd, p. 113; Works Progress Administration, New York City, "Illiteracy: The 1930 Census," Report, 1939, p. 2, Works Progress Administration papers, RG 69, National Archives, Washington, D.C. The New York black figure had fallen from 8 percent in 1910: Jones, p. 1. Nationally, 23 percent of all blacks over age 10 were illiterate. *Negro Year Book 1925–26,* vol. 7 (Tuskeegee Institute, 1925), p. 296. Economics: Herbert Gutman, *The Black Family in Slavery and Freedom, 1750–1925* (New York, 1977), pp. 453–54; Kiser, pp. 198–99, 201; Hubert, p. 45. Census' 321 occupations: Charles Johnson, p. 643.

23. Spero and Harris, pp. 160, 161; Dutcher, pp. 70, 76, 121. Nationally blacks were 4 percent of carpenters, 1 percent of machinists, and 8 percent of masons. U.S. Department of Commerce, Bureau of the Census, *Fourteenth Census of the United States, 1920* (Washington, D.C., 1920), 4: 344–47; Ira Reid, "Child Dependency as Affected by Race, Nationality and Mass Migration: The Negro in the United States," in the White House Conference on Child Health and Protection, *Dependent and Neglected Children* (New York, 1933), Section

IV, p. 297; Gary Becker, *The Economics of Discrimination,* 2nd ed. (Chicago, 1971), p. 137; *Fourteenth Census,* 4: 1170–71; Domingo p. 21; National Industrial Conference Board, p. 4. Nationally, too, blacks made up approximately 1 percent of machinists. There are certain dangers in relying on the census for comparative purposes. Every decade the census bureau changed enumeration categories and instructions to census takers. For example, a female farm worker in 1910 was considered in the work force if she worked on a regular basis, even if she worked without pay. In 1920, she was only counted as such if she worked for pay, and for most of her time. Other dangers include incorrect reporting of people's occupations, misrepresentation by those being surveyed, and the change in the meaning of a job over time.

24. George Schuyler in Wayne Cooper, ed., *The Passion of Claude McKay* (New York, 1973), p. 255. Randolph: Jervis Anderson, *A. Philip Randolph* (New York, 1973; reprint ed., Berkeley, 1986), pp. 65–66.

25. Gutman, pp. 453–54; Domingo, p. 21; National Industrial Conference Board, p. 4; Richard Sterner, *The Negro's Share: A Study of Income, Consumption, Housing and Public Assistance* (Westport, Conn., 1943), p. 28. Black men in manufacturing, 1930: 22 percent. Non-skilled and service, 1925: 72 percent.

26. Black wages: Roi Ottley and William Weatherby, *The Negro in New York* (New York, 1967: reprinted from the Federal Writers' Project ed.), p. 286; Kiser, p. 199. NYUL study: Reid, NYUL, pp. 20, 23. The Urban League sent questionnaires to 3,000 black families known to it or to the Harlem branch of the New York Tuberculosis and Health Association. Responses came from 2,326 households containing 12,501 individuals living between Lexington and Convent Avenues from 110th to 150th streets. $33 a week: National Industrial Conference Board, p. 72.

27. Black and white wages similar: Kennedy, p. 97; Charles Johnson, *The Negro in American Civilization* (New York, 1930), p. 55. N.Y.C. "common labor" wage estimated by taking the city median (36 to 55 cents an hour), assuming the highest figure of 55 cents and 48-hour work week, the reported average. National Industrial Conference Board, *The Economic Status of the Wage Earner in New York and in Other States* (New York, 1928), p. 27. Industrial wage: ibid., p. 103. Black wages: see, for example, Sterner; Reid, NYUL; Todd, p. 92. Overall wage rates did rise slightly over the decade. Powell, p. 185.

28. Native-born white women: 17 percent worked; foreign-born: 18 percent. Dutcher, p. 33; Reid, NYUL, p. 20; Kiser, p. 34; Federal Writers' Program, New York City, "History of Negroes in New York," draft n.d., p. 2, papers of the WPA, Federal Writers' Program, "Negroes of New York," box 4, Schomburg Archives; Owen Lovejoy, *The Negro Children of New York* (New York, 1932), p. 18. Joint Committee on Negro Child Study in New York City, *A Study of Delinquent and Neglected Negro Children Before the New York City Children's Court, 1925* (New York, 1927), p. 12. Age: Sterner, p. 32; YWCA et al., "A New Day for the Colored Woman Worker: A Study of Colored Women in Industry in New York City," Pamphlet, March 1919, p. 8, Nannie Helen Burroughs papers, box 322, Library of Congress Manuscript Collection, Washington, D.C. Married women: 32.5 percent of black and 6.5 percent of white women worked. By 1930, those figures had risen to 33.2 percent and 9.8 percent, respectively. Claudia Goldin, "Female Labor Force Participation: The Origin of Black and White Differences, 1870 and 1880," *Journal of Economic History* 37 (March 1977): 88 (from census data).

29. Mary White Ovington, *Half a Man: The Status of the Negro in New York* (New York, 1911; reprint ed., 1969), p. 77. Many have taken this to mean that black families were dominated by women. If anything, equal responsibility for family maintenance made these families more egalitarian, not female-dominant. Yet even this much is questionable. Black women earned less than their husbands did. Although they may have been better able to resist the worst forms of male domination because of their economic position, there is little indi-

cation that either men or women perceived the actual position of the male as head of the household as threatened. In fact, Elise McDougald argued that males' economic frustration resulted in more, rather than less, domination of their wives. Elise McDougald, "The Task of Negro Womanhood," in Alain Locke, ed., *The New Negro* (New York, 1925; reprint ed., 1969), p. 380.

30. McDougald, p. 369; Dutcher, p. 79.

31. Dutcher, pp. 90 (U.S. black), 102 (U.S. white), 105 (U.S. foreign-born), 97 (N.Y.C. black), 106 (N.Y.C. foreign-born). N.Y.C. white (actually, total population): National Industrial Conference Board, *Cost of Living*, p. 4.

32. Increase from 1910: Dutcher, pp. 80–84. Occupation statistics: ibid, p. 97; Mayor's Commission on Conditions in Harlem, "The Negro in Harlem," Report, 1935, p. 21, LaGuardia papers, box 2550.

33. George Stigler, *Domestic Servants in the United States, 1900–1940* (New York, 1946), p. 6. The Manhattan figure is close to the national rate for employed black women, excluding agricultural laborers. Sterner, p. 352; Gunnar Myrdal, *An American Dilemma* (New York, 1944; reprint ed., 1969), p. 1082. Including agricultural labor, Stigler estimates 45 percent of black women nationally worked in domestic service.

34. Domestics: Kiser, p. 199. Laundry wages: National Board of the YWCA, Industrial Department, "National Industry Assembly Bulletin #3," 1930, p. 14, National Negro Congress papers, box 2, Schomburg Archives. Pressers: "Colored Women Pressers in Downtown Factory Work Under Very Bad Conditions," *New York Age*, 11 February 1925, p. 3. Committee: Frank Crosswaith, Trade Union Committee to Organize Negro Workers, "Report in Full, Covering Activities from June 1, 1925–Dec. 31, 1925," n.d., p. 5, National Urban League papers, Industrial Relations Department, series 4, box 1, Library of Congress Manuscript Collection, Washington, D.C.

35. Ovington, pp. 88–89. Industry: Dutcher, pp. 70, 79; YWCA et al., pp. 5–6, 11, 13–15. From the start, the ILGWU unionized blacks in the needle trades, often working closely with the NUL, the NAACP, and the YWCA. Spero and Harris, pp. 338, 341.

36. YWCA et al., pp. 9–11, 13, 19, 21–23.

37. Ibid., pp. 21, 24. 1928 (figures for Manhattan women reported by the New York State Industrial Commission): YWCA, "National Industry Assembly," p. 14. 1919 wages: YWCA et al., pp. 37, 39.

38. Michael Goldstein, "Black Power and the Rise of Bureaucratic Autonomy in New York City Politics: The Case of Harlem Hospital, 1917–1931," *Phylon* 41 (June 1980): 188–89, 193.

39. Ibid., pp. 191–98; "Harlem Hospital Leads Country in Recognizing Negro Doctors and Nurses," *Dunbar News*, 26 February 1930, p. 1; Charles McCarthy, "'Sui Generis': A History of Harlem Hospital" (Master's thesis, Columbia University, 1969), p. 53.

40. Early survey: Myrtle Pollard, "Harlem As It Is" (M.B.A. thesis, City College of New York, 1937), pp. 194–95. The 1929 study: Melville Weiss, "'Don't Buy Where You Can't Work': An Analysis of Consumer Action Against Employment Discrimination in Harlem, 1934–1940" (Master's thesis, Columbia University, 1941), p. 16. Dr. Louis Wright of Harlem Hospital, a black physician, claimed 120 black doctors practiced in New York City in 1929 (over a sixth of the nation's total). Louis Wright, "The Negro Physician," *Crisis* 36 (September 1929): 305. Sales: Census, *Negroes*, pp. 518–19, 524–26. This net sale figure, though small, was higher than that of any other large black urban center: p. 519. Domingo believed West Indians most often ran grocery stores and tailoring establishments, while native-born blacks most often operated barber shops and pool rooms. Domingo, p. 649.

41. "Boost Harlem," *American Recorder*, 8 December 1928, p. 6. The boost came at the end: ". . . [But] we can boast of having some well-edited newspapers, large and magnificent

church edifices, two banks operating exclusively within the colored area, many substantial and growing business enterprises; many outstanding individuals honor the learned professions of medicine and dentistry, law and theology, and there are many men of ability and high moral purpose engaged in public affairs." Less than 20 percent: Weiss, p. 16.

42. Kiser, p. 201. Black wages higher than in the South: Kennedy, pp. 95–96. Cost estimates based on man, woman, and two children, 12 and 2 years old. Sundries include transportation, recreation, medical care, charity, furniture, books, insurance, and cleaning materials. Conference Board, *Cost of Living,* pp. 43, 72, 73, 76–82, 84–85, 87, for family; 92, 97, for singles. Native-born white spending: Conference Board, *Economic Status,* pp. 82, 85. New York City Department of Health, *Annual Report, 1926* (New York, 1926), p. 27; President's Conference, p. 64. Family earnings include earnings from all employed family members.

43. Powell, p. 173.

44. Judge Davies and United Neighborhood Houses study: President's Conference, p. 16. Price differential confirmed by WPA, Federal Writers' Project, *New York City Guide* (New York, 1939), p. 258. 1915: National League on Urban Conditions Among Negroes, *Housing Conditions Among Negroes in Harlem, New York City* (New York, 1915), p. 16. Rent rise, 1919–1927: Lovejoy, p. 20. Average Harlem rent, heat: Reid, NYUL, p. 15. Average Manhattan rent, heat: National Industrial Conference Board, *Cost of Living.*

45. NYUL survey, moving, Housing Commission: Reid, NYUL, pp. 8–10, 17; Charles Johnson, *The Negro in American Civilization,* p. 211. Violations: Larry Greene, "Harlem in the Great Depression: 1928–1936" (Ph.D. dissertation, Columbia University, 1979), p. 209.

46. NYUL, p. 19. U.N.H. study: Kiser, p. 32. Owen Lovejoy, "Justice to the Negro Child," *Opportunity* 7 (June 1929): 175. Also see James Ford, *Slums and Housing: With Special Reference to New York City,* 2 vols. (Cambridge, 1936), 1: 300, 324, 326; Winthrop Lane, "Ambushed in the City," *Survey [Graphic]* 53 (1 March 1925): 693–94.

47. A household includes all individuals dwelling in a single apartment or house. A family is also related by blood, marriage, or adoption. Lodgers include all those who live in an apartment but are unrelated by blood or marriage to the family head. Reid, NYUL, pp. 4–5, 11; Gutman, p. 454. (He found one-third of West Indian and two-fifths of native-born black households held only two parents and their child or children.) A Tenement House study reported by Woofter found almost a third of the 1,627 black families they interviewed had lodgers. Thomas Woofter, *Negro Problems in Cities* (New York, 1928; reprint ed., 1969), p. 87. Osofsky, p. 138. The 1915 study: National League on Urban Conditions Among Negroes, pp. 17, 19. Both quotation and invitation from Kiser, p. 45.

48. YWCAs: Julia Skinner, "Facts about Negro Working Women," Memorandum, 25 February 1927, pp. 1–2, Phelps-Stokes Fund papers, "Jones-Tobias" box 33, Schomburg Archives. Crowding: Weaver, p. 35; Charles Johnson, *Negro in American Civilization,* p. 208. Of 276 Manhattan census tracts, only 40 held over 300 per acre, eight of which were in Central Harlem (and another eight in East Harlem): Cities Census Committee, *Population of the City of New York, 1890–1930* (New York, 1932), p. 223.

49. Ford, p. 336; Harry Schulman, *The Slums of New York* (New York, 1938), pp. 55–56; "Harlem Home Conditions Bad," and "Sees Negro Housing Crisis," *New York Times,* 13 January 1928 (clipping), Gumby collection, Part III, box 40, Columbia University Rare Book and Manuscript Library. Quotation: Osofsky, p. 135. Mortality: Nathan, p. 59, for black ("colored"); Department of Health, Bureau of Records, "Vital Statistics: Condensed Annual Reports, 1930–1939," Public Health Library, New York City; Ransom Hooker, *Maternal Mortality in New York City: A Study of All Puerperal Deaths 1930–1932* (New York, 1933), p. 7, for general (11.4 in 1925). These rates stayed fairly stable throughout the 1920s. To stan-

dardize for age means to calculate what the rate would be if the given population had the same age distribution as the general (U.S.) population. Calculations done by the Department of Health.

50. U.S.: For blacks, the general death rate in 1925 was 18.2; for whites, 11.2. Manhattan: 14.3. Nathan, pp. 19, 27. In this study, Nathan defines Harlem (sometimes calling it "north Harlem") as 21 census tracts including roughly the area between 118th and 155th streets, from Amsterdam Avenue to Park Avenue (that is, all but the southern portion of the area my study uses). This "predominantly Negro" area contained an estimated 200,474 people in 1925, on 1,011 acres: p. 18. Harlem's white rates: Kiser, p. 36 (who defines Harlem slightly differently from Nathan) standardized black and white mortality rates for age. Doing so illuminates the difference between the races in Harlem. He found Harlem's white crude death rate to be 14.4 per thousand; and black, 16.0. Standardized for age, 13.8 whites died per thousand, compared with 19.7 blacks. The differences widened similarly in each disease category. Thus the high white death rate seems due to the fact that the white population was older.

51. Study: U.S. Public Health Service, *Mortality Among Negroes in the United States,* by Mary Gover, Public Health Bulletin #174, June 1927 (Washington, D.C., 1928), pp. 22, 24. Harlem and N.Y.C.: my calculations, and Nathan, pp. 8, 24, 26–27; Welfare Council, Exploratory Committee on Negro Welfare, "Report of the Committee on Negro Welfare," January 1939, p. 7, Columbia University Social Work Library; Kennedy, p. 175; Johnson, *Negro in American Civilization,* pp. 147, 153. In some cases the estimates in each study differ by a few percentage points. I used Harlem black rates (which were available for 1926 and 1927 only) when possible. Otherwise, I relied on N.Y.C. black rates, or general Harlem rates. Suicide: see, for example, Eugene Genovese, *Roll Jordan Roll: The World the Slaves Made* (New York, 1976), pp. 639–40.

52. Table: Population statistics from Drolet and Lowell, p. 3; total birth and death figures from Department of Health, *Annual Reports;* black figures from DeLamar Institute of Public Health, "Population, Births, Notifiable Diseases, and Deaths, Assembled for New York City, New York, 1866–1938," Report, January 1941, Public Health Library; Department of Health, *Quarterly Bulletins, 1935* (New York, 1935), p. 98, for some tuberculosis figures. N.Y.C. rates from Health Department, "Vital Statistics." Harlem's rates and black infant mortality rates from Nathan, pp. 25, 26, 60, 61. Harlem's suicide and homicide rates are 1923–1927 averages. Manhattan figures are 1923–1927 averages. Nathan, pp. 18, 20, 26, 27, 61. U.S. figures: Nathan, pp. 59, 60, 62; *Negro Year Book, 1926–27,* p. 304; Harold Dorn, "Changes in Infant and Child Mortality Rates," in James Bossard, ed., *Children in a Depression Decade: The Annals of the American Academy of Political and Social Science,* 212 (November 1940): 32; Johnson, *Negro in American Civilization,* p. 142.

53. Department of Health: Jones, p. 3. AICP, *Health Work for Mothers and Children in a Colored Community,* Publication #131 (New York, 1924), p. 9.

54. NYUL, *The Negro in New York: Annual Report, 1931* (New York, 1931), pp. 17–18. Harlem Tuberculosis and Health (part of N.Y. Tuberculosis and Health Association): Welfare Council, *Health Inventory,* p. 286. Convalescent care: ibid., p. 126. Nathan, p. 10; Hubert, p. 44. The city paid convalescent homes to care for poor patients. In 1925, 96 percent of such patients were white. Of the 13 homes so supported, only 3 contained any black patients. Welfare Council, *Health Inventory,* p. 126. Clinics: ibid., p. 128; AICP, *86th Annual Report: 1928–29* (New York, 1929), p. 29. See appendix for number of free clinics by type.

55. Lane, pp. 713–14. Nathan, pp. 10, 32, 38. Comparing death rates in different sections of Harlem (all poor), Nathan rejected economic differences as the determining factor. She claimed differing rates among census tracts in Harlem correlated most closely with population density. However, an analysis of all Harlem tracts reveals that no significant correlation

exists between death rate and population density. A correlation does exist between death rates and percent black by census tract (that is; in general, the higher the black proportion of a tract, the higher the death rate), but it is not perfect. Analysis done by Irwin Greenberg.

56. Nathan, pp. 10, 32, 39. Block quotation: pp. 31, 40. Similar points: Osofsky, p. 143; Ovington, p. 31.

57. Kiser, p. 39; Johnson, *Negro in American Civilization,* p. 335; E. Franklin Frazier, *The Negro Family in the United States* (Chicago, 1939; revised ed., New York, 1948), p. 277; "Harlem Home Conditions Bad," p. 40; Lovejoy, "Justice," p. 176; Jones, p. 4.

58. Nancy Weiss, *National Urban League, 1910–1940* (New York, 1974), pp. 13–14; Hollingsworth Wood, "The New York Colored Mission—Good Samaritan Inn," *Opportunity* 3 (March 1927): 83; Federal Writers' Program, New York City, "Welfare and Public Relief," draft, 1939, p. 4, WPA, Federal Writers' Program, "Negroes of New York," box 10. Child care: Reid, NYUL, pp. 28–29. Included in the group left alone were 7 percent who were told to go to the library, and another 9 percent instructed to stay in school. Mary White Ovington reminds us of the benefits of the black extended family network: by taking care of children, grandparents felt useful, and freed mothers to work. Ovington, p. 78. Children's Aid Society, *The CAS 77th Annual Report,* 1929 (New York: 1930), p. 19. Joint Committee on Negro Child Study, pp. 17, 32–35.

59. Poor defined as having family earnings of less than $25 per week. Income: New York City Children's Court, *Annual Report, 1926* (New York, 1927), p. 32. Delinquency rates: Mayor's Committee on Juvenile Delinquency, "First Interim Report: Analysis of the Statistics of the Children's Court Division of the Domestic Relief Court of the City of New York," 8 July 1943, chart B, Municipal Reference and Resource Center, New York City; N.Y.S. Temporary Commission, pp. 132, 134; Children's Court, *Annual Report, 1925* (New York, 1926), p. 60; ibid., *1927* (New York, 1928), p. 22; ibid., *1928* (New York, 1929), p. 22; ibid., *1929* (New York, 1930), p. 26. NYUL study: Utopia Children's House, "Report of the UCH," 1933, p. 1, LaGuardia papers, box 35. Percent in population: in 1920, black children were 1.6 percent of all city children. In 1930: 3.9 percent. In 1925, 12 percent of the city's black population, 13 percent of its white population and 11 percent of Harlem's black population were between the ages of 5 and 14. In 1930: 13 percent, 17 percent, and 11 percent, respectively. Joint Committee on Negro Child Study, p. 17; New York Tuberculosis and Health Association, p. 4; Nathan, p. 17. Migration: Lovejoy, *Negro Children,* pp. 37, 39.

60. Joint Committee on Negro Child Study, p. 20. Different studies find the same facts throughout the five-year period from 1925–1929. "Harlem Home Conditions Bad"; Gardner Jones, Federal Writers' Program, New York City, "Delinquent and Neglected Negro Children," draft, 4 October 1937, p. 1, WPA, Federal Writers' Program, New York City, "Negroes of New York," box 9. Frazier, *Negro Family,* p. 277; Johnson, *Negro in American Civilization,* p. 335. Robbery: snatching purses or similar acts. Burglary takes place inside a building. Theft: burglary with forced entry. Stealing: burglary without forced entry.

61. N.Y.C. black population: NYUL, *A Challenge to New York: Annual Report, 1927* (New York, 1927), p. 5, estimates it at 259,800. The total population from which juvenile delinquents could come is 30,000 for blacks and 789,000 for whites. Cases: Black: Joint Committee on Negro Child Study, p. 20. White: Children's Court, *Annual Report, 1924,* pp. 16–19. Guilt: in 1925, 32.5 percent of black youths charged with delinquency were dismissed or discharged. In 1924 (closest statistics available) either 38.6 percent or 45.8 percent of whites were, depending on what counts under the delinquency heading. Numbers vary slightly according to the definition of juvenile delinquency ("ungovernable," for example, sometimes appears under "delinquent," and sometimes not). Proportional arraignments: 81 white children per 10,000 (145 per 10,000 white boys) and 172 black children per 10,000 (268 boys).

"Serious" delinquents: Sylvia Robison, *Can Delinquency Be Measured?* (New York, 1936), p. 141. Blacks were 9.8 percent of the Manhattan child population and 19.5 percent of the "serious" truant population. Still, the real numbers were small: only 142 black children were serious truants.

62. Kiser, p. 40; Robison (includes Reid's comments), pp. 58, 63, 64.

63. In 1924 and 1925, for children found delinquent, 12.3 percent of blacks and 67.1 percent of whites received probation. Committed to institution: 29.2 and 11.5 percent, respectively. Suspended sentence: 41.4 and 8.7 percent. Other (fine, bail, etc.): 17.1 and 12.7 percent. Children's Court, *Annual Report, 1924,* pp. 16–19; Joint Committee on Negro Child Study, p. 20; Robison, p. 28; Johnson, *Negro in American Civilization,* p. 330; Lovejoy, "Negro Children," pp. 35, 37. 1930 figures: Robison, p. 93. In Manhattan in 1930, 57 percent of blacks and 47 percent of whites under care were in institutions. Robison's findings show a shorter sentence for blacks than whites in institutions. It is not clear why her figures disagree with the others'.

64. N.Y.S. Temporary Commission, pp. 132, 134; Children's Court, *Annual Report, 1925,* pp. 32, 60; ibid., *1927,* p. 22; ibid., *1928,* p. 22; ibid., *1929,* p. 26; Joint Committee on Negro Child Study, pp. 19, 20. In 1927 and 1928, black neglect cases were approximately 8 percent of all such cases, rising to almost 10 percent in 1929. Proportion of population: ibid., pp. 12–13.

65. Prisons and rates per population: Kiser, p. 40. Black prisoners constituted almost 5 percent of the total black population between 20 and 45. White prisoners were 1.5 percent of the comparable white population. Women were 11 percent of all white prisoners and a quarter of black: p. 41. Bail, etc.: ibid.; Kennedy, p. 187. Police arrest blacks: see, for example, Kennedy, p. 188. Lodgers, childless: Shulman, pp. 19, 308–9.

66. Kiser, p. 41; Shulman, p. 309; Lane, p. 692; Claude McKay, *Harlem Glory,* (Chicago, 1990), pp. 12–15.

67. The Committee of Fourteen was organized in 1905 for the suppression of vice (usually prostitution) and supported solely by voluntary contributions. Committee of Fourteen, *Annual Report, 1925* (New York, 1926), cover. Investigation conducted from March to September of 1928, from 126th to 152nd Streets (in some cases south to 111th) between Fifth and St. Nicholas Aves.: ibid., *1928* (New York, 1929), pp. 31–34. Its 1926 report (New York, 1927), makes the same points: p. 31. 1905: from ibid., *1929* (New York, 1930), p. 15. McKay, *Harlem Glory,* p. 15.

68. The number of arrests for prostitution rose each year, probably due more to better police work than to a rise in prostitution, the Committee of 14 explained in *Annual Report, 1927* (New York, 1928), p. 32. In fact, the number of women arraigned in Women's Court for all crimes rose each year. New York City Magistrate's Court, *Annual Report, 1925* (New York, 1926), p. 135; ibid., *1926,* p. 109; ibid., *1927* (New York, 1928), p. 111; ibid., *1928,* p. 114; ibid., *1929,* p. 107; Committee of Fourteen [1930?]. Harlem arrests: ibid., *1925,* pp. 44–45; ibid., *1926,* p. 47; ibid., *1927,* p. 41; ibid., *1928,* p. 45; ibid., *1929,* p. 67. Under cover: ibid., *1926,* p. 30; ibid., *1928,* pp. 3, 6; ibid., *1929,* p. 56.

69. "Cocaine Main Harlem Drug," *Lincoln News,* 15 July 1929, p. 9. "Dope" refers here to opium.

70. Edna Lonigan, *Unemployment in New York City* (New York, 1931), p. 12 (data from N.Y.S. Department of Labor); AICP, *84th Annual Report, 1926–1927* (New York, 1927), p. 17; *Annual Report, 1927–28* (New York, 1928), p. 14; Ira Reid, NYUL Industrial Department, "Industrial Newsletter: The Flyleaf," 1 October 1927, p. 1, National Urban League papers, series 4, box 32, Library of Congress Manuscript Collection. The NYUL placed only 32 percent of its male applicants, and 36 percent of its female. Ira Reid, NYUL, "Annual

Report, Industrial Department, 1926," 1 November 1927, p. 1, National Urban League papers, series 5, box 10. 1928 figures: Louise Kennedy, Commission for the NYUL Study, "The NYUL Story," draft, 1935, National Urban League papers, series 4, box 32.

71. Kate Huntly, Welfare Council, *Financial Trends of Agencies Engaged in Giving Outdoor Relief in New York City*, Study 4 of the Research Bureau (New York, 1931), pp. 10, 36, 41, 49–50; AICP: *84th Annual Report, 1926–27*, pp. 17, 19. It provided health services, money, nursing, vocational guidance, old-age homes, and a children's camp for the poor of both races. COS: *43rd Annual Report, 1924–25* (New York, 1926), pp. 15, 19; ibid., *48th Annual Report, 1929–30* (New York, 1931), pp. 10, 22.

72. The Welfare Council described itself as a "voluntary association of the public and private social agencies in New York City who are willing to pool their information, experiences, plans and ideas in order to secure: better team work and elimination of duplication; better standards of social work; better public understanding of social work; and a better factual basis for community planning of social service." Begun in 1925, in three years it had over 640 member agencies out of approximately one thousand in the city. *The Welfare Council* (New York, 1928), p. 1. The conference and quotations: Welfare Council, Committee on Employment, "Report of the Committee on Employment of the Welfare Council Concerning the Employment Situation," 28 May 1928, pp. 1–3, Mayor James Walker's papers, box 281, Municipal Archives.

73. Board of Child Welfare of the City of New York, *Tenth Annual Report*, 1925 (New York, 1926), pp. 3, 5, 26–27; BCW, *Annual Report* [1941?]. NYSES: Federal Writers' Program, New York City, "Social Adjustments of Negroes," draft, n.d., p. 1, WPA, Federal Writers' Program, "Negroes of New York," box 9; Federal Writers' Program, New York City, "History of Negroes in New York," p. 1. Of course, not all job applicants were placed; this documents need, not service. Magistrate's Court, *Annual Report, 1925*, p. 137; ibid., *1926*, p. 111; ibid., *1927*, p. 113; ibid., *1928*, p. 116; ibid., *1929*, p. 109. A BCW "Memorandum to Mayor LaGuardia," 25 January 1934, LaGuardia papers, box 658, stated that illegitimate children were not eligible for BCW relief. This practice dates from at least the 1920s, since the Charity Organization Society voted in 1928 to support illegitimate children because the BCW did not. COS, Central Office Committee Meeting Minutes, 7 December 1928, COS papers, box 97, Columbia University Rare Book and Manuscript Library.

74. Charity Organization Society, *Harlem Number*, Bulletin #667 (New York, 1929), p. 3. It also employed black social workers, one of the few to do so: p. 4. Private services: Joint Committee, pp. 20–28; James Hubert, NYUL, "Newsletter to Executive Board Members," 25 September 1926, p. 1, National Urban League papers, series 5, box 10.

75. "The Reminiscences of George S. Schuyler," 1962, p. 232, Columbia University Oral History Research Office.

Chapter 2

1. U.S.: Charles Lawrence, "Negro Organizations in Crisis: Depression, New Deal, World War II" (Ph.D. dissertation, Columbia University, 1952), p. 193. N.Y.C.: Edna Lonigan, *Unemployment in New York City* (New York, 1931), p. 4; New York City WPA Advisory Council, "Reports on Public Assistance to the Administrator, WPA for the City of New York," 14 March 1939, p. 266, Columbia University Social Work Library, New York City. Blacks: Richard Sterner, *The Negro's Share: A Study of Income, Consumption, Housing and Public Assistance* (Westport, Conn., 1943), p. 362. 1931: Joint Legislative Committee on Unemployment, *Preliminary Report*, Document #69 (Albany, 1932), p. 38.

2. Lilian Brandt, *An Impressionistic View of the Winter of 1930–1931 in New York City*

(New York, 1932), pp. 7–9, 13; Mayor's Committee on Unemployment Relief, *Report of Mayor LaGuardia's Committee on Unemployment Relief* (New York, 1935), p. 14; New York City Department of Health, *Quarterly Bulletins, 1935* (New York, 1935), p. 15.

3. Charity Organization Society, *Annual Report, 1928–1929* (New York, 1930); ibid., *1929–1930* (New York, 1931); E. Franklin Frazier, *The Negro Family in the United States* (Chicago, 1939; revised ed., New York, 1948), p. 251. Quotation: Brandt, p. 18. Delinquency: J. B. Maller, *Juvenile Delinquency in New York City* (revised reprint from the *Journal of Psychology* 3 [November 1936]), p. 11, Vertical File: "Juvenile Delinquency Clippings," Municipal Reference and Resource Center, New York City; Children's Court, *Annual Report, 1928* (New York, 1929), p. 22; ibid., *1930* (New York, 1931), p. 22; ibid., *1931* (New York, 1932), p. 24; ibid., *1932* (New York, 1933), p. 24. Cases before Children's Court:

	1928	1930	1931	1932
delinquent	7,481	8,179	7,434	7,437
neglected	4,463	4,569	4,660	4,854

In 1933 the Children's Court moved to the Domestic Relations Court, and the numbers from that year seem based on different and non-comparable information. See, for example, Katherine Hildreth, Children's Court, "The Negro Problem as Reflected in the Functioning of the Domestic Relations Court of the City of New York," Report, 2 June 1934, p. 3, U.S. Department of Labor papers, Division of Negro Labor, RG 183, USES box 1391, National Archives, Washington, D.C.

4. WPA Advisory Council, p. 79; N.Y.C. [Budget office?], "Memorandum *In Re* City's Aid to the Unemployed," March 1931, p. 6, Mayor Walker papers, box UW 1926–30, Municipal Archives, New York City; N.Y.C. Department of Public Welfare, *Annual Report, 1930* (New York, 1931), p. 20; ibid., *1931* (New York, 1932), p. 13.

5. In New York City, the two fields with the highest unemployment were construction and manufacturing, with 27 percent each. Domestic service declined 13 percent. By contrast, trade and professional service had rates of 7 percent each, and public service suffered virtually no drop. Lonigan, p. 5. Factory production: Brandt, p. v. Joint Legislative Committee, p. 35.

6. Table 2.1: Sterner, p. 362. First fired: see, for example, Carita Roane, Testimony before Mayor's Commission on Conditions in Harlem, 20 April 1935, p. 4, Mayor LaGuardia papers, new box 3770, Municipal Archives; Frank Byrd, "Harlem's Employment Situation," *Crisis* 40 (May 1931): 160; Ira Reid and T. Arnold Hill, "The Forgotten Tenth," Pamphlet, May 1933, pp. 62–63, Columbia University Social Work Library. Welfare Council: Lester Granger, *The Negro Worker in New York City* (New York, 1941), p. 6. The *Herald Tribune* reported that five times as many black workers as white lost their jobs: Federal Writers' Program, New York City, "Social Adjustments of Negroes," notes, n.d., p. 2, papers of the WPA, Federal Writers' Program, "Negroes of New York," box 9, Schomburg Archives, New York City; Alfred Smith, Federal Emergency Relief Administration, "Reasons for the Disproportionate Number of Negroes on the Relief Rolls," Report, April 1935, p. 7, National Negro Congress papers, box 2, Schomburg Archives; Sterner, pp. 29, 362. Chapters 3 and 6 document numerous instances of job discrimination based solely on race. Clyde Kiser, *From Sea Island to City: A Study of St. Helena Islanders in Harlem and Other Urban Centers* (New York, 1932; reprint ed., New York, 1969), p. 199: "Despite the depression there have been very few cases of returns home," testifying to harder times elsewhere.

7. Health Area 12: Clyde Kiser, "Diminishing Family Income in Harlem: A Possible Cause of the Harlem Riot," *Opportunity* 13 (June 1935): 172. The shifts were small. Sample size of

1,579 in 1928 and 1,845 in 1932. Employment figures: Charles Franklin, *The Negro Labor Unionist of New York* (New York, 1936), p. 54; Mayor's Commission on Conditions in Harlem, "The Negro in Harlem," Report, 1935, p. 21, LaGuardia papers, box 2550; Lois Helmbold, "Making Choices, Making Do: Black and White Working Class Women's Lives and Work During the Great Depression" (Ph.D. dissertation, Stanford University, 1982), pp. 217, 222–24. George Stigler, *Domestic Servants in the United States, 1900–1940* (New York, 1946), p. 7. NYSES: Carita Roane, "Negro Relief Work in New York," *Crisis* 39 (January 1932): 451, 453. For a fuller discussion of job market dynamics, see Chapter 3.

8. Roane, pp. 451, 453; Byrd, p. 160; Miriam Carpenter II, "Some Aspects of the Depression on Negroes" (Master's thesis, Columbia University, 1937), p. 79. Salary by occupation level: Kiser, "Diminishing Income," p. 172.

9. New York State Temporary Commission on the Condition of the Urban Colored Population, *Second Report,* Legislative Document #69 (Albany, 1939), p. 136; Frazier, pp. 276–77; Mayor's Commission on Conditions in Harlem, "Juvenile Arrests in Police Precincts # 23, 24, 26, 28, 30, 32, 34 Classified by Type of Crime, Age Group, Residence and Sex: 1930, 1931, 1932, 1933," Tables, 1935, LaGuardia papers, box 34; Mayor's Committee on Juvenile Delinquency, "First Interim Report," 8 July 1943, Chart B, Manuscript Reference and Resource Center. (Court appearances for delinquency from 1928–1933 are higher than those of any other nearby year.) Black proportion (up from 8–10 percent in the earlier 1920s): Children's Court, *Annual Report, 1928,* p. 22; ibid., *1929* (New York, 1930), p. 26; ibid., *1930,* p. 22; ibid., *1931,* p. 24; ibid., *1932,* p. 24; Kiser, *Sea Island,* pp. 39–40. Unemployed youths: Lawrence, p. 194.

10. Incomes: Kiser, "Diminishing Income," p. 172; National Industrial Conference Board, *The Cost of Living in the United States in 1931* (New York, 1932), p. 4.

11. Sydney Axelrad, League of Mothers' Clubs, "Tenements and Tenants," Report, 1933, pp. 2–3, 9–10, 13, Vertical File: "Tenement Houses," Municipal Reference and Resource Center.

12. Beverly Smith, "Harlem's Distress Intensified as Growing Property Values Threaten Impoverished Tenants," *Dunbar News,* 26 February 1930, p. 1; James Hubert, "Harlem Faces Unemployment," *Opportunity* 9 (February 1931): 42, 44. Nels Anderson, Welfare Council, "The Homeless in New York City," Report, February 1934, p. 138, Community Service Society papers, box 132, Columbia University Rare Book and Manuscript Library.

13. Actually, the children were brought to court; the court listed "neglect" and "parents' whereabouts unknown" as categories of juvenile delinquency. Sample cases: Mayor's Commission on Conditions in Harlem, "Neglected Children—Police Report," notes, 1935 (1930 cases), LaGuardia papers, box 755. The list also includes incest victims, runaways, and "wayward" and homeless children. COS: Frazier, p. 251. Quotation: N.Y.S. Temporary Commission, p. 136. Statistics: Children's Court, *1928,* p. 22; ibid., *1930,* p. 22; ibid.,*1931,* p. 24; ibid., *1932,* p. 24. Again, 1933 statistics are calculated differently. See Hildreth, p. 3.

14. Utopia Children's House, "Report of the UCH," 1933, p. 4, LaGuardia papers, box 35; New York Association for Improving the Condition of the Poor (AICP), *86th Annual Report: 1930–1931* (New York, 1931), p. 27.

15. New York City Department of Health, *Births and Infant Mortality, Tuberculosis Causes and Deaths: Boroughs of Manhattan and Brooklyn* (New York, 1932), pp. ii, xvii, xviii, xx; Owen Lovejoy, *The Negro Children of New York* (New York, 1932), p. 27; Roi Ottley and William Weatherby, *The Negro in New York: An Informal Social History, 1626–1940* (New York, 1967; reprinted from the Federal Writers' Project ed.), p. 272. Most of the figures remained unchanged, or had declined slightly from 1920 figures. Harry Shulman, *The Slums of New York* (New York, 1938), p. 63. Quotation: "Force Negroes to Live in Foul Hovels," *Hunger Fighter,* 25 September 1933, p. 2, International Labor Defense papers, box 2, Schomburg Archives.

16. New to aid: Hubert, p. 44. Relief population: National Urban League, "How Unemployment Affects Negroes," Report, March 1931, p. 15, U.S. Dept. of Labor papers, Division of Negro Labor, box 1394A. Unemployed estimates (for 1932): Granger, p. 7; Ottley and Weatherby, p. 270.

17. WPA Advisory Council, p. 67. Some federal money was made available under President Hoover, but New York City received too little to make any difference. Welfare Council: William Hodson, Welfare Council, to Mayor James Walker and the New York City Board of Estimate, 9 January 1932, p. 3, Mayor Walker papers, box 280, Municipal Archives. Hodson became the head of the Department of Public Welfare under Mayor LaGuardia.

18. Roane, pp. 451–52; New York State Governor's Commission on Unemployment Relief, *Administration of Home Relief in New York City* (New York, 1935), pp. 34, 35, Russell-Sage collection, City College of New York. New York City [Budget Office?], "Memorandum," p. 3, Mayor's Official Committee for Relief of the Unemployed and Needy, *Report of the Activities of the Mayor's Official Committee, October 1930–June 1931* (New York, 1931), pp. 1, 13, 27, 41, 59, 65; Mayor's Official Committee, *Annual Report, July 1931–June 1932* (New York [1932]), pp. 1–3; ibid., *Annual Report, July 1932–June 1933* (New York [1933]), pp. 1–3. March and rally: "Reds Battle Police in Union Square," *New York Times,* 7 March 1930, pp. 1–2; "Reds Invade City Hall," *New York Times,* 17 October 1930, p. 1.

19. "City Teachers Add Relief to 3 R's By Raising $1,000,000 for Needy," *New York Herald Tribune,* 25 November 1931 (clipping), Columbia University Microfilm VF 517; "Relief Work in Public Schools," *New York Sun,* 5 December 1931 (clipping), Columbia University Microfilm VF 517.

20. N.Y.S. Commissioner: David Adie, "Some Aspects of Child Welfare Services," *Proceedings of the Conference on State Child-Welfare Services, Washington, D.C., April 4–6, 1938* (Washington, D.C., 1938), p. 60. Interviews with social workers (including quotations): Brandt, pp. 54–56. COS: *1933–34* (New York, 1935), p. 22. Needs versus rights: See, for example, William Gaylin, Ira Glasser, Steven Marcus, and David Rothman, *Doing Good: The Limits of Benevolence* (New York, 1978), particularly Rothman's "The State As Parent," pp. 67–96.

21. "Largest" depending on which services one includes. To take 1934 as an example, the AICP provided 3 percent of all public and private relief granted. AICP, *90th Annual Report: 1932–1933* (New York, 1933), p. 6. Unemployment as cause: 80 percent in 1931, 85 percent in 1932. All data from the AICP, *Annual Report 1928–29* (New York, 1929), p. 5; ibid., *1929–1930* (New York, 1930), p. 5; ibid., *1930–1931,* p. 5; ibid., *1931–1932* (New York, 1932), pp. 3, 26, 27; ibid., *1932–1933,* p. 36; AICP, "Index Numbers Indicating an Increase in Demands on the Resources of the AICP Since Oct. 1, 1928" [1933?], Community Service Society papers, box 26; COS, *Annual Report, 1924–25* (New York, 1926), p. 15; ibid., *1929–30,* pp. 10, 18, 22; ibid., *1930–31* (New York, 1932), p. 11; ibid., *1931–32* (New York, 1933), pp. 10, 11; ibid., *1932–33.* (New York, 1934), pp. 13, 14. AICP, *Annual Report, 1932–1933,* states it ran out of money often in the early Depression. The AICP and the COS merged in 1939.

22. See Children's Aid Society *Annual Reports* at the Municipal Reference and Resource Center for details.

23. Bailey Burritt, Emergency Work Bureau, to Mayor Walker, 15 January 1931, p. 1, Walker papers, box 280. "Impending need": Hodson, p. 3.

24. Emergency Unemployment Relief Committee, p. 3; Emergency Work and Relief Bureau of the Emergency Unemployment Relief Committee, "Report, October 1, 1931–August 1, 1932," pp. 3, 6, Columbia University Social Work Library; "Old Work Bureau Will Close Today," *New York Times,* 1 November 1934 (clipping), Columbia University Social Work Library; Governor's Commission on Unemployment Relief, pp. 18, 33; Sadie Hall, Federal Writers' Program, New York City, "Public Relief Development," draft, 26 October 1939, pp. 1–2, WPA, Federal Writers' Program, "Negroes of New York," box 10; W. H. Mat-

thews, "The Story of the Emergency Relief Bureau, October 1, 1930–August 31, 1933," Pamphlet, 1933, pp. 49–50, Columbia University Social Work Library; Barbara Blumberg, *The New Deal and the Unemployed: The View from New York City* (Lewisburg, Pa., 1979), pp. 19, 25, 27.

25. Matthews, pp. 10, 13, 15, 16, 20, 30, 38, 40, 43; Emergency Work and Relief Bureau of the E.U.R.C., pp. 11, 13, 18, 19; New York City Emergency Employment Committee, *Report of the Emergency Employment Committee, October 1, 1930–July 1, 1931* (New York, 1931), p. 8, 27, 29, 32. Sandwiches: ibid., p. 16. The Women's Bureau was organized and run by Mrs. Belmont. White-collar: Emergency Unemployment Relief Committee, "The New Step on the Stair," Report, 1932, p. 3, Columbia University Social Work Library.

26. Governor's Commission on Unemployment Relief, p. 45; Department of Public Welfare, *Annual Report, 1934* (New York, n.d.), p. 8; Department of Public Welfare, Emergency Home Relief Bureau, "Preliminary Report for Six Months December 28, 1931–June 30, 1932," p. v, Columbia University Social Work Library. Outdoor relief was instituted in 1929. Hall, p. 1. N.Y.C. Board of Child Welfare, *15th Annual Report,* 1930 (New York, 1931), pp. 6–7; ibid., *16th,* 1931 (New York, 1932), pp. 3, 6; ibid., *17th,* 1932 (New York, 1933), pp. 5–6 (quotation p. 6).

27. Godias Drolet and Louis Weiner, New York City Health Department, Committee on Neighborhood Health Development, *Vital Statistics in the Development of Neighborhood Health Centers in New York City* (New York, 1932), pp. 59, 60. Placements: Roane, p. 452; Department of Public Welfare, *Annual Report, 1930,* p. 1. Women fared better. Ibid., *Annual Report, 1932* (New York, 1933), p. 13. Over 600 women a night appeared at women's shelters. This lower number reflected the lack of beds for women, not less need. Welfare Council, Research Bureau, "Confidential Memorandum: Temporary Shelter of Homeless in New York City," March 1933, pp. 1, 2, and Tables 1, 3, Community Service Society papers, box 131; Roane, pp. 451–52; Department of Public Welfare, *Annual Report, 1930,* pp. 61, 64; ibid., *1931,* p. 8.

28. Mayor's Committee on Unemployment Relief, p. 24; Department of Public Welfare, *Annual Report, 1932,* p. 9. Money provided: New York State Temporary Emergency Relief Administration, *The State in Public Unemployment Relief,* Legislative Document #59, 1 March 1934 (Albany, 1934), p. 9; William Hodson, Welfare Council, "How New York City's Funds for Relief Are Being Spent," Memorandum, 17 October 1932, p. 1, Community Service Society papers, box 123. (He claims $24 million was spent by the city, but this figure seems not to include all city services.) City Affairs Committee of New York, "Report on Unemployment Relief Under the Walker Administration," Press release, 27 January 1931, pp. 1–4, Vertical File: "New York City Unemployment Relief Measures, 1914–1939," Municipal Reference and Resource Center. COS minimum budget: *Annual Report, 1931–32,* p. 14. AICP total: AICP, *89th Annual Report, 1931–32,* p. 27.

29. HRB: Governor's Commission, pp. 88–89. Wicks Act: ibid., p. 35. The board had also considered needy many of those rejected, but these applicants had not fulfilled the two-year residency requirement. Hodson to Walker and Board of Estimate, p. 3. E.U.R.C., "Report," pp. 3–4, for quotation; E.U.R.C., "Report as of May 1933," p. 4, Columbia University Social Work Library.

30. Welfare Council: Hodson to Walker and Board of Estimate, p. 1. WPA Advisory Council, p. 19; New York State Department of Social Welfare, *Volume, Distribution and Cost of Child Dependency in New York State for the Year Ending December 31, 1932* (Albany, 1934), p. 60, in *New York State Welfare Department Publications,* vol. 1, Columbia University Social Work Library.

31. AICP, *Annual Report, 1929–1930,* p. 27; New York State Temporary Emergency Relief Administration, *Relief Today in New York State* (Albany, 1933), p. 9, in *New York*

State TERA Publications, vol. 1, Columbia University Social Work Library; Matthews, p. 9.

32. Hubert, p. 44; T. Arnold Hill, National Urban League, to Porter Lee, President's Emergency Committee for Employment, 22 January 1931, National Urban League papers, series 4, box 7, Library of Congress Manuscript Collection, Washington, D.C.; "New Hope for Negro Race Born in Melting Pot That Is Harlem," *New York Herald Tribune,* 14 February 1930 (clipping), Gumby collection, part 3, box 40, Columbia University Rare Book and Manuscript Library; E. Franklin Frazier, *The Negro in the United States,* revised ed. (New York, 1957), p. 602. Although the Communist party charged that "relief agencies openly discriminate against Negroes," there is no factual basis to support such a statement, at least for home relief. "Negro Jobless Discriminated Against by City," *Hunger Fighter,* January 1933, ILD papers, box 2.

33. Governor's Commission on Unemployment Relief, p. 35. The survey, taken in April of 1932, is presented in Larry Greene, "Harlem in the Great Depression: 1928–1936" (Ph.D. diss., Columbia University, 1979), p. 385. Residence: Nels Anderson, p. 141. Although migration slowed dramatically, a continued stream of newcomers did contribute to Harlem's high levels of need.

34. NYUL: Hubert, p. 45. White-collar: "The Gibson Committee operated their Emergency Work Bureau not only with a distinctly racial bias, but also with a class bias which probably had an equally negative impact on the Harlem poor." Greene, pp. 380–82 (includes NYUL placement findings). The Communist party's Unemployed Council went farther, accusing the Gibson Committee, the NYUL, and the Red Cross of "regularly turn[ing] applicants away, on any excuse or none," but I found no evidence of such behavior. "Negro Jobless." Illegitimacy: in New York State in 1930, 62 black illegitimate births per one thousand live black births, 13.8 for white. S. J. Holmes and E. R. Dempster, "The Trend of Illegitimate Birth-Rate in the United States," *Population* 2 (November 1936): 14. In 1940, nationwide, 2 percent of white and 17 percent of black births were registered as illegitimate. Harry Ploski and Ernest Kaiser, *The Negro Almanac* (New York, 1971), p. 382. Neither reflect actual illegitimacy, but both document the higher rate of acknowledged or reported illegitimacy in the black population, which affected black opportunities for relief.

35. Mission: 8 West 131st Street. L. Hollingsworth Wood, "The New York Colored Mission–Good Samaritan Inn," *Opportunity* 3 (March 1927): 82, 83; Federal Writers' Program, New York City, "Welfare and Public Relief," draft, 1939, p. 4, WPA, Federal Writers' Program, "Negroes of New York," box 10; Mayor's Official Committee, p. 17; New York Colored Mission, *Annual Reports of the Colored Mission, 1925–1933* (New York, 1926–1934), New York Public Library. Precincts: The 32nd Precinct at West 136th Street had 1,269 cases, and the 28th on West 123rd St. had 376. The next-highest had 254 cases, and was outside Harlem. Mayor's Commission on Conditions in Harlem, "Report to Mayor on Home Relief by Race," draft, 28 August 1936, p. 2, LaGuardia papers, box 2550. For private caseloads, see above, and Miriam Carpenter II, "Some Aspects of the Depression on Negroes" (M.A. thesis, Columbia University, 1937), pp. 10–11; Mayor's Commission on Conditions in Harlem, "The Negro in Harlem," pp. 21, 35.

36. The Colored Orphan Asylum, *90th Annual Report: 1925–1926* (New York, 1926), pp. 7, 14; COA, *95th Annual Report, 1930–1931* (New York, 1931), p. 5; ibid., *1931–1932* (New York, 1932), p. 5. Its money and support, at least in the Depression, also came from the Welfare Council, the Greater New York Fund, and the Federation of Protestant Welfare Agencies. COA, *"If... any child lacks...": Annual Report: 1938–1939* (New York, 1939), p. 15. Boarding out began in 1918. *Annual Report: 1918* (New York, 1919), p. 15. Department of Public Welfare, *Annual Report, 1930,* p. 22; ibid., *1931,* pp. 18, 20. SPCC: New York City Domestic Court, *Annual Report, 1933* (New York, 1934), p. 46.

37. New York State Temporary Commission, pp. 132, 134, 136; Frazier, *The Negro Family*, pp. 276–77; Sylvia Robison, *Can Delinquency Be Measured?* (New York, 1936), pp. 61, 73; Mayor's Commission on Conditions in Harlem, "Complaints against the Police Department," notes, 1935, LaGuardia papers, box 755.

38. The Center opened in 1929. Children's Aid Society, *Off Harlem's Streets* (New York, 1940), p. 2; Children's Aid Society, *79th Annual Report, 1931* (New York, 1932), p. 3; ibid., *80th Annual Report, Summer Work Number, 1932;* ibid., *81st Annual Report, 1933* (New York, 1934), p. 29; George Gregory, "The Harlem Children's Center," *Opportunity* 10 (November 1932): 341, 342. Recreation: Lovejoy, p. 41; Winfred Nathan, *Health Conditions in North Harlem, 1923–1927,* National Tuberculosis Association Social Research Series #2 (New York, 1932), p. 57.

39. "Fight Jim Crow Attack on Negro Jobless," *Hunger Fighter,* September 1932 (clipping), ILD papers, box 2. Lodging: Nels Anderson, p. 175; Welfare Council, "Confidential Memorandum," p. 1; Wood, p. 83.

40. Hubert, p. 44. NYUL, "Statistical Report of the Employment Department of the NYUL for the Year 1933" [1934?], pp. 1–3, NUL papers, series 4, box 32.

41. NYUL, *An Adventure in Economic and Race Adjustment: Annual Report, 1934* (New York, 1934), pp. 5, 7; Samuel Allen, NYUL, "Report of the Industrial Secretary, Annual Meeting, 10 January 1934," pp. 1–3; NUL papers, series 4, box 32; NYUL, *Annual Report 1927* (New York, 1928), p. 7; ibid., *Report* [1931?]; James Hubert, "Newsletter to Executive Board Members," 25 September 1926, pp. 3, 6, NUL papers, series 5, box 10; NYUL, "Report on Work by NYUL Departments, Year of 1932," pp. 1–3, Arthur Schomburg papers, box 16, Schomburg Archives; NYUL, "Statistical Report of Work by NYUL Departments, Jan. 1, 1933, to May 31, 1933," pp. 1–2, Arthur Schomburg papers, box 16; NYUL, *The Negro in New York: Annual Report, 1931* (New York, 1931), pp. 21, 31. The NYUL had been providing most of these services for years, but for many fewer people. Fund raising: Hill to Lee. Description in "Editorials," *Survey [Graphic]* 53 (1 March 1925): 698–99.

42. Daisy Reed, "For Harlem Negro Children," *Opportunity* 6 (August 1928): 246; Utopia Children's House, *Fifth Annual Campaign for $5000* (New York, 1933), pp. 1–2, LaGuardia papers, box 35; Utopia Children's House, "Report," 1933, pp. 1–2. Hope Day Nursery, "Card Party and Dance Given by Hope Day Nursery for Colored Children," Invitation, 1 February 1929, NAACP papers, series C, box 269, Library of Congress Manuscript Collection. UCH self-description: Utopia Children's House, "1937: A Report," Pamphlet, n.d., p. 4, W. Adams papers, box 5, Schomburg Archives. White Rose Mission: "Welfare and Public Relief," pp. 3–4; Mayor's Committee on City Planning, "West Harlem Community Study," Report, 1937, p. 40, Municipal Reference and Resource Center.

43. *The Katy Ferguson House* (New York, 1929), pp. 1–2; Katy Ferguson House, Untitled pamphlet, 1932, p. 1, Russell-Sage collection. The house staff tried to find these women employment after the birth of their children. Women stayed an average of five months. Other institutions: Joint Committee on Negro Child Study in New York, *A Study of Juvenile Delinquent and Neglected Negro Children Before the New York City Children's Court, 1925* (New York, 1927). (These are 1925 figures, but later reports by the Katy Ferguson House note that no more accepted black women or their illegitimate children a decade later.)

44. Hubert, "Harlem Faces Unemployment," p. 44. Twelve churches had over a thousand members. William Welty, "Black Shepherds: A Study of the Leading Negro Clergymen in New York City, 1900–1940" (Ph.D. dissertation, New York University, 1969), p. 242. Size: U.S. Department of Commerce, Bureau of the Census, *Negroes in the United States 1920–1932* (Washington, D.C., 1935), p. 546; William Wright, Jr., "The Negro Store-fronts: Churches of the Disinherited: A Study of the Store-front Churches of East Harlem, New York" (Ph.D. dissertation, Union Theological Seminary, 1942), p. 57. United Holy Church: "Prompt Aid for the Needy," *Harlem Evening Star,* 1 March 1932, p. 1.

45. Welty, p. 285; Greater New York Federation of Churches, *The Negro Churches of Manhattan* (New York, 1930), pp. 22–25; *Mother AME Zion Church Bulletin*, February 1936, Universal Negro Improvement Association papers, box 12, Schomburg Archives; Baxter Leach, Federal Writers' Program, New York City, "Negro Churches in Harlem," draft, n.d., WPA, Federal Writers' Program, "Negroes of New York," box 2; Myrtle Pollard, "Harlem As It Is" (B.B.A. thesis, City College of New York, 1936), pp. 188, 192, 195, 196. Sister Josephine Becton: ibid., p. 181. Mother Horn: Abram Hill, Federal Writers' Program, New York City, "Elder Horn," draft, 24 August 1939, pp. 1, 4, WPA, Federal Writers' Program, "Negroes of New York," box 1; Pollard, p. 183. Although 48,000 is probably exaggerated, certainly her church fed thousands.

46. Claude McKay, *Harlem: Negro Metropolis* (New York, 1940), pp. 48–49; Pollard, p. 211; Ivan Light, *Ethnic Enterprise in America: Business and Welfare Among Chinese, Japanese, and Blacks* (Berkeley, 1972), p. 145. For more on Divine, see Father Divine's newspaper, *Spoken Word* (many of which are in LaGuardia's papers, box 34); John Hoshor, *God in a Rolls Royce: The Rise of Father Divine: Madman, Menace or Messiah* (New York, 1936); Wilbur Young, Federal Writers' Program, New York City, "Sketch of Father Divine," 22 August 1939, WPA, Federal Writers' Program, "Negroes of New York," box 1; Robert Parker, *The Incredible Messiah: The Deification of Father Divine* (Boston, 1937); Claude McKay, "'There Goes God!' The Story of Father Divine and His Angels," *Nation* 140 (6 February 1935): 151–53. The best book on his life is Robert Weisbrot's *Father Divine and the Struggle for Racial Equality* (Urbana, Ill., 1983). Quotations from Weisbrot, pp. 48, 53.

47. Adam Clayton Powell, Sr., *Against the Tide: An Autobiography* (New York, 1938). Sermon, church programs: ibid., pp. 198–99, 227–28; Roi Ottley, *New World A-Coming* (Boston, 1943), pp. 225–26; "Relief for Harlem," *Dunbar News*, 17 December 1930, p. 1; Hubert, "Harlem Faces Unemployment," p. 45.

48. Shelton Hale Bishop, "Harlem Cooperating Committee on Relief and Unemployment," Report, 25 June 1931, pp. 1–5, Community Service Society papers, box 123; "Help the Work of Relief," *New York Age*, 7 February 1931 (clipping), Community Service Society papers, box 158; "Relief for Harlem," p. 1; Powell, p. 227. John D. Rockefeller, Jr., contributed $15,000 to the committee.

49. John Gillard, *The Catholic Church and the American Negro* (Baltimore, 1929), pp. 59, 61, 157, 198, 200, 202; Central Registration Bureau [Welfare Council], "Report of a Study Made by the CRB on Intake of Unattached Women in the HRB Precinct 32 During the Month of April, 1935," p. 7, LaGuardia papers, box 33. Seven percent of all black Harlem church members were Catholic. A black Hebrew congregation with approximately eight hundred members, the Commandment Keepers (87 West 128th Street), served its community as well. Leach; S. Michelson, Federal Writers' Program, New York City, "The Black Jews and Their Synagogues in New York," n.d., pp. 1–2, WPA, Federal Writers' Program, "Negroes of New York," box 2; Greater New York Federation of Churches, p. 22.

50. Vishnu Oak, *The Negro Entrepreneur*, vol. 2: *The Negro's Adventure in General Business* (Yellow Springs, Oh., 1949), pp. 60, 62–64; Greene, pp. 168–70; Byrd, p. 161.

51. Letters between Walter White of the NAACP and Commissioner of Hospitals William Greeff: 3 November 1932 (from White); 14 November 1932 (from Greeff); 18 November 1932 (from White); 6 December 1932 (from White); 9 December 1932 (from Greeff), NAACP papers, Group 1, series C, box 275. Allen testimony: James Allen, Testimony before Mayor's Commission on Conditions in Harlem, 20 April 1935, LaGuardia papers, new box 3770. The questioning continued:

Q. You don't place jobs. What do you do when organizations send back men? Just drop it?

A. Some go to the Supreme Court of the U.S.

Q. When persons come to your organization with complaints of discrimination is it that [you] have no success in correcting them?

A. Many are corrected.

Q. Have you placed any?

A. . . .we do not place people directly.

52. "Fight Jim Crow Attack on Negro Jobless"; Mark Naison, *Communists in Harlem During the Depression* (Urbana, Ill., 1983), pp. 35–37.

53. Shulman, pp. 66, 340. His survey covered areas in south Harlem, and not all the families were black.

54. Welty, p. 286; NYUL, "Statistical Report . . . for 1933," pp. 1–3.

Chapter 3

1. Citywide Citizens' Committee on Harlem, "Report of the Subcommittee on Employment," 1942, p. 1, Municipal Reference and Resource Center, New York City.

2. Mayor's Committee on Unemployment Relief, *Report of Mayor LaGuardia's Committee on Unemployment Relief* (New York, 1935), p. 9.

Percent of Civilian Labor Force
Unemployed, 1937

	U.S.	*N.Y.C.*	*Urban Areas*
Total	16	20	
Male	15	20	21
Female	19	21	19

U.S. Public Health Service, National Public Health Survey, *The Socio-Economic and Employment Status of Urban Youth in the United States, 1935–36* (Washington, D.C., 1941), pp. 13, 39. If N.Y.C. 1929 Unemployment Index = 100, 1933 = 1,423, 1934 = 1,147, 1935 = 1,064, 1936 = 914, and 1937 = 698. N.Y.C. WPA Advisory Council, "Reports on Public Assistance to the Administrator, WPA for the City of New York," 14 March 1939, p. 266, Columbia University Social Work Library, New York City; Mayor's Committee on Unemployment Relief, p. 6. Data from 1937 (what I called "white" is actually total): Clayton Cook, Director, Counseling and Employment Service of the Children's Aid Society, "A Recent and Brief Study of the Employment, Educational and Economic Conditions in Harlem," Memorandum to Walter White, NAACP, 1 May 1937, p. 1, NAACP papers, series C, box 311, Library of Congress Manuscript Collection, Washington, D.C. Unemployment rates: Florence Murray, ed., *The Negro Handbook* (New York, 1942), p. 148; Federal Security Agency, Social Security Board, "Statistics of Family Composition in Selected Areas of the United States, 1934–36, New York, New York," Bureau Memorandum #45, n.d., pp. 8, 204, Municipal Reference and Resource Center. WPA Federal Writers' Project, *New York Panorama* (New York, 1938), p. 142; U.S. Department of Commerce, Bureau of the Census, *Sixteenth Census 1940: Population,* vol. 2, part 5 (Washington, D.C., 1943), p. 160. In 1940 of the total population over 14, 24 percent of New York City's blacks were unemployed or in emergency work jobs. In Chicago, 28 percent were; in Detroit, 29 percent. For whites, the figures were 15 percent for New Yorkers, 12 percent in Chicago, 11 percent in Detroit. Richard Sterner, *The Negro's Share: A Study of Income, Consumption, Housing and Public Assistance* (Westport, Conn., 1943), p. 363.

3. DPW, *Annual Report, 1937* (New York, 1938), p. 105; ibid., *1935* (New York, 1936), p. 84. Length of stay from 1935 report. White male: WPA Division of Research, *Workers on Relief in the United States in March 1935*, vol. 2: *A Study of Industrial and Educational Backgrounds* (Washington, D.C., 1939), p. 17. Note, too, that women stayed longer than men. Usual occupations: U.S. Federal Emergency Relief Administration, "Survey of the Occupational Characteristics of Persons Receiving Relief in New York City," Press release, 8 May 1935, p. 4, Municipal Reference and Resource Center, Vertical File: "NYC Unemployment, Relief Measures, 1914–1939." Employed figures: 1940 data, Manhattan: Department of Health and Neighborhood Health Development, "Health Center Districts, New York Handbook of Statistical Reference Data: Ten Year Period, 1931–1940," 1944, pp. 14, 17, Public Health Library, New York City. See also: Joint Committee on National Recovery, "Unemployment Among Negro Male Workers at the End of 1934," Report [1935?], p. 2, National Negro Congress papers, box 2, Schomburg Archives, New York City; New York State Temporary Commission on the Condition of the Urban Colored Population, *Second Report*, Legislative Document #69 (Albany, 1939), p. 35. Unemployed domestics: Central Registration Bureau [Welfare Council], "Report of Study Made by the CRB of the Intake of the Unattached Women in the HRB Precinct 32 During the Month of April, 1935" [1935], pp. 1, 3, Mayor LaGuardia papers, box 33, Municipal Archives, New York City. Household heads: WPA Division of Research, *Workers on Relief in the United States in March 1935*, vol. 1: *A Census of Usual Occupations* (Washington, D.C., 1938), pp. 988—89.

4. The raw data can be found in the Bureau of Labor Statistics papers, RG 257, BLS #807, National Archives, Washington, D.C. The New York City black families sampled are scattered through boxes 31–51. I selected all cases in which the family was labeled "Negro" and had an address in Harlem. Aggregate data can be found in the published final study: U.S. Department of Labor, Bureau of Labor Statistics, *Money Disbursements of Wage Earners and Clerical Workers in the North Atlantic Region, 1934–36*, vol. 1: *New York City* (Washington, D.C., 1939). All families interviewed, white and black, had at least one wage-earner working a minimum of 1,008 hours in 36 weeks, with a minimum average income of $500, at least $300 of which was earned by one person. No family could be included if one worker earned over $2,000 annually or $200 in any one month. Less than a quarter of the family's total income could come from sources other than earnings (lodgers, gifts, investments, etc.). At no time during the year could the family have received relief. Incomplete families (those without both husband and wife) were included, but no one-person households: ibid., p. 2.

5. For details see appendix. Almost two-thirds of foreign-born white families relied on one income. United States Department of Labor, Bureau of Labor Statistics, *Family Income and Expenditure in New York City, 1935–1936*, vol. 1: *Family Income*, Bulletin #643 (Washington, D.C., 1941), pp. 120, 184. Depending on income level, between one-third and two-thirds of black families relied on one income, compared to between three-quarters and 90 percent of native-born white families. Not unexpectedly, the average supplementary earner (any worker in the family other than the principal or highest earner) in white families earned two times as much as the average black supplementary earner, and a third again as much as a foreign-born white supplementary earner ($815, $443, $562, respectively). The average earnings (income from wages) for white families totalled $1,681; and for black, $1,349. Yet white families had fewer wage-earners than did black; white wages must therefore have been higher. For each race, the higher the income, the greater the number of workers and the higher their contribution. At each level, though, the number of black workers per family surpassed white. BLS, *Disbursements*, pp. 72, 79, 102–5.

6. Black four-adult families also had four workers slightly more often than white. Most

frequently for these black households, two members of the four held jobs. Over half of white four-adult families had three employed workers (Federal Security Agency, p. 203). The average number of earners per family is higher for this group than for the other BLS study, *Family Income,* which found 40 percent of black families had more than one earner. The Harlem sample includes only wage earning and clerical families who presumably required more workers to achieve the same economic level because each worker's wages would be low.

7. Children in school: One child of 17 years was not listed as employed or unemployed, yet had only completed the ninth grade. It is not clear whether she was still in school, having been left back, or whether she had in fact left school for work but had not found any. City-wide, 7 percent of all blacks over 14 years old were in school, compared to 6 percent of whites. (This excludes those both working and in school.) If all those not in the labor force for unknown reasons were in fact in school, the figures would change to 10 percent of the black population, and 11 percent of the white. U.S. Department of Commerce, Bureau of the Census, *Negroes in the United States, 1920–1932* (Washington, D.C., 1935), p. 298; Bureau of the Census, *Sixteenth Census,* pp. 158–60.

8. While for some supplementary earners this underemployment was probably voluntary, undoubtedly many would have preferred steadier employment. Non-nuclear members of the economic household worked less often than nuclear relatives, which probably helps explain why they lived with another family in the first place.

9. Black women had had a long tradition of work, but for women overall the Depression brought a questioning of old assumptions. The impact of the Depression on women's work has been much discussed recently. In brief: women had been entering the work force in increasing numbers before this time; economic need encouraged over two million more to overcome their (and society's) traditional reluctance to enter a "man's" world of work. Yet the Depression also slowed women's move into the work force. With so many men seeking employment, many felt women ought not take what few jobs were available. In some cases, such feelings became official policy—three-fourths of public school districts refused to hire married women as teachers, for example. Robert McElvaine, *The Great Depression: America, 1929–1941* (New York, 1984), p. 182. Such bars, added to tradition and a general lack of training, meant that even in hard times many women chose not to seek jobs. (The fact that women's new wage-earning role was so clearly linked in the public mind with economic hard times also ensured that once things were "back to normal" traditional roles would reassert themselves with more force. The image of women at home became associated with healthy economic times.) Still, women, especially married women, did enter the work force in larger numbers between 1930 and 1940, attesting to the strength of their need. Because they entered jobs in the "female sphere" and because many of these jobs were less affected by the Depression, overall, women obtained jobs more easily than men. Yet these jobs were more likely to be temporary and lower paid. For more detailed discussion, see, for example, Ruth Milkman, "Women's Work and the Economic Crisis: Some Lessons from the Great Depression," in Nancy Cott and Elizabeth Pleck, eds., *A Heritage of Her Own* (New York, 1979); Winifred Wandersee, *Women's Work and Family Values, 1920–1940* (Cambridge, Mass., 1981); McElvaine, pp. 182–83; Susan Ware, *Holding Their Own: American Women in the 1930s* (Boston, 1982).

10. See, for example, Mary White Ovington, *Half a Man: The Status of the Negro in New York* (New York, 1911; reprint ed., 1969), p. 77. BLS, *Family Income,* pp. 120, 184; Bureau of the Census, *Negroes in the United States,* p. 298. Marriage and work: NYUL, *The Negro in New York: Annual Report, 1931* (New York, 1931), p. 31. See appendix for correlations. These figures are all higher than the national black average, but all black figures resemble each other more than they resemble any figures for white women. Foreign-born white single women also had high employment rates, in some areas even higher than black, but foreign-

born married women worked less often. Lois Helmbold, "Making Choices, Making Do: Black and White Working Class Women's Lives and Work During the Great Depression" (Ph.D. dissertation, Stanford University, 1982), p. 198.

11. Alfred Smith, Federal Emergency Relief Administration, "Reasons for the Disproportionate Number of Negroes on Relief Rolls," Report, 1935, pp. 6–7, 10–11, National Negro Congress papers, box 1. Luther Burton, Testimony before Mayor's Commission on Conditions in Harlem, 4 May 1935, pp. 9–11, Mayor LaGuardia papers, new box 3770, Municipal Archives, New York City. Grammar is as it appears in transcript. Historians and sociologists, recognizing the racially segmented labor market, usually argue it broke down to the advantage of blacks after the creation of the CIO and particularly during World War II. The data I have suggest instead that the dual labor market first broke down in the Depression, to the blacks' disadvantage.

12. Mr. Haines, Testimony before Mayor's Commission on Conditions in Harlem, n.d., LaGuardia papers, new box 3770.

13. Mayor's Commission on Conditions in Harlem, "The Negro in Harlem," Report, 1935, pp. 21–22, 29–30, LaGuardia papers, box 2550; NYSES, Harlem Branch, "Annual Report," 1936, U.S. Department of Labor papers, Division of Negro Labor, RG 183, box 1387, National Archives; N.Y.S. Temporary Commission on the Condition of the Urban Colored Population, *Report,* Legislative Document #63 (Albany, 1938), p. 16.

14. Discussion of this topic is plentiful. See below, and Ray Marshall, *The Negro Worker* (New York, 1967); Marshall, *The Negro and Organized Labor* (New York, 1965); Sterling Spero, Abram Harris, *The Black Worker* (New York, 1931); Ira Reid, *Negro Membership in American Labor Unions* (New York, 1930); Herbert Northrup, *Organized Labor and the Negro* (New York, 1944), Philip Foner and Ronald Lewis, eds., *The Black Worker During the Era of the American Federation of Labor and the Railroad Brotherhoods* (Philadelphia, 1979); Foner and Lewis, eds., *Black Workers* (Philadelphia, 1989).

15. James Allen, Testimony before Mayor's Commission on Conditions in Harlem, 20 April 1935, LaGuardia papers, new box 3770; Mr. Haines, Testimony; N.Y.S. Temporary Commission, "Report," p. 22. Also see James Hubert (Urban League), Testimony before the Mayor's Commission on Conditions in Harlem, 20 April 1935, LaGuardia papers, new box 3770.

16. Public utilities quotations: N.Y.S. Temporary Commission, *Second Report,* pp. 64, 66; Mayor's Commission, "Negro in New York," pp. 24–25; Floyd Snelson, Federal Writers' Program, New York City, "Occupations from Which Negroes Are Barred," 16 May 1938, p. 1, papers of the WPA, Federal Writers' Program, "Negroes of New York," box 2, Schomburg Archives. Allen, Testimony; Hubert, Testimony. New York Telephone: B. J. Stern, N.Y.C. Board of Education, "An Industrial and Occupational Survey of Selected Industries in the City of New York" [1945?], p. 2, Columbia University Business Library. NAACP: Walter White, telegrams to John L. Lewis and Mayor LaGuardia, 16 March 1940, LaGuardia papers, new box 3666. He reminded them: "Use of Negroes on city-owned subways has, as you both know, been eminently successful." All this arose in reference to the attempt to unify the BMT and IRT workers with those in IND unions.

17. Mayor's Commission on Conditions in Harlem, "The Negro in Harlem," pp. 22, 29–30; N.Y.S. Temporary Commission, *Report,* p. 16.

18. Robert Weaver, U.S. Department of the Interior, Office of the Adviser on Negro Affairs, *The Urban Negro Worker in the United States, 1925–1936,* vol. 2: *Male Negro Skilled Workers* (Washington, D.C., 1939), pp. 19–20. Doctors: National Urban League (NUL), "The Negro Working Population and National Recovery: A Special Memorandum to Franklin Delano Roosevelt, President of the United States by the National Urban League for Social Service Among Negroes," 4 January 1937, p. 6, National Urban League papers, series 1, box

1, Library of Congress Manuscript Collection. Edna Lonigan, *Unemployment in New York City* (New York, 1931), p. 5, notes the black unemployment figure is higher than white, but does not cite that rate. Carita Roane, "Negro Relief Work in New York," *Crisis* 39 (January 1932): 451; N.Y.S. Temporary Commission, *Second Report,* p. 43; Mr. Lange, NYSES, "Memo to Mr. William Wilkinson, Administrative Assistant," 14 December 1936, pp. 19–20, U.S. Dept. of Labor papers, Division of Negro Labor, USES, Oxley box 1387. NYUL: Louise Kennedy, Commission for the NYUL Study, "The NYUL Study, 1935: First Draft," n.d., pp. 15–16, NUL papers, series 4, box 32. For placements, 83.4 percent of women in domestic work, 70.2 percent of men in unskilled jobs.

19. Smith, pp. 9–10. Also noted by National Urban League, "The Negro Working Population," p. 5. Claude McKay, "Labor Steps Out in Harlem," *Nation* 145 (16 October 1937): 399.

20. Arnold Rose, "Non-Domestic Service Occupations," 1 September 1940, in "Negro Labor and Its Problems," vol. 3, p. 355, Typewritten collection, Carnegie-Myrdal papers, Schomburg Archives. NUL: Ira Reid and T. Arnold Hill, "The Forgotten Tenth," Pamphlet, May 1933, p. 17, Columbia University Social Work Library. Richard Wright, *Lawd Today* (New York, 1963), p. 115.

21. Figures for 1940: N.Y.C. Health Department, "Health Center Districts," p. 15. Figures from text and table are from p. 17. Personal service includes waiting tables, shoe shining, working as a porter or hairdresser, or similar work. Since the economy had improved by that time, these figures reflect an economic picture better than that of the Depression. Manhattan: professional and service rates were the same as in 1930, clerical higher than in 1930. Nationally, although both wages and the percent of the black population employed declined, blacks did not reverse the slight occupational improvements they had made in the 1920s. Between 1930 and 1940 the proportion in professional, managerial, and skilled work remained fairly stable (except for a decline in black farm owners and tenants). Clerical jobs increased slightly, but the biggest shift was from unskilled labor, both farm and non–farm, to semi-skilled positions. Committee on Fair Employment Practice, *First Report: July, 1943–December, 1944* (Washington, D.C., 1945), p. 139.

22. More wives and husbands worked in semi-skilled occupations than did other black workers in the family; otherwise, the occupational structure of all black earners mirrored that of the husband and wife. (The entire Harlem sample is made up of blue-collar and clerical workers, so these proportions are higher than they would be if the entire working population were considered. Yet as most blacks worked in these areas, the figures are not as skewed as a comparable study of the white community would be.)

23. Almost half of BLS survey wives with at least some high school education worked in such jobs, compared with just over half of those with less than a fifth grade education. UNIA: of sixty-two domestics or "cleaners," thirteen had had at least some high school education. Nine others also had some high school, and worked as pressers, "entertainer," pianist, factory worker, and housewives. UNIA clients had had an average of six and a half years of education, five months less than the average for the larger black population. UNIA papers, boxes 6–7, Schomburg Archives. Study of thirty-nine families: Edna Burge, Welfare Council, "Economically Independent Negro Families in the Boroughs of Manhattan and Brooklyn," Report, 1939, Columbia University Social Work Library.

24. UNIA papers, boxes 6–7: 13 laborers (0 to 9 years of school), three handymen (5, 12, and 12 years), 4 painters (3 to 11 years), 3 elevator operators (6 to 8 years), 2 cooks (5, 7 years), 2 mechanics (7, 10 years). One each of varied occupations: one actor (no education), one college-educated clerk, an errand boy, a carpenter (both 8 years), rock driller (9), waiter (10), and so on.

25. Every survey taken documents the higher illiteracy rate among immigrant whites, and

low education levels. See, for example, Works Progress Administration, New York City, "Illiteracy, the 1930 Census," Report, 1939, p. 2, WPA papers, RG 69, National Archives. Some suggest that blacks' lack of economic mobility was due to the poorer quality of their education or training. This may certainly be true, although discrimination and racial exclusion played a greater role. For a general discussion of these issues, see Stanley Lieberson, *A Piece of the Pie: Blacks and White Immigrants Since 1880* (Berkeley, 1980). NYUL: Anne Loop, "Does Educational Background Influence the Career of Negroes?" *Journal of Negro Education* 10 (April 1941): 212.

26. Reid and Hill, p. 18.

27. Mayor's Commission, "Negro in Harlem," p. 22. Table 3.2: Olivia Frost, "An Analysis of the Characteristics of the Population in Central Harlem," Report of the Urban League of Greater New York, pamphlet, August 1946, pp. 28–29, Microfilm 312-U, Schomburg Archives.

28. Edwin Harwood and Claire Hodge, "Jobs and the Negro Family: A Reappraisal," in Doris Wilkinson and Ronald Taylor, eds., *The Black Male in America* (Chicago, 1977), pp. 329–30; Milkman, pp. 512–13, 516. Operators had a 2.5 percent unemployment rate; laundresses, 3 percent. Carpenters had an 80 percent rate; road laborers, 13 percent. The latter two categories were 99 percent male. Rates for N.Y.C., 1930: Lonigan, p. 5. Approximately 85 percent of black women not in agriculture worked in service occupations in the U.S. in 1930.

29. George Stigler, *Domestic Servants in the United States, 1900–1940* (New York, 1946), pp. 16, 41. "Downtrodden": Marvel Cooke, "Modern Slaves," *Amsterdam News*, 16 October 1937, p. 19. "Conditions of Negro Domestics," Policy statement, 27 September 1933, National Negro Congress papers, box 1; Louise Mitchell, "'Slave Markets' Typify Exploitation of Domestics," *Daily Worker*, 5 May 1940, p. 5; "Building the Domestic Workers' Union," *Harlem Organizer* (November 1934): 3, LaGuardia papers, box 755. In Burge's study and the UNIA files, domestic workers reported equally low wages.

30. N.Y.S. Temporary Commission, *Second Report*, p. 37. The Urban League found 10–20 cents. NUL, "Negro Working Population," p. 5. Relief rejections: see UNIA papers, for example—Sadie Jefferson, 27, or Malinda Prunell, 33, both widowed. Ella Baker and Marvel Cooke, "The Bronx Slave Market," *Crisis* 42 (November 1935): 330–31, 340. Cheating: see, for example, Vera Jones, letter to the editor in the *Nation* 141 (17 July 1935): 75.

31. N.Y.S. Temporary Commission, *Report*, pp. 14–15, *Second Report*, p. 37; Jane Filley and Therese Mitchell, League of Women Shoppers, *Consider the Laundry Workers* (New York, 1937), pp. 25, 40, 46, National Negro Congress papers, box 1. The league described itself as "an organization of consumers whose purpose is to provide its members with impartial and authentic information about labor conditions in factories and stores so that the public can use their buying power for justice." From 1936 to 1937 the league personally investigated 32 steam laundries and 12 hand laundries: ibid., p. 5. A state minimum-wage law in place by 1939 mandated $16 a week. N.Y.S. Department of Labor to Captain King of the UNIA [1939], UNIA papers.

32. Frank Crosswaith, "Looking Around and Beyond," *Guardian*, 24 July 1939 (clipping), Negro Labor Committee papers, box 23, Schomburg Archives. Other quotations: Filley and Mitchell, pp. 24, 48.

33. Roane, pp. 451, 453. Employment Service of the Riverside Church and the Charity Organization Society, "Report of the Employment Service for the Years 1931–1935," n.d., pp. 1, 6, 29, Community Service Society papers, box 123, Columbia University. (Not all the COS placements were black.)

34. See appendix for BLS figures. The Johnsons: Burge, appendix B. N.Y.S. Department of Labor, Division of Women in Industry and Minimum Wage, "Adequate Maintenance and

Protection of Health for Women Workers in New York State," Report, January 1938, pp. 25–26, Columbia University Social Work Library. This estimate did not include income taxes.

35. The relationship between age and wage rates existed for men in each occupational category, but for women only in unskilled factory work (where presumably seniority did play some role in determining wages). NYUL and WPA: Loop, p. 221. Larger BLS survey: BLS, *Family Income*, pp. 20, 21, 23, 24. Judd, Johnson, shipping clerk, truck driver, from Burge, appendix. Pelmore from UNIA files. Some shipping clerks did earn more.

36. NNC: Anonymous, "The Position of the Negro in Our National Economic Crisis," notes for speech [1934?], pp. 1, 5, National Negro Congress papers, box 1. Barred because of race: see N.Y.S. Temporary Commission, *Second Report*, pp. 38–39 and earlier discussion of union and employer restrictions.

37. These figures are earnings of "principal earners." Other, supplementary earners generally earned less, and worked for fewer weeks. BLS, *Family Income*, pp. 111, 112, 175, 176. For professional workers, see below.

38. BLS, *Disbursements*, pp. 112, 114. These figures vary from the other studies because they include only wage-earning and clerical workers.

39. For example, for the $500 to $749 bracket, the principal earner in the white family worked an average of 34 weeks (with a range of 24 to 42 weeks). Black principal earners had to work for 49 weeks (range: 42–52) to achieve the same income level. Black families in which the principal earner worked as short a time as did the white counterpart presumably earned so little they were forced to turn to relief. For clerical families, white families earning between $500 and $999 worked between 20 and 45 weeks. Blacks in the same income category worked between 51 and 52 weeks. In fact, blacks worked that much at every income level; poorer black families were poorer because they received lower wages, not because they worked less, as was the case with many whites. BLS, *Family Income*, pp. 20, 21, 23, 24. The only white group whose earnings did not rise directly with the number of weeks worked was the business and professional class, discussed separately below. Ibid., pp. 110–13, 174–77. These data came from both non-relief families and families receiving some relief but still working sometime during the year. Smith, pp. 6–7.

40. See appendix. BLS, *Family Income*, p. 6, presents average wages for whole group—includes all occupation groups, and relief and non-relief families. Virgin Islands family: BLS Harlem sample. The *Family Income* figures are for two-parent families. The N.Y.C. figures are higher than black earnings in the South, but lower than for city whites: $1,830 native white, and $1,610 foreign-born white.

41. For BLS figures see appendix. UNIA, boxes 6–7. In these files fewer West Indians held either factory or white-collar employment than was true for the BLS sample.

42. See appendix for figures. The fact that more of the foreign-born over 16 worked is significant for what it suggests about the different roles and expectations of family members in the two populations. Either foreign-born blacks were more successful in finding work or their lower incomes made them stress work for every family member more strongly. Their desperation may have led them to more readily accept the lowest jobs. Whatever the reason, family roles in foreign-born families must have been slightly different than in native-born because everyone worked.

43. Percent of each race earning specified income, New York City, 1935:

	"Colored"	White
less than $1,000	22.0	13.7
$1,000–$1,999	26.6	40.0

	"Colored"	*White*
$2,000–$2,999	4.6	16.1
$3,000 or more	2.3	9.7

(Remainder were on relief, or not reported). U.S. Public Health Service, "The Relief and Income Status of the Urban Population of the United States, 1935," Preliminary Report, Population Series Bulletin C, 1938; revised, 1939, p. 7, National Health Service papers, Public Health Library, New York City. The BLS survey found similar results. The Federal Security Agency's study of New York City non-relief families in the same year found higher percentages of both races in the lowest bracket, but the relationship between the two remained the same. Federal Security Agency, "Statistics of Family Composition," p. 206. Its figures, broken down by numbers of workers per family, confirm that blacks earned less than whites per working person.

44. These black families earned less than whites even with a greater number of workers per family; the average black family had 1.49 workers, compared with 1.25 for whites. BLS, *Family Income,* pp. 148–49. This is for all occupation groups combined. Note that despite a higher unemployment rate, more blacks per family worked at least some time during the survey year. U.S. WPA, Division of Social Research, *Intercity Differences in Costs of Living in March 1935, 59 Cities,* by Margaret Stecker, Works Progress Monograph 12 (Washington, D.C., 1937), pp. 172–74. Frazier: His figures are from 1940 when, presumably, income had increased from earlier years. E. Franklin Frazier, *The Negro in the United States,* revised ed. (New York, 1957), p. 611. Still, this figure for blacks, 14 percent under the minimum, was in fact closer to that minimum than were black average earnings in any other city studied except Philadelphia and Washington, D.C. Charles Lawrence, "Negro Organizations in Crisis: Depression, New Deal, World War II" (Ph.D. dissertation, Columbia University, 1952), p. 199.

45. Black professional and business men earned $20 more than black women, on average. BLS, *Family Income,* pp. 113, 177. Principal earners only. Gunnar Myrdal, *An American Dilemma* (New York, 1944; reprint ed., New York, 1962), p. 304. Professionals: Arthur Gary, Federal Writers' Program, New York City, "Negroes in the Professions," Report, 4 April 1938, pp. 10, 13, 16, 24, 25, WPA, Federal Writers' Program, "Negroes of New York," box 3; Mayor's Commission on Conditions in Harlem, "Summary of Colored and White Business [in Harlem]," notes, tallies, interviews, LaGuardia papers, box 755. Of 1,928 black-owned businesses, 704 were in "personal service," and 355 in "basic needs." Urban League: "The Negro Working Population," pp. 5–6. Businesses: U.S. Department of Commerce, Bureau of the Census, "New York City—Retail Stores Operated by Negro Proprietors: 1935," Press release, 28 October 1937, Municipal Reference and Resource Center, for Harlem figures. U.S.: Murray, p. 18; Myrdal, p. 307. (Note the different figures of each report.) Harlem: 960 retail stores owned by black proprietors in 1935, largest number of any city. But the average annual sales per store totaled only $3,964, and together these stores employed 793 people other than the proprietors.

46. William Hodson, Commissioner, Department of Welfare, to Lester Granger, Welfare Council, 14 May 1939, pp. 1–2, LaGuardia papers, box 131; Hodson, Press release, 15 May 1939, p. 1, LaGuardia papers, box 131. LaGuardia: Claude McKay, *Harlem: Negro Metropolis* (New York, 1940), p. 122, N.Y.S. Temporary Commission, *Report,* p. 33. Burge: the musician, Mr. Haynes, earned $50 a week plus royalties. Advertisement in *Opportunity* 7 (November 1929): 355. Signers included Adam Clayton Powell, Sr., Eunice Carter, Charles Roberts, Myles Paige, James Hubert, and Fred Moore. City service quotation: N.Y.S. Tem-

porary Commission, *Second Report,* pp. 54–55. NAACP and LaGuardia: Roy Wilkins, "Watchtower," *Amsterdam News,* 12 August 1939 (clipping), LaGuardia papers, new box 3666. White to LaGuardia, 21 November 1941, LaGuardia papers, new box 3666.

47. N.Y.S. Temporary Commission, *Report,* p. 34; Estelle Riddle, "Negro Nurses: The Supply and Demand," *Opportunity* 15 (November 1937): 327. They were also accepted to one specialty training program at Bellevue but not to general nursing training. See Chapter 2 for early NAACP efforts in this regard.

48. This information is in correspondence between Roy Wilkins of the NAACP and Commissioner Goldwater of the Department of Hospitals. The reply to Greene was dated 24 September 1934. Wilkins to Goldwater, 23 October 1934, NAACP papers, Group I, series C, box 275; Goldwater to NAACP, 31 October 1934. The NAACP asked, 22 November, what would happen to the candidate. Goldwater reiterated the next day he would not intervene. A further letter from Wilkins, 26 November, was the last letter to appear in the file. Other support: National Business and Professional Women's Club, "Resolution," 25 May 1935; Alpha Kappa Alpha Resolution, 1 March 1935; Reveille Club of New York (resolved to approve the A.K.A. sorority resolution), 12 April 1935; Boys of Yesteryear Resolution, 27 April 1935. All in LaGuardia papers, new box 3529.

49. Walter White, NAACP, to Mayor LaGuardia and Commissioner Goldwater, 27 November 1936, LaGuardia papers, box 786; Goldwater to White, 28 November 1936.

50. Goldwater to LaGuardia, 1 December 1936; LaGuardia to Walter White, 10 December 1936. Mrs. Roberts, National Association of Colored Graduate Nurses, Testimony before the N.Y.S. Temporary Commission [December 1937], p. 1, National Association of Colored Graduate Nurses papers, box 1, Schomburg Archives. At a fifth hospital, Queens, they could do outpatient work, she noted.

51. Goldwater, Testimony at N.Y.S. Temporary Commission Public Hearing, 13 December 1937. Commission findings: N.Y.S. Temporary Commission, *Second Report,* p. 55.

52. Goldwater, Testimony, 13 December 1937, pp. 3, 5, 8.

53. Goldwater, Testimony, pp. 7, 8, 12, 15. N.Y.S. Temporary Commission, *Second Report,* p. 55.

54. Ibid., p. 56; Ira Reid, "The Negro in the American Economic System," Report, 1 August 1940, p. 223, Carnegie-Myrdal study, Reid, vol. 1, Schomburg Archives; Riddle, p. 327; National Association of Colored Graduate Nurses, "Evaluation Committee Report," 1941, pp. 3–6, National Association papers, box 1.

55. The NYSES received all job requests, and referred them to appropriate local branches. N.Y.S. Temporary Commission, *Report,* p. 20; *Second Report,* pp. 43–44; James Flemming, "10,000 Get Jobs at Free Office," *Amsterdam News,* 27 March 1937, p. 1; Cook, p. 2. October, 1935: Lange, pp. 19–20; Mayor's Commission on Conditions in Harlem, "The Negro in Harlem," p. 48.

56. Special position: Lange, p. 1. Harlem office: Flemming, p. 1.

57. Carita Roane, "Negro Relief Work in New York," *Crisis* 39 (January 1932): 450. N.Y.S. Temporary Commission, *Report,* p. 18.

58. Hubert, Testimony.

59. N.Y.S. Temporary Commission, *Report,* p. 14.

Chapter 4

1. WPA Federal Writers' Project, *New York Panorama* (New York, 1938), p. 141.

2. W.E.B. DuBois, *Black Folk Then and Now* (New York, 1939), p. 216; Claude McKay, *Harlem: Negro Metropolis* (New York, 1940), pp. 125–27; Nancy Weiss, *Farewell to the*

Party of Lincoln: Black Politics in the Age of FDR (Princeton, 1983), p. 94, Gilbert Osofsky, *Harlem: The Making of a Ghetto,* 2nd ed. (New York, 1971), pp. 169–70; Charles McMillan, "Introduction to an Era: A Study of the Political Development of the Negro in New York City, 1917–1936" (A.B. thesis, Princeton University, 1967), pp. 21, 64; Ralph Bunche, *The Political Status of the Negro in the Age of FDR* (Chicago, 1973), p. 605; Sutherland Denlinger, "Heaven Is in Harlem," *Forum and Century* 95 (April 1936): 211–12.

3. Osofsky, pp. 169–71, 177; Weiss, p. 94. Quotation: Osofsky, p. 169. In 1925, 51 percent of Harlem was registered Democrat, 48 percent Republican. I suspect, though, that the Democratic majority can be accounted for by the heavily Democratic Jewish population still in the area. For example, Nancy Weiss, who analyzed black Harlem voting, believes 51 percent of blacks were Democrats in 1932, although Harlem's total Democratic figure for that year was 67 percent. Weiss, p. 206. John Morsell, "The Political Behavior of Negroes in New York City" (Ph.D. dissertation, Columbia University, 1950), Appendix table 28, for overall Harlem figures. Assembly: Five Republicans, one Democrat.

4. NYUL, "Eleventh Vocational Opportunity Campaign," Radio broadcast, WMCA Radio, 18 March 1943, p. 4, Radio transcripts, box 2, Schomburg Archives, New York City. For more on public housing and segregation, see Joel Schwartz, "Tenant Unions in New York City's Low Rent Housing: 1933–1949," *Journal of Urban History* 12 (August 1986): 414–43; and Peter Marcuse, "The Beginnings of Public Housing in New York," *Journal of Urban History* 12 (August 1986): 353–90.

5. Marcuse, p. 371.

6. Weiss, pp. xvi, 62, 63, 227, 229; Nancy Weiss, *National Urban League: 1910–1940* (New York, 1974), p. 295. Advertisement: *Opportunity* 7 (November 1929), p. 355. Roy Wilkins, "Watchtower," *Amsterdam News,* 12 August 1939 (clipping), Mayor LaGuardia papers, new box 3666, Municipal Archives, New York City. A party committed to reform and clean government, the Fusion Party joined with the Republican Party on behalf of LaGuardia's candidacy.

7. William Stevenson, Federal Writers' Program, New York City, "A Brief History of the Citizen's Democratic Club," 1 July 1937, p. 1, papers of the WPA, Federal Writers' Program, "Negroes of New York," box 8, Schomburg Archives. Canvass of clubs by Myrtle Pollard, "Harlem As It Is" (B.B.A. thesis, City College of New York, 1936), pp. 319, 321; Simon Williamson, Federal Writers' Program, New York City, "A Brief History of the Coalition Democratic Club," n.d., p. 1, WPA, Federal Writers' Program, "Negroes of New York," box 8. For a good overview of local black political action prior to the Depression, see Osofsky, Chapter 11. Mainstream: see, for example, Robert McElvaine, *The Great Depression: America, 1929–1941* (New York, 1984), p. 195.

8. James Gardner, Federal Writers' Program, New York City, "Brief History of the Harlem Workers' Center, Headquarters of the Communist Party," 7 March 1937, pp. 1–2, WPA, Federal Writers' Program, "Negroes of New York," box 8; James Ford and Louis Sass, "Development of Work in the Harlem Section," *Communist* 14 (April 1935): 317–19; Mark Naison, *Communists in Harlem During the Depression* (Urbana, Ill., 1983), pp. 34–37, 50–51, 95, 149, 258; Naison, "Communism and Black Nationalism in the Depression: The Case of Harlem," *Journal of Ethnic Studies* 2 (Summer 1974): 25, 27; Larry Greene, "Harlem in the Great Depression: 1928–1936" (Ph.D dissertation, Columbia University, 1979), p. 453; August Meier and Elliott Rudwick, "The Origins of Nonviolent Direct Action in Afro-American Protest: A Note on Historical Discontinuities," in Meier and Rudwick, eds., *Along the Color Line* (New York, 1976), pp. 333–35. Scottsboro: p. 57; ACLU to Mayor LaGuardia, 17 March 1934, LaGuardia papers, box 2550. Naison's book provides an excellent description and analysis of party activities in Harlem. Tenants League: Greene, pp. 239–40, 244–46.

9. James Ford, speech delivered at meeting of Joint Conference Against Discriminatory Practices, Abyssinian Baptist Church, New York City, 23 October 1935, pp. 4–7, LaGuardia papers, box 35.

10. Ford and Sass, pp. 312–13; Harvey Klehr, *The Heyday of American Communism: The Depression Decade* (New York, 1984), p. 341; Naison, "Communism," pp. 30–31; Naison, *Communists,* pp. 126, 129, 138, 185; Adam Clayton Powell, Sr., "Riots and Ruins," Manuscript, n.d. [preface dated 1945], p. 168a, Typescript collection, box 33, Schomburg Archives. Father Divine sent 3,000 to march in Communist rallies between 1934 and 1936. While not a supporter of the party, Divine explained that both supported racial equality and the common people: Will Irwin, "Harlem's Man from Heaven," *Liberty* (September, 1935): 15, LaGuardia papers, box 35; Robert Weisbrot, *Father Divine and the Struggle for Racial Equality* (Urbana, Ill., 1983), pp. 133, 148–49, 151. Tenants: Naison, "Communism," p. 25; Ray George, "500 Negro and White Workers in Harlem Hold Relief March," *Hunger Fighter,* April 1933, p. 2, International Labor Defense papers, box 2, Schomburg Archives; Tim O'Connor and Leon Goodelman, "41 Harlem Families Strike for Decent Housing," *PM,* 4 May 1941, p. 12; Margaret Reynolds, Interview with Consolidated Tenants League, n.d., LaGuardia papers, box 35; Joel Schwartz, "The Consolidated Tenants League of Harlem," *Afro-Americans in New York Life and History* 10 (January 1986).

11. "Reds Fight Police in Bronx Evictions," *New York Times,* 2 February 1932, p. 6; Marcuse, p. 356; Richard Boyer and Herbert Morais, *Labor's Untold Story,* 3rd ed. (New York, 1980), p. 261, for 77,000 figure.

12. Schwartz, "Consolidated Tenants League," pp. 31–36. Quotation: Schwartz, "Tenant Unions," p. 427. CTL purpose: Margaret Reynolds, Mayor's Commission on Conditions in Harlem, "Consolidated Tenants League," Report, n.d., p. 1, LaGuardia papers, box 35.

13. Ford and Sass, p. 312. Umbrellas: Naison, *Communists,* pp. 121–23; Mayor's Commission on Conditions in Harlem, "Character of the Negro Community," notes and clippings, 1935, LaGuardia papers, box 755.

14. Ford and Sass, p. 325. Naison claimed Harlem contained 300 black members in 1935: *Communists,* p. 134. Also see Klehr, p. 348. Workers' Center: Gardner, p. 1. Olivia Pearl Stokes, Interview, Black Women's Oral History Project, 25 September 1979, p. 16, Schlesinger Library, Radcliffe College, Cambridge, Mass.

15. "What Happens at a Communist Party Branch Meeting in the Harlem Section," *Daily Worker,* 16 August 1937; Neil Hickey and Ed Edwin, *Adam Clayton Powell and the Politics of Race* (New York, 1965), pp. 48, 57. McKay: "Negro Author Sees Disaster If the Communist Party Gains Control of Negro Workers," *New Leader,* 10 September 1938, p. 5. End of alliance: Naison, *Communists,* p. 287; Frank Crosswaith, "Communists and the Negro," notes for speech to Catholic Moderators' Labor School, n.d., pp. 3–4, Frank Crosswaith papers, additions, box 1, Schomburg Archives; Gary Hunter, "'Don't Buy from Where You Can't Work': Black Urban Boycott Movements During the Depression, 1929–1941" (Ph.D. dissertation, University of Michigan, 1977), pp. 57–59; Schwartz, "Consolidated Tenants League," pp. 40–41; Jervis Anderson, *A. Philip Randolph* (New York, 1973; reprint ed., Berkeley, 1986), pp. 235–39.

16. Garvey and UNIA preamble: "The Negro's Place in World Reorganization," in Sterling Brown, Arthur Davis, Ulysses Lee, eds., *The Negro Caravan* (New York, 1970), pp. 678, 680–81. McKay quoted in Wayne Cooper, ed., *The Passion of Claude McKay* (New York, 1973), pp. 234–39. Adam Clayton Powell, Sr., *Against the Tide* (New York, 1938), p. 71.

17. For further detail, see National Negro Congress papers at the Schomburg, especially John Davis, "Let Us Build a National Negro Congress," 1936, p. 30, National Negro Congress papers, box 2. Also Klehr, pp. 345–46, 412; Raymond Wolters, *Negroes and the Great Depression: The Problem of Economic Recovery* (Westport, Conn., 1970), pp. 358–72;

Charles Lawrence, "Negro Organizations in Crisis: Depression, New Deal, World War II" (Ph.D. dissertation, Columbia University, 1952), pp. 296–300; Gunnar Myrdal, *An American Dilemma* (New York, 1944; reprint ed., 1969), pp. 817–18; Naison, *Communists in Harlem*, pp. 178, 182; Hunter, pp. 235–40.

18. McKay, *Harlem, Negro Metropolis*, pp. 112–13; Greene, pp. 173–75. NAACP: Mr. Fishman, "Prostitution," Memorandum to Walter White, 9 May 1932, p. 4, NAACP papers, series C, box 305, Library of Congress Manuscript Collection, Washington, D.C.

19. See, for example, John Clarke, "The Early Years of Adam Clayton Powell," in Clarke, ed., *Harlem: A Community in Transition*, 3rd ed. (New York, 1970), pp. 229–41. Schwartz, "Tenant Unions," p. 457. Naison makes a similar argument: see *Communists*, Chap. 2 et passim.

20. Stokes, p. 11.

21. Benjamin Mays and Joseph Nicholson, *The Negro's Church* (New York, 1933; reprint ed., New York, 1969), p. 1. According to official statistics, approximately 42 percent of Harlemites belonged to a church. This membership figure is probably low since every "official" list of Harlem churches in the 1930s gave a different number of them, and usually omitted a majority of the smaller storefront churches. American blacks were primarily Baptist (41 percent), Methodist (20 percent), and Protestant Episcopal (11 percent). Most West Indians belonged to Lutheran, Moravian, Protestant Episcopal, and Catholic churches. Each denomination had different structures, but all types of churches became politically involved. For more detailed information, see Greater New York Federation of Churches, *The Negro Churches of Manhattan* (New York, 1930), pp. 7, 22, 25; Ira de Augustine Reid, *The Negro Immigrant: His Background Characteristics and Social Adjustment, 1899–1937* (New York, 1939), p. 124; *Negro Year Book, 1931–32*, vol. 8 (Tuskeegee Institute, 1931), p. 264; U.S. Department of Commerce, Bureau of the Census, *Negroes in the United States, 1920–1932* (Washington, D.C., 1935), p. 546; William Wright, Jr., "The Negro Store-fronts: Churches of the Disinherited: A Study of the Store-front Churches of East Harlem, New York," (Ph.D. dissertation, Union Theological Seminary, 1942), p. 57; William Welty, "Black Shepherds: A Study of the Leading Negro Clergymen in New York City, 1900–1940," (Ph.D. dissertation, New York University, 1969), p. 242; Elmer Clark, *The Small Sects in America*, revised ed. (New York, 1949), p. 163; Arthur Fauset, *Black Gods of the Metropolis* (Philadelphia, 1944); Joseph Washington, Jr., *Black Sects and Cults* (Garden City, N.Y., 1972). Specific leaders studied by WPA, Federal Writers' Program, New York City, "Negroes of New York," boxes 1, 2. Storefronts and sects can be found also in newspaper advertisements: see, for example, *Harlem Reporter*, 3 January 1930, p. 2; *Harlem Evening Star*, 1 March 1932, p. 3.

22. Roi Ottley and William Weatherby, *The Negro in New York: An Informal Social History, 1626–1940* (New York, 1967; reprinted from the Federal Writers' Project ed.), pp. 290–91. Mays and Nicholson, pp. 9, 279–88; E. Franklin Frazier, *The Negro in the United States*, revised ed. (New York, 1957), pp. 360, 366; Pollard, pp. 183–99; Welty, p. 286; Federal Writers' Program, New York City [Ottley and Weatherby?] "I Too Sing America," n.d., pp. 18, 21, WPA, Federal Writers' Program, "Negroes of New York," box 4. Powell: Adam Clayton Powell, Jr., *Marching Blacks: An Interpretive History of the Rise of the Black Common Man* (New York, 1945), p. 89; Hickey and Edwin, pp. 36–37; Clarke, p. 234; Adam Clayton Powell, Jr., *Adam by Adam* (New York, 1971), pp. 58–59. Louise Meriwether, *Daddy Was a Number Runner* (New York, 1986), p. 56.

23. See Father Divine's newspaper, *Spoken Word* (many issues of which are in LaGuardia papers, box 34), especially 17 August 1935, A.D.F.D., p. 24; McKay, pp. 38, 47; Wilbur Young, Federal Writers' Program, New York City, "Sketch of Father Divine," 22 August 1939, pp. 10–11, WPA, Federal Writers' Program, "Negroes of New York," box 1; Robert Parker, *The Incredible Messiah: The Deification of Father Divine* (Boston, 1937), pp. 246–

49. Divine's politics is the subject of Weisbrot. He claimed to oppose unions because they were undemocratic, limiting workers' rights to sell their goods or labor for as little as they chose, and because they "oppressed" workers by forcing them to pay dues. Probably, too, he wanted his followers to have no other loyalties.

24. Mays and Nicholson, p. 101; "I Too Sing America," p. 77; McKay, *Harlem,* p. 77. In 1926 in urban New York State, 42,000 black men and 65,700 black women reported belonging to a church. Census, *Negroes in the United States,* p. 16. Overall, 73 percent of black women belonged to churches, compared with 45 percent of men (U.S. figures). In New York, the ratio of women to men was just over 2 to 1. These ratios ranged from Catholics, with 79 men per 100 women, to the AME Zion Church, with 56 men per 100 women. The smaller sects generally had even fewer men. Census, pp. 531, 536; *Negro Year Book, 1931–1932,* p. 264; John Gillard, *Colored Catholics in the United States* (Baltimore, 1941), p. 216.

25. Mary McLeod Bethune, "A Century of Progress of Negro Women," 1933, quoted in Gerda Lerner, ed., *Black Women in White America* (New York, 1973), p. 583; Richard Wright, *Twelve Million Black Voices* (New York, 1941; reprint ed., New York 1969), p. 131. Ottley and Weatherby, p. 290.

26. Stokes, p. 44.

27. Storefronts were as active as more-established churches. Many were in fact headed by women. Contemporary black newspapers listed hundreds of Spiritualist churches, for example, a large minority of which were led by women. See, for example, *Harlem Reporter,* 3 January 1931, p. 2. McKay, *Harlem,* pp. 38, 47, 77; Stokes, p. 45; Miles Fisher, "Organized Religion and the Cults," *Crisis* 44 (January 1937): 10; Wilbur Young, pp. 10–11; Pollard, pp. 181, 183. Faithful Mary ultimately fell from grace in 1937. Weisbrot, p. 105. *Mother AME Zion Church Bulletin,* February 1936, Universal Negro Improvement Association papers, box 12, Schomburg Archives.

28. Elise McDougald, "The Double Task: The Struggle of Negro Women for Sex and Race Emancipation," *Survey [Graphic]* 53 (1 March 1925): 691; Nannie Burroughs quoted in Lerner, p. 553. The "Queen" quotation is the end of the "let us as women" quotation above. These articles reflect both the activism and the traditionalism of these women. The Schomburg has this and other churches' minutes in which such emerging political interest appears. White women also used this "feminine" rhetoric of motherhood, of course, reflecting the times. Catholic women were similarly active: Gillard, p. 235; John Gillard, *The Catholic Church and the American Negro* (Baltimore, 1929), pp. 48, 61, 157, 198, 200; Catherine de Hueck, *Friendship House* (New York, 1946), p. 43.

29. He ran in the 19th District, and lost the election by 240 votes. Election flyer, Schomburg Archives. He was involved in the "Don't Buy Where You Can't Work" campaign, the topic of Chapter 5. Women in political clubs: Pollard, p. 319. Father Divine: Irwin, p. 12. Female party workers: Morsell, p. 48. Speaks: Chase Mellen, Jr., to Lester Stone, Mayor LaGuardia's secretary, 26 March 1934, LaGuardia papers, new box 3529. City Hall rally: "Reds Invade City Hall," *New York Times,* 17 October 1930, p. 1.

30. McDougald, p. 691.

31. Laundry leaflet and pro-union leaflet enclosed in: Trade Union Committee for Organizing Negro Workers, "Report in Full Covering Activities from June 1, 1925–December 31, 1925" [1926], National Urban League papers, series 4, box 1, Library of Congress Manuscript Collection. Background on TUC: Negro Labor Committee, *Negro Labor Committee: What It Is—and Why!* (New York [1936?]), pp. 10–11; Negro Labor Committee, "History, Trade Union Committee for Negro Workers—1925," pp. 1–2, Negro Labor Committee papers, box 1, Schomburg Archives; TUC, "Report in Full," pp. 1–6; John Walter, "Frank R. Crosswaith and the Negro Labor Committee in Harlem 1925–1939," *Afro-Americans in New York Life and History* 3 (July 1979): 36–37, 40; Ira Reid, *Negro Membership in Amer-*

ican Labor Unions (New York, 1930), pp. 131–32. TUC and others: Leaflet enclosed in "Report in Full." Crosswaith: Walter, pp. 35–36; Negro Labor Committee, "Organizations of which Frank R. Crosswaith was a member," n.d., NLC papers, box 28. Randolph: See Jervis Anderson; William Harris, *Keeping the Faith* (Urbana, Ill., 1977).

32. Charles Johnson, "Black Workers and the City," *Survey [Graphic]* 53 (1 March 1925): 719; Sterling Spero and Abram Harris, *The Black Worker* (New York, 1931; reprint ed., New York, 1974), pp. 182, 198–89; Reid, *Negro Membership,* pp. 49, 95. Local 306: Reid, *Negro Membership,* pp. 96–98; Herman Bloch, *The Circle of Discrimination: An Economic and Social Study of the Black Man in New York* (New York, 1969), p. 103.

33. Blacks constituted almost 8 percent of the national work force. Johnson, p. 719; Reid, *Negro Membership,* pp. 33–34, 130–32; Charles Franklin, *The Negro Labor Unionist of New York* (New York, 1936), pp. 113–14; Spero and Harris, pp. 58, 61. Similar numbers and studies: Florence Murray, ed., *The Negro Handbook* (New York, 1942), pp. 134–35; Reid, *Negro Membership;* Mr. Oxley, Chief, Division of Negro Labor, "*Re:* Nationals and Internationals in Building Construction Trades . . . Which Bar Negroes by Ritual or Constitution," Memorandum to Mr. Hinrichs, Bureau of Labor Statistics, 3 March 1935, U.S. Department of Labor papers, Division of Negro Labor, RG 183, USES box 1391, National Archives, Washington, D.C. (reported 22 unions excluding blacks or admitting them to separate locals only); Reid, *Negro Membership,* pp. 49, 53, 74, 85, 87, 88, 95–98, 100, for blacks in specific unions. National: In 1930, 56,000 blacks in the U.S. belonged to unions, 1 percent of the black work force. In the same year, 3,360,000 whites belonged, 8 percent of the white work force. Blacks constituted less than 2 percent of the total union population (down from 1910). Orly Ashenfelter and Lamond Godwin, "Some Evidence on the Effect of Unionism on the Average Wage of Black Workers Relative to White Workers, 1900–1967," 24th Annual Meeting, Industrial Relations Research Association [1971?], pp. 218–19. Still, even these figures were a striking improvement over the 1,385 black union members in 1906 and 12,000 in 1926.

34. Guichard Parris and Lester Brooks, *Blacks in the City: A History of the National Urban League* (Boston, 1971), p. 250; Weiss, *National Urban League,* pp. 283–85, 292, 295–96. Negro Labor Committee, *NLC: What It Is,* pp. 4–5. "Economic" quotation: "Harlem Emerges as Stronghold of Trade Unionism," *New York Post,* 13 May 1938, p. 6.

35. Edith Kine, "The Garment Union Comes to the Negro Worker," *Opportunity* 12 (April 1934): 107–9; Negro Labor Committee, "History, 1930s," notes, n.d., NLC papers, box 1. Mayor's Commission on Conditions in Harlem, "The Negro in Harlem," Report, 1935, pp. 31–33, LaGuardia papers, box 2550.

36. Frank Crosswaith, "Harlem Labor Center—Labor's Home in Harlem," notes for speech, n.d., p. 1, Crosswaith papers, box 1; Negro Labor Committee, "Report of the Harlem Labor Committee, Dec. 1934–March 1935," n.d., pp. 1–4, NLC papers, box 25; Walter, pp. 40–42; Franklin, pp. 142, 145, 147; "I Too Sing America," pp. 7–10.

37. Negro Labor Committee to WPA, 6 June 1938, NLC papers, box 4; "Harlem Emerges" (includes signs). Franklin, p. 157; NLC to WPA, 6 June 1938; NLC, "Harlem Labor Committee, 1934–35," notes, n.d., NLC papers, box 1; NLC, "General Facts," notes, n.d., NLC papers, box 4. Press examples: "Job for Dewey" (editorial), *Amsterdam News,* 9 October 1937, p. 14; "Harlem Emerges."

38. Welfare Council: Lester Granger, *The Negro Worker in New York City* (New York, 1941), p. 14. Franklin, pp. 126, 247; Federal Writers' Project: *New York Panorama,* p. 150. The Committee for Industrial Organization, part of the AFL, later left the AFL to become the Congress of Industrial Organizations (CIO).

39. New York State Temporary Commission on the Condition of the Urban Colored Population, *Second Report,* Legislative Document #69 (Albany, 1939), p. 46. Most of the formally restricted unions were related to railroads and construction.

40. In 1940, 600,000 blacks, or 11 percent of all working blacks, belonged to unions, making up 7 percent of all union members. Ashenfelter and Godwin, p. 221. Blacks constituted almost 9 percent of the total U.S. work force; U.S. Department of Labor, Bureau of Labor Statistics, *War and Post-War Trends in Employment of Negroes,* Serial # R1723 (Washington, D.C., 1945), p. 3, National Negro Congress papers, box 94. Apprenticeship: N.Y.S. Temporary Commission, *Second Report,* p. 33. Limited black participation: Franklin, pp. 234–37.

Chapter 5

1. The movement has been known variously as "Don't Buy Where You Can't Work," "Don't Buy from Where You Can't Work," and "Buy Where You Work." I have used Powell's term. Aldon Morris, *The Origins of the Civil Rights Movement* (New York, 1984).

2. NYUL: Ira Reid, NYUL, "Annual Report, Industrial Department, 1926," 1 November 1927, p. 3, National Urban League papers, series 5, box 10, Library of Congress Manuscript Collection, Washington, D.C.; "League of Equal Political and Civic Rights to Tackle Employment Problem," *March of Events* 1 (January 1928): 12–13; NYUL et al., "Employment Mass Meeting," Transcript, 24 April 1930, pp. 3–4, 10–11, NUL papers, series 7, box 21.

3. NYUL et al., "Employment Mass Meeting," pp. 4, 10–11; Guichard Parris and Lester Brooks, *Blacks in the City: A History of the National Urban League* (Boston, 1971), p. 208. In Chicago, blacks owned 3 of 45 groceries, 4 of 15 service establishments, and 8 of 49 furniture stores on State Street. Gary Hunter, "'Don't Buy from Where You Can't Work': Black Urban Boycott Movements During the Depression, 1929–1941" (Ph.D. dissertation, University of Michigan, 1977), p. 52. For a good discussion of the Chicago efforts, see Hunter.

4. Harlem Housewives League, "The Harlem Housewives League," Report [1931?], pp. 1–2, NUL papers, series 4, box. 32.

5. NYUL et al., "Employment Mass Meeting," pp. 2–4, 9, quotation, p. 10; "Relief for Harlem," *Dunbar News,* 17 December 1930, p. 1. NAACP: Hunter, p. 48.

6. *Harlem Business Men's Bulletin* 1 (March 1931): 1–3. Advertisement: *American and West Indian News,* 19 January 1929, p. 5, Black Newspapers collection, box 1, Schomburg Archives, New York City. August Meier and Elliott Rudwick, "The Origins of Nonviolent Direct Action in Afro-American Protest: A Note on Historical Discontinuities," in Meier and Rudwick, eds., *Along the Color Line* (New York, 1976), pp. 346, 380. E. Franklin Frazier, "Some Effects of the Depression on the Negro in Northern Cities," *Science and Society* 2 (Fall 1938): 496. Johnson: sermon given 8 April 1934, printed in John Johnson, *Harlem, the War and Other Addresses* (New York, 1942), pp. 62, 68.

7. William Muraskin, "The Harlem Boycott of 1934 and Its Aftermath" (M.A. thesis, Columbia University, 1966), pp. 11–12; Melville Weiss, "'Don't Buy Where You Can't Work': An Analysis of Consumer Action Against Employment Discrimination in Harlem, 1934–1940" (M.A. thesis, Columbia University, 1941), p. 61. The *Crisis* presented a debate on the merits of picketing and boycotting that raises many of these points. Vera Johns (pro), George Schuyler (con), "To Boycott or Not to Boycott," *Crisis* 41 (September 1934): 258–60, 274. Businessmen: Melville Weiss, p. 62.

8. Johns and Schuyler, p. 274. The NLC did not participate in the coalition until the end of the decade.

9. Mark Naison, "Communism and Black Nationalism in the Depression: The Case of Harlem," *Journal of Ethnic Studies* 2 (Summer 1974): 26–29; NYUL, "Newsletter," 12

November 1940, p. 2, NUL papers, series 4, box 33; Nancy Weiss, *National Urban League: 1910–1940* (New York, 1974), pp. 306–7. League strategy: Ira de Augustine Reid and T. Arnold Hill, "The Forgotten Tenth," Pamphlet, May 1933, p. 6, Columbia University Social Work Library, New York City. The league used similar tactics in other black areas.

10. James Hubert, testimony before Mayor's Commission on Conditions in Harlem, 20 April 1935, Mayor LaGuardia papers, new box 3770, Municipal Archives, New York City. "Conservative" quotation: Reid and Hill, p. 55.

11. Quotation: WPA Federal Writers' Project, *New York Panorama* (New York, 1938), p. 148. NAACP Minutes, William Pickens' papers, box 16, Schomburg Archives; Harvard Sitkoff, *A New Deal for Blacks* (New York, 1978), p. 249.

12. William Imes, Testimony before Mayor's Commission on Conditions in Harlem [1935], LaGuardia papers, new box 3770; "Blumstein's to Hire Negro Clerks," *New York Age,* 4 August 1934, p. 9. The *Age* reports Manley's group as the Harlem Women's Association, while Hunter places her in the Harlem Housewives League.

13. The history and activities of the Citizens' League are discussed in Muraskin; Melville Weiss; Hunter, as well as in the primary sources cited here. Names of participating groups taken from Citizens' League for Fair Play flyer advocating Blumstein's boycott, Schomburg Archives. The NAACP considered a shift toward more activist tactics in 1933, but decided instead to continue its focus on the judicial process. Hunter, p. 63.

14. Hunter, pp. 85–89, for Hamid (in Chicago known as Bishop Conshankin). The *Defender* and the Urban League refused to participate in the Chicago efforts. Ultimately, Chicago blacks won 10,261 jobs: Hunter, p. 299. Hunter claims it was Hamid who prompted the organization of Harlem's Citizens' League; Effa Manley, shocked at the ferocity of Hamid's rhetoric, asked Reverend Johnson to organize a "respectable" jobs campaign. Hunter, p. 183. Hamid: Wilbur Young, Federal Writers' Program, New York City, "Activities of Bishop Amiru Al-Mu-Minin Sufi A. Hamid," n.d., pp. 1–2, papers of the WPA, Federal Writers' Program, "Negroes of New York," box 1, Schomburg Archives; Claude McKay, *Harlem: Negro Metropolis* (New York, 1940), pp. 185–86; Charles Franklin, *The Negro Labor Unionist of New York* (New York, 1936), p. 135; Muraskin, pp. 1–4. "Ira Kemp Insists He Will Send One Harlemite to Congress," *Amsterdam News,* 13 November 1937, Crosswaith papers, additions, box 2, Schomburg Archives. Clashes: *New York Age,* 13 August 1932. Hamid's group was sometimes called the Negro Industrial *and* Clerical Alliance.

15. Kemp: "Kemp Insists." John Johnson, sermon given 4 August 1934, in *Harlem, the War and Other Addresses,* pp. 62, 68. Note that the issue was identified as that of women obtaining jobs.

16. Imes testimony; Franklin, p. 130; Mayor's Commission on Conditions in Harlem, L. M. Blumstein, Interview [1935], p. 1, LaGuardia papers, box 33; Federal Writers' program, New York City [Ottley and Weatherby?], "I Too Sing America," n.d., p. 2, WPA, Federal Writers' Program, "Negroes of New York," box 4; Roi Ottley and William Weatherby, *The Negro in New York: An Informal Social History, 1626–1940* (New York, 1967; reprinted from the Federal Writers' Project ed.) , pp. 281–82; Roi Ottley, *New World A-Coming* (Boston, 1943), pp. 114–15; Charles Lawrence, "Negro Organizations in Crisis: Depression, New Deal, World War II" (Ph.D. dissertation, Columbia University, 1952), pp. 284–85; Muraskin, pp. 9–11, 13; Melville Weiss, pp. 58–59; Mark Naison, *Communists in Harlem During the Depression* (Urbana, Ill., 1983), pp. 115–19. The progress of the pickets can be followed in the *New York Age.* See, for example: "Blumstein's Bans Negro Clerks," 26 May 1934, p. 1; "Negro Clerks for 125th Street Store," 9 June 1934, p. 1 (Koch's Department Store); "Pickets to Continue Activity in Front of L. M. Blumstein Co. Store," 16 June 1934, p. 1; "Blumstein's Said to Be Weakening as Citizens' Committee Pushes Boycott," 23 June 1934, p. 1; "Harlem's Campaign for Jobs Gets Added Support," 30 June 1934, p. 1; "Push Fight on

Blumstein's," 7 July 1934, pp. 1–2; "'Blumstein's Must Go!' Shouted by 500 Harlemites at Meeting for Citizens' League," 16 July 1934, pp. 1, 3; "Blumstein's Patrons Assaulted," 21 July 1934, p. 1; "Parade and Mass Meeting Set to Climax Boycott Against the Blumstein 125th Street Store," 28 July 1934, p. 1; "Blumstein's to Hire Negro Clerks," 4 August 1934, pp. 1, 9; "Honor Roll of Pickets in 125th Street Boycott," 4 August 1934, p. 9.

17. Larry Greene, "Harlem in the Great Depression: 1928–1936" (Ph.D. dissertation, Columbia University, 1979), pp. 459, 462. Slave masters did not favor lighter-skinned slaves for aesthetic reasons only; often these slaves were in fact the master's children. "Negroes" quotation: "Renegade 'Boycott Committee' Runs Wild, Assaults Shoppers," New York Age, 22 September 1934, p. 1. HLU: "Kemp Insists"; Muraskin, pp. 49, 51–52. Incorporated in 1936. Power: Melville Weiss, pp. 70–71. For a defense of Hamid, Kemp, and Reid on the color issue, see Muraskin, pp. 39–41, 43 ("there is ample reason for assuming total sincerity on their [Kemp's and Reid's] part" becaue Reid was West Indian and a Garveyite, and Kemp dark and a Garveyite.)

18. Mr. Snyder, Interview, 22 April 1935, by R. J. McBride. LaGuardia papers, new box 33. Also see "Citizens' League for Fair Play to Continue Employment Fight," New York Age, 11 August 1934, pp. 1, 3, about Hamid; and "Picket Weisbecker's Store," New York Age, 25 August 1934, p. 1, about Kemp and Reid.

19. Bernard Deutsch, President, Board of Aldermen, to Mayor LaGuardia, 25 September 1934, LaGuardia papers, box 658. Merchants' claims: Myrtle Pollard, "Harlem As It Is" (B.B.A. thesis, City College of New York, 1936), p. 22 (interview with Mr. Blumstein and Mr. Berler, president of Koch's Department Store, July and August, 1935). "Renegade 'Boycott Committee' Runs Wild," p. 1.

20. "Racial Picketing Barred," New York Times, 1 November 1934, p. 12. The article noted it was the nation's first such decision. Similar decisions would be handed down in other cities, including Cleveland, Baltimore, and Newark. Hubert to Eunice Carter, 16 April 1935, LaGuardia papers, new box 3529. Muraskin, p. 48; Greene, pp. 455, 471; Ira Reid, "The Negro in the American Economic System," Report, 1 August 1940, p. 149, Carnegie-Myrdal study, Reid, vol. 1, Schomburg Archives; Melville Weiss, pp. 64–66; Franklin, p. 134. Johnson: Muraskin, p. 48. Rev. Imes called it "an unfortunate altercation among the elements that originally composed [the League]." Imes testimony.

21. "Plane Crash Kills Sufi Hamid," New York Age, 6 August 1938, p. 1; "Plane Crash Fatal to 'Harlem Hitler,'" New York Times, 1 August 1938, p. 1; Melville Weiss, pp. 75–77, 80; Franklin, pp. 131, 140–41; McKay, Harlem, pp. 133, 201; Muraskin, pp. 14–17, 33–38; Young, pp. 3–8. The Lerner Company brought the suit against Hamid's group.

22. Melville Weiss, p. 78; "I Too Sing America," p. 3; Greene, p. 472. Elsewhere: Hunter, pp. 120–21, 142.

23. Both quotations: Cecilia Saunders, Testimony before Mayor's Commission on Conditions in Harlem, 13 April 1935, LaGuardia papers, new box 3770.

24. Melville Weiss, p. 87. Elsewhere: Hunter, pp. 142, 146.

25. Hamid in court: McKay, Harlem, pp. 210–11. Hamid and anti-Semitism: Muraskin, p. 18; "Plane Crash Kills Sufi Hamid"; Ottley, p. 118; McKay, Harlem, p. 200; Hunter, p. 189. Complaints: see, for example, Amsterdam News, 29 September 1934, and 13 October 1934; Jewish Day, 22 September 1934; "Shopkeepers Are Heard," New York Times, 26 September 1934, p. 44. HLU: Ottley, pp. 119, 121–23; Charles Segal, representative of a committee of Eighth Avenue merchants, to Police Commissioner Lewis Valentine, 27 July 1938, LaGuardia papers, box 89. The speeches in question took place in "public addresses on Eighth Avenue between West 115th Street and West 116th Street" in 1938. Mayor LaGuardia responded with a sympathetic letter. Harlem Merchants' Association: merchants

between 110th and 155th Streets, between St. Nicholas and Third Avenues. It claimed a membership of over 500, few of whom were black. Imes testimony. Crusade: "I Too Sing America," pp. 3, 4, 6. Communists and merchants: McKay, *Harlem,* pp. 195–96; Naison, *Communists,* pp. 102, 121–22.

26. The Sufi's defense: McKay, *Harlem,* pp. 198, 208. Bribery and pressure: Deutsch to LaGuardia; Franklin, p. 138; Ottley, p. 117.

27. "Job for Dewey" (editorial), *Amsterdam News,* 9 October 1937, p. 14. NLC and Owl Shoe Co.: [Crosswaith?] "Harlem Labor Union," notes, n.d., Negro Labor Committee papers box 28, Schomburg Archives; Deutsch to LaGuardia; Muraskin, pp. 46–48; Melville Weiss, pp. 71–72; Franklin, p. 138 (testimony from employees threatened by Hamid).

28. Arthur Reid, Interview with Muraskin, n.d., in Muraskin, pp. 32–33.

29. HLU organizer, Interview with Lawrence, 15 April 1943, in Lawrence, pp. 288–89.

30. Reid: Wendell Malliet, "Big Job Drive Seems Headed for the Rocks," *Amsterdam News,* 29 October 1938, p. 11; Melville Weiss, p. 92. Crosswaith: Malliet, p. 11; Frank Crosswaith, Testimony before Mayor's Commission on Conditions in Harlem [1935], p. 46, LaGuardia papers, new box 3770.

31. Malliet, p. 11; Melville Weiss, p. 110.

32. Sitkoff, p. 249; NAACP minutes, n.d., William Pickens' papers, box 16; Naison, *Communists,* p. 59.

33. Naison, *Communists,* pp. 102, 108. Quotation: Adam Clayton Powell, Jr., "Soapbox," *Amsterdam News,* 30 October 1937, p. 13. James Ford's speech delivered at meeting of Joint Conference Against Discriminatory Practices, Abyssinian Baptist Church, New York, New York, 23 October 1935, pp. 4–7, LaGuardia papers, box 35 (quoted in Chapter 4), was referring specifically to participation in the "Don't Buy" campaign.

34. At Weisbecker's also the police stopped the picket line. "Open Fight on Weisbecker's," *Amsterdam News,* 15 June 1935 (clipping), LaGuardia papers, new box 3538. Empire Cafeteria: "1,500 in Harlem Protest," *New York Times,* 1 September 1934, p. 17 (306 Lenox Ave.); Naison, *Communists,* pp. 100, 120, 122; Naison, "Communism," pp. 27–29; Alliance and UNIA: Melville Weiss, p. 67; Lawrence, p. 287; James Ford and Louis Sass, "Development of Work in the Harlem Section," *Communist* 14 (April, 1935): 313. Empire handbill: in LaGuardia papers, new box 3538. Franklin, p. 139.

35. Mayor's Commission: quoted in Alain Locke, "Harlem, Dark Weather-Vane," *Survey Graphic* 25 (August 1936): 460. Myrdal, p. 313; McKay, *Harlem,* pp. 210–11, 228; Hunter, pp. 131–42; Hubert, Testimony; Muraskin, p. 53; "Open Fight on Weisbecker's." The New Negro Alliance was a group of young students and lawyers in Washington, D.C., including William Hastie and Thurgood Marshall, who organized in 1933 to ensure equal access to government programs and private employment.

36. Sydney French, Federal Writers' Program, New York City, "Biographical Sketch of Rev. A. C. Powell, Jr., " 1939, pp. 3, 17, WPA, Federal Writers' Program, "Negroes of New York," box 1; Melville Weiss, p. 95; Neil Hickey and Ed Edwin, *Adam Clayton Powell and the Politics of Race* (New York, 1965), p. 53; Adam Clayton Powell, Jr., *Marching Blacks: An Interpretive History of the Rise of the Black Common Man* (New York, 1945), pp. 93, 96. Poor: Powell, *Marching Blacks,* p. 98; French, "Biographical Sketch," p. 96. The number of members was undoubtedly inflated, but certainly participation was enormous. Members: Matthew Eder, Secretary, Uptown Chamber of Commerce, to Mayor LaGuardia, 20 July 1938, p. 1, LaGuardia papers, box 89; Charles Collier, Jr., New York Urban League, "Report of Industrial Secretary for Board Meeting, May 11, 1938," pp. 3, 4, NUL papers, series 4, box 33. Chicago moderates organized similarly in the Council of Negro Organizations. It claimed 100,000 members, and also launched mass demonstrations and pickets after the *New Alli-*

ance decision. Often working with the Negro Labor Relations League, a group of younger blacks committed to improving black employment opportunities, black Chicagoans won important victories such as the placement of black managers in the local newspapers. Hunter, pp. 270–71. These efforts across the country were not isolated or separate; just as the *Whip's* editor helped spark Harlem's efforts, Powell's address to the NLRL in 1938 spurred Chicago blacks to rejoin the struggle.

37. Crosswaith to LaGuardia, 30 April 1938, LaGuardia papers, box 89; Melville Weiss, p. 101.

38. "Consolidated Gas Co. to Put 4 Negroes to Work As Clerks," *New York Age,* 7 May 1938, p. 1; Alyse Abrams, Federal Writers' Program, New York City, "Rev. Adam Clayton Powell, Jr." [1939?], p. 1, WPA, Federal Writers' Program, "Negroes of New York," box 1; Melville Weiss, pp. 97–99; "I Too Sing America," p. 17; Ottley and Weatherby, pp. 268, 288; Ottley, p. 228–29; Hickey and Edwin, p. 54; Reid, "The Negro in the American Economic System," p. 154; Miriam Carpenter II, "Some Aspects of the Depression on Negroes" (Master's thesis, Columbia University, 1937), pp. 50–51; N.Y.S. Temporary Commission on the Condition of the Urban Colored Population, *Second Report,* Legislative Document #69 (Albany, 1939), p. 64. Powell quotation: "Negroes Win Jobs with Utility in Harlem When Anti-Bias Group Threatens Boycott," *New York Times,* 29 April 1938, p. 8. "Job Discrimination on Negroes Charged," *New York Times,* 2 November 1938, p. 25; NUL, "Number Please? Employment of Negro Workers in the Telephone Industry in 44 Cities," Report, January 1946, p. 5, Columbia University Social Work Library. For more information on phone company, see Venus Green, "The Impact of Technology upon Women's Work in the Telephone Industry, 1880–1980" (Ph.D. dissertation, Columbia University, 1990). There is no evidence the jamming threat was carried out.

39. Copy of this letter (on Abyssinian Baptist Church letterhead), dated 28 April 1938, sent to Mayor LaGuardia from Frank Crosswaith, LaGuardia papers, box 89. Pickets also reported in "Negroes Win Jobs."

40. "Memorandum of Understanding Between the Uptown Chamber of Commerce and the Greater New York Co-ordinating Committee for Employment, in Relation to the Employment of Negroes in Harlem Stores," 20 July 1938, LaGuardia papers, box 89, and NUL papers, series 4, box 6. See also "Negroes Win Help in Fight for Jobs," *New York Times,* 28 August 1938, Section IV, p. 10; "Merchants Sign Employment Pact," *New York Age,* 16 July 1938, pp. 1, 5.

41. Employees: NYUL, "Annual Report, 1938," New York Public Library; Melville Weiss, p. 102. HLU: "Harlem Emerges as Stronghold of Trade Unionism," *New York Post,* 13 May 1938, p. 6; Melville Weiss, pp. 104, 106–8, 111–14. Complaints continued to trickle into the Attorney General's office until 1946. In that year, Crosswaith was called to testify at an investigation into the HLU. The problems may have continued still longer, but no information is available for later dates. Negro Labor Committee, "HLU."

42. Powell, *Marching Blacks,* p. 101; Hunter, p. 278. This was less than a total victory, though, as most of the jobs did not in fact go to clerks but to unskilled workers.

43. Hickey and Edwin, p. 60; Powell, *Marching Blacks,* p. 99; Meier and Rudwick, p. 32; NYUL, "Executive Board Minutes," 17 December 1937, pp. 2–3, Arthur Schomburg papers, box 16, Schomburg Archives. By the middle of the 1940s, blacks held clerical and sales positions in Alexander's, Macy's, Lane Bryant, Lord and Taylor, Bloomingdale's, and B. Altman. LeRoy Jeffries, NUL, "Integration of Negroes in Department Stores," Report, July 1946, Columbia University Social Work Library.

44. Hunter, p. 285.

45. For an eloquent argument that black political action in the New Deal period did bring changes in race relations, presaging the modern civil rights movement, see Sitkoff.

Chapter 6

1. New York State Temporary Emergency Relief Administration, *Administration of Public Unemployment Relief in New York State* (New York, 1935), p. 7, in *New York State TERA Publications,* vol. 2, Columbia University Social Work Library, New York City.

2. New York City WPA Advisory Council, "Reports on Public Assistance to the Administrator, WPA for the City of New York," 14 March 1939, p. 67, Columbia University Social Work Library.

3. N.Y.C. Emergency Relief Bureau, "Final Report of the ERB: June 6, 1934, to December 31, 1937," p. 43, Columbia University Social Work Library; Department of Health and Neighborhood Health Development, "Health Center Districts, New York Handbook of Statistical Reference Data: Ten Year Period, 1931–1940," 1944, pp. 14, 17, Public Health Library, New York City. Table 6.1: Federal Emergency Relief Administration, "Survey of the Occupational Characteristics of Persons Receiving Relief in New York City," Press release, 8 May 1935, Appendix, Vertical File: "New York City Unemployment," Municipal Reference and Resource Center, New York City.

4. Relief: Guichard Parris and Lester Brooks, *Blacks in the City: A History of the National Urban League* (Boston, 1971), p. 239. White family heads varied from 12 percent on relief at ages 50–59, to 16 percent at 20–29. Blacks: 36 percent of those 50–59 years old, to 65 percent of those over 70. U.S. Department of Labor, Bureau of Labor Statistics, *Family Income and Expenditure in New York City, 1935–36,* vol. 1: *Family Income* (Washington, D.C., 1941), pp. 139, 203. Of New York State blacks on relief, 7 percent had no formal education, 22 percent had one to four years, 21 percent had five to six, 30 percent had seven to eight, 20 percent had some high school years, 1 percent had more than 12 years. The median education for New York State: 7.1 for blacks, 8.3 for whites, WPA Division of Research, *Workers on Relief in the United States in March 1935,* vol. 2: *A Study of Industrial and Educational Backgrounds* (Washington, D.C., 1939), p. 71; Mayor's Commission on Conditions in Harlem, "The Negro in Harlem," Report, 1935, p. 112, LaGuardia papers, box 2550.

5. Blacks turn sooner to relief: Nettie McGill and Ellen Matthews, *The Youth of New York City* (New York, 1940), p. 44. NYUL, "Annual Report, 1940," 1940, p. 1, National Urban League papers, series 13, box 19, Library of Congress Manuscript Collection, Washington, D.C.; Dominic Capeci, Jr., *The Harlem Riot of 1943* (Philadelphia, 1977), p. 35.

6. East Harlem District Health Committee, "Health, Social and Economic Conditions in Health Area 20, East Harlem Health District, New York City," Report, 1942, p. 8, Public Health Library. Male and female heads.

7. BLS, *Family Income,* pp. 38–39, native-born families. Also Richard Sterner, "Standard of Living of the Negro," Research memorandum, 1940, p. 381, Carnegie-Myrdal study, Sterner, vol. 2, Schomburg Archives, New York City. Families earning $500: U.S. Department of Labor, Bureau of Labor Statistics, *Money Disbursements of Wage Earners and Clerical Workers in the North Atlantic Region, 1934–1936,* vol. 1: *New York City* (Washington, D.C., 1939), p. 21.

8. Mayor's Commission on Conditions in Harlem, "Relief Administration," Report, n.d., Mayor LaGuardia papers, box 755.

9. WPA Advisory Council, p. 79, and DPW, *Annual Report* for each year. The Board of Child Welfare rolls increased by approximately 1,000 to 2,000 cases per year (except 1934–35). Mayor's Committee on Unemployment Relief, *Report of Mayor LaGuardia's Committee on Unemployment Relief* (New York, 1935), p. 10. April 1934: 14,399 singles on relief. January 1935: 43,287. The 1935 Social Security Act and subsequent legal changes made recipients eligible for aid at 65 rather than 70. The BCW dropped its citizenship requirement and shortened in-state residency requirements.

10. New York State Department of Social Welfare, *Democracy Cares: The Story Behind Public Assistance in New York State* (Albany, 1941), p. 70, in *New York State Department of Social Services Publications,* vol. 8, Columbia University Social Work Library. ERB, "Final Report," p. 22; DPW, *Annual Report, 1935,* pp. 8–9; Federal Writers' Program, New York City, "Welfare and Public Relief," draft, 1939, p. 4, papers of the WPA, Federal Writers' Program, "Negroes of New York," box 19, Schomburg Archives. In 1935 the Wicks Act amended TERA, and the next year a permanent system of state aid was established. ERB, "Annual Report, June 1, 1935, to May 31, 1936," p. 3, Columbia University Social Work Library; New York State Governor's Commission on Unemployment Relief, *Administration of Home Relief in New York City* (Albany, 1935), pp. 41, 45, Russell-Sage collection, City College of New York. For more detail, see "A High School Student Views Relief and City Government," Report, 1936, LaGuardia papers, box 2539; "Welfare and Public Relief," p. 4; ERB, "Final Report," p. 12; *Democracy Cares,* p. 71. The HRB became an ERB subdivision. In 1937 both joined the DPW.

11. "Welfare and Public Relief," p. 4. "Works Progress" became "Work Projects" in 1939.

12. One million: DPW, *Annual Report, 1938–1939* (New York, 1939), p. 12; ERB, "Annual Report," p. 4; ERB, "Final Report," p. 16. Examples of budget-related work cuts: in 1934 the agency fired half of all public works employees because of cost overrruns. In 1939 the Relief Act mandated that all WPA workers employed there longer than 18 months be let go. Almost 800,000 lost their jobs. A survey three months later found less than an eighth had found private-sector work. Robert McElvaine, *The Great Depression* (New York, 1984), p. 308. Budget: *Democracy Cares,* p. 73.

13. U.S.: Joint Committee on National Recovery, "Statement" [1934], National Negro Congress papers, box 1, Schomburg Archives. White: ten percent on relief. N.Y.C. 1935: Alfred Smith, FERA, "Reasons for the Disproportionate Number of Negroes on the Relief Rolls," Report, April 1935, p. 8, National Negro Congress papers, box 2; BLS, *Family Income,* pp. 38–39. Home Relief: Federal Writers' Program, New York City, "Depression," n.d., p. 12, WPA, Federal Writers' Program, "Negroes of New York," box 4; Mayor's Commission on Conditions in Harlem, "The Negro in Harlem, " p. 36. Northern cities: Ira Reid and T. Arnold Hill, "The Forgotton Tenth," Pamphlet, p. 24, May 1933, Columbia University Social Work Library.

14. *Democracy Cares,* pp. 86, 88. To get a sense of comparison with other years, the 1938 monthly average figures were 428,016; 196,448; 73,238; and 167,241, respectively. WPA Advisory Council, p. 67. Categorical relief: money provided for the blind, disabled, elderly, and for female household heads with dependent children. Other figures, even from the same sources, vary for the same categories. Most are in the same range, but why they are not identical is not clear. For example, the DPW's *Annual Report, 1938–1939,* reports that 1 January 1938, 167,226 families received home relief, and 137,906 worked on some public works job: p. 8. Governor's Commission, p. 43, lists 220,216 families on home relief, December 1934. Work: 119,619. DPW and BCW: 46,713, not including 22,659 children in institutions. ERB, "Final Report," p. 16, reports, January of 1934: 321,000 on relief. *Democracy Cares,* p. 72: average monthly total on relief: in 1937, 339,738; in 1938, 354,779 (probably does not include DPW and BCW). These figures do not include the non-monetary services also provided by New Deal agencies. In 1936, for example, 220,000 relief families received free medical care, compared with 30,000 in 1933. ERB, "Final Report," p. 26.

15. TERA, *Administration of Public Unemployment Relief,* p. 27. ERB, "Annual Report," p. 7. Other years similar: Board of Survey on Transfer of Relief Administration, "58 Questions on Relief in New York City," draft, 1 February 1938, p. II F 1, Columbia University Social Work Library.

16. The steadily increasing numbers on the BCW rolls also masked a great amount of turbulence: Board of Child Welfare, *17th Annual Report,* 1932 (New York, 1933), pp. 5–6; *19th*

Annual Report, 1934 (New York, 1935), pp. 3, 5, 25; *20th Annual Report,* 1935 (New York, 1936), pp. 5–6; *21st Annual Report,* 1936 (New York, 1937), pp. 5–6; *22nd Annual Report,* 1937 (New York, 1938), pp. 4, 8; *23rd Annual Report,* 1938 (New York, 1939), pp. 7, 25, 40; "Quarterly Report, Oct. to Dec. 1933," 1934, LaGuardia papers, box 658; *24th Annual Report,* 1938, pp. 20, 36–37. Average payment, size of rolls:

Year	Pay Per Child	Women Served	Children Served
1933	$18.65	18,500	43,500
1934	$18.63	18,700	43,300
1935	$18.66	19,000	43,100
1936	$18.65	19,100	43,000
1938	$25.41	25,400	47,000
1939–40	$25.60	26,500	49,000
In 1934–35, 3,200 women entered rolls, 2,900 left.			
1936	3,400		3,300
1938	4,200		4,500
1939–40	4,400		6,700

Two-thirds: "58 Questions," p. II E 2, taken from survey sample by ERB. Not clear if it is a randomly chosen, representative sample of total relief population.

17. Mayor's Committee on Unemployment Relief, *Report,* p. 9. City Affairs Committee (no author) to Mayor LaGuardia, 1934, LaGuardia papers, box 2539. Russell-Sage: New York City League of Women Voters, "Summary of the Report of the Mayor's Committee on the Relief Administration," April 1935 [though labeled 1934], p. 1, Vertical File: "New York City Unemployment Relief Measures," Municipal Reference and Resource Center. NYSES: *Democracy Cares,* pp. 49–50.

18. Joint Committee on National Recovery, "Statement."

19. Without knowing why these families did not receive help, discrimination is still difficult to prove. "Corsi Relief Facts Branded as Misleading," *Daily Worker,* 6 May 1935, p. 36, LaGuardia papers, box 755. Mayor's Commission, "The Negro in Harlem," pp. 36, 44; "First to Be Fired—Last to Be Hired" (editorial), *HRB Employee* 2 (April 1935): 1, LaGuardia papers, box 755; Capeci, p. 35.

20. Complaints and grants: Mayor's Commission on Conditions in Harlem, "The Negro in Harlem," pp. 44–45, LaGuardia papers, box 2550. Harlem complaints: 26 per 1,000 cases. Brooklyn, Bronx: 13–14. Fred Benedikt, Testimony before Mayor's Commission on Conditions in Harlem, 11 May 1935, LaGuardia papers, new box 3772.

21. These cases found in UNIA Central Division, Unemployment Unit, UNIA papers, boxes 6–7, Schomburg Archives; "UNIA Propaganda Bureau," Pamphlet [1941?], p. 1, UNIA papers, box 7. Also responses from the WPA on some of these cases.

22. Hodson to Captain A. L. King of the UNIA, Central Division, 20 January 1938, about a complaint referred by the UNIA. UNIA papers, box 13.

23. Mark Naison, *Communists in Harlem During the Depression* (Urbana, Ill., 1983), p. 76.

24. Ray George, "500 Negro and White Workers in Harlem Hold Relief March," *Hunger Fighter,* April 1933, p. 2, International Labor Defense papers, box 2, Schomburg Archives; "Harlem Council Gets Real Results," *Hunger Fighter,* 24 March 1934, p. 2, ILD papers, box 2. James Ford, speech delivered at Mass Meeting of Joint Conference Against Discriminatory Practices, Abyssinian Baptist Church, New York, New York, 23 October 1935, p. 4, LaGuardia papers, box 35.

25. Mayor's Commission on Conditions in Harlem, "Character of the Negro Community," notes and clippings, 1935, LaGuardia papers, box 755; UNIA papers, box 12; Mark Naison, "Communism and Black Nationalism in the Depression: The Case of Harlem," *Journal of Ethnic Studies* 2 (Summer 1974): 30–31; Naison, *Communists,* pp. 121–23; Mass meeting: "26 and 28 Precincts," *HRBEA Bulletin* 1 (21 January 1935). Ford, speech, pp. 3–4. Battles: Naison, "Communists," p. 26.

26. ERB, "Final Report," p. 29; James Ford, Secretary, Harlem Section of the Communist Party, "Unemployment and Discrimination on Relief and Work Jobs," Testimony before Mayor's Commission on Conditions in Harlem, 27 April 1935, pp. 1, 3, LaGuardia papers, box 805. Edmund Butler, ERB, "Response of Edmund Butler, Secretary of NYC E. R. Bureau to Commission's Report, 7 May 1936," 14 May 1936, p. 4, LaGuardia papers, box 2550.

27. ERB, "Final Report," p. 29. Battles: UNIA files. The UNIA intervened, arguing that such stories were completely plausible, and all too common. No outcome reported. Several such cases in the records.

28. Hugh Jackson, Director of Public Assistance, Department of Welfare, to Ethel Epstein, Administrative Assistant to Mayor LaGuardia, 5 January 1940, p. 1, LaGuardia papers, box 142. Reasonable standards: Department of Welfare, Home Relief Division, "Manual of Policies Relating to Relief: Manual for Relief Workers," 1938, Section 39, Columbia University Social Work Library. Sarah Wilson: UNIA files.

29. ERB, "Final Report," p. 30; "A High School Student." Testimony: *Unemployment in the United States: Hearings Before a Subcommittee on Commerce,* U.S. Senate, 71st Congress, 2nd session, 1930 (Washington, D.C., 1930), Testimony, Mrs. Charles Marquis Merrell, p. 85.

30. Divine follower quoted in McKay, *Harlem: Negro Metropolis* (New York, 1940), p. 65. Sterner, "Standard of Living," p. 24, for national figures. Attesting to their great need, even with these restrictions, N.Y.S. blacks over 65, 1 percent of the total elderly population, constituted almost 5 percent of Social Security recipients: p. 273. Illegitimacy: BCW, *23rd Annual Report,* p. 7.

31. Rates for each agency differed slightly. AICP, *92nd Annual Report, 1934–35* (New York, 1935), p. 29. Board of Survey: "58 Questions," p. II D 4.

32. HRB's November 1934 instructions for figuring allowances (by month): a man received $14.30 for food; a woman, $13.45; a child of nine, $10.40; and a child of three, $8.68. Household supplies for this family: $1.74. Fuel: $3.47. Light: $2.82. Clothing allowances early in the decade were allocated sporadically, when money became available. Insert, "1934—November," in DPW, Emergency Home Relief Bureau, "Preliminary Report for Six Months, December 28, 1931–June 30, 1932," Columbia University Social Work Library. The $61.16 figure for 1937 was calculated on the basis of two adults, with children of eight and thirteen. "Maintenance": for our hypothetical family of four this was estimated by the WPA in 1937 to be $116.64 a month. "58 Questions," p. II D 3. ERB, "Final Report," p. 24; New York State TERA, "Budget Manual: The Family Budget as a Basis for Home Relief," 1 November 1935, pp. 7, 11, 17, 23, in *New York State TERA Publications,* vol. 1, Columbia University Social Work Library; ERB, "Annual Report," p. 10; "New York Relief Held 40 Percent Too Low for Marginal Needs," *Crusader News Agency,* 14 February 1938, p. 9, National Negro Congress papers, box 93, Schomburg Archives; Mayor's Committee on Unemployment Relief, pp. 1, 7, 22. CP: "Do You Know," *Hunger Fighter,* 24 February 1934, p. 4, ILD papers, box 2. The relief amount does not consider the free health care available to the relief family, nor that the unemployed saved the cost of transportation to work, included in the emergency and maintenance budgets.

33. The 1935 survey of Harlem non-relief families revealed a per-person food expenditure of $12.78 a month, a figure well under white expenditures but significantly higher than relief

payments. Raw data for published study, BLS, *Money Disbursements:* Bureau of Labor Statistics papers, RG 257, BLS #807, New York City, boxes 31–51, National Archives, Washington, D.C. White: BLS, *Money Disbursements,* reported the average white family spent $55.83 a month on food. With an average white non-relief family size of 3.8 (p. 102), costs totaled $13.94 per person (p. 106). The Bureau's figure for black families, $451 a year (p. 107), divided by 3.5 members, comes to $12.80 a person. This survey considers only wage-earning and clerical families. General rates: East Harlem District Health Committee, p. 11. The data are for Health Area 20, March 1939. Shelter: Central Registration Bureau [Welfare Council], "Report of Study Made by the CRB of the Intake of the Unattached Women in the HRB Precinct 32 During the Month of April, 1935" [1935], p. 8, LaGuardia papers, box 33.

34. ERB, "Final Report," p. 24. East Harlem District Health Committee, p. 11; Ford, "Unemployment and Discrimination," pp. 1–2; "A High School Student" (includes quotation). Social Service Housing Committee (formerly Welfare Council Housing Department), "Rent Practices in Family Agencies: A Summary of a Study of Rent Practices and Policies in Nine Family Agencies in the City of New York," 27 June 1941, p. 10, Community Service Society papers, box 419, Columbia University Rare Book and Manuscript Library. Welfare Council, Exploratory Committee on Negro Welfare, "Report of the Exploratory Committee on Negro Welfare," January 1939, p. 3, Columbia University Social Work Library. Home Relief Manual: "Manual of Policies Relating to Relief," Section 12, p. 13.

35. All examples from UNIA files. League of Women Voters, p. 2; Mayor's Committee on Unemployment Relief, pp. 14, 15, 18, 22. Relief grant figures: Department of Welfare, *Annual Report, 1938–1939,* p. 8; "58 Questions," p. I A 1; ERB, "Final Report," p. 12; BCW, "Budget Schedules for Monthly Allowances," 1 February 1940, Schedule I and V, LaGuardia papers, box 849. Two years earlier, the family would have received half that amount for rent, or $13.75. The BCW provided slightly more. J. M. Cunningham, Deputy Comptroller, to Lillian Robbins, Chairman, Unemployment Committee of United Neighborhood Houses of New York, 15 May 1940, p. 1, LaGuardia papers, box 692: "The City is now taking much better care of its fatherless children than it did in past years." U.S. Department of Labor, Bureau of Labor Statistics, *Family Income and Expenditure in New York City, 1935–1936,* vol. 2: *Family Expenditure* (Washington, D.C., 1939), pp. 113, 155.

36. CWA unskilled workers earned 50¢ an hour in 1934, while skilled workers earned $1.20. All worked an average of thirty hours a week. WPA Advisory Council, p. 147; *Hearings before the Subcommittee of the Committee on Appropriations,* House of Representatives, 75th Congress, 1st session, on the Emergency Relief Appropriation Act of 1937 (Washington, D.C., 1937), p. 181 (cumulative through March 1937). Average earnings overall for WPA workers came to 70¢. This was higher than the national average, but costs in the city were also higher: Barbara Blumberg, *The New Deal and the Unemployed: The View from New York City* (Lewisburg, Penn., 1979), pp. 32–33. Non-relief figures are for white earnings in the private sector. BLS, *Family Income,* pp. 20, 21. This is earnings, not total income, which of course was even higher. On the other hand, these figures for independent workers include only those who did not receive any relief for the entire year prior to the survey. Thus these people must be the better-off wage earners. CCC men earned $30 a month; NYA workers usually earned $20 to $22 a month for 40 to 44 hours of work. Students received $3 to $6 a month in scholarships. "Manual for Relief Workers," Sections 35, 36.

37. UNIA papers, boxes 6–7: eight of 143 complaints involved the amount of relief received.

38. Raw data, BLS, Harlem survey; WPA Advisory Council, p. 147; "58 Questions," p. II D 3; McElvaine, p. 193; Edna Burge, Welfare Council, "Economically Independent Negro Families in the Boroughs of Manhattan and Brooklyn," Report, 1939, Appendix, Columbia University Social Work Library.

39. Testimony, Fred Benedikt. Samuel Allen, Industrial Secretary, NYUL, "Report of the Industrial Secretary: Annual Meeting, 10 January 1934," p. 4, NUL papers, series 4, box 32.

40. Charles Collier, Jr., Industrial Secretary, NYUL, "Report of the Industrial Secretary for Board Meeting, 11 May 1938," NUL papers, series 4, box 33; NYUL Executive Board, "Minutes of Meeting, 22 November 1934," p. 1, Arthur Schomburg papers, box 16, Schomburg Archives.

41. Lemuel Foster, Executive Officer, WPA Race Relations Bureau, "Report to Administrator Ridder," 31 July 1936, p. 5, Arthur Schomburg papers, box 16; Mayor's Commission on Conditions in Harlem, "The Negro in Harlem," pp. 37–41.

42. Mary Irvin, Testimony before the Mayor's Commission on Conditions in Harlem, 27 November 1935, LaGuardia papers, box 33. National Urban League, "The Negro Working Population and National Recovery: A Special Memorandum to Franklin Delano Roosevelt, President of the United States, by the National Urban League for Social Service among Negroes," 4 January 1937, p. 11, NUL papers, series 1, box 1.

43. Mayor's Commission on Conditions in Harlem, notes, LaGuardia papers, box 755; "Response of Edmund Butler," pp. 1–4.

44. ERB, Advisory Committee on Negro Problems, "Summary of the Activities of the Advisory Committee," 25 September 1936, p. 1, Vertical File: "NYC Negroes," Municipal Reference and Resource Center; ERB, Press release, 19 June 1935 (for release 20 June), pp. 1–3, LaGuardia papers, box 43.

45. Ford, speech, p. 4; Naison, *Communists*, p. 123; Collier, NYUL, p. 1.

46. NAACP, "HOLC Injects Color Question in Denying Loan in Harlem," Press Service of the NAACP, 23 November 1934, p. 2, National Negro Congress papers, box 3. Rooming houses could not receive HOLC loans. Shelters: "Unemployment Discrimination on Relief and Work Jobs," Ford, Testimony, pp. 1–2, and typed lists in the Mayor's papers, relief files. Women: Central Registration Bureau, "Report," p. 6.

47. "20 Will Get Big WPA Jobs," *Amsterdam News* (clipping) [April 1936], WPA papers, RG 69, NYC box 2062, National Archives. Foster (WPA Race Relations Bureau) also reported it.

48. New York City WPA, *Final Report of the WPA for the City of New York, 1935–1943* (New York, 1943); Blumberg, p. 79; Foster, p. 1. The Advisory Committee on Negro Problems, a community group headed by the Rev. John Johnson, requested black participation in an investigation of racism in WPA practice. The group became the advisory group to the WPA at the latter's request. 1936: WPA, *Final Report,* p. 98; Foster, p. 9.

49. FERA: NUL, "The Negro Working Population," p. 7. Nationwide: ibid., p. 9. Alain Locke, "Harlem: Dark Weather-Vane," *Survey Graphic* 25 (August 1936): 459; Harvard Sitkoff, *A New Deal for Blacks* (New York, 1978), pp. 69–71.

50. Allen, NYUL, p. 5; NUL, "The Negro Working Population," p. 11; NAACP to Union Mechanics' Association, 14 August 1935, LaGuardia papers, box 2550. Bridge subcontractors: McClintic–Marshall Construction Co. PWA response quoted in James Allen, Testimony before the Mayor's Commission on Conditions in Harlem, 20 April 1935, LaGuardia papers, new box 3770.

51. Mayor's Commission on Conditions in Harlem, "The Negro in Harlem," pp. 47–51. James Allen testimony; Frank Crosswaith, Testimony before the Mayor's Commission on Conditions in Harlem, n.d., LaGuardia papers, new box 3770. Allen testified the 12 projects were done in 1932, but this may have been a transcription error.

52. Allen testimony: Mayor's Commission on Conditions in Harlem, "The Negro in Harlem," pp. 48–52. (It listed the findings of the TERA report of 5 December 1934). Memo cited: Project #188, 22 August 1935, quoted in ibid., p. 51.

53. William Dammond to Mayor LaGuardia, 9 April 1935; Albert Dillard to Mayor

LaGuardia, 8 October 1935, both in LaGuardia papers, new box 3531. There are several boxes of such correspondence. TERA: Mayor's Commission on Conditions in Harlem, "The Negro in Harlem," pp. 47–51.

54. Garfield Freeman, Testimony before the Mayor's Commission on Conditions in Harlem, n.d., LaGuardia papers, new box 3537. Blanshard to Frazier, 8 October 1935, LaGuardia papers, new box 3529. WPA: Charlotte Carr, Executive Director, ERB, to Mayor LaGuardia, 28 August 1936, p. 2, Vertical File: "NY Unemployment Relief," Municipal Reference and Resource Center; Welfare Council, "Memorandum Suggested for Presentation to Foundations Requesting Funds for a Placement and Study Bureau for Negro Children and Youth in New York," March 1937, p. 13, Community Service Society papers, box 104, Columbia University Rare Book and Manuscript Library; Foster, pp. 2, 5; Mayor's Commission on Conditions in Harlem, "Report to Mayor on Home Relief by Race," 28 August 1936, p. 2, LaGuardia papers, box 2550. Race relations: ibid., pp. 2, 3—23,000 of 60,000 blacks moved to work relief, and 191,000 of 306,000 whites.

55. First memorandum: WPA, "Memo to Mrs. Woodward [Washington, D.C.] from Lawrence Morris [N.Y.C.] *re:* Mrs. Hutchinson, Director, Historical Records Survey, NYC" (marked "Confidential"), 22 April 1937, p. 1, WPA papers, box NYC 651.35. Second: Luther Evans, National Supervisor, Historical Records Survey, to Employees of Historical Record Survey, New York City, 21 April 1937, p. 1, WPA papers, box NYC 651.35.

56. Allen, NYUL, p. 4. This particular situation occurred with ERB work relief.

57. See NYUL Executive Board minutes for each year in NUL papers, series 4, boxes 32 and 33. These examples taken from the 19 December 1935 meeting, pp. 1–2. CP: see, for example, Naison, *Communists,* p. 148.

58. James Hubert, Testimony before Mayor's Commission on Conditions in Harlem, 20 April 1935, LaGuardia papers, new box 3770. Black proportion in population (5 percent in New York City based on 1930 census) was used as a base by PWA, U.S. Housing Authority, Federal Works Agency, Committee on Fair Employment Practice, and as the proportion of blacks to be eligible for PWA public housing projects (in black areas). National: Sitkoff, p. 67.

59. "Those Housing Jobs" (editorial), *Amsterdam News,* 11 April 1936, U.S. Department of Labor papers, Division of Negro Labor, RG 183, USES Oxley box 1387, National Archives (includes Ickes quotation). Practice: Naison, *Communists,* p. 105.

60. Foster, pp. 5, 6; Mayor's Commission on Conditions in Harlem, "Report to Mayor on Home Relief," p. 2; Carr to LaGuardia, p. 2; Welfare Council, "Memorandum Suggested," p. 13. Memo: November 1935, quoted in Foster, p. 4. PWA also had rules against discrimination but obviously did not enforce them. FDR: Sitkoff, p. 69; McElvaine, p. 193. In February of 1939 Congress amended the Emergency Relief Act to make it illegal to discriminate "on account of race, creed or color." Sitkoff, p. 69. Although this amendment was often ignored, it did put the two elected branches of government on record as opposing discrimination.

61. Ridder: "20 Will Get Big WPA Jobs," p. 1. Butler: "Response of Edward Butler," pp. 1–4. Race Relations: Foster, p. 3.

62. Blumberg, pp. 82–83: In 1937, three-fourths of blacks were classified as "common laborers." Five percent held professional and technical classifications, 0.5 percent were supervisors. Early 1940s: *Democracy Cares,* p. 86; Citywide Citizens' Committee on Harlem, "Report of Subcommittee on Employment," 1942, Municipal Reference and Resource Center. True nationally: Florence Murray, ed., *The Negro Handbook* (New York, 1942), p. 161.

63. NYA, N.Y.C., "NYC NYA Student Aid Application Survey Form B," Chart, NYA papers, RG 119, Division of Finance and Statistics, Reports Unit, National Archives; Murray, p. 163. Federal government: McElvaine, p. 193.

64. WPA, "Reports, 1935–41," letters and pamphlets, pp. 14, 24, 36 (1938); p. 22 (1939), Columbia University Social Work Library; John Van Deusen, *The Black Man in White America* (Washington, D.C., 1938), p. 52. Harlem River Houses opened in 1937.

65. Commission for the NYUL Study, "The NYUL Study, 1935: First Draft," n.d., pp. 31, 46–48, NUL papers, series 4, box 32; Blumberg, p. 154.

66. WPA Federal Writers' Project, *New York City Guide* (New York, 1939), p. 257; McElvaine, p. 273; Jervis Anderson, *This Was Harlem* (New York, 1981), pp. 277–78; WPA and Harlem Sponsoring Committee, "Harlem Festival and Exhibit June 8–13, 1936," Program, pp. 1, 10–11, WPA papers, NYC 651.3, box 2062. Private agencies also provided educational programs; the NYUL had been running literacy classes since 1934, as did Father Divine. NYUL, "Minutes, Executive Board Meeting, 22 November 1934," p. 2; Gustav Stumpf, "Harlem Tops New York WPA Classes," *Crisis* 45 (January 1938): 10. Quotation: Vivian Morris, Federal Writers' Program, New York City, "History of Harlem Art Center," 1937, p. 1, WPA, Federal Writers' Program, "Negroes of New York," box 1.

67. Mrs. Henry Breckenridge, Chairperson, Municipal Arts Committee, to Mayor LaGuardia, 7 December 1936, Harlem Neighborhood file, Municipal Reference and Resource Center. General figures: "Harlem Festival" cover and pp. 1, 9–11. The projects employed 158 teachers in 1936. The art center discussion based on Vivian Morris, pp. 1–2; Simon Williamson, Federal Writers' Program, New York City, "Harlem Art Center Opens," 1936, p. 2, WPA, Federal Writers' Program, "Negroes of New York, " box 1; S. Michelson, Federal Writers' Program, New York City, "The Federal Art Project in Harlem," 1936, pp. 1–3, WPA, Federal Writers' Program, "Negroes of New York," box 1. Jacob Lawrence: Ellen Wheat, *Jacob Lawrence, American Painter* (Seattle, 1986), pp. 14–15, 24.

68. "Harlem Festival," pp. 13–15; WPA, "Monthly Report of NYC WPA Nursery School and Parent Education," January 1941, p. 1, WPA papers, NYC 651.3142, box 2101. Angels: Emergency Unemployment Relief Committee, "The Story of the Emergency Work Bureau, Oct. 1, 1930–August 1, 1933," Pamphlet, 1933, p. 34, Columbia Social Work Library.

69. Applications: approximately 15,000 to 16,000 until 1933. They dropped by a fifth the first year of the New Deal and remained between 9,000 and 10,000 for the remainder of the decade. The proportion of cases accepted fell from 40 percent in 1930 to 33 percent in 1937. For figures, see DPW, *Annual Reports, 1929–1937.* None needed: *Annual Report, 1937,* p. 22. Relief: ibid., *1935,* p. 18. The proportion committed because of death, illness, incarceration, or abandonment of at least one parent, remained virtually identical: 90 percent in 1934 and 1937 (although only 10 percent were full orphans). Those committed solely because of unemployment or poverty: 8 percent in 1934, 5 percent in 1935, then 4 percent, and 3 percent in 1937: ibid., *1934* (New York, 1935), p. 17; ibid., *1935,* p. 54; ibid., *1936* (New York, 1937), p. 92; ibid., *1937,* p. 87. In 1925, in comparison, only 24 percent of all applicants were approved for commitment. Of them, 7 percent were orphaned or abandoned; less than 1 percent were committed because of family unemployment. Ibid., *1925* (New York, 1926), p. 12. Similarly for 1926; ibid., *1926* (New York, 1927), p. 16. Block quotation: New York State Department of Social Welfare, *Volume, Distribution and Cost of Child Dependency in New York State for Year Ending December 31, 1932* (Albany, 1934), p. 9, in *New York State Welfare Department Publications,* vol. 1, Columbia University Social Work Library. "Rescue": WPA Advisory Council, p. 151. "Keep families together" quotation: Governor's Commission on Unemployment Relief, p. 18.

70. Child Welfare League of America, *Child Care Facilities for Dependent and Neglected Negro Children in Three Cities: New York City, Philadelphia, Cleveland* (New York, 1945), pp. 45, 54.

71. Caseloads: Welfare Council, "Memorandum Suggested," p. 12. COS and AICP: the

Annual Report for each group, both at Columbia University Social Work Library; James Brown, Community Service Society Institute of Welfare Research, *Analysis of Family Service Statistics, 1939–1942* (New York, 1944), pp. 4, 33, 36, Russell-Sage collection. AICP, *90th Annual Report, 1932–1933* (New York, 1933), p. 3.

72. COS and Welfare Council, *Directory of Social Agencies, 1927–28; 1933–34; 1937–38; 1940* (New York, 1928, 1933, 1937, 1939). An annual list of private welfare organizations in the city, this directory documented the rise and fall of these groups, as well as changes in nomenclature and address. The body was not all-inclusive though: for example, Utopia Children's House was not in the list of day nurseries. CSS, "The First Year," pp. 14–18, 43; CSS, "A Changing World," Annual Report, 1940–1941 [1941?], p. 49, Columbia University Social Work Library. Needs: "The First Year," p. 3.

73. CSS, "Bulletin #36: Harlem Speaks Up," 1 April 1940, p. 11, Russell-Sage collection; Floyd Snelson, Federal Writers' Program, New York City, notes, November 1937, p. 4, WPA, Federal Writers' Program, "Negroes of New York," box 6; N.Y.C. Colored Mission, *Annual Report, 1925* (New York, 1925), p. 11; ibid., *1936* (New York, 1936), p. 13; ibid., *1937* (New York, 1937), p. 19; ibid., *1938* (New York, 1938), p. 19; Clayton Cook, Director, Counseling and Employment Service of the CAS, "A Recent and Brief Study of the Employment, Educational and Economic Conditions in Harlem," Memorandum to Walter White, NAACP, 1 May 1937, p. 4, NAACP papers, series C, box 311, Library of Congress Manuscript Collection; Phelps-Stokes Fund, "Minutes of Conference Between a Committee of the Trustees of the Phelps-Stokes Fund and Members and Officers of the Association to Promote Proper Housing for Girls, Inc.," 2 December 1943, pp. 6–7; APPHG papers, box 3, Schomburg Archives.

74. NYUL services: See, for example, Commission for the NYUL Study, pp. 28, 31, 48, 50, 71–72; NYUL, *Annual Report, 1934* (New York, 1934), pp. 5–17; ibid., *1940* (New York, 1940), pp. 2–3, both in NUL papers, series 13, box 19; Nancy Weiss, *National Urban League, 1910–1940* (New York, 1974), pp. 253, 255; James Hubert, Executive Director, NYUL, "Newsletters # 1 and 2," 1 July and 1 October 1939, NUL papers, series 5, box 10; NYUL, "Newsletter," 12 November 1940, p. 1, NUL papers, series 4, box 33; NYUL "Minutes, 17 December 1937"; NYUL, "Minutes, 22 November 1934," p. 2. Other black groups: see, for example, "Welfare and Public Relief," pp. 3, 4; Mayor's Committee on City Planning, "West Harlem Community Study," Pamphlet, 1937, p. 41, Municipal Reference and Resource Center; Katy Ferguson House, *Annual Report*, p. 1, of each year from 1934–38, and p. 2 of 1941 and 1942, Russell-Sage collection. In 1935, the Mayor's Committee on Conditions in Harlem conducted a survey of Harlem's institutions and which races they served.

	Both	*White*	*"Colored"*
Schools and libraries	33 public,		
	4 Catholic	11	
HRBs	11		
Social agencies	9	13	6
Hospitals, clinics	10	12	1
Playgrounds	5		1
Adult recreation	3	66	33
Political clubs	7	7	8
Municipal depts., branches	20		
Mutual welfare lodges	10	9	11

Mayor's Commission on Conditions in Harlem, "Institutions in Harlem," statistics, 1935, LaGuardia papers, box 755. Social agencies include nurseries, old age homes, and so on. Adult recreation includes billiard and pool halls, clubs, theaters and similar entertainments. Certainly there were more playgrounds than listed here. It is not clear, then, how inclusive the rest of the list is. Also see "Relief Bureaus in Harlem," *Dunbar News* 3 (9 March 1932): 7.

75. Myrtle Pollard, "Harlem As It Is" (B.B.A. thesis, City College of New York, 1936), pp. 276–77; "Welfare and Public Relief," p. 4; Utopia Children's House, "1937: A Report," Pamphlet [1938?], pp. 2–4, W. Adams papers, box 5, Schomburg Archives.

76. CAS, *85th Annual Report,* 1937 (New York, 1938), pp. 36–37; *83rd Annual Report,* 1935 (New York, 1936), p. 17; CAS, *Off Harlem's Streets* (New York, 1940), pp. 4, 6; CAS, *The Home Front: 88th Annual Report,* 1940 (New York, 1941), p. 21; *84th Annual Report,* 1936 (New York, 1937), p. 15.

77. "Incomes": CAS, *82nd Annual Report,* 1934 (New York, 1935), p. 18. "Realizing:" CAS, *Off Harlem's Streets,* p. 8.

78. All quotations: CAS, *84th Annual Report,* pp. 15–17. Also see Cook, p. 2.

79. "Ample proof": *Off Harlem's Streets,* p. 4. Foster placement and Valhalla: CAS, *80th Annual Report: Summer Work Number,* 1932 (New York, 1932), n.p.; CAS, *84th Annual Report,* 1936, p. 23; Andrew Billingsley and Jeanne Giovannoni, *Children of the Storm: Black Children and American Child Welfare* (New York, 1972), p. 113. Household service: "Harlem Festival," p. 14. Mayor's Committees: also donated to the Police Department's Juvenile Aid Bureau, Bellevue's special relief fund, the Italian Board of Guardians, and other, similar groups. William Cohen, Executive Vice-Chairman of Mayor's Committee on Welfare, to Mayor LaGuardia, 23 May 1938, p. 2, LaGuardia papers, box 98; Bureau of Municipal Investigation and Statistics, "Report on Examination of Accounts of Mayor's Special Committee for the Period from May 1, 1938, to January 21, 1940," pp. 3–8, LaGuardia papers, box 142. Walkill: CAS, *84th Annual Report,* 1936, p. 11. One of the few: CAS, *Off Harlem's Streets,* p. 8. In perhaps the most blatant example of racist generosity, the Cotton Club, which did not permit blacks to sit in its audience, distributed 3,000 Christmas food baskets in 1934 to Harlemites, filled with chicken, vegetables, fruit, bread, and sugar. Anderson, p. 243.

80. CAS, *79th Annual Report,* 1931 (New York, 1932), p. 17.

81. Valhalla: CAS, *79th Annual Report,* 1931, p. 18. Both quotations from Katherine Hildreth, Special Examiner, N.Y.C. Children's Court, "The Negro Problem as Reflected in the Functioning of the Domestic Relations Court of the City of New York," Report, 2 June 1934, p. 11, Department of Labor papers, Division of Negro Labor, USES Oxley box 1391. SPCC figures: ibid., p. 12. In 1937, the Child Welfare League estimated of 2,000 Protestant black children under care:

	In Institutions	In Foster Homes
COA	322	436
Edwin Gould Foundation*		500
CAS	65	124
N.Y. Children's Foster Home Service		200
Five Points House of Industry*		142
Nursery and Infants Hospital	?	?

*Would not allow blacks in its institutions. The Five Points House seems to be part of the Gould Foundation.

Catholics: The New York Foundling Hospital was Catholic, and had another 700 black children. St. Benedict's Home in Rye, New York, all black, took Protestant as well as Catholic children, as did Little Flower House in Brooklyn. Child Welfare League of America, p. 39. Blacks comprised 55 percent of the total dependent Protestant population: p. 38. By raising the age limits, the COA grew from 340 children in 1925 to 702 in 1937. COA, *90th Annual Report: 1925–26* (New York, 1926); COA, *102nd Annual Report: 1937–1938* (New York, 1938).

82. DPW, *Annual Report, 1936,* p. 30; ibid., *1937,* p. 22. COA: Child Welfare League, p. 43. Welfare Council: "Memorandum Suggested," pp. 1, 14, 15. Conditions for black dependent children in other cities were generally even worse. The Child Welfare League described facilities in Philadelphia as "appallingly insufficient." Child Welfare League, p. 140.

83. Welfare Council, "Memorandum Suggested," p. 16. The Exploratory Committee on Negro Welfare echoed the Welfare Council's plea: Exploratory Committee on Negro Welfare, "Report," January 1939, p. 3. Joint Committee on Negro Child Study in New York City, *A Study of Delinquent and Neglected Negro Children Before the New York City Children's Court, 1925* (New York, 1927), p. 29, note 48; COA, *"If... any child lacks": Annual Report, 1938–39* (New York 1939), p. 6; COA, *102nd Report, 1937–38,* p. 8.

84. TB: COA, *99th Annual Report, 1935* (New York, 1935), p. 6. While the average daily population in the institution or boarded out fluctuated a bit, it hovered around 700, limited by the institution's physical capacity. Children released: see *98th... 1934* (New York, 1934), pp. 7–8, 13; *99th... 1935,* pp. 7–8, 12, 14; *100th... 1936* (New York, 1936), pp. 6–10; *101st ... 1937,* pp. 5–6, 13, 15; *"If... any child lacks",* pp. 14, 15; *102nd Annual Report, 1937–1938,* p. 6; *104th ... 1940* (New York, 1940), pp. 5, 7; *"Tomorrow's Resources": Annual Report, 1940–41* (New York, 1941), pp. 5–10.

85. Agnes Inglis to Justine Wise Polier, Judge, Domestic Relations Court, "Memorandum," 10 November 1939, pp. 1–2, LaGuardia papers, box 142. Delinquents: Wiltwyck: p. 3. Opened by the New York Protestant Episcopal City Mission Society. The court concluded that much more money would be needed to create adequate facilities: ibid., pp. 3–4.

86. CAS, *The Home Front,* p. 17 (including quotation), p. 58; Billingsley and Giovannoni, p. 115 (State Charities Aid Association). Service Bureau: DPW, *Annual Report, 1936,* p. 30. It intended to incorporate itself into the Department of Welfare in a few years but that did not happen. The bureau remained part of the CAS and by 1943 had a black director, three black supervisors, and seven black caseworkers. Billingsley and Giovannoni, p. 114.

87. DPW, *Annual Report, 1938–1939,* pp. 187–88; DPW, *Annual Report, 1939–1940* (New York, 1940), p. 142. Rise: COA, *104th Report,* p. 5. In 1942 the Citywide Citizens' Committee prevailed upon the city to pass a law denying funding to any child care organization that did not accept black children. See Chapter 8.

Chapter 7

1. In five "typical" Harlem blocks, for example, the percentage of families on relief varied from 16 to 58. New York Housing Authority, Harlem Branch, "Harlem Family Income Survey," Report, May 1935, pp. 21, 23, 25, 27, 29, 31, U.S. Department of Labor papers, Division of Negro Labor, RG 183, USES box 1392, National Archives, Washington, D.C. Between 137th and 138th, Seventh and Lenox, 16 percent were on relief, and average annual family income was $1,059. Between 133rd and 134th streets, Seventh and Lenox, 42 percent were on relief, and average family income totaled $842.52. Mayor's Commission on Conditions in Harlem, "Negro in Harlem," Report, 1935, p. 59, Mayor LaGuardia papers, box 2550, Municipal Archives, New York City. Grocery credit: NAACP, "Food Costs More in

Harlem," Pamphlet [1942?], p. 19, Columbia University Social Work Library, New York City. Quotation: Vernal Williams, Testimony before Mayor's Commission on Conditions in Harlem, during testimony of the Rev. Mr. Garner, 22 May 1935, LaGuardia papers, new box 3770. Johnson: UNIA Central Division, Unemployment Unit, UNIA papers, boxes 6–7, Schomburg Archives, New York City.

2. Federal Writers' Program, New York City, "Housing of Negroes in New York," notes, n.d., p. 1, papers of the WPA, Federal Writers' Program, "Negroes of New York," box 4, Schomburg Archives. U.S. Department of Labor, Bureau of Labor Statistics, *Family Income and Expenditure in New York City, 1935–1936,* vol. 1: *Family Income* (Washington, D.C., 1941), pp. 106, 108–9, 170, 172–73. This study documents the proportion of families with lodgers by race, family type, and income level. Not all lodgers lived with the family for an entire year, so it is impossible to calculate what a typical lodger paid for rent. These rents made up 6 percent of the black non-relief family's total income, 3 percent of the black relief family's. For all white families, lodger rents made up less than 1 percent of total income. BLS survey: see appendix. Raw data in Bureau of Labor Statistics papers, RG 257, BLS #807, boxes 31–51, National Archives.

3. BLS data. Other supplementary earnings (investments, insurance, gifts, interest, pensions, and so on, excluding lodgers): 15 percent of non-relief black families and 26 percent of white reported such supplements. In these black families, supplements provided 2.1 percent of the total income. In these white families: 5.7 percent. *Family Income,* pp. 98–99, 106, 129, 161–62, 193.

4. Richard Sterner, *The Negro's Share* (Westport, Conn., 1943), p. 393 (over $3,000 too few black cases):

Percent of Families That Contributed
to the Support of Relatives

Income Level	Black Families	White Families
$500–$999	8	5
$1,000–$1,499	34	8
$1,500–$1,999	30	12
$2,000–$2,999	42	24

These are non-relief families. Examples of borrowing and exchange: UNIA files. Philadelphia and Chicago: Lois Helmbold, "Making Choices, Making Do: Black and White Working Class Women's Lives and Work During the New Deal" (Ph.D. diss., Stanford University, 1983), p. 87.

5. Louise Meriwether, *Daddy Was a Number Runner* (New York, 1986), pp. 17–18. Loften Mitchell, "Harlem Reconsidered," *Freedomways* 4 (Fall 1964): 469. Myrtle Pollard, "Harlem As It Is" (B.B.A. thesis, City College of New York, 1936), p. 9.

6. Welfare Council study: Burge, p. 50, and Appendix B. Mayor's Commission on Conditions in Harlem, "Negro Arrests in Police Precincts # 23, 24, 26, 30, 32, 34 in Harlem Area, 1930–First 6 Months of 1935," statistics, 1935, LaGuardia papers, box 755; Holmes: UNIA papers, box 13. Francie: Meriwether, p. 46.

7. U.S. Department of Labor, Bureau of Labor Statistics, *Money Disbursements of Wage Earners and Clerical Workers in the North Atlantic Region, 1934–1936,* vol. 1: *New York City* (Washington, D.C., 1939), pp. 101–7. Per person: U.S. Department of Labor, Bureau of Labor Statistics, *Family Income and Expenditure in New York City, 1935–36,* vol. 2: *Family Expenditure* (Washington, D.C., 1939), pp. 114, 116, 155–57. "White" is only native-born.

In the BLS sample, total income determined spending to a greater extent than did family size, although both were significant. See appendix for more detailed figures.

8. BLS, *Money Disbursements,* pp. 101–7. Moving: UNIA papers, boxes 6–7. Commission study: Mayor's Commission, "The Negro in Harlem," pp. 59–60: 374 families in the block bounded by 137th and 138th Streets, Seventh and Lenox Avenues, and 301 families living between 133rd and 134th Streets, Seventh and Lenox Avenues.

9. Adam Clayton Powell, Jr., *Adam by Adam* (New York, 1971), p. 62. Reverend Garner, Testimony; Roi Ottley, *New World A-Coming* (Boston, 1943), p. 157. U.S. Department of Labor, Bureau of Labor Statistics, "Retail Prices of Food, July 2, 1935," Press release, July 1935, National Negro Congress papers, box 1, Schomburg Archives; U.S. Department of Labor, Bureau of Labor Statistics, *Changes in Cost of Living: November 1935* (Washington, D.C., 1935), p. 8, NNC papers, box 1. BLS Harlem survey expenditures: see appendix.

10. Interestingly, a slightly higher proportion of blacks reported having medical or accident insurance at each income level, and paid higher premiums. Sterner, pp. 138, 148, 391; U.S. Department of Labor, Bureau of Labor Statistics, "Expenditures of Negro Families in New York City," by Faith Williams, *Labor Information Bulletin* 5 (August 1938): 9. Clinics, dentists: Sterner, p. 389; Burge, pp. 39–40. Sterner found white medical costs exceded black for all income levels except $500 to $999, in which black medical costs just topped white. Blacks spent between 2.5 percent and 3.6 percent of their income on medical expenses, and whites between 4.1 percent and 4.6 percent. Sterner, p. 148. For the total sample, food costs were affected directly by both family size and income. See appendix. Poorest blacks: those earning less than $1,860, well under half the highest black income of $4,376. This group includes all the foreign-born in the sample, and 42 American-born. The average income for the poor native-born group was $1,309; for the foreign-born, $1,280; for whole sample, $1,633.

11. BLS data.

12. Deficits: 75.3 percent. Dividing families into those that saved and those that did not, the average savings per family that saved was $41, while the average deficit among debtor families was $54. These deficits do not include mortgages or similar sorts of debts, but rather small-scale borrowing or buying items on credit. By race: BLS, *Money Disbursements,* pp. 103, 105. Also see Sterner, p. 92, who found at every income level fewer blacks in debt than whites, and their average debts lower. At income levels where the white family typically still had debts, the average black family had savings, and the average savings were higher than white savings at each income level. Gunnar Myrdal, *An American Dilemma: The Negro Problem and American Democracy* (New York, 1944; reprint ed., New York, 1962), pp. 368, 370. Pollard, p. 5.

13. UNIA files. The UNIA did not report on the disposition of this case.

14. City Affairs Committee: "1,500,000 in NYC Live in Tenements," *Hunger Fighter,* March 1933, p. 3, International Labor Defense papers, box 2, Schomburg Archives. Neighborhood Health Committee: Godias Drolet and Marguerite Potter, New York City Health Department, and the Committee on Neighborhood Health Development, *Health Center Districts: Statistical Reference Data, 1929–1933* (New York, 1935), pp. 95, 107; Harry Shulman, *The Slums of New York* (New York, 1938), pp. 63–64. The COS found its clients paid an average of $23.75 a month for rent in 1931, down from $25.27 in 1929, but rents were "highest in uptown New York—north of 125th Street." COS, *Annual Report, 1931–32* (New York, 1933), p. 13. Sydney Axelrad, League of Mothers' Clubs, "Tenements and Tenants," Report, 1933, Municipal Reference and Resource Center, New York City. Porters: Jervis Anderson, *This Was Harlem: A Cultural Portrait, 1900–1950* (New York, 1982), pp. 244–45.

15. Larry Greene, "Harlem in the Great Depression, 1928–1936" (Ph.D. dissertation, Columbia University, 1979), pp. 249; Mark Naison, *Communists in Harlem During the Depression* (Urbana, Ill., 1983), p. 41.

16. Anson Phelps-Stokes, "Informal Memorandum *re* Association to Promote Proper Housing for Girls," 1 November 1943, pp. 1–4, Phelps-Stokes papers, Association to Promote Proper Housing for Girls, box 3, Schomburg Archives; Association to Promote Proper Housing for Girls, "History of the APPHG," Report [1941?] p. 2, Phelps-Stokes papers, APPHG box 1; APPHG, "Club Caroline," Report, 1943, pp. 1–2, Phelps-Stokes papers, "Jones-Tobias," box 33; Anson Phelps-Stokes, *Negro Status and Race Relations in the United States, 1911–1946* (New York, 1948), p. 28. Quotation: APPHG, *Annual Report, January 1, 1931–January 1, 1932* (New York, 1932), p. 3, Phelps-Stokes papers, APPHG box 1.

17. Frazier, p. 251; Lilian Brandt, *An Impressionistic View of the Winter of 1930–31* (New York, 1932), p. 9. Association to Promote Proper Housing for Girls, Minutes of Annual Meeting, 15 April 1930, p. 2, Phelps-Stokes papers, box 3; Shulman, p. 64.

18. New York City Housing Authority, "Report of the New York City Housing Authority," 25 January 1937, pp. 51, 67, 68, LaGuardia papers, box 80. Temporary Commission: New York State Temporary Commission on the Condition of the Urban Colored Population, *Second Report,* Legislative Document #69 (Albany, 1939), pp. 78–79; New York State Temporary Commission on the Condition of the Urban Colored Population, *Report,* Legislative Document #63 (Albany, 1938), p. 48. Jecter: UNIA files. "Living quarters" quotation: BLS, "Expenditures of Negro Families," p. 9.

19. N.Y.S. Temporary Commission, *Report,* p. 48; Ellen Tarry, Federal Writers' Program, New York City, notes, 23 February 1938, p. 12, WPA, Federal Writers' Program, "Negroes of New York," box 4. Health Dept.: Federal Writers' Program, New York City, "Depression and New York City Negroes," n.d., pp. 6–7, WPA, Federal Writers' Program, "Negroes of New York," box 9. NAACP: Clayton Cook, Director, Counseling and Employment Service of the CAS, "A Recent and Brief Study of the Employment, Educational and Economic Conditions in Harlem," Memorandum to Walter White, NAACP, 1 May 1937, p. 4, NAACP papers, series C, box 311, Library of Congress Manuscript Collection, Washington, D.C. ERB, "Preliminary Report to the Board of Estimate and Apportionment on Relief Population Housing Conditions," 23 June 1937, pp. 2–3, and summary table, Municipal Reference and Resource Center. The study surveyed 54 percent of the caseload of 28 May 1937.

20. Mayor's Commission, "The Negro in Harlem," p. 60; New York City Housing Authority, "Harlem Family Income Survey," p. 3. Manager: James Dickson to Eunice Carter, n.d., LaGuardia papers, new box 3529. Citizens' Committee: Algernon Black, "The Citizens' Committee on Harlem: Beginnings," 4 September 1974, p. 16, Algernon Black papers, Columbia University Rare Book and Manuscript Library. Findings: May 1941. Mayor's Commission: Federal Writers' Program, New York City, "Depression," notes, n.d., pp. 4–5, WPA, Federal Writers' Program, "Negroes of New York," box 4.

21. "Good": 34 percent of Harlem and 30 percent of Manhattan apartments; "Fair": 49 and 48 percent respectively; "Poor": 18 and 22 percent. Note that more in Harlem received a "good" rating than the 25 percent in 1927. It is not clear why, as housing certainly deteriorated in this period. Figures also available for one- and two-family houses and rooming houses. This study was based on relief families only. Perhaps the high "good" rating reflects the fact that more black than white families who had skills or white-collar jobs had lost their jobs and turned to relief. ERB, "Preliminary Report," summary table. WPA study: N.Y.C. WPA and N.Y.C. Housing Authority, *Housing in New York City* (New York, 1939), Table VIII, "Manhattan Summary" and "Areas 8 and 9" (Harlem).

22. Notes for article to be written by Mayor LaGuardia, 5 October 1944, LaGuardia papers, box 2550. (This article, never published, was a response to an article by Walter Davenport, "Harlem . . . Dense and Dangerous," *Collier's* (September 1944): 11–13, 92.) WPA Federal Writers' Project, *New York City Guide* (New York, 1939), p. 392; Peter Marcuse, "The Beginnings of Public Housing in New York," *Journal of Urban History* 12 (August 1986): 372, 375.

23. Federal Writers' Program, "Housing of Negroes in New York," p. 7; Langdon Post, Testimony before Mayor's Commission on Conditions in Harlem, 6 April 1935, LaGuardia papers, new box 3770; "Harlem Block of 3,871 City's Most Crowded," *Herald Tribune,* 16 September 1935, pp. 1, 3; Black, p. 16; Housing Authority, "Report," p. 50. Sancton in Ottley, p. 150.

24. Langdon Post, Chairman, Housing Authority, to Mayor LaGuardia, 30 April 1936, LaGuardia papers, box 2550. Slum Clearance: quoted from NAACP press release [April 1934?], p. 1, NAACP papers, series C, box 307.

25. Housing Authority, "Harlem Family Income Survey," p. 3; Mayor's Committee on City Planning, *West Harlem Community Study* (New York, 1937), p. 28.

26. Department of Health, *Quarterly Bulletin #1, 1935* (New York, 1935), p. 17, Public Health Library, New York City. Abortions: Department of Health, *Annual Report, 1937* (New York, 1937), Table XXIX. Malnutrition: Abby Leland, Principal of P.S. 157 to Mayor LaGuardia, 25 April 1934, p. 1, LaGuardia papers, box 724. The 1936 study: Guichard Parris and Lester Brooks, *Blacks in the City: A History of the Urban League* (Boston, 1971), p. 239. City-wide figures: *Quarterly Bulletin,* p. 15; Mayor's Committee on Unemployment Relief, *Report of Mayor LaGuardia's Committee on Unemployment Relief* (New York, 1935), p. 14, Columbia University Social Work Library.

27. The rates were significantly higher than for rural areas. Clinics: Department of Health, *Annual Report, 1935* (New York, 1935); WPA, *New York City Guide,* p. 263. Use: Sterner, p. 389. For example, at $500 to $999, 34 percent of blacks and 12 percent of whites attended a clinic. At $2,000 to $2,999, 8 percent of blacks and 7 percent of whites did. Atlanta: 27.8 percent blacks and 10.5 percent whites reported free-clinic use. Tuberculosis: Health Department and Neighborhood Health Development, "Health Center Districts, New York Handbook of Statistical Reference Data: Ten Year Period, 1931–1940," 1944, p. 63, Public Health Library. Central Harlem had one municipal hospital, three proprietary hospitals (charging fees), and three voluntary hospitals, some of which also contained public clinics. In the larger Harlem area there were 17 voluntary hospitals, 8 proprietary, one municipal, one state institution. Mayor's Commission, "Negro in Harlem," p. 82. Narrowing the gap: Drolet and Potter, pp. 92–94.

28. The tuberculosis figures are 1929–1933 and 1936–1940 averages. The earlier Manhattan rate is for pulmonary tuberculosis, the rest for all forms. Second set of pneumonia rates are 1936–1940 averages. The homicide rate is for blacks and whites city-wide and the later figures are averages of male and female rates, given separately. Department of Health, "Statistics on Infant and Maternal Mortality in New York City by Health District and Health Area, 1930–38," 1939, Table 17, Public Health Library; Department of Health, *Annual Report, 1937,* Tables XII, XXXIII, LXV; Department of Health, *Quarterly Bulletin #4, 1937* (New York, 1937), p. 83; "Health Center Districts," pp. 25, 30, 35, 44, 47, 48. Winfred Nathan, *Health Conditions in North Harlem, 1923–1927,* National Tuberculosis Association Social Research Series #2 (New York, 1932), p. 27. As in the 1920s, Harlem's black death rates surpassed white in infant mortality, stillbirths, and maternal mortality. Overall death rates of blacks and whites in Harlem were virtually identical, due to the older average age of white Harlemites. "Health Center Districts," pp. 56–57. Whites had higher death rates only for cancer, heart disease, and pneumonia, diseases striking the elderly more often. Ibid., Tables XII, XVIII.

29. Infant mortality dropped to 56 for Harlem, 42 for Manhattan, although the rate of stillbirths rose for both populations. Department of Health, *Annual Report, 1940* (New York, 1940). Relief: Frazier found a positive correlation between what he called the dependency rate and the death rate, but a negative correlation between dependency and infant mortality. E. Franklin Frazier, "Some Effects of the Depression on the Negroes in Northern Cities,"

Science and Society 2 (Fall, 1938): 495. Correlations: .83 for death rate, − .60 for infant mortality.

30. Citywide Citizens' Committee on Harlem, "The Story of the Citywide Citizens' Committee on Harlem" [1943?], p. 10, Schomburg Archives.

31. Mrs. Aspinall, Mrs. William Burroughs, Ira Kemp, Testimony before Mayor's Commission on Conditions in Harlem, 9–10 April 1935, LaGuardia papers, new box 3770. Commission quotation in "Petition to the Board of Education," 1936, NAACP papers, series C, box 292.

32. Union: Charles Hendley to NAACP, 31 January 1936, p. 1, and broadside, 9 January 1936, NAACP papers, series C, box 292. "Petition," *New York Telegram,* 18 February 1936, covered this petition drive. Roscoe Conkling Bruce of the Dunbar Apartments, to Walter White, NAACP, 25 January 1936, included this one-page "Petition to the Board of Education of the City of New York," NAACP papers, series C, box 292. COA: *101st Report, 1936–37* (New York, 1937), p. 17. Unfortunately comparable statistics from earlier years are not available, nor are the geographic origins of these children. IQ tests unreliable: see, for example, Stephen Jay Gould, *The Mismeasure of Man* (New York, 1981); R.C. Lewonton, Steven Rose, Leon Kamin, *Not in Our Genes: Biology, Ideology, and Human Nature* (New York, 1984).

33. Permanent Committee for Better Schools in Harlem, Meeting announcement, 5 June 1937, NAACP papers, series C, box 292; Charlotte Morgan, "Finding a Way Out: Adult Education in Harlem During the Great Depression," *Afro-Americans in New York Life and History* 8 (January 1984): 18; Naison, *Communists,* p. 214.

34. Citywide Citizens' Committee on Harlem, "Report of the Subcommittee on Education and Recreation," 1942, pp. 9, 11, 12, Municipal Reference and Resource Center. Staying in school: in Manhattan, 41 percent of whites over age 25 had more than an eighth grade education, compared with 32 percent of blacks. For those aged 14 to 24, 39 percent of black children and 40 percent of white were still in school. U.S. Department of Commerce, Bureau of the Census, *Sixteenth Census of the United States, 1940, Population,* vol. 2, part 5 (Washington, D.C., 1943), pp. 158, 159. Considering those over 16, the legal minimum age to leave school, the same proportion of 16–24-year-olds in Central Harlem, both relief and non-relief, attended school as did Manhattan adolescents as a whole in 1935 (20 percent): Nettie McGill and Ellen Matthews, *The Youth of New York* (New York, 1940), pp. 55, 65.

35. "Harlem's Block of 3,871," p. 3; Walter White to Mayor LaGuardia, 3 October 1936, pp. 2–3, NAACP papers, series C, box 311.

36. Actually, "special care" had the second highest number of arrests. This undefined term may refer to material witnesses, abandoned or otherwise needy children, or perhaps include neglected children. Blacks comprised between 8 and 12 percent of the total delinquent population, far higher than their proportion in the youth population (at least until 1934 when the courts stopped providing figures by race). For white boys also, "stealing," "burglary," and similar crimes were the commonest charges. For girls of both races, the commonest charges fell under "misconduct: home." For raw numbers, see: Mayor's Commission on Conditions in Harlem, "Juvenile Arrests in Police Precincts # 23, 24, 25, 28, 30, 32, 34 in Harlem Area, 1930–1934," LaGuardia papers, box 755; Mayor's Committee on Juvenile Delinquency, "First Interim Report: Analysis of the Statistics of the Children's Court Division of the Domestic Relations Court of the City of New York," 8 July 1943, Chart B and Appendix Table IV, Municipal Reference and Resource Center. Numbers down between 1930 and 1935: Mayor's Commission on Conditions in Harlem, "Harlem Riot Report," draft, n.d., p. 15, LaGuardia papers, new box 3529; U.S. Department of Labor, Children's Bureau Publication #280, *Children in the Courts* (Washington, D.C., 1942), p. 7. In general the decline was true for other cities as well. Nationwide, blacks constituted 20 percent of the total delinquent population, ibid., p. 9.

37. Lucy and Wooley: Agnes Sullivan, Welfare Council, "An Inquiry into the Provisions for Care of Negro Boys Under 12 Years of Age and Judged Delinquent by the Children's Court," Report, June 1935, pp. 28, 32, Columbia University Social Work Library. 1931 study: James Ford, *Slums and Housing: With Specific Reference to New York City,* 2 vols. (Cambridge, 1936), I:408–9, 418. Over half of the 2,966 prostitutes arrested in 1940 who claimed Manhattan residence were black. Marguerite Marsh, Welfare Council, "Prostitutes in New York City: Their Apprehension, Trial, and Treatment, July 1939–June 1940," Report, June 1941, Public Health Library, p. 104: 1,705 white, 1,965 black. Of the total, 3,217 were arrested in the four Health Districts around Central Harlem: ibid., pp. 105–6. And more of the black prostitutes were convicted: ibid., p. 47. While sentencing did not differ substantially by race for those convicted for the first time, of those arraigned several times, blacks received jail terms more often and suspended sentences less often than white prostitutes did: ibid., p. 114. (Black prostitutes also charged clients less: 97 percent of all black prostitutes charged less than $3, compared with 57 percent of whites: ibid., p. 156.) Arrests in Harlem: data from Mayor's Commission on Conditions in Harlem, "Negro Arrests."

38. Ferdinand Morton, "Memorandum *re* Conditions in Harlem," 25 April 1932, pp. 2–3; Assistant Commissioner of Correction Fishman to Walter White, Memorandum, 9 May 1932, pp. 1–5, NAACP papers, series C, box 305. Morton also mentioned black-owned Small's Paradise in his list of prostitution centers, but this was later crossed out with the words "better not mention Smalls at all . . . prostitution there is at a minimum," p. 2.

39. Mayor's Commission, "Harlem Riot Report," pp. 15–16; Mayor's Commission on Conditions in Harlem, "Complaints Against Police Department," 1935, p. 3, LaGuardia papers, box 755. Telegram, White to LaGuardia and Valentine, 27 July 1939; Valentine to LaGuardia, 5 October 1939, LaGuardia papers, new box 3666.

40. Powell Jr. to Arthur Garfield Hayes, 28 March 1935; Police Department, Aiken arrest transcript (includes Aiken's statement, 9 April 1935; police report, 13 March 1935; witness's testimony: Buck Brown, Testimony before Mayor's Commission on Conditions in Harlem, 20 April 1935; and Dr. Epstein's report, 9 April 1935); Valentine to LaGuardia, 30 April 1935, all in LaGuardia papers, new box 3666. Brown had never met Aiken before. Other witnesses reportedly saw nothing.

41. Morton, pp. 1–2.

42. Garner, Testimony. Societies: see, for example, any issue of the *American and West Indian News* or *Fraternal Echo,* both in Black Newspapers collection, Schomburg Archives; Mayor's Commission on Conditions in Harlem, "Institutions in Harlem," statistics, 1935, LaGuardia papers, box 755; Clyde Kiser, *From Sea Island to City* (New York, 1932; reprint ed., New York, 1969), p. 212. Pollard, pp. 79, 81–84, 120–47, also provides a partial list. These lists contradict Ivan Light's findings in *Ethnic Enterprise in America: Business and Welfare Among Chinese, Japanese and Blacks* (Berkeley, 1972). He argues native-born blacks only rarely formed mutual aid societies.

43. Richard Wright, *Twelve Million Black Voices* (New York, 1941; reprint ed., New York, 1969), p. 130; Mitchell, p. 469.

44. Female-headed figures for U.S. almost identical. But total "broken" black families in 1930 (one parent of either sex) were 35 percent of all black families, 41 percent of all black relief families in 1933 (U.S.). Federal Writers' Program, "Depression and New York City Negroes," p. 17; Cook, pp. 5, 6; Frazier, "Some Effects," p. 494; Richard Sterner, "Standard of Living of the Negro," Research memorandum, 1940, p. 378, Carnegie-Myrdal study, Sterner, vol. 2, Schomburg Archives; Alfred Smith, FERA, "Reasons for the Disproportionate Number of Negroes on the Relief Rolls," Report, April 1935, p. 20, NNC papers, box 2. The 675 families: Mayor's Commission on Conditions in Harlem, "Negro in Harlem," p. 59. The 374 families on one block earned an average of $1,059; the 301 on the other, $843. One-third female-headed families in each. Delinquency: although for both boys and girls, those

arrested for delinquency had both parents at home less often than did the general youth population, the difference was far more pronounced for female delinquents than for male. Mayor's Commission on Conditions in Harlem, "Harlem Study," notes [1935], LaGuardia papers, new box 2550; Domestic Court, *Annual Report, 1935* (New York, 1936), p. 65; ibid., *1936* (New York, 1937), p. 107; ibid., *1937* (New York, 1938), p. 99; ibid., *1940* (New York, 1941), p. 110. As for illegitimacy, not only are all available figures suspect, the marital status of the parents is irrelevant to the question of the family's economic viability. Presence or absence of a parent, married or not, is the more important issue.

45. N.Y.S. Temporary Commission, *Second Report*, p. 8.

Chapter 8

1. Robert Weaver, *The Negro Ghetto* (New York, 1948), p. 78.

2. Henry Alsberg, "Relief Needs in New York City Still Are Serious . . . Employment on Defense Projects Has Helped Little," *PM*, 19 May 1941 (clipping), Mayor LaGuardia papers, box 173, Municipal Archives, New York City. Relief: (September 1940) New York State Department of Social Welfare, *Democracy Cares: The Story Behind Public Assistance in New York State* (Albany, 1941), pp. 74, 81, 88, in *New York State Department of Social Services Publications*, vol. 8, Columbia University Social Work Library. Forty-four percent of relief families had one employable member, 10 percent had two, 3 percent had three or more. Of the employables, 25 percent unskilled, 23 percent service, 15 percent clerical, 14 percent semi-skilled, 12 percent skilled, 4 percent managerial and professional, 7 percent not reported: ibid., pp. 82, 84. Alsberg claims 460,000 of the city unemployed could work as of 19 May 1941. Cases closed: *Democracy Cares*, p. 85: 79,000 of 228,000. U.S.: Weaver, p. 77. Military contracts: *Democracy Cares*, p. 46. By contrast, Baltimore employment rates rose 78 percent between 1940 and 1942. Edward Schwartz, Eloise Sherman, "Community Health and Welfare Expenditures in Wartime," U.S. Department of Labor, Children's Bureau Publication #302, 1944, p. 1, Columbia University Social Work Library, New York City. Also see Dominic Capeci, Jr., *The Harlem Riot of 1943* (Philadelphia, 1977), pp. 62–63. City unemployed in July of 1942: 368,000—50,000 more than in July of 1939. In 1941, 375,000 unemployed. In U.S., 1941, 9.9 percent mean unemployment. Robert McElvaine, *The Great Depression* (New York, 1984), p. 320.

3. "What About Harlem?" (editorial), *Nation* 154 (6 June 1942): 645; Capeci, pp. 58, 62. The native-born white proportion on the rolls dropped from 47 to 43 percent between 1940 and 1942, while the native-born black group rose from 14 to 17 percent. *Democracy Cares*, pp. 73, 88–89. In 1941, 238,454 received some sort of non-work public relief: *Democracy Cares*, p. 86. CSS: James Brown, Community Service Society Institute of Welfare Research, *Analysis of Family Service Statistics, 1939–1942* (New York, 1944), pp. 4, 7, 31, 33, Russell-Sage collection, City College of New York.

4. New York City Department of Health and Neighborhood Health Development, "Health Center Districts, New York Handbook of Statistical Reference Data: Ten Year Period, 1931–1940," 1944, pp. 70–71, Public Health Library, New York City; *Democracy Cares*, p. 86. For New York as a whole, 18 percent had no private sector employment. Barbara Blumberg, *The New Deal and the Unemployed: The View from New York City* (Lewisburg, Pa., 1979), pp. 268, 277. Citywide Citizens' Committee on Harlem, "Report of the Subcommittee on Employment," 1942, p. 4, Manuscript Reference and Resource Center, New York City: in 1942, 26 percent of the WPA was black. Nationally, blacks made up 16 percent of the WPA in 1941. Florence Murray, ed., *The Negro Handbook* (New York, 1942), p. 161.

5. William Hodson, Commissioner, Department of Welfare, "Relief, Public Assistance

and Social Insurance: Retrospect and Prospect," 12 January 1943 [speech?], pp. 3–4, Russell-Sage collection, City College of New York.

6. National Urban League, "Eleventh Vocational Opportunity Campaign," Radio broadcast, 18 March 1943, for WNYC Radio, p. 1, Radio transcripts, box 2, Schomburg Archives, New York City. The NUL began VO campaigns in the Depression, as it explained, to find jobs for blacks on all levels, encourage unions and employers to hire and accept blacks, and encourage blacks to obtain training in new areas. "Ninth Vocational Opportunity Campaign," 18 March 1941, for WEVD, p. 1, Radio transcripts, box 2.

7. Citywide Citizens' Committee on Harlem, "Preliminary Report of the Subcommittee on Employment [1942], p. 3, Schomburg Archives; Citizens' Committee, "Report of the Subcommittee on Employment," pp. 2–3, black placements: 83 percent female, in temporary and domestic jobs. "What About Harlem?" p. 645. NUL, "Ninth VOC," 19 March 1941, pp. 4–5. Delany: NUL, "Ninth Vocational Opportunity Campaign," Radio broadcast, 19 March 1941, for WNYC, p. 3, Radio transcripts, box 2.

8. Training programs: Committee on Fair Employment Practice, *First Report, July 1943–December 1944* (Washington, D.C., 1945), p. 140. Schools can't place black graduates: NUL, "Ninth VOC," 19 March 1941, p. 2; Committee on Fair Employment Practice, p. 90; NUL, "Eleventh VOC," p. 4. Bureau of Employment Security: Roi Ottley, *New World A-Coming* (Boston, 1943), p. 289; Committee on Fair Employment Practice, p. 89. Collier: NUL, "Ninth VOC," 18 March 1941, p. 2. Jobs: Ottley, p. 289. *Nation:* "What About Harlem?" p. 645.

9. John Johnson, *Harlem, the War and Other Addresses* (New York, 1942), pp. 18, 19, 22–23. Sermon, 16 November 1941.

10. Weaver quoted in Ottley, p. 289. Since no numbers of trade unionists in Harlem exist, one can only speculate on comparative percentages. Approximately 40,000 Harlemites belonged to unions by the late 1930s. Given an employed black labor force of just under 200,000, it appears there were more unionists there by the early 1940s. New York Urban League, "Newsletter," 12 November 1940, p. 15, National Urban League papers, series 4, box 33, Library of Congress Manuscript Collection, Washington, D.C.; Guichard Parris and Lester Brooks, *Blacks in the City: A History of the Urban League* (Boston, 1971), pp. 286–87. In 1943, five AFL unions excluded blacks tacitly, and seven segregated blacks. Two non-AFL unions segregated them. Herbert Northrup, "Organized Labor and the Negro," in Bernard Sternsher, ed., *The Negro in Depression and War: Prelude to Revolution, 1930–1945* (Chicago, 1969), pp. 129–30. Black members: *Negro Year Book, 1941–46* (Tuskeegee, 1947), p. 146. Harlem unionists: John Morsell, "The Political Behavior of Negroes in New York City" (Ph.D. dissertation, Columbia University, 1950), p. 141.

11. According to Gary Hunter, in 1932 Amos Mosley of Virginia State College had suggested a march on Washington to demand equal rights for blacks, but his call was rejected as too militant. Gary Hunter, "'Don't Buy from Where You Can't Work': Black Urban Boycott Movements During the Depression, 1929–1941" (Ph.D. dissertation, University of Michigan, 1977), p. 292. MOWM: See, for example, Harvard Sitkoff, *A New Deal for Blacks* (New York, 1978), pp. 314–21; Neil Hickey and Ed Edwin, *Adam Clayton Powell and the Politics of Race* (New York, 1965), pp. 63–65; Parris and Brooks, pp. 290–91; Jervis Anderson, *A. Philip Randolph* (New York, 1973; reprint ed., Berkeley, 1986), pp. 248–61.

12. Bureau of Labor Statistics, *War and Post-War Trends in Employment of Negroes,* Serial #R1723, January 1945, pp. 2, 3, National Negro Congress papers, box 94, Schomburg Archives. Black women declined as a proportion of women workers, but this was because white women joined the work force in huge numbers while large numbers of black women had already been working.

13. Committee on Fair Employment Practice, p. 89; Charles Lawrence, "Negro Organi-

zations in Crisis: Depression, New Deal, World War II" (Ph.D. dissertation, Columbia University, 1952), p. 361a. Trainees: Committee on FEP, p. 140. NYA: Citywide Citizens' Committee, "Report ... on Employment," p. 9. NYSES: Olivia Frost, "An Analysis of the Characteristics of the Population in Central Harlem," Report of the Urban League of Greater New York, August 1946, p. 34, Microfilm 312-U, Schomburg Archives. Weaver, p. 78, for skilled and semi-skilled.

14. First year: Ottley, p. 302. N.Y.C.: Committee on Fair Employment Practice, pp. 31, 37, 43, 118. Black women were 14 percent of all working women. Sixty-eight percent of them worked in service.

15. Ottley, pp. 232–33; Hickey and Edwin, pp. 75, 83; Adam Clayton Powell, Sr., "Riots and Ruins," Manuscript, n.d. [preface dated 1945], pp, 149, 152, Typescript collection, box 33, Schomburg Archives; Capeci, pp. 11–13, 16.

16. See, for example, Sitkoff, pp. 298–99. Governor's Committee began in March of 1941. Frieda Miller, Chairman, New York State Council of National Defense, Committee on Discrimination in Employment, to Cecelia Saunders, Executive Secretary of West 137th Street Branch, YWCA, 27 July 1941, Cecelia Saunders (Small collections), Schomburg Archives; "Bias Seen Barring Many from Committee on Discrimination in Jobs," New York Times, 17 May 1941, p. 9. Channing Tobias and Randolph served on it.

17. Mabel Staupers, "The Negro Nurse," Opportunity 20 (November 1942): 332, 333; NYUL, "Steadily Forward: Annual Report, 1943," 1943, pp. 8, 11, NUL papers, series 13, box 19; Capeci, p. 60. For more on black nurses, see Darlene Clark Hine, Black Women in White (Bloomington, Ind., 1989).

18. Joshua Freeman, In Transit (New York, 1988), pp. 255–56. This is the best source on the TWU. Also: Miriam Carpenter II, "Some Aspects of the Depression Upon Negroes" (M.A. thesis, Columbia University, 1937), p. 50; Hickey and Edwin, pp. 61–62; Adam Clayton Powell, Jr., Marching Blacks: An Interpretive History of the Rise of the Black Common Man (New York, 1945), pp. 99, 102; August Meier and Elliott Rudwick, "Communist Unions and the Black Community: The Case of the Transport Workers Union, 1934–1944," Labor History 23 (Spring 1982): 166–81.

19. Citywide Citizens' Committee on Harlem, "The Story of the Citywide Citizens' Committee on Harlem" [1943?], pp. 3–4, 24, Schomburg Archives; Algernon Black, "The Citywide Citizens' Committee on Harlem: Beginnings," 4 September 1974, pp. 1–3, 10, 13–16, Algernon Black papers, box 7, Columbia University Rare Book and Manuscript Library; Powell, "Riots and Ruins," p. 153. Meeting held 12 November. Over 200 blacks and whites attended. For more on their activities, see also "Harlem Problems Held One of Jobs," New York Times, 27 May 1942, p. 24; "Practical Action on Harlem Urged," New York Times, 26 May 1942, p. 23; "Harlem Week" (editorial), New York Times, 26 May 1942, p. 20. State agency: "Anti-Bias Bill Is Passed, 109–32, by Assembly Without Amendment," New York Times, 1 March 1945, pp. 1, 16; "Anti-Racial Bill Passed by Senate and Sent to Dewey," New York Times, 6 March 1945, p. 1; "Summary of Ives Bill As Passed" (includes quotation), New York Times, 6 March 1945, p. 17; "Anti-Racial Bill Signed by Dewey," New York Times, 13 March 1945, p. 38; "Anti-Bias Agency Begins Job Monday," New York Times, 29 June 1945, p. 17.

20. NUL, "Number Please? Employment of Negro Workers in the Telephone Industry in 44 Cities," Report, January 1946, p. 5, Columbia University Social Work Library. For more information see Venus Green, "The Impact of Technology upon Women's Work in the Telephone Industry, 1880–1980" (Ph.D. dissertation, Columbia University, 1990).

21. (Note there were fewer agencies than during the Depression.) John Hill, Presiding Justice, Domestic Relations Court, "Memorandum in re: Institutional Facilities for the Placement of Delinquent Children," 26 June 1942, p. 5, LaGuardia papers, box 2585. Several

other institutions placed children in foster care. At start of 1941, 2,142 black children "under care." For numbers at each institution, see Special Committee of the Section on Care of Dependent Children, Welfare Council, "The Adequacy of Foster Care for NYC's Dependent and Neglected Negro Protestant Children," Report, July 1941, p. 5, in *New York City Welfare Council Publications,* vol. 6, Columbia University Social Work Library. CAS: Child Welfare League of America, *Child Care Facilities for Dependent and Neglected Negro Children in Three Cities: New York City, Philadelphia, Cleveland* (New York, 1945), p. 68. Amendment: Department of Welfare, "Report on the Enforcement of the Race Discrimination Amendment," 14 October 1942, cover letter, Columbia University Social Work Library; Ottley, p. 163; Mayor's Committee on Juvenile Delinquency, "Report in Four Parts," 5 June 1944 (this from 1 October 1942, "Race Discrimination Amendment"), Manuscript Reference and Resource Center.

22. Andrew Billingsley and Jeanne Giovannoni, *Children of the Storm: Black Children and American Child Welfare* (New York, 1972), pp. 112–13; Hodson to LaGuardia, 14 October 1942, p. 1, LaGuardia papers, box 2546; Department of Welfare, "Report on Enforcement," pp. 1, 2; Child Welfare League, pp. 44, 79–80.

23. Cook: "Hiring Hall Aimed at Slave Markets," *New York Times,* 27 April 1941, p. 35. Department of Health, Bureau of Child Hygiene, "Report on Existing Facilities for Day Care of Children in Groups in New York City," November 1942, p. 4, Public Health Library; New York City Committee on Wartime Care of Children, "Report of the Committee to Mayor LaGuardia," 20 October 1942, pp. 2–3, Society for the Prevention of Crime papers, box 64, Columbia University Rare Book and Manuscript Library; Children's Aid Society, *Children in Wartime: 89th Annual Report,* 1941 (New York, 1942); *90 Years Ago . . . 90th Annual Report,* 1942 (New York, 1943).

24. Citizens' Committee, "Preliminary Report . . . on Employment," p. 1. Mrs. Duncan, President, Association to Promote Proper Housing for Girls, to supporters of the association, 27 May 1944, pp. 1–2, Phelps-Stokes papers, Jones-Tobias, box 33, Schomburg Archives.

25. Judge Bolin made the comments about black women in the city's war industries in 1943. Williams and Bolin: NUL, "Eleventh VOC," pp. 1–3. 1944: BLS, *War and Post-War Trends,* p. 3. April 1940 and April 1944: blacks as percent of all employed males: 8.6 in 1940, 9.8 in 1944. Of domestic workers, blacks were 60.2 percent in 1940, and 75.2 percent in 1944; of personal and other service: 22.8 and 31.4 percent, respectively; of laborers (excluding farm): 21.0 and 27.6 percent; of professional and semi-professional: 2.8 and 3.3 percent.

26. Spending averages: News Syndicate Company et al., *New York City Market Analysis* (New York, 1943), Sections 1, 22. Elderly study: Federation of Protestant Welfare Agencies, "A Study on the Needs of the Negro Aged in New York City," Pamphlet, May 1946, pp. 2, 6, 8, Schomburg Archives. Forty-four percent of this population worked. Over 65: 34 percent received Social Security, 22 percent worked, 24 percent supported by children or other relatives, 4 percent received home relief, 16 percent "other." Social Security: 1940 statistics. Blacks, 2 percent of the state population, were 4.6 percent of Social Security recipients. Sterner, pp. 273, 417–18. For U.S., blacks were 7.1 percent of the population, 11.2 percent of Social Security recipients. CAS: Billingsley and Giovannoni, pp. 13–14.

27. *Negro Year Book,* p. 321; Department of Health, "Service and Vital Statistics Tables, 1941–1946: Health Center Districts, New York City," n.d., p. 11, Public Health Library. In each of the three years after 1940, the mortality rates of the Lower East and West Side equalled or surpassed those of Central Harlem: ibid., p. 2. Infant mortality in Manhattan was higher than city-wide: 30 N.Y.C. per thousand live births, 37 Manhattan, 52 Central Harlem: ibid., p. 3. Tuberculosis deaths (all forms) in Central Harlem, 1943: 201. Manhattan: 84. New York City: 47. Citywide Citizens' Committee, "Report of the Subcommittee on Health and Hospitals," 1942, pp. 16–18, Municipal Reference and Resource Center.

28. NAACP, "Food Costs More in Harlem," Pamphlet [1942?], pp. 4–10, 19–21, Columbia University Social Work Library; Citywide Citizens' Committee, "Report . . . on Health & Hospitals," p. 12; Arnold Beichman, "Harlem Pays More Money for Less Food," *PM*, 23 February 1942, p. 6. Follow-up: Sara Mann, "Harlem: Runaway Prices, Shoddy Stuff Are Found in *PM* Check of Merchandise," *PM*, 15 October 1943; Department of Markets, "Comparative Price List," for week ending 17 July 1943, pp. 1–2, LaGuardia papers, box 2547. Store rents were between 10 and 100 percent higher in Harlem than anywhere else in New York City: NAACP, "Food Costs," p. 19.

29. Average-stay quotation: N.Y.C. Department of Investigation and the Committee on Institutions of the Domestic Relations Court, "Shelter Care of Children by the New York SPCC," Report, 4 January 1944, p. 5, in *New York City Department of Investigations Publications,* Columbia University Social Work Library. "Grave" quotation and the 887 children: Hill, "Institutional Facilities," pp. 1–2. Study done of Society for the Prevention of Cruelty to Children's shelters, 1943. Department of Investigation, p. 5 and Table 6; NYSPCC, "A Reply by the NYSPCC to Criticisms Contained in 'A Report to Mayor LaGuardia,' dated 4 January 1944," March 1944, pp. 70, 73, Municipal Reference and Resource Center.

30. Hill, pp. 2–5.

31. McKay: Wayne Cooper, ed., *The Passion of Claude McKay* (New York, 1973), p. 277. Letter quoted in Jervis Anderson, *This Was Harlem* (New York, 1981), p. 291.

32. Walter Harding, Police Captain, 28th Precinct, "Report on Harlem Disturbance Which Began 8:05 P.M. August First 1943," 16 August 1943, pp. 2–4, LaGuardia papers, box 2550. Capeci provides more detail. Marjorie Polite, after leaving the hotel because she did not like her room, received a refund but demanded an additional dollar, which she had given the elevator operator as a tip. The manager refused; she became angry, "boisterous, disorderly and profane" (Capeci's words). A policeman asked her to leave, she refused, and he arrested her for disorderly conduct. Mrs. Florine Roberts, there to visit her soldier son Robert Bandy, demanded Polite's release. Her son argued with the officer as well, hit him and ran. Because he refused to stop, the policeman threw his nightstick, then drew a gun and shot him: pp. 99–100.

33. Capeci, pp. 100–8. The 28th Precinct at the riot's center reported 254 civilian and three soldiers' arrests; four killed; 812 stores attacked; and 144 injured. Of those arrested, 234 were male. Captain Harding, "Report," pp. 34, 36, 47. Race, sex (according to the report): pp. 1, 7. Totaling crimes and arrests in all the Harlem precincts affected, 1,469 stores attacked, 606 civilians arrested, 4,587 windows broken, 189 injured (including 24 whites, presumably police and passers-by). Police Department, Sixth Division, "Report on Cause, Location, Crimes, Injuries, Police Details, Etc. in Connection with the Harlem Disturbance, August 1, 2, 1943," Memorandum to Police Commissioner, 21 August 1943; Fifth Division, "Harlem Disturbance," Memorandum to Police Commissioner, 16 August 1943, LaGuardia papers, box 2550. "Decent citizens": Fifth Division, "Harlem Disturbance," p. 2.

34. Powell, "Riots and Ruins," pp. 37, 42–44. "Resentment" quotation: Hickey and Edwin, p. 81.

35. Powell, "Riots and Ruins," pp. 45–49. "The Shape of Things" (editorial), *Nation* 157 (14 August 1943): 170. Harold Orlansky, "The Harlem Riot: A Study in Mass Frustration," *Social Analysis* Report #1, 1943, pp. 8–9.

36. Orlansky, pp. 11–15, 26. Orlansky acknowledged he overgeneralized about who stole what, but suggested that this was the overall pattern. Store owners: Harlem Chamber of Commerce, Statement, 1 September 1943, LaGuardia papers, box 2550; "Fear Mass Exodus of Retail Stores Out of Harlem," *Uptown in New York* (Uptown Chamber of Commerce mag-

azine) 24 (August–September, 1943): 1–2, LaGuardia papers, box 2550; "UCC Officers Deride Claim That Economic Conditions Caused Riot," *Uptown*, p. 4.

37. Capeci. This discussion has relied a good deal on his work, especially pp. 115, 121–25, 134–35, 157–59, 167.

38. See Nancy Weiss, *Farewell to the Party of Lincoln* (Princeton, 1983). I am referring to the switch in affiliation in national elections; many had already turned to the Democrats in local elections, and in fact swung back to the Republicans to vote for Mayor LaGuardia. Percent of families on relief, 1935: In New York City, 42.0 percent of blacks, 13.8 percent of whites; Chicago: 36.3 and 11.8 percent; Detroit: 34.2 and 10.8; Atlanta: 33.6 and 15.2; Birmingham: 34.5 and 13.5. In rural areas, in many cases white relief rates surpassed black. In the South, black relief grants usually totaled less than white, both urban and rural. Richard Sterner, *The Negro's Share: A Study of Income, Consumption, Housing and Public Assistance* (Westport, Conn., 1943), pp. 222, 236, 371.

39. Ira Reid and T. Arnold Hill, NUL, "The Forgotten Tenth," Pamphlet, May 1933, pp. 42–43, Columbia University Social Work Library.

40. Walter Davenport, "Harlem . . . Dense and Dangerous," *Collier's* (23 September 1944), pp. 11–12, LaGuardia papers, box 2550. Davenport's last comment referred, of course, to the Harlem riot of 1943.

Index

Unemployment: among black professionals, 84–85; data on, 227–30; during Depression, 42–43, 65–66, 73; gender differences in, 77–79; in 1942, 199; rise in 1920s, 39–40

Unions, 137; black women and, 25–26; discrimination by, 43, 71–73; "Don't Buy" campaign and, 129–30; increase in black membership of, 113, 201; NNC and, 81; relief program discrimination and, 148; struggle to lift restrictions of, 108–13, 201, 203–5; women and, 25–26, 109, 206. *See also specific unions*

United Association of Colored Motion Picture Operators, 110

United Bus Strike Committee, 204, 205

United Holy Church of America, 58–59

United Neighborhood Houses, 29, 30

United Tenants' League of Greater New York, 184

Unity Democratic Club, 121

Universal Negro Improvement Association (UNIA), 13, 76, 83, 93, 121, 131; nationalist goals of, 101; relief program discrimination and, 147, 148; Unemployed Unit of, 177; unemployment services and, 81

Upper Harlem Council of the Unemployed, 62–63, 97, 147

Uptown Chamber of Commerce, 135

Urban League. *See* Hubert, James; National Urban League; New York Urban League

Utopia Children's House (UCH), 46, 58, 169

Valentine, Lewis, 193–94

Visiting Nurses Association, 33

Vocational Opportunity Campaigns, 119

Vote. *See* Political activity

Wages: of blacks employed in Harlem stores, 61–62; of black women, 24, 25, 78, 79, 80; disparity between black and white, 21–22, 70, 81; employment discrimination and, 82; failure to meet expenses, 68, 84, 175, 176–95, 208, 230–31; of foreign-born blacks, 83–84; gender and, 79; impact of Depression on, 44–45; paid by WPA, 152–53; unionization and, 111

Wagner, Robert, Jr., 149, 205

Walker, James, 48, 153; black employment by city government under, 95

Walkill Cottage and camp, 170, 210

Walk Together, Chillun (Wilson), 164

Washington, march on, proposed by Randolph, 202–3

Weatherby, William, 22, 104, 105

Weaver, Robert, 201

Weisbecker's Market, 131

Weiss, Nancy, 11, 96

Welfare Council, 40, 44, 46, 48, 52, 112, 171, 172

White, Walter, 62, 86, 87, 190–91, 193–94, 202, 205

White businesses, 61–62; food prices and, 209. *See also* "Don't Buy Where You Can't Work" campaign

White Rose Mission, 58, 168

Wicks Act of 1931, pp. 50, 52

Wilkins, Roy, 85–86; praise for LaGuardia, 97

Wilkinson, William, 89

Williams, Aubrey, 163

Williams, Vernal, 99, 176

Wilson, Frank, 164

Wilson, John Louis, 96

Wolters, Raymond, 11

Women: aid provided by black organizations for, 58; churches and, 105–7, 108; "Don't Buy" campaign and, 116–17, 120; employment discrimination and, 76, 77–80; employment of, 22–26, 44, 66, 69, 78–80, 207; housing of, 155, 177, 182, 207; political activity of, 105–8; unions and, 25–26, 109, 206; wages of, 24, 25, 78, 79, 80; working conditions of, 78, 79–80

Women's Bureau of EURC, 54

Women's clubs, 105. *See also specific clubs*

Women's Emergency Shelter, 150, 155

Women's Trade Union League, 109, 206

Woolworth's, 116, 122

Workers' Council, 110–11

Works Progress Administration (WPA), 143; Advisory Council of, 166; art, music, and education programs of, 164–65; benefits provided by, 163–65; blacks employed by, 199; Division of Social Research studies of, 84; hiring discrimination and, 156–57, 158–60, 161–62; studies conducted by, 184; wages paid by, 152–53; Writers' Program of, 168

World's Fair Corporation, 136, 137

World War II, changes brought by, 198–204, 207, 218

Wright, Richard, 73, 100, 105, 196

W. T. Grant Company, 123

YMCA, 16, 18, 133, 168, 189

Young Communist League, 3–4

Young Liberators, 3

Young West Indian Congress, 121

YWCA, 16, 18, 25, 79, 105, 148, 155, 168, 189, 206